Songs for Dead Parents

Songs for
Dead Parents

Corpse, Text, and World in Southwest China

ERIK MUEGGLER

The University of Chicago Press
Chicago and London

The University of Chicago Press, Chicago 60637
The University of Chicago Press, Ltd., London

Published 2017
Printed in the United States of America

26 25 24 23 22 21 20 19 18 17   1 2 3 4 5

ISBN-13: 978-0-226-48338-2 (cloth)
ISBN-13: 978-0-226-48100-5 (paper)
ISBN-13: 978-0-226-48341-2 (e-book)
DOI: 10.7208/chicago/9780226483412.001.0001

Library of Congress Cataloging-in-Publication Data

Names: Mueggler, Erik, 1962– author.
Title: Songs for dead parents : corpse, text, and world in southwest China /
    Erik Mueggler.
Description: Chicago ; London : The University of Chicago Press, 2017. | Includes
    bibliographical references and index.
Identifiers: LCCN 2017010952 | ISBN 9780226483382 (cloth : alk. paper) |
    ISBN 9780226481005 (pbk. : alk. paper) | ISBN 9780226483412 (e-book)
Subjects: LCSH: Mourning customs—China, Southwest. | Death—China, Southwest.
    | Funeral rites and ceremonies—China, Southwest.
Classification: LCC GT3283.A3 S659 2017 | DDC 393/.90951—dc23
    LC record available at https://lccn.loc.gov/2017010952

♾ This paper meets the requirements of ANSI/NISO Z39.48-1992 (Permanence of Paper).

For my mother
Rosalie Ryan Mueggler
1934–2015

Contents

Acknowledgments

The community described in this book has welcomed me back repeatedly since 1993, feeding and housing me, tolerating my presence at many events, and patiently handling my persistent, clueless, annoying, embarrassing questions. I owe so many of its members an enormous debt of gratitude.

A writing residency at Deep Springs College granted me the time and tranquility needed to begin this book; a Michigan Humanities Fellowship allowed me to complete it. Parts of the book were presented at University of Michigan venues—talks at the Lieberthal-Rogel Center for Chinese Studies and the Doctoral Program in Anthropology and History, workshops in the Sociocultural Anthropology and Linguistic Anthropology subfields, and four lectures for the Department of Anthropology in memory of our late, beloved colleague Roy Rappaport. Parts were also presented at colloquia at Deep Springs College, Cornell University, the University of Toronto, Webster University, the University of Virginia, the Max Planck Institute for Social Anthropology, the Max Planck Institute for the Study of Religious and Ethnic Diversity, Academia Sinica, National Taiwan University, and Colorado College. While failings of memory make it impossible to thank most of those whose ideas, incitements, enthusiasm, or skepticism enriched this book on those occasions, a few whose contributions stand out sharply are Fred Damon, Christian du Pee, Gillian Feeley-Harnik, Krisztina Fehervary, Matthew Hull, Judith Irvine, Webb Keane, Alaina Lemon, Michael Lempert, Jianxiong Ma, Bruce Mannheim, Martin Powers, Elizabeth Roberts, Warren Rosenblum, P. Steven Sangren, Lee Schlesinger, Oliver Tappe, Thomas Trautmann, Peter van der Veer, and Wang Zheng.

Treehouse discussions with the always intellectually effervescent David Porter provided episodic spurts of inspiration. Ashley Lebner's curious, intelligent, incisive, and encouraging engagement with the ideas in this book influenced it in more ways than I can say; I owe her the warmest thanks. In her typically timely fashion, Nadine Hubbs contributed a small, peaceful writing refuge, where a mysterious, intensely productive vibe spurred me on to finish a draft of the manuscript. Frances Kai-Hwa Wang read scrupulously through the entire manuscript, improved nearly every sentence, and firmly schooled me on the value of the Oxford comma. Tim Vachon created the elegant line drawings and diagrams.

The University of Michigan's Office of Research and Lieberthal-Rogel Center for Chinese Studies provided publication-subvention grants to illustrate the book and keep its retail price reasonably low. Much of chapter 1 has been previously published in the *Journal of Asian Studies*, and most of chapter 4 has been published in the *Journal of the Royal Anthropological Institute*. I am grateful for their permissions to republish.

Introduction

The Yipao River slices through the Baicaoling Mountains of north-central Yunnan before meeting the great Jinsha on its way down from the Tibetan Plateau.[1] The mountains crowd closely on both sides, leaving only a few narrow valleys suitable for rice cultivation. During the Ming and Qing dynasties, this rough country was the northern hinterland of Baiyanjing 白鹽井, an important complex of salt wells, where a magistrate was tasked with maintaining the state monopoly on salt. This local authority also directly governed the uncouth mountain peoples to the north, giving them different histories and fates than mountain residents in the surrounding counties, ruled by hereditary native chiefs ratified by the Imperial state. By the nineteenth century, the sustained defiance the people of the Yipao River gorge had shown the Ming state as it established suzerainty over the basin-and-range social system of central Yunnan had been largely forgotten (Ma 2014). A local gazetteer published in 1845 depicts their descendants as harmless, if immoral of habit:

> White Luoluo (白倮倮) have foolish and docile dispositions. Men and boys wrap their heads, go barefoot, and wear black goatskin vests. Women plait their hair and wrap their heads with black cloth. . . . Unmarried men and women leave the house and sit together drinking liquor. When the drinking is over, the women return again to their mothers' houses to wait . . . . They trade in hemp cloth, hemp thread, honey, pine torches, and the like. They live from the eastern and northern borders [of Dayao County] to some sixty li from the city. (Liu 1845, juan 7)

1. The Yipao River 一泡江 is also called the Yupao River 魚泡江.

These "Luoluo" proved far from docile twelve years later when, following the
Taiping Rebellion, they seized much of this mountain territory, established
their own governing council, and defied the Qing armies for eighteen years
(Liu 1980). After this rebellion was crushed and the ethnic demography of the
mountains was transformed by a flood of Han migrants, any further threat
from the Luoluo seemed negligible. Another official local history, from 1922,
speaks of them in passing, remarking succinctly upon their clothing, houses,
marriage customs, and healing practices:

> Yi (夷) men wear goatskins and hemp cloth. The women and children dress
> in colored cloth and wear goatskins on their backs. Their dwellings are all
> thatched or have wooden roof shingles; thus they are called "wood-shingled
> houses." Men and women choose freely whom to marry. When ill they do not
> use medicine; instead they perform spirit dances and pray to avert misfortune
> (qirang 祈禳), vastly different from Han. (Guo 1968 [1922], 251)

Without fail, all such accounts make prominent mention of the goatskin
garment that men, women, and children all wore: a long, sleeveless vest or jer-
kin, open at the front, the goat's tail and hind feet dangling behind, the glossy
black hair turned outward against damp, cold, and heat. More than anything
else, its unhemmed edges and black color identified these people of the Yipao
River valley to outsiders' eyes. (Other peoples, closer to the plains, wore their
goatskin jerkins hemmed and with the smooth, buff-colored leather turned
outwards, the hair inward.) Had these histories' authors inquired further into
the ways the people in the mountains lived and, especially died, they might
have noticed that the glossy black garments were a product of highly elaborated practices of wrapping corpses. Goats were bred in all-black herds and
sacrificed at funerals, anchoring exchanges that made corpses into fully social
dead bodies by enveloping them in clothing, hemp cloth, cotton quilts, coffins, lamenters, and dancers. Their meat was eaten at funeral feasts and their
skins returned to the donors to be tanned and worn as vests.

The goatskin-clad residents of the district, who knew themselves as Lipò
and Lòlopò, also reflected on customs of clothing and sacrifice they observed
among the class of literati and officials who wrote these histories.[2] For them, a
potent symbol of state authority was a statue of the "god of salt" that had once
stood over the wells of Baiyanjing. In a story widely told in the uplands, this
statue memorialized an old shepherd who discovered the salt there. Out with

2. These endonyms are usually transliterated into Chinese as Lipo 里颇 and Luoluopo
罗罗颇.

his sheep, the old man noticed that one of his rams disappeared for days at a time and returned alone, fatter than the others. He tied a bell around its neck and followed it to a spring. The water had a strange pleasant taste, and food boiled in it tasted delicious. After learning of this discovery, the officials built the wells of Baiyanjing, not forgetting to reward the old man by transforming him into a god, an old Lòlopò in a goatskin:

> They gave him a feast and made congratulatory speeches. Then they killed an ox, wrapped the man in the hide, and stood him up in the sun. As the hide dried, it compressed and preserved him. They made offerings to him, standing there. A flood later washed him away, but they built a stone statue of him, wrapped in ox hide and wearing a goatskin vest.[3]

Memorialization in stone was promoted by the officials of Baiyanjing and their allies among the rural Confucian elite and adopted by upland "Luoluo" or "Yi" in the eighteenth and nineteenth centuries during a momentous shift from cremation to burial. Lipò and Lòlopò elaborated, making their tombstones into petrified corpses, borrowing Chinese characters to inscribe their skins with histories of life and kinship, wrapping them in silk, bearing them to the graveyard on litters, and standing them up there to receive offerings. The language was borrowed and so was the land, both skin and depth. Presiding over every burial site was a Confucian official in the form of a stone or tree, the surface manifestation of Yan Luo Wang 閻羅王, or Yama (locally pronounced Yàlòwù), king of the new underground state, who understood no local language. All "prayers" to him, though perhaps "vastly different" from Han ways of speaking, were nevertheless enunciated in Chinese, the language of officialdom.

In the local language, which its speakers called Liŋo or Lòloŋo (ŋo means "tongue"), the petrified corpse of the god of salt was a bu, a fearsome expression of the central problem of death: how bodies might be unmade and remade, dematerialized and rematerialized. (See the appendix for a description of the romanization conventions used in this book and for a discussion of Lòloŋo.) On journeys to haul salt or engage in trade, Lipò and Lòlopò often encountered bu: statues in Confucian and Buddhist temples with the power to trap and crush a soul, resulting in lethargy, depression, or death. Yet Lipò and Lòlopò also fashioned bu, and not only in the relatively new and unsettlingly permanent form of tombstones. Until 1958, Lòlopò gathered in the winter sun below a hill of graves to hold a third major funeral ritual for each adult who

---

3. As told by people in Júzò recalling how their fathers hired on as muleteers to haul salt cakes from Baiyanjing to the lowlands. I have told this story once before (Mueggler 1998a).

had died that year. They built an effigy, a *bu*, for the dead, of twenty-four pine and chestnut saplings, wrapped in white hemp and black cotton and clothed in layers of trousers, shirts, aprons, and baby-carrying cloths. A ritualist made a long speech to this effigy: not q̠irang—prayer to avert misfortune—as in the 1922 local history, but *pi̠*, a meticulous and consequential negotiation with this no-longer-human being. This speech raised the troubling question of what a dead body was and how it must be treated in the context of the switch from cremation to burial. It engaged this question most directly in a story about the first great shaman, Pi̠mæ̀nelì. The story was long, distributed over several of the speech's seventy-two "songs," but it can be told briefly.

Pi̠mæ̀nelì discovered a powerful medicine with which he cured all his kin and friends of death by bringing breath back into their lifeless bodies. Hearing of his, the dragon invited Pi̠mæ̀nelì to the sky to treat his crest, which was hurting him. The shaman climbed to the sky on an apple-pear tree, leaving his medicine in the care of his son. Naturally, the son ignored his father's warning not to leave the jars of medicine out in the sunlight, and the sun stole the medicine away. The shaman's son, who was relying on the medicine to make his living, soon died of cold and hunger. The smoke of his cremated body and the cries of his grief-stricken kin drifted up to the sky, reaching the ears of his father, who descended as fast as he could, although not very fast, as evil yellow ants had chewed down the tree on which he had ascended so he had to go the long way around. At home he found only the cremated ashes of his dead son and empty jars of medicine. He rinsed the jars with water, which he sprinkled over the ashes, and the ashes reassembled themselves into a corpse, a *bu*, perfect except that it lacked breath. Pi̠mæ̀nelì called his kin together, dressed his son's corpse in hemp stockings so it might walk to the underworld, and invented the ritual procedures for burial.

Yet burial was not so final as all that. After assembling and wrapping the *bu* of the tenth lunar month, the ritualist attempted to animate it as his shamanic ancestor Pi̠mæ̀nelì had done with the corpse of his son. He struck each part of it, head to foot, with his knife, chanting:

0.1	pi̠ pi̠ ŋo wú no	I speak and my head hurts
	ts'ì wú ŋo gə̀ lɔ	give me medicine for my head
	pi̠ pi̠ ŋo lu no	I speak and my tongue hurts
	ts'ì lu ŋo gə̀ lɔ	give me medicine for my tongue
	pi̠ pi̠ ŋo ji no	I speak and my skin hurts
	ji kɔ̀ tsú gə̀ lɔ	stick my skin back together . . .

And so on, through feet, heart, liver, lungs, and penis, exchanging his body part for part with the body of the *bu*, head to foot and outside to inside. And then,

0.2	bɛ pi̱ æ̀ lè tṳ	I speak and it rises up
	bɯ pi̱ í lè tṳ	I speak to the *bɯ* and its hands move
	í lè tṳ lɔ ga	its hands begin to move
	mṳ̀ do mṳ̀ hə	to the top of heaven
	mi gə mi tè lɔ	through earth's corners
	bɯ pi̱ bɯ tṳ ga	I speak and the *bɯ* emerges
	bɯ pi̱ bɯ kó ga	I speak and the *bɯ* begins
	bɯ pi̱ bɯ lí ga	I speak and the *bɯ* flourishes

Reanimating the corpse, repeating nearly word for word a passage he had voiced hours before when singing of the creation of the world and the emergence of people, replacing only the word *bu*, living people, with its near homonym *bɯ*: corpse, statue, tombstone, body reconstituted from ashes but given no breath, body assembled of saplings, wrapped in clothing and reanimated through speech—body.

These bodies were all dead (*shr*), even those on the cusp of reanimation, which nobody expected would ever really have breath and warmth like living people wrapped in their own clothing and goatskins. Dead bodies—assembled, wrapped, animated—were the central material artifacts of Lòlop'ò ritual life. It might even be said that they were the only actual bodies in Lòlop'ò ritual life—the only bodies that were explicitly theorized, assembled, inscribed, voiced, sung. Living bodies lay hidden as though in shadows cast by the dead: mysterious assemblages of potential attributes, awaiting death to be exposed, dissected, elaborated, compiled, celebrated, defeated. Bridges of intricate architecture were suspended over the gulf that separated the actual bodies of the dead from those who were as yet only potentially dead. This was an architecture of words and acts: counted, aligned, repeated, reversed, filigreed into elaborate formal structures, and attended to with assiduous care. And the affects that pulsed across these bridges—especially sadness at death and the force of new life—powered the domestic world, of house and courtyard, open to the cosmos. Each of the dead bodies in these examples required the construction of such a bridge. In the case of the god of salt, a compressed image of the authority of the imperial and republican states, the bridge would be a small but elaborate effigy and a quick formal chant to free a soul trapped by the *bɯ*. The gulf between the living and the silk-wrapped tombstones that were the god of salt's twentieth-century analogues was bridged with verses inscribed in Chinese characters into their stone skins. The first shaman, Pi̱mæ̀nelì, created an elaborate set of funeral procedures to reach across to the reconstituted corpse of his son, and Lòlop'ò would continue to elaborate as they buried their dead from the late nineteenth through the early twenty-first centuries. As to the great effigy that joined the image of the shaman's son with the body of a recently dead kinsperson, the bridge was the spectacular collection of seventy-two songs for the dead, near the end of which a living shaman attempted the reanimation of this dead body. These communicative constructions were live wires that drew force to animate the living out of the bodies of the dead.

Bodies Actual and Virtual

This book examines practices of making and unmaking dead bodies in a community in north-central Yunnan called Júzò, or "little valley" in the local language, Zhizuo 直苴 in Chinese.[4] Throughout the period in question, from the early twentieth century to the present, people in this community used sacrifice, exchange, performance, inscription, and poetic vocalization to make bodies for the dead in an exuberant variety of ritualized practices. In these contexts, to assemble dead bodies was to actualize social relations. We can think of persons as being composed of the relations that create and sustain them—relations of alliance that produce households, relations of generation and nurture that make children's bodies, relations of labor that sustain these bodies, relations of descent that create the conditions to make new alliances, new households, new children, and so on. All these categories are mere short-hand for a great variety of branching forms of relationality in which each person is suspended. This—persons as objectifications of the gendered relations that produce them—has been a common way for anthropologists to think of persons, following the work of Marilyn Strathern (especially 1988, 1991, 1992a, 2005). It is a convenient tool to use as I attempt to translate into comprehensible anthropological idioms what Lòlopò seem to think and do about living and dead persons. Yet for most Lòlopò, especially those who have lived for a while, the most engaged, rigorous, and conscientious form of thought about what we have come to call "persons" is the work of making dead bodies.

This work reveals and formalizes relations that are otherwise implicit, potential, or obscured. It is complex, undertaken through several major and many minor ritualized events spread out over many years, but it might be divided into three steps. First, a soul is captured and materialized: a singular but impersonal essence that has no content and no inherent internal relationality. Second, a bodily core is assembled of materials expressive of fundamental

---

4. The character 苴, pronounced jū in standard Chinese, is pronounced zùo locally. It appears in many place names in north-central Yunnan as a transliteration of the Lipo zò, "little."

forces in the universe, including those concentrated in domestic spaces and those that extend through the earth, waters, and sky. Third, this core is wrapped in formal images of the social relations presumed to have engaged the person while alive. Images of social relations are built up in order to be dissevered, with the ultimate aim of disengaging living persons from the dead, as though by cutting the body of the dead out of the person of the living. This work is explicit, involving a great deal of naming and performing of specific relations. The work is also comprehensive, beginning with dead's most intimate relations and following relations of relations through multiple branching pathways until an entire social world is defined. The dead body is made into the formal image of this world, and as it is cut out of the person of each participant the social world it materializes is cut out as well. Work for the dead is ultimately intended to make them into others—into the kind of strangers with which one may enter into formal contracts. Stasch's useful definition of otherness as a social relation applies to these dead; they are ultimately remade as different and distant, and their distance attracts, repels, or otherwise moves those in relation with them. "To engage with what is other is to participate in some sort of reflexive questioning, definition or redefinition of one's familiar world-apprehending categories and one's position in a categorical order" (Stasch 2009, 15). In this sense, work for the dead does not restore a social order fractured by death, as the tradition of the anthropology of death would have it. Work for the dead creates a formal and objectified image of the social world in the dead body, which participants can perceive as other to themselves. This process of assembly and disengagement, carried out over several decades, is the source of generative power, producing living bodies as effects of work on the dead.

Among the tools for this work are hemp, grain, rice loaves, and the bodies of domestic animals: goats; chickens, seen as less valuable and more distant substitutes for goats; and pigs, which are seen as more valuable and more intimate versions of goats. In other words, central to assembling bodies for the dead are other bodies, especially the bodies of rice loaves and goats, each a clarifying version of the other. Dead bodies are made through anatomical operations on these other bodies, operations that disassemble and distribute them in order to make explicit social relations presumed to exist in potential or obscured form. The bodies of goats and rice loaves are thus partial analogues of dead bodies. Together, all the goats and rice loaves sacrificed during a funeral occasion, superimposed upon each other as it were, form an image of a dead body disassembled into its constituent parts. From the perspective of work on the dead, a living goat is merely a virtual body. It is, to be sure, composed of the relations that produced it (between the father and sons who raised it, among the kin who helped buy it), but these relations are made manifest, comprehended *as* relations, only after the goat is killed and its meat distributed to all those who participated in them. A rice loaf too is a virtual body, composed of potential relations, actualized by its division among those who labored to grow, harvest, thresh, and winnow the rice. Among the central functions of the poetry performed at funerals is to make explicit the relations of labor and suffering that have contributed to the various bodies through which the dead body is fashioned as an image of the social relations that composed it in life.

Like goats and rice loaves, living human bodies might also be understood to be virtual bodies. Bodies become actual only after they are dead, the histories of the relations that composed them made formally explicit, built into them and wrapped around them so as ultimately to be cut out of them. This is true of corpses, wrapped in hemp, swaddled in quilts, contained in coffins, surrounded by lamenters and dancers, accompanied by myriad acts of sacrifice and exchange. It is true of empty places where coffins once stood, of tombstones, of ancestral effigies, and of the great *bu* of the tenth lunar month. From the perspective of work on the dead, these are the only actual, concrete, material bodies; living bodies are merely potential dead bodies. The extent to which this way of thinking systematically permeates modes of understanding what bodies are can be seen in a story of genesis told in the great speech to the dead of the tenth month. The earth was made by a deaf-mute who trapped, slaughtered, butchered, and distributed an ox. The ox's head became the earth, its eyes the stars, its breath the wind, its teeth the cliffs, its saliva the pine pitch, its skin the earth's skin, its fat the earth's fat, its intestines the vines, its heart the earth's heart, its hooves the rocks, its blood the rivers. There is more to this story (elaborated in chapter 6), but even given this much, we might understand the earth itself as a body, an effigy, a *bu*, assembled and actualized through the sacrifice and distribution of an ox's body. Dead bodies— and the images of social worlds they materialize—exist in the same way as the earth: the material effects of processes that actualize prior virtual forms.

Since this book is about social relations with the dead, one of its aims is to find ways to speak of the dead as Lòlopò do, as nonhuman social beings engaged with the living and with each other. This has required a difficult shift of perspective. In an earlier ethnography of Júzò, I was chiefly interested in how people there employed unique cultural resources to come to terms with the past violence of socialist campaigns (Mueggler 2001). Central among these resources was a kind of dead being, the ghosts of those who had died of starvation and the effects of malnutrition during the famine precipitated by the Great Leap Forward. Because these dead were never properly buried or mourned, they afflicted their descendants with great harm. Ways of being affected by this harm, ways of talking about it, and ways of using ritualized procedures to counter it appeared to be potent means to recall the violence of the Great Leap Forward, which could not often be spoken about directly, and to create ethical responses to its lasting effects, both for individual people and for their community. In that work, I approached ghosts as imaginary beings with real effects, a status they seemed to share with the socialist state, which appeared in experience as an imagined unity whose effects were nevertheless omnipresent.

There was much in the nature of wild ghosts (*chènè*) that made this procedure feel right, since people often spoke of them as illusions that appeared and disappeared, although their appearance, unlike many imaginings, always had consequences. And thinking of the socialist state as a parallel imaginary entity had many analytical advantages, among the most attractive of which was, ironically, a certain power of demystification: the state was not experienced in this deeply marginalized community as some potent, unified, organized force but as an illusion that came and went, leaving in its wake effects that were often difficult to absorb or explain. Yet I have come to understand that this procedure also produced serious distortions. Simply put, thinking of wild ghosts as imaginary as opposed to the reality of living people shifted the center of analytical gravity to living *society* focusing attention on the effects of a *belief* in ghosts on the relations of living people and making it difficult to think of ghosts as fully social beings. Wishful thinking among my Lòlopò interlocutors may have influenced this analytical choice, for they very much did not *want* ghosts to be social beings, and the ritualized procedures with which they encountered these entities were designed to restrain or undermine their nevertheless incorrigible sociality.

Many in Júzò found my interest in wild ghosts unseemly: ghosts are a perversion of the natural order, better not spoken about much, and hardly an appropriate topic for a book-length study. A far more solid focus of interest, they advised, would be the wealth of procedures used to care for the dead, which, if carried out conscientiously and with a degree of luck, would prevent the dead from becoming wild ghosts. Beginning in 1993 and extending over repeated visits through 2012, many in Júzò became my conscientious guides to these procedures and the poetics that accompany them, enumerating, reciting, explaining, and translating, displaying intense interest and subdued pride in this extraordinary body of inherited knowledge. As I worked

through this material, it became clear that my nearly instinctual approach to
the dead as imaginary beings was an obstacle to understanding. It flattened
out the rich and varied terrain of work on the dead, focusing my attention
on the effect of this work on relations among the living rather than where
Lòlop'ò placed theirs: relations with the dead. Lòlop'ò do not see their dead as
imaginary as opposed to the real of the living. The living too are manifest to
the senses of others only at times and across shifting material forms: bodies,
faces, voices, photographs, texts. The living too require materializing procedures to make them actual, to concretize them in time and space so they
might be nurtured, cared for, communicated with, exchanged with, and killed
or helped die. In Júzò at least, and possibly anywhere, an ontological distinction between the living and the dead is a distortion. Rather than to speak of
either living or dead as real or imaginary it is more accurate to speak of both
as moving continuously between material and immaterial forms.

Opening an essay about structuralism published in 1967, Gilles Deleuze
noted that the binary real/imaginary is deeply embedded in received ways of
thinking in the Euro-American West. He put it forcefully: "We are used to,
almost conditioned to, a certain distinction or correlation between the real
and the imaginary. All of our thought maintains a dialectical play between
these two notions" (Deleuze 2004 [1967], 171). Habits of thought so embedded in our traditions as these cannot be banished with a word, continuing
to operate implicitly in thought and discourse despite all moves to deny or
counter them until the philosophical traditions in which they are rooted are
deliberately and painstakingly unmade. Deleuze's own oeuvre is testament to
this—an enormous project dedicated to flattening such ontological distinctions through a series of intimate generative engagements with a vast selection of texts from the history of Euro-American philosophy and literature.
The correlative distinction between real and imaginary has been fundamental
to the approach of Western secular thought to beings like spirits, demons, and
the dead, and I am not under the illusion that it can be easily dissolved. The
terms that I adopt instead—material and immaterial, actual and virtual, extensive and intensive—may appear at times simply to replace that distinction,
smuggling it back into my analysis under new names. Still, I am convinced
that the exercise of applying close and sustained ethnographic attention to the
ways Lòlop'ò work on the dead, the words they used to speak to the dead, and
the modes they have developed to exchange with the dead do reveal, over the
course of this study, how the dead are involved with the living in a common
social world: how relations with the dead are necessary for and internal to relations among the living.

Thought About Being, Thoughts About Ritual

In its exuberant variety and exhaustive repetition, Lòlopò work on the dead creates a series of consistent questions and answers about problems such as what the world is, what bodies are, what spirits are, what persons alive and dead are. It is almost certain that similar approaches are shared by many Tibeto-Burman-speaking and Miao-Yao-speaking communities in the immensely varied landscape of China's southwest, though we unfortunately do not yet have sufficient ethnography to confirm this guess. If we interpret these questions and answers to be chiefly about signs, we might call them, collectively, a semiotic ideology (Keane 2003, 2007) or a regime of reference (Mueggler 1998a, 2002). If we interpret them to be centrally about what might be known and how it can be known, we might call them an epistemology (Toren and Pina-Cabral 2011, Strathern 1991). If we see them as largely about what exists and how it exists, we might call them an ontology. Since many of these questions and answers deliberately address the problem of what the world is and what place the living and dead occupy in it, some might find this last designation appropriate. Yet the connotations the term "ontology" has recently acquired in anthropology open up any use to quick misinterpretation. For instance, although Lòlopò work on the dead expresses the idea that living humans and dead people exist in the same social world while their bodies are made of different things, it cannot be said to participate in an "animist ontology" that expresses one of several fundamental possibilities for the human mind, as in the recent influential work of Philippe Descola (Descola 2013, Sahlins 2013). Lòlopò work on the dead is the product of a shift from cremation to burial, encouraged by state administrators and made inevitable by Han migration into the Yunnan-Guizhou plateau from the seventeenth through the nineteenth centuries. During this transformation, Lòlopò created an uneasy compromise between cremation and burial, combining ideas about shamanic and bureaucratic authority, as they worked out a practical poetics of body and world. Their procedures for work on the dead are products of a historical process rather than expressions of an underlying possibility of mind.

Or, to take another example, it is not productive to treat Lòlopò work on the dead as expressing one ontology in a plurality, where groups or societies fashion worlds that are ontologically distinct from each other (a sampling of the varied scholarship that argues for this possibility or something like it would include Viveiros de Castro 2004, Henare et al. 2007, Pedersen 2011, Holbraad 2012, Candea and Alcayna-Stevens 2012, Kohn 2013, Paleček and Risjord 2013). Ontology, or thought about being, has been the defining preoccupation of the Euro-American philosophical tradition, of which recent anthropological musings about ontology are a late expression.[5] While this investigation of work on the dead does reflect on Lòlopʼò thought about phenomena that might be grouped under the term "being" (a term with no true Lòloŋo equivalent), I make no claims that it describes a different "Lòlopʼò ontology," attaching this concept as an afterthought to description. Instead, this book attempts to immerse the reader in a "continuing struggle with the language of description" (Strathern 1999, xi) while refusing to elevate grand concepts too far above the terrain of description.[6] At the same time, it draws selectively on one productive strand in the European tradition of ontological thought, that of Gilles Deleuze (whose consistent formula was "ontologically one, formally distinct"), to work through some problems of description that might otherwise be thornier.

The sites where people work on the dead are ritualized sites. The Lòloŋo term that most accurately translates "ritual" is *cìpe̠ mope̠*, which can be glossed "rules and procedures," or, more comprehensively, "the action of following rules and procedures." People in Júzò often express the sense that the rules and procedures that govern work on the dead have been passed down from their ancestors through the agency of smart, skilled people, particularly clever old women. A fragment from the "song of rules and seeds," one of the seventy-two songs that made up the long speech made to the dead during the tenth lunar month, discusses the origins of "rules and procedures."

0.3	à sà cì shŕ sṳ	who made these rules?
	shř ts'i mo mæ̀ cì shŕ sṳ	a woman of seventy made these rules
	à sà cì shŕ tsæ	who made such fine rules?
	mó mi he mo cæ cì shí tsæ	the little yellow mouse of the underworld made these fine rules

The cleverest old woman I knew was one of my most valued guides to the intricacies of work on the dead, a ritualist born around 1930, whom I knew as Àp'ìmà, Grandmother. She delighted in this passage for the way it evoked

5. An anthropological effort to locate distinct ontologies in different societies, it has been claimed, "privileges a consummate Euro-American philosophical concept (and a rather unitary one at that, thus evoking society, the individual and comparison) and assigns it to the task of ethnographic description" (Lebner 2016, 136n17).

6. In an essay responding to some anthropological attempts to develop ideas about "plural ontologies," Strathern writes, "Can one imagine a universe of scholars where this (caring for concepts) is not a primordial duty? . . perhaps the locus of truth is found elsewhere than in concepts. That would put moral concern elsewhere too" (Strathern 2012, 403, quoted in Lebner 2016, 138).

a balance of close attention to the details of sequential action and the arbitrary chaos of the little yellow mouse's scurrying feet, making tracks whose
purpose no human can comprehend. This balance was the essence of funeral
"rules and procedures." In the "song of rules and seeds," ritual rules arise as
the world takes form, preceding the emergence of human persons. Rules (ci)
are seeds ($shí$), sown across the earth to clothe the valleys and hills in trees,
the original materials out of which bodies for all dematerialized beings are
fashioned—protobodies for spirits and the dead.

Anthropologists have spilled buckets of ink on the topic of ritual. Talal
Asad has shown how ritual was constituted as a unified object of study for
anthropology in the long process of modernizing and secularizing Christianity. In this process, the concept of ritual grew from the idea of a book or
manual for action to the idea of an essentially signifying behavior: action that
stands for something else and a "type of activity to be classified separately
from practical, that is technically effective, behavior" (Asad 2009, 58). The
idea that ritual is signifying, communicative practice has been the foundation
for most influential theories of the concept in anthropology, including those
of Clifford Geertz (1973), Victor Turner (1967, 1969, 1974, 1982), and Roy Rappaport (1999). Working against the grain of this received wisdom, Humphrey
and Laidlaw explicitly reject the idea that ritual is essentially communicative.
Ritual is a quality of action, they argue, rather than a class of events. Ritualized action has a particular structure of intention. "Instead of being guided
and structured by the intentions of actors, ritualized action is constituted and
structured by prescription, not just in the sense that people follow rules, but
in the much deeper sense that a reclassification takes place so that only following the rules counts as action." As a result, "in ritual one both is and is not
the author of one's own acts" (Humphrey and Laidlaw 1994, 106). In working out this definition, Humphrey and Laidlaw borrow a distinction from
Atkinson (1989, 14–15) between liturgy-centered rituals, such as the highly
scripted puja ceremonies of Jains, where no act has a "meaning" that any participant can name with certainty, and performance-centered rituals, such as
séances or shamanic performances, where most participants can agree on the
intended effects. The crucial distinction is that the question most appropriate
to ask of liturgical ritual is Have we got it right? while the central question
for performative ritual is Has it worked? Humphrey and Laidlaw insist that
performance-centered rituals are only weakly ritualized. While prescribed actions are important, they are less a "pre-ordained progression of steps" than a
repertoire of acts available to participants. And intention is not entirely displaced; the intentions of the participants often do guide and structure their actions (Humphrey and Laidlaw 1994, 10–11).

This helps clarify in what sense it is appropriate to translate *cìpẹ mopẹ*, "rules and procedures," with the concept of ritual, at once taken for granted and hotly contested. Funerals in Júzò are clearly ritualized in the sense that Catherine Bell gives the term: they are scripted, repetitive, formalized, and bounded (Bell 1997). For this reason, almost any anthropologist—indeed almost anyone—would immediately recognize Lòlopò funerals as sharing characteristics with ritualized events in every place on earth. Yet Lòlopò funerals are only weakly ritualized in Humphrey and Laidlaw's more limited sense. The intentions of participants in funeral events are extremely varied. Some might want to honor the funeral's focal dead, others to honor their own dead, others to uphold the prestige of their own descent group, others to repay a debt or put another into debt, others to have a meal of meat and alcohol, others to "help" by suffering and shedding tears. Most combine several of these aims and shift the focus of their intentions as the night or day goes on. Nevertheless, there is one central unifying goal that everyone is clear about and that almost everyone serves in his or her own fashion: the dead must be separated from the living effectively and sent on their way properly so they will grant their descendants generative capacity and not return to harm them. At the same time, while it is not always clear to all participants how a certain operation might contribute to this unifying intention, everyone has the sense that it is clear to *someone*—usually a clever old woman like Àp'imà or, if not to her, to the "underworld" (*mómi*), personified by the little yellow mouse. The answer to the question that Humphrey and Laidlaw claim dominates performative rituals, Has it worked?, is always contingent upon the answer to the question, Have we got it right?, crucial for liturgical rituals. If we have gotten it right, it is far more likely to have worked, and if it works, then we have clearly gotten it right. (The difficulty of knowing with confidence the answer to either question is one reason that funerals are repeated again and again until the dead finally fade from memory.) Funerals in Júzò are both "performative" and "liturgical" in Atkinson's sense, each aspect depending upon the other.

While Lòlopò funerals are scripted in the sense that they follow prescribed rules thought to have been handed down from the ancestors, they do not share the characteristic that Asad claims has undergirded the secular concept of ritual: they are not different from practical, technically effective behavior. The "rules and procedures" of funeral ritual are technical procedures in the same sense as are the routines of agricultural or pastoral work. Like farmers and herders nearly everywhere, Lòlopò engage in many repetitive, bounded and formalized, generative, nurturing, and life-taking activities without always being able to give a full account of how they work. Yet they do work, at least sometimes, if conditions are favorable and if they are performed with appropriate skill, care, and intelligence. Funeral rituals are much the same: practical, skilled activity following procedures taught by trusted and knowledgeable people. Like agricultural and pastoral work in a place where land is scarce and marginal, magnifying the catastrophic effects of serious errors, funerals are deeply conservative. While innovation does occur, it is usually limited except when forced by outsiders with little at stake in the outcome. As in farming and herding, a great deal of communication occurs in funeral ritual—and indeed, much of this book is devoted to the poetics of lament and *nèpi*, the art of speaking to unseen beings. But this communication too is intended to have practical effects. The sense that nearly everything in funerals, even the most scripted words and acts, is a practical technique intended to make specific things happen, underlies all the explorations of this book.

Settling, Burning, Burying

Lòlopò in Júzò's oldest village, Chemo, say their ancestors once traveled every year from their homes in the Baicaoling mountains to Júzò's fertile little valley to hunt wild pigs. They would drive the pigs into the fertile mud at a spring in the forested valley's center and club them to death. One year, one of the hunters dropped his knife sheath to drink and two grains of rice fell out. He shook out more grains, chanting, "Let the green rice grow long as a horses tail; let the rice stalks grow thick as a horse's penis!" When, on returning in the autumn, the hunters found the rice had grown taller than a man, they brought their families back to settle. These ancestors immigrated to Júzò sometime in the seventeenth century as the inhabitants of their homeland scattered in the wake of a military disaster.

Their home had been the villages of Vèli/Yeli 野利 and Laba 拉巴 in the Yipao River's rough watershed, the Tiesuo Valley 鐵索箐. The mountains of Tiesuo had been a refuge for indigenous peoples who spent much of the Ming dynasty resisting the state's penetration and transformation of central Yunnan. As Jianxiong Ma (2014) has shown, these mountains were linked, to the south and west, to three basins of central importance to the Dali Kingdom and its successor, the province of Yunnan under the Yuan (still governed by the royal Duan lineage of Dali): the basins of Zhaozhou, Midu, and Weishan. During the early Ming, local society in the basins was transformed, dividing into descendants of military garrisons allied with a new Confucian elite, now identified as Han, and descendants of the former inhabitants of the Dali Kingdom, largely Buddhist and known as Minjia 民家 or Bai 白, "common people." In most of the mountains linking these basins, the Ming governed indirectly, leaving the population under the control of native hereditary chiefs.

The Tiesuo Valley had no such chief and was nominally subject to the direct rule of local Ming authorities. Rugged and deeply forested, the Tiesuo region became a gathering place for peoples in rebellion against the Ming state. The Ming knew its residents collectively known as Lisuo 力些 in distinction from the Laluo 臘倮, mountain peoples governed by native hereditary chiefs. Lisuo peoples developed a highly militarized and politically organized society that prevented the Ming from penetrating the Tiesuo Valley for more than two hundred years. Although the peoples of the Tiesuo Valley were isolated from the basin markets and thus had difficulty obtaining such crucial items as salt and iron, they traded and cooperated militarily with the residents of districts governed by native hereditary chiefs, such as Wuding, whose chiefs episodically resisted Ming authority.

Between 1522 and 1572, Ming authorities organized two military expeditions against Tiesuo; both failed. Finally in 1573, the first year of the Wanli reign, Yunnan's military governor commanded forces from the county centers of Dayao to the east and Binchuan and Zhaozhou to the west to invade the Tiesuo Valley. The troops burned the villages, killed more than a hundred leaders, and captured the residents of some four hundred households. Most of the escaped Lisuo fled, some moving west into the valley of the upper Mekong, which became another center of armed resistance, others scattering to other mountain places. Ma attributes the origins of the peoples now known as Lisu 傈僳 to this diaspora. Some remained, submitting to Ming authority and becoming the ancestors of the Lipo (Lipò, "Li people"), who still farm and herd in the Tiesuo Valley's rugged mountains.[7] The ancestors of Júzò's Lòlopò immigrated from Tiesuo not long after this defeat, the ethnonym Lòlopò replacing Lipò as the valley absorbed migrants from elsewhere. The descendants of the original settlers used the Chinese-style surname Li, and when they first learned to write on tombstones they used the character 力, "strength," rather than the conventional 李 to inscribe this name, echoing the appellation Lisuo 力些 coined by Ming officials to suggest the formidable military power of their ancestors.

An allusion to this migration was made in the speech chanted during the funerals of the tenth lunar month, which sent dead souls on a long looping journey through the surrounding terrain (described in chapter 6). One arc of this journey began in the centers of government to which the Tiesuo Valley

7. The source for these two paragraphs is Jianxiong Ma (2013, 2014). Ma's chief source on Tiesuo during the Ming dynasty is essays by Li Yuanyang 李元陽 in the Wanli and Yongzheng-era gazetteers of Zhaozhou and Binchuan Counties.

became subject, then meandered through clusters of Lìp'ò villages on the region's high mountain slopes:

0.4	chì mi mí k'o jǫ	we've heard of such a land
	tsì jɔ k'o le jɔ	officials live there
	mà jɔ k'o le jɔ	kings live there
	mi m p'ò tsʼò n̄ la	land where fathers cannot eat salt
	mi m mo tsʼò n̄ shǫ	land where mothers cannot swallow salt
	mi jù mi ma yi	foothills follow the river
	sí kʼə sí mà hǫ	stacks of firewood burned to ash
	mi jù yi ma hǫ	foothills stand by the river
	mi sò yi ma hǫ	stand and mark the land
	mi sò mi wo dǫ	the land is marked and owned
	mi ji mi wo dǫ	all that land is owned

"Come back to this land of Júzò," the speech continues. "Land to drive and herd pigs, . . . long riverbeds where oxen plow, where grain springs from furrows, where corn hangs heavy before harvesting, where rice falls without threshing." Escaping the defeated Tiesuo region did not release Lòlop'ò ancestors from the hands of kings and officials, however. During the Qing dynasty, Júzò and its environs became firmly embedded in the regular administrative system of Dayao County. Yet this little valley also retained and developed a local form of political organization developed by the ancestors from Tiesuo. The descendants of the first immigrants put the remains of their parents' cremated bones in a small box with a lid shaped like the mountains that surrounded their valley. This rectilinear body, a small model of the cosmos, traveled through the valley, circulating each New Year to a different household elected to undertake a series of ritual and political duties Called huotou 伙頭 or 火頭 in Chinese, this system echoed the local political structure that had organized the Lisuo of Tiesuo, who also had communal chiefs called huotou 火頭 (Ma 2014). In Júzò, this system was used to mediate the local representatives of the Qing and republican states. The household selected as huotou was responsible for hosting official visitors, aiding them with their business and sending them peacefully on their way, negotiating settlements of minor disputes, arresting and holding serious wrongdoers, and seeing to it that taxes were paid (Mueggler 2001, 2002).

Shortly after the first Li families immigrated to the valley, a Han family named Wu joined them, building homes in the same village, Chemo. Others soon followed, both Lìp'ò from the mountains to the west and Han from

Sichuan and other parts of Yunnan. The Qing period saw mass migration to the Yunnan-Guizhou plateau from other provinces. The plateau's population quadrupled between 1700 and 1850, the migrants seeking livelihoods in mines, cities, and trade but also swelling the farming population. The most rapid migration occurred from 1775 to 1825, when the rate of increase rose from seven per thousand in 1775 to twenty per thousand twenty years later. By the mid-nineteenth century, migrants made up some 20 percent of the region's aggregate population. In semi-peripheral Chuxiong Prefecture, which included Dayao County, the population density rose from ten people per square kilometer in 1775 to twenty-seven in 1825 (Lee 1985). The authors of Dayao County's official history took a local perspective on this regional phenomenon in 1845. Han migrants, they remarked, were overwhelming the indigenous population of "various types" (zhongren 種人), distinguished from the unmarked Han by character, dress, and customs:

> During the Yuan and Ming, three out of ten people were Han, six out of ten were various types, and one was a migrant. . . . These last ten years, [migrants] have come from Guizhou, from western Chuxiong, and from Sichuan, filling the county to its borders, and the numbers of the various types diminish daily. Previously, all profits from harvesting bamboo and wood went to the various types, but today migrants have so diligently invaded the market that those who don felt capes and wear animal furs make not a tenth of what they did before. The rest goes to Han. (Liu 1845, juan 7)

Most Han who found their way to Júzò were absorbed like Lipò newcomers into the Lòlopò population, intermarrying with locals, learning the Lòloŋo language, leaving funerals clad in goatskin vests, and, when wealthy, participating in the valley-wide huotou system. But a few—the Wu who arrived in the seventeenth century, the Gu who came in the 1820s, the Zhang who turned up between 1820 and 1850—resisted, struggling to retain a Han identity. Their central resources in this struggle were the corpses of their dead. Having built their houses on the hillside above the little marsh where the first rice grew, the first Li families selected a twin hillside for their dead, separated from their village by a gully, eventually calling it called Kàlìbò, "hill of graves." They cremated corpses at the foot of the hill and buried their ashes above, marking the spot with a small square stone.

The Wu emphasized their Han identity by burying their uncremated corpses on the opposite side of the shared village of Chemo. As Lòlopò from Chemo tell it, after watching the Li flourish for several generations while their own numbers stagnated, the Wu demanded to share their geomantically favorable burial ground. They disinterred the corpse of a Wu ancestor and moved it to Kàlìbò:

> They buried a bowl with a live goldfish together with him. But the Wu clan still didn't thrive, so they dug the corpse up again, finding the goldfish still alive. The fish lept out and became a torrent that triggered a landslide that made a deep gully that still separates the Wu graves from the Lòlop'ò graves.

The Wu patrilineage remained tiny, and other immigrant Han chose separate gravesites. Eventually some Han began to erect inscribed tombstones over their graves. The oldest remaining is the stone for Wu Xixian, who passed away in 1776, leaving two sons and three grandsons, all of whom married Lòlop'ò women. It is likely that this stone was erected decades or even generations after Wu Xixian's death. The earliest dated stone is for a woman, Yang Long, born into a Lòlop'ò family in 1762 but married to a Wu and buried in 1821, leaving five sons, two of whom married Lòlop'ò neighbors and two of whom found women from outside the valley, possibly Han. Yang Long's stone was erected in 1832. In the late nineteenth century, around the time that Qing troops defeated an eighteen-year Lòlop'ò rebellion in the mountains to the south, Lòlop'ò in Júzò began to follow the example of Han immigrants and bury their dead.

This transformation generated the efflorescence of techniques for working on the dead described in this book. Whether a body was rendered into smoke that drifted into the sky or enclosed in a coffin, buried in a grave, and memorialized on stone had everything to do with the social fates of the dead—the ways they were remembered and forgotten and their relations with the living and each other. An older way of understanding the material nature of the dead, in which bodies were raised up into the sky to sleep among the trembling leaves of apple-pear trees, was placed in tension with a new understanding in which bodies resided forever beneath the ground in stone houses, uncanny doubles of the houses of the living. A vision of shamanic power in which words did battle with forces of death in the sky was placed in tension with a vision of bureaucratic power where gates were guarded by soldiers, bribes paid to officials, and the dead made to live forever under the watchful eyes of an official whose instrument of power was the pen he used to record who owed how much life to whom. Burial, tombstones, and inscription created a new form of body for the dead, where the sense of permanent corporeal memorialization under official eyes evoked by the story of the god of salt competed with an earlier sense of transient corporeal materiality—the tension captured so eloquently in the story of the shaman Pìmænèlì recomposing the cremated ashes of his son into a corpse to be buried.

Socialist Reform and the Unmourned Dead

On the eve of the socialist revolution (1950), people in Júzò engaged in a lively series of ritualized events after the death of any adult who passed away properly at home and not of violence, starvation, suicide, childbirth, or another form of bad death. These events began at the bedside of a dying person, where intimate kin planned her funeral and did what they could to ease her suffering. This vigil continued for two or three days after breath ceased while the death was announced to affines. On an astrologically propitious date, hundreds of kin gathered in the courtyard of a host household for the rites of Emerging from the House (*hek'ədǫ*) and Emerging from the Courtyard (*kukædǫ*). These lasted an afternoon, evening, and night, after which the encoffined corpse was taken up to the gravesite to be buried. Three days later, close friends and relatives gathered for a second night vigil, Third-Night Return (*sahèlò*), to welcome the wandering soul home for a night. Seven days after the burial, for a woman, or nine, for a man, hundreds of kin and friends gathered again for the day-long Dawn-to-Dusk Sacrifice (*nihèpi*), after which the dead soul was given a home in an ancestral effigy, hung high on the innermost wall of a descendant's house. After the harvest, during the crisp, sunny weather of the tenth lunar month, hundreds of kin and friends gathered below the hill of graves for Tenth-Month Sacrifice (*ts'iho nèpi*). Several years after both members of a married couple had died, when their descendants had gathered enough resources to prepare a tombstone, they gathered again to transport this new body for the dead to the gravesite, erecting it in a ceremony with the Chinese name libei 立碑, Raising the Tomb. Every year after that, during the rains of the seventh lunar month, close kin gathered again to make sacrifices to the stone, an event with another Chinese name, shangfen 上坟, Climbing to the Grave. Several decades after the death, the grandchildren or great-grandchildren of the dead couple called their kin and friends together during the tenth lunar month for a final occasion, Sleeping in the Forest (*likádùhè*), held at night in a grove of old trees below the valley's central hill of graves. This event, held only when resources were available, finally and completely severed relations between the dead and their living descendants.

Gifts and sacrifices were the central work of these events. Every participant brought a gift ranging in value from several bags of grain to a goat. Some gifts were given to and redistributed by the host household; others were given to other central participants. All were to be repaid at other funerals, involving nearly every household in the valley in a dense network of obligation and counter-obligation. Poetic language, also understood as a gift, was central. During Emerging from the Courtyard, people sang "orphans' verse" (*chr̀mèkò*), dialogues between men and women about the life and suffering of the dead. At Dawn-to-Dusk Sacrifice a male mourner performed "weeping for the dead" (*shrtsiŋə*) for a fee, at the foot of the place where the coffin had lain; then women sang "weeping songs" (*ɔchaŋə*) for their own intimate dead. These three kinds of lament were also performed at all other funeral events except those centered on tombstones, where Chinese was the only appropriate language to communicate with the dead. At the center of Tenth-Month Sacrifice and Sleeping in the Forest was a great chant to the dead, a virtuosic display of memory and poetic skill, taking up to eight hours to perform. This was a form of poetic art called *nèpi*, "speaking to ghosts"; many other, shorter *nèpi* were used during funeral occasions to negotiate with spirits, make announcements to the dead, call back the wandering souls of the living, and perform other tasks that engaged unseen beings. In the twentieth century, Lòlopò developed another kind of linguistic art, inscriptions in Chinese characters on tombstones: biographical eulogies, mortuary poetry, and long lists of descendants. All this poetry communicated with the dead, fashioning them as social beings and transforming their relations with the living.

During the first few years of Liberation (1950–1956), rationalizing funeral ritual was a priority for the new local government. Mindful of the revolutionary state's intention to ally with "minority nationalities," its local representatives initially voiced respect for the ritualization of death in Júzò. Yet they soon began to complain of its extravagance, particularly during the tenth lunar month, when hundreds of people gathered below the graveyards during the day for Tenth-Month Sacrifice and in a wooded grove at night for Sleeping in the Forest. In 1950, the new local government prohibited Sleeping in the Forest and began vigorously to discourage Tenth-Month Sacrifice. Still, the sites of Tenth-Month Sacrifice stayed busy for the next four years, and the major rites of Emerging from the Courtyard and Dawn-to-Dusk Sacrifice, less visible because they were held within courtyard walls, continued undisturbed.

Land was collectivized into small agricultural producers' cooperatives in November 1955, and collective units expanded over the next few years until they became the size of counties in 1958. Still, people in Júzò managed to continue staging funerals, using grain allocated to households to make rice loaves and three small goats (one for each central group of kin) donated by their production teams as sacrificial animals. But the entire system of rites for the dead collapsed in the autumn of 1958, as the grain harvest was directed to collective dining halls, all livestock were gathered into collective farms, and large numbers of men left to work on waterworks projects. During the Great Leap Forward and the devastating famine that followed (1958–1961), people in Júzò wrapped their dead in old quilts, carried them to the graveyard, and buried them without ceremony. In 1962, after production teams, the size of neigh-borhoods, again became the unit of procurement and redistribution, Lòlopò again began to hold Emerging from the Courtyard and Dawn-to-Dusk Sacri-fice, in severely curtailed style. In the early 1990s, an elderly male resident of Júzò recalled those years, beginning with the period from 1955–1958:

> After all, production-team leaders had deaths in their families too. So, even though higher levels forbade it, they would donate three small goats, and no one would let outsiders know. Then from 1958 to 1965 it was the Great Leap Forward and "eating from one big pot" [collective dining halls replaced by strict collective control over agricultural produce]. So at best we used three chickens instead of three little goats. And when we didn't have chickens we used rabbits—very difficult! Emerging from the Courtyard and Dawn-to-Dusk Sacrifice were held in one evening, and there was no exchange, since there was nothing to exchange. The three "thieves" (*tsapò*) [who led a night-long dance around the coffin] would dance a few turns and then stop, and the whole affair was done in fear of activists [young locals radicalized in mid-dle schools during the Cultural Revolution]. You wouldn't even announce a death, because if you did activists would come make trouble for you. Things went on this way until 1979.

During the radicalized years of the Cultural Revolution, those ritualists who had mastered the great chants for Tenth-Month Sacrifice and Sleeping in the Forest were targeted in struggle sessions and condemned to hard labor. The few who survived the great physical and psychological stress of those years developed other problems: the spirit familiars who had possessed them with the words of the great chants, abandoned and insulted, made them ill with chronic disease. The dead of the Great Leap Famine and all those who died between the famine's end and 1979 became wild ghosts, afflicting their de-scendants with pain and difficulty. People in Júzò learned to use a ghostly id-iom to understand the socialist state (a condition explored in Mueggler 2001).

In the wake of the Great Leap Forward, the region that residents called Júzò, united by endogamous kinship, common language, and a former local political system, was transferred from Dayao County to Yongren County and divided into the large central township (later to become an administrative village) of Zhizuo 直苴 and the small peripheral administrative village of Bo-zhedi 波者地. This region's population more than doubled in the second half of the twentieth century due to decreased infant mortality, relatively relaxed local birth control rules, and the household registration system that kept most rural people in place. Farmers compensated by growing hemp in shady mountain gullies unsuitable for other crops and producing hemp cloth for the market, aided by high hemp procurement prices. In 1978, the state ended price supports for hemp, prices plunged, and people in Júzò came to rely on grain production for nearly their entire income (Mueggler 1998b). Collective land was contracted to households in 1980, each person receiving an average 0.36 mu of irrigated land, farmed in rice in the summer and wheat or barley in the winter, and 0.93 mu of dry land, farmed in maize or potatoes in the summer and wheat or barley in the winter. The poorest production teams distributed no irrigated land and 1.1 mu per person of dry land. Few households could feed and clothe their members with this land, and most depended on relief grain from the state, receiving twenty to eighty kilos per person each year. By 1992, the total population was 3,433 in 860 households, clustered into the two large villages of Chemo ("big village") and Chezò ("small village") and fifty-one small villages and hamlets, many with only two to ten households (Yongren Xian Renmin Zhengfu 1992).

When land was apportioned to households, families gained control over grain and animals for the first time since 1958. This, and the relatively relaxed policies of the Deng Xiaoping government towards ritualized activities, made it possible for people in Júzò to invest again in Emerging from the House, Emerging from the Courtyard, and Dawn-to-Dusk Sacrifice. During the 1980s many Lòlopò families held these ceremonies for those who had died during the past two decades and never been properly mourned. As rural prosperity increased in the 1980s, the scale of these events grew, surpassing that of the early twentieth century. Lòlopò began to set up tombstones again and, beginning in 1989, to inscribe them with Chinese characters, continuing and elaborating a practice begun in the mid-twentieth century. The poetic language of death also revived. Women who had learned lament before 1958 taught it to their granddaughters and grandnieces. By the 1990s, lament was thriving, and funeral rituals were being held on a very large scale. Yet the most treasured poetic inheritance from the early twentieth century was never performed in context again after 1958. The ritualists in Júzò's central valley who had mastered the great chants for Tenth-Month Sacrifice and Sleeping in the Forest were all dead or gravely ill, and without their participation, these two forms of work for the dead could not be revived.

Learning Humiliation

This small valley and its smaller tributaries, never isolated but always looking inward to a lively sense of self-identity, were pulled apart by state-sponsored resettlement and economic out-migration during the first two decades of the twenty-first century. After the serial failure of a long string of schemes to eradicate what they saw as the valley's incorrigible poverty, county officials developed a plan to move a third of the population to new villages in the wide stretches of uninhabited terrain near the south bank of the Jinsha River, where people from other mountain places would also be resettled. This region presented a sharp ecological contrast to the lushly forested little valley discovered by the first Lòlopʼò ancestors. The botanist Joseph Rock traversed it in March 1924:

> We crawled today over an undulating sandy low hilly plateau . . . a weird haziness filled the atmosphere, which made the sun appear as a dull red fiery ball suspended in a grey mist caused by the dust-filled air. Bare hills wherever one looked, sandstone and yellow earth, much eroded low hills with old graves.[8]

Due to the difficulty of moving water up from the deep gorges of the Jinsha River and its tributaries, the region had remained mostly uninhabited (notwithstanding Rock's characteristically despondent mention of graves). By 2005, due to a large capital investment by state agencies, the hills were sparsely crosscut with aquifers, electric lines, and asphalt tracks, and a few villages surrounded by greening fields dotted the arid bluffs. The state promised those who would resettle here the "three connections" (san tong): water, electricity, and roads, still absent or inadequate in Júzò. In most new villages the state provided one mu of irrigated land per person, a building site for every household, a stretch of mountain land (some distance away) on which to cut timbers for building, and a partial subsidy for other building materials. Even so, relocating required a significant cash investment from each household, which most gathered by selling their contracted land to others in Júzò. By 2010, over 800 people from Zhizuo and 300 from Bozhedi had moved into the area, built houses, and begun terracing fields—approaching the target third of the population.

Some aspects of Lòlopʼò heritage thrived in this new setting. In the new village of Yangyuhe, for instance, with forty-four households from Júzò and seventy-three from other mountain places, a new culture center featured classes where women from Júzò taught their lavish style of embroidery. Inside the center, a wall mural titled "The Development of Yi Embroidery" narrated at length a sanitized version of the story of Júzò's founding "1,300 years ago" and the emergence shortly thereafter of the "age-old clothing competition festival" (which Lòlopʼò invented in the late 1980s).[9] Weddings in the new villages, filmed with digital cameras, became visually stunning events where women showcased

8. Joseph Frances Charles Rock, diary, March 1924. Royal Botanic Garden, Edinburgh.

9. In Mueggler (2002), I describe the invention of this festival, taken by many in Júzò to be a partial revival of some of the ceremonial events held during the lunar New Year to mark the transfer of the huotou leadership position from one household to another.

innovations in embroidery and youths openly sang antiphonal courting songs, underground in Júzò proper since the 1950s. The new villages brought to fruition a new regime of visibility that administrators had been trying to achieve in Júzò for decades. When representatives of county and prefectural agencies arrived with video cameras and commands to don embroidered clothing and perform circle dances, Lòlopò women became "signifiers to" rather than "signifiers of," a distinction Althusser made while thinking through the workings of ideology (Laplanche 1989, 44). Their task was not to signify anything in particular; it was merely to signify with as much energy and color as possible. In their habitually cheerful demeanor, maintained even under stress, and their undeterred enthusiasm for the arts of embroidery, they became the county's representative "nationality" (minzu) people, standing in for all the drabber and less willing mountain peoples, such as Lisu, Miao, and Nuosu. In the county center, a long way physically and culturally from Júzò, retired townsfolk passed their time learning Lòlopò circle dances beneath gigantic murals featuring "Yi" women embroidered head to foot. This new visibility placed Lòlopò in a tight circuit of recognition and legitimacy (Santner 2011, 54), granting them an identity not of their making and sanctioning them as exemplary representatives of "minority nationality" people. And it made them particularly vulnerable to bureaucratic arbitrariness, as evidenced by the many intensified social programs in the new villages, designed to undo their backwardness.

Lòlopò had learned to protect funerals from outsiders, fearing activists in the socialist period and official disapproval afterwards. The action of funerals was intentional and effective; it did not lend itself to the colorful, empty display of the kind demanded of "minority nationalities" by the reform state. Now for the first time, funerals were exposed to the gaze of others, whose eyes reflected the judgments most people were conditioned to make about minorities: enticingly exotic and shockingly backwards. Lòlopò learned the required lesson in response: humiliation. In nearly every aspect, funerals seemed designed to confirm the judgment of backwardness in the eyes of others, especially Han others. Funerals were loud, drunken, unruly, and wastefully excessive. The public grief that Lòlopò crafted with such artful poetic skill offended the modernizing sensibilities that nearly everyone around them was striving to develop, in which emotion is internal, spontaneous, private, and sincere. Lòlopò spoke of the Han funerals they encountered with disdain: "Han merely wrap their brows in white cloth, bump their heads a few times, and take the coffin out to be buried. As simple as that. And only immediate descendants bother to attend: most people stay away. Han dead are truly pitiful." Yet those living in diaspora villages worried that, soon enough, their own sons and daughters would be treating their dead parents the same way.

In the first two decades of the twenty-first century, Júzò joined the millions of villages that formed a vast labor reservoir for urban economic expansion, absorbing excess labor in periods of slow growth and providing meager livelihoods for ill, disabled, and elderly migrant returnees. This process, which Yan Hairong has called the "emaciation of the countryside," supplied "a flexible army of migrant laborers for a carnival of accumulation in which Chinese and transnational businesses share in the banquet of profits" (Yan 2008, 43). In Júzò, as in poor and minority villages across the province, nearly every young woman with ability or ambition departed to seek employment in service or manufacturing in county towns, the provincial capital, or the coastal cities, responding to the pervasive sense that reform-era development had robbed the countryside of opportunities for youth to construct any meaningful form of identity (Yan 2008, 51).[10] Many young men left too, but construction, the main sector that would employ peasant men, was shrinking. Many youths, unable to find unskilled labor, returned to squat on their parents' land. Though largely endogamous, Júzò had once been known among youths in nearby villages as a target for nighttime raids to try to sleep with pretty Lòlomo girls, said to welcome temporary alliances.[11] People in Júzò knew such youths as Kújupò, outsiders of low morals. "Now there are no pretty girls left," a former rake, now a county official, told me in 2012, during a banquet spent swapping comic tales about youthful conquests in Júzò. "And for outsiders, it's strictly hands off. Zhizuo youth band together and rough up anyone from outside who attempts to court a girl, as they are precious few. That place is full of men in their thirties without wives, children, or responsibilities. It's a big social problem."

Many in Júzò had long dreamed of finding metal ore in their mountains—a cure for poverty. But when the Zhizuo Copper Mine opened in 2007, about twenty kilometers above the central villages, it brought few benefits. Most of its 327 workers were from outside, and they lived at the mine itself or in the township center far below Júzò. A few young men from Júzò joined the 85 laborers in the pit; some died there, one on his first day. Others invested in trucks or vans to transport workers along the new mine road, the first reliable road into the valley. But elderly people complained that the road killed or maimed many young men who bought motorcycles to drive in and out of the valley.

10. In her compelling study of migrant domestic laborers, Yan Hairong asks the pertinent question about migration: "Why was the countryside in the 1990s often invoked by rural young women as a symbolic field of death, compelling them to seek a modern subjectivity elsewhere?" (Yan 2008, 26).

11. Lòlomo are Lòlo women, as Lòlopò are Lòlo men, and the full and proper endonym, frequently used in Júzò, is Lòlopò Lòlomo, for "Lòlo men and women."

Mine tailings polluted the river that flowed through the valley and centered so much poetic language. People in Júzò said that livestock who drank the river water became sick and died. Potable water for humans came from smaller tributary streams, but the river irrigated most of the rice fields. The lengthy and complex exorcism rite held by the riverside had once been performed only for those who had died badly: death from childbirth, suicide, or starvation, death by crushing, drowning, wounding, or falling from the path, death in an unknown place. And though these were many, they were always a minority, always exceptions. Now, beginning around 2000, exorcism became routine for every person who died, held a day or two after Emerging from the Courtyard. Accidents were so frequent, so many died in faraway places, and the state of being a wild ghost was so contagious, that anyone at all might return to afflict her descendants with pain, chronic illness, or death by violence. It was an expression of a pervasive sense that social relations were becoming increasingly fragmented and dangerous.[12]

As Júzò proper contracted, retaining mainly the elderly, children living with their grandparents, and adults who did not have the ability to find work outside or the resources to resettle, work for the dead became even more central. People spent more time dying, waiting to die, caring for others as they died, and planning funerals. No public events had replaced the mass rituals of socialism: meetings, classes, public education sessions, even gatherings for an occasional outdoor film. Aside from a festival at the lunar New Year and weddings, now infrequent, death rituals were the only events for which people gathered as a community. The elderly now dying had lived through repeated radical historical transformations, from the socialist revolution forward. Their deaths and their funerals became sites where these events could be collectively reprised and evaluated, opportunities to reassess what persons were in relation to national history, how they had changed, what they might become. The absent dead had long had a role at funerals for others. Now, while those who had resettled in nearby villages returned for funerals, many who had migrated out to find work did not, and room had to be made for the absent living as well. The sisters of deceased men or sisters-in-law of deceased women took on the crucial role of daughters at funerals, marking the places of actual daughters who had disappeared into the cities. Laments incorporated lists of intimate kin who had gone and not returned. The names of the absent living were inscribed on the tombstones of their parents, grandparents, and parents' and grandparents'

---

12. Exorcism rituals are omitted from the analysis of death rituals in this book, as they were explored in *The Age of Wild Ghosts* (Mueggler 2001).

siblings; these stone surfaces became the only places where all the living descendants of the deceased could gather. Death rituals became sites where the
threads of diaspora could be gathered and descent groups reconstituted.

The Plan of this Book

These historical transformations might be summed up in a few sentences.
Responding to pressure from local officials, the prestige of a regional Confucian elite, and the example of Han migrants, Lòlop'ò ceased burning their
dead late in the nineteenth century. Techniques for working on the dead pro-
liferated with the shift to inhumation, turning on the problem of the newly
durable corpse and the troublesome issues of political cosmology it raised.
Burial brought the image of the state into the center of death ritual. Lòlop'ò
created a lively and varied corpus of poetic language around their relations
with the dead, which they continued to refine through the first half of the
twentieth century. Work for the dead dwindled during the socialist period as
ritual activity was banned and ritualists humiliated or destroyed. The ghosts
of those who died during the Great Leap Famine and the following two decades multiplied, and relations with the state came to depend upon a ghostly
idiom. During the first two decades of the reform period, some major funeral
forms revived and expanded as work for the dead centered on putting these
ghosts to rest. Some kinds of poetic language thrived, as older women made
concerted efforts to remember and teach lament. Other funeral forms could
not be revived, as those few people who knew the poetry on which those
forms centered had died or fallen ill. Resettlement and emigration in the first
two decades of the twenty-first century exposed death ritual to the eyes of
many different outsiders, bringing new forms of self-consciousness into work
for the dead. In Júzò proper, death ritual became even more central—the site
where a difficult recent history might be reprised, a community in diaspora
reconstituted, and relations with the dead reshaped to be more "modern."

Yet these changes were not experienced in chronological succession. They
were sedimented into techniques and verses in close strata that exerted force
on each other. The image of the imperial state that found its way into death
ritual during the shift to burial shaped the way the socialist state was received
and appraised in the language of ghosts. Styles of narrating history migrated
from the "speaking bitterness" narratives of the early socialist era into lament
and became templates for narrating a turn to prosperity during the reform
era. The entire edifice of work on the dead, built up, torn down, and rebuilt
over a century and a half, became central to the ways Lòlop'ò confronted the
difficult transformations of the early twenty-first century. The task of this

book is to excavate these strata and describe their mutual influence rather than to impose a successive chronology upon them. While this book is centrally concerned with history, I have not arranged it chronologically.

In part I, chapter 1 spans the entire period in question, from the adoption of burial through the present, as it investigates the introduction of writing into Júzò in the form of Chinese-language inscription on tombstones. Stone inscriptions shifted textual agency from skilled readers to knowledgeable or powerful writers and created links between state authority and the bodies of the dead. Stones became analogues of corpses, doors to the underworld, narratives of lives, and textual diagrams of kinship relationships. Lòlopò used stones to create new ways of understanding and reaffirming relations among living descendants, and they used the association of writing with state authority to insert their dead into the national time of revolution as the state's victims or beneficiaries.

Chapters 2, 3, and 4 describe work on the dead as it was practiced during the reform era, focusing on Emerging from the House, Emerging from the Courtyard, and Dawn-to-Dusk Sacrifice. Chapter 2 shows how a dead body is assembled—how an impersonal but singular soul is captured, fleshed out with materials that hook it into the elements of immanent experience, and wrapped in the clothing of social relations. Chapter 3 investigates the sacrifices and exchanges that continue to wrap this assemblage, transforming it into a formal image of an entire social world. Anatomical operations of division and distribution transform virtual (living) bodies into actual (dead) bodies, opening up the body to reveal the relations of which it is composed. The relations of generativity at the heart of kinship emerge from this procedure, creating the conditions for making new living bodies. Chapter 4 shifts the focus to poetic language, specifically the art of lament. It compares laments from the 1990s, when the revitalization of work on the dead was thoroughly underway, with laments from 2012, after closer contact with others had given people in Júzò a sense of self-consciousness about lament. Laments fashion grief in a public setting by framing relations with the dead in vivid poetic language. Laments from the early 1990s described these relations as a circuit of suffering that connected children with their dead parents. By 2012, innovative lamenters had reoriented their understanding of suffering to be personal, internal, and intimate, reshaping their relations with the dead to take on some of the attributes associated with "modern" forms of authentic, sincere, internalized emotional expression.

Part II excavates deeper strata, describing the techniques and poetics of the two major funeral events that were abandoned during the 1950s and never revived: Tenth-Month Sacrifice and Sleeping in the Forest. Chapter 5 touches on some of the ethical and methodological questions raised by my acquisition of the great chants at the centers of these two events from a ritualist who fled Júzò's central valley during the 1950s, as well as by my attempts, in concert with others, to transcribe and translate them. In fifty-eight out of an original seventy-two songs, the chants construct a world for the dead, assemble an architecture for dead souls, and theorize the construction of dead bodies. Chapter 6 looks at the first twelve songs, which create the world and establish the possibility for human persons. It shows how the relations involved in death do not end with the concrete, personal relations between the dead and their intimate kin examined in part I. These relations also invove wider geographies and histories of migration, settlement, and ownership. Chapter 7 examines the fates of dead souls projected in these chants. In closely structured sets of parallel songs, images from cremation and images from inhumation intersect in several immaterial bodies for the dead: raised high in a monkey's nest, raised high in a courtyard, raised high in an eagle's nest, buried underground under the watchful eyes of the underworld king. These songs subject the dead to the imperialism of life, binding them to life by means of gifts from the living that force them into unending repayments for unending imbursements. Yet these songs also sketch out lines of movement that might provide the dead with routes of escape. Chapter 8 investigates the ways these songs theorize the material bodies for the dead, the ancestral effigy and the great *bu* effigy for Tenth-Month Sacrifice. Songs about these effigies' origins were performed in close connection with techniques for building and transporting them, and chapter 8 outlines the ritual action of Tenth-Month Sacrifice and Sleeping in the Forest, based on the memories of elderly Júzò residents and my attendance at one Tenth-Month Sacrifice event, briefly revived in an outlying settlement. Here, while the ritualist engaged in his long, weighty dialog with the dead, others performed other poetry with cleverness and good humor. By describing these songs as they assemble a world for the dead, these chapters attempt to reconstruct a rich, methodical, and thorough Lòlopò account of the genesis of human subjects, living and dead.

The perspective taken on the dead develops through this book. In part I the dead are, as is conventional in the anthropology of death, seen mainly from the situation of the living. Work on the dead is understood chiefly through its effects on the living; communication with the dead is seen as for the sake of the living, transformations in the personhood of the dead are taken as attempts to transform living persons. The speech described in part II is a sustained, detailed, and consequential engagement with the dead, an attempt to make a world for them and create their material and immaterial bodies. While it is an interested speech with a practical orientation, intended to establish and enforce a contract between the living and the dead, it also appears to be a sympathetic speech, an attempt to give the dead a voice, share in their perspective, and empathize with their position—even to allow their eventual escape from the iron-clad requirements the living seek to impose on them. In some ways, then, this speech might be seen as analogous to an anthropological description of the world of the dead. My task is to show how it moves away from a view of the dead as entirely instrumental to the interests of the living towards a closer perspective on beings with their own fates and experiences.

Ultimately, my aim is to understand the questions Lòlopò ask and answer about these mysterious others at the center of their social world. What are they? How are they embodied, in material and immaterial terms? In what ways is our existence intertwined with theirs; in what ways might they be untangled? What are their demands, their due, their powers? In what ways must they be imprisoned within a social existence, and under what conditions may they be helped to escape, to melt away?

PART I

1

Corpse, Stone, Door, Text

In 1877, Liu Yuqing, a formidable local chief in the Ailao Mountains of central Yunnan, erected a tombstone for the founder of his patrilineage. He was in a victorious mood, having recently helped the Qing army crush an extended rebellion of the farmers and herders of his district. The rebels had been inspired by the Taiping Rebellion (1850–1864) and led by a determined young farmer named Li Zixue. They had seized an iron mine, manufactured weapons, and established a local government that controlled the northern Ailao Mountains from 1856 through 1874. As a reward for his aid in destroying them, Liu Yuqing had been returned extensive lands lost by his paternal ancestors.

On the stone, Liu inscribed a long text in the meter of the Three Character Classic, memorized by every schoolboy. The text begins with the mountain landscape, forested and wild.

南山中，林木茂，野獸多[1]

In the southern mountains, The forests were profuse, The game abundant.

The inscription continues, telling of how Liu's lineage led its nomadic people into these mountains to hunt during a time when they wore hemp and goatskins, ate buckwheat and meat, warred with neighbors on their borders, and were happy from dawn to dusk. Liu's ancestors and their followers were among those known to the Ming as the rebellious Lisuo 力些, who fled the Tiesuo Valley after their defeat by the Ming armies in 1573. Seeking to convey a sense of autochthonous origins, the inscription implies that the Liu lineage discovered the land's fertility and settled down to plow and plant during the time of

---

1. The entire stone is quoted in Liu (1980, 29–30), who transcribes it in simplified characters, which I have converted back to the original traditional characters.

Hongwu, the first Ming emperor. It tells of how Liu's ancestor Pu Kai (1628–1662) built rice fields and markets and of how Pu Kai's sons gambled away their father's property after his death. After listing the lands returned to the lineage as Liu Yuqing's reward for defeating the rebellion of his own people, the inscription concludes:

楷父體，火化后，無著落，楷遺體，原葬處，塔枝樹，地不利，乖事出，
移此后,龍脈旺，萬事昌，南山強，惟我庄.

The body of Patriarch Kai, After its cremation, Has no resting place. The remains of Kai, Their original place of burial, Is marked by a stupa and a branching tree. But the site was not auspicious, Perverse events occurred. After the remains were moved here, Where the dragon veins are splendid, All things prospered. The power of the Southern Mountains, Belongs only to our house.

Liu Yuqing's lineage and its rebellious subjects were of the people known locally as Black Luoluo (Liu 1845, juan 7), Lòlopʼò in their own language. Prior to the nineteenth century, Lòlopʼò wrapped the corpses of their dead in clothing and quilts and carried them to a forested mountainside to be burned. The corpses were raised on a wooden frame and firewood was piled beneath. Some of the burned bones and ash were placed in an earthen urn or cloth bag and buried two or three inches below ground in a graveyard. In most places, a small, square stone, uncut and unmarked, was placed on the ground above the remains. Pu Kai's ashes had been removed from such a site and reinterred in a new lineage graveyard for buried corpses.[2]

Pu Kai's stone memorial was a heartfelt repudiation of this practice. The shift from cremation to burial coincided with the encroachment, at first gradual then overwhelming, of Han traders and settlers into the domain controlled by Liu Yuqing's lineage and its simultaneous loss of political autonomy. Liu Yuqing's descendant Liu Yaohan has chronicled his ancestors' struggle to retain control of their mountain territory in the face of the flood of immigrants who quadrupled the region's population in the eighteenth and nineteenth centuries. In the seventeenth century, Pu Kai's district measured about forty by sixty li, with several villages of Lòlopʼò tenants. Pu Kai welcomed Han craftsmen but forbade trade with the merchants who were moving out from garrison villages into the mountains; he is said to have had many merchants killed. After his death, his five sons traded and gambled freely, selling off four-fifths of their father's land to Han families who brought in more Han settlers. Understanding

2. Alfred Lietard (1913, 24) describes cremation practice among Lòlopʼò of Liu Yuqing's region. Yang Fuwang (2008) gives a brief description of cremation practices among Lipo in Lianchi Township of Yongren County, near Júzò.

that his family's survival depended upon identifying with the Han ruling class, Pu Kai's grandson Pu Zhongxin (1736–1795) took the Han surname Liu, abandoned his native dress, and married a Han woman. Liu Yuqing, whose mother was also Han, was Pu Zhongxin's grandson (Liu 1980, 12–30).

Seeking to create a Han identity, Liu Yuqing's ancestors found Han wives from elsewhere, opting out of the endogamous system of bilateral cross-cousin marriage pursued by ordinary Lòlop'ò. This strategy simplified the complex Lòlop'ò process of making kinship, shed the networks of relations among affines it generated, and focused inheritance and descent on a single patrilineage. On the tombstone erected over buried remains, Liu Yuqing inscribed this patrilineage in enduring material form. His memorial makes it clear that the stone could serve as a medium for stable relations among lineage, land, and landscape in a way that Pu Kai's cremated remains alone could not. Bodies—both the living bodies of fathers and sons and the remains of dead forebears—were material anchors for the virtual relations of patrilineage. Stones stabilized bodily remains, rendered visible their relations to the living, and channeled the forces of the landscape to manifest in the fates of the living. The "perverse events" that plagued the lineage after Pu Kai's death—the loss of most of its land and the rebellion of those who served it—were due to the improper placement of his cremated remains. To rebury them in a new place beneath an inscribed stone was to reject a practice that did not anchor the corpse solidly in the soil and to re-found the lineage after decades of loss and rebellion in secure connections among corpse, stone, land, and landscape.

During the eighteenth and nineteenth centuries, non-Han peoples across the Yunnan-Guizhou plateau learned the power of inscribed writing to fix corpses in the landscape, connect lineages to bodily remains, and make claims of land ownership founded on these links. But it was not only elites like Liu Yuqing who were beginning to inscribe on stone. Ordinary people, less constrained by the imperative to reassert or consolidate power, were learning the practice as well. Their stones did not always follow the custom—common in the models adopted from Han immigrants—of focusing kinship exclusively on patrilineage. Instead, they improvised, finding in the circumscribed surface of the stone the space to reaffirm other, more elaborate, practices of making kinship as well as constraints that began to transform these practices.

In Júzò, on the periphery of the Baicaoling Mountains, which extend the Ailao range northward into Dayao and Yongren Counties, the abandonment of cremation in favor of burial under stones layered new dimensions into worlds constructed for the dead to inhabit. Before people began to inscribe stones, writing was used in Júzò almost entirely for bureaucratic purposes. It was associated with tax records, land deeds and surveys, and the materialization of state authority in artifacts like stone road markers and a stone inscription memorializing the Qing victory over Li Zixue's rebellion. When ordinary people in Júzò began to inscribe their tombstones, they adopted Chinese-language script for their own purposes for the first time. Inscribed stones became durable analogues of corpses, doors to the underworld, narratives of lives, and textual materializations of networks of kinship relations. An understanding of textuality in which writing appeared as transient material traces of unseen nonhuman beings on the surfaces of the world, subject to creative interpretation, came into contact with a new understanding, where text was permanent inscription of durable meaning on stone and paper, subject to manipulation beforehand by the powerful and knowledgeable. Inscription on stone shifted textual agency from readers to writers and created durable links between state authority and dead bodies.

Recent literature in the ethnography of literacy questions previous attempts to establish global distinctions between orality and literacy influenced by Jack Goody and Ian Watt's (1963) proposal that the introduction of writing into societies previously dominated by orality created new possibilities for distancing and critique, and encouraged logical and critical cognition. This argument emerged from a long history of scholarly efforts to clearly distinguish writing from other material-semiotic practices such as picture-making, particularly in the context of logographic scripts in Mesoamerica (a comparable case in Yunnan is Naxi <u>dongba</u> script).[3] In recent years, the lively interdisciplinary reaction provoked by these arguments has deepened and diversified to produce a rich array of ethnographic and historical case studies describing the varied ways writing and literacy participate in specific social practices. This literature has moved away from looking for cognitive implications for literacy in general to understanding how particular practices of writing and reading are implicated in social relations, especially relations of power.

Of particular relevance is the large literature on imperial peripheries, where written colonial languages, vehicles for state power, are adopted by indigenous-language communities.[4] An examination of tombstone inscriptions in Júzò reinforces three points in this scholarship. First, as Mathew Hull (2012) points out in an ethnography of practices of bureaucratic writing and

3. See, for example, Marcus's (1976) proposed definition of writing in her influential review of the scholarship on Mayan script. For some descriptions of Naxi <u>dongba</u> script, see Mueggler (2011b) and the essays in Oppitz and Hsu (1998).

4. A sampling of productive recent interventions in this literature from dispersed geographical locations would include Ahearn (2001), Ballantyne (2011), Besnier (1995), Blomaert (2008), Brose (2005), Burns (2010), Rappaport and Cummings (2011), and Solomon and Nino-Murcia (2011).

reading in Pakistan, the category of writing tends to dissolve internally when specific graphic practices are examined in their social context. Second, as the category of writing fragments into particular practices, its external boundaries also blur: very little analytical purchase can be gained by drawing rigid distinctions between writing and other material-semiotic practices, a point made eloquently in Barbara Mundy's (1996) study of maps produced by Spanish, Creole, and native elites in Mesoamerica in the late sixteenth century. Third, material-semiotic practices like inscription on stone are emphatically material practices. It matters very much whether writing is inscribed on bone, skin, leaves, paper, or stone; indeed, the weight of a text may lie nearly entirely in its material substrate.

I begin this story of relations between the living and the dead with tombstones, since stones, unwritten and written, span its chronological scope and condense many of its themes. The immense value of inscribed stones as historical sources in China is well known. Yet, despite their ubiquity, stones from the contemporary era have been neglected as ethnographic sources. Moreover, little attention has been paid to how cultures of stone inscription spread—to how different peoples in China learned to write on stone and to how the significance of stone as an inscriptive surface differed from that of shell, bone, leaves, wood, metal, or paper. In Júzò, the stone inscription was introduced by a tiny minority, struggling like Liu Yuqing's lineage to produce and sustain elite Han identity, materializing the memory of patrilineal ancestors in the face of established Lòlopò habits of deliberate genealogical forgetting. When ordinary Lòlopò adopted this practice in the twentieth century, they elaborated it in several directions. They created lengthy biographies of the deceased that blended elements from oral laments and from the midcentury narrative practice of "speaking bitterness" (suku). These biographies placed the dead in a new relation to the state and to national time. They also transformed the Han custom of listing the sons of the deceased by creating extended diagrams of kin relations, including as many as eighty people, living and dead, absent and present. After Júzò lost more than half its population to resettlement and migration in the first decades of the twenty-first century, stones became tools for creating a virtual universe of kinship that reconnected all the departed to those who stayed behind.

Learning to Bury

Abundant archaeological and textual evidence suggests that residents of the southwest had been cremating their dead since at least the time of the Nanzhao Kingdom (653–902). In the *Man shu* 蠻書, or "Book of Barbarians," cremation and burial were already correlated with relative degrees of civilization. The Baiman ("white barbarians") who lived in the basins "bury their corpses three days after death in tombs in the style of the Han." The Wuman ("black barbarians") of the mountains "do not use tombs. They burn the corpse three days after death and cover the ashes with soil, retrieving only the two ears" (Fan 1962 [864], quoted in Gu 2007, 217). In the Dali Kingdom (937–1253), which succeeded the Nanzhao, many elites adopted a form of esoteric Buddhism transmitted from India and Tibet called asheli 阿闍黎 after achārya, a Sanskrit term for spiritual masters. A Jingtai-period (1449–1457) gazetteer, *Yunnan tujing zhishu* 雲南圖經志書, briefly describes burial practices among the region's elites: "After a man dies he is placed in a room; then the achārya master recites incantations. Three days later, the corpse is cremated outdoors; golden foil is attached to the bones, and spells are written in Sanskrit on them; thereupon they are placed in an urn and interred" (Chen 1995 [1455], quoted in Howard 1997, 47). Writing on bones and stone pillars was central to these funerals. Archaeologists have found graveyards containing urns of cremated bones and inscribed pillars throughout west Yunnan, in Dali, Chuxiong, and Lijiang, and north into the Liangshan ranges in Sichuan, ascribing them to the ethnic groups that the *Man shu* called Baiman, which included the elites of the Nanzhao and Dali Kingdoms. The *Yunnan tujing zhishu* describes funeral rituals among the Luo Yi in Luo Zhou, Guizhou:

> When they die they do not use a coffin. The great wrap their corpses with tiger and leopard skins, the mean with cattle and goat skins, carrying them in bamboo mats to the wilds to burn. Friends and relatives gather and kill livestock as sacrifices. They leave the bones without gathering them. The chiefs and the wealthy order slaves to stand guard for a period of two or three months, a month for children. They hide the bones in a place that non-kin do not know. Though Luoluo are scattered in many places, their customs are all the same; this is not unique to this prefecture alone. (Chen 1995 [1455])[5]

Cremation was not restricted to the barbarians of the southwest. Patricia Ebrey has shown that cremation was common during the Song period in many other parts of China. Confucian scholars objected to the practice as "cruel, a desecration of the corpse, barbaric, Buddhist, and unfilial" (Ebrey 2003, 159). Philosophers argued that the body was a gift from the parents, to be returned to them whole at death. The Song state imposed the penalty of strangulation for burning a corpse in 962, with an exemption for foreigners and Buddhist monks, initiating a proscription that would be renewed and

5. On the history of the Yi-dominated polities of Luo Zhou, see Herman (2007).

reinforced repeatedly until the end of the Qing. While such injunctions in the Song and the Yuan seem to have had little influence on the popularity of the practice, the Ming and Qing were far more effective at social reform. The Ming founder Zhu Yuanzhang was a determined opponent of cremation, and the official history of his rule, the *Ming Taizu shilu* 明太祖實錄, states, "In modern times a more flagrant instance of corrupt morals has yet to be found than the wild and rustic nonsense of burning the dead and throwing their bones in the water" (quoted in Yang and Yang 2000, 66). The Ming legal code made the penalty for cremating a senior relative beheading and for cremating a child eighty strokes of the cane. Most Han communities abandoned the practice by the end of the dynasty.

Ritual reform among the non-Han peoples of the southwest was far slower, awaiting the imposition of direct imperial rule. At the beginning of the Ming a third of Yunnan, half of Guizhou, and most of western Sichuan were governed by native hereditary officials ratified by the state under the <u>tusi</u> system. The imperial state gradually gained influence in these areas during the Ming era, intervening more directly in the appointment of native chiefs and replacing them with court-appointed officials wherever possible. During the early decades of the Qing dynasty, native chiefs continued to lose political autonomy to the state, which created new divisions among them and weakened their ties to their subjects, resulting in increased violence both among native chiefs and between Han and non-Han communities (Herman 1997). In response, the Yongzheng emperor determined in 1728 to abolish the <u>tusi</u> system once and for all. Local administrators responded with alacrity and sometimes with considerable violence, deposing or demoting most chiefs on the plateau. Though Dayao County, where Júzò was located, had not been governed by native hereditary chiefs since the beginning of the Ming, when it was placed under the special administration (<u>tijusi</u>) of the nearby salt-mining town of Baiyanjing, it was surrounded by indirectly administered regions. To the south, the once-powerful Gao lineage of Yaozhou (now Yao'an) was deposed in 1792; the Duan lineage of Zhennan (now in Nanhua) lost power in 1795. To the east, the Li lineage of Dingyuan (now in Yuanmo) was demoted in 1785 and deposed in 1805. Several minor lineages in the counties of Binchuan and Xiangyun to the west were demoted in the same period (Gong 2000, 526–527, 532). Only the formidable Liangshan ranges to the north escaped direct state rule until the socialist revolution: Nuosu people there continue to cremate their dead into the twenty-first century.

The new local officials who replaced <u>tusi</u> encouraged non-Han peoples to adopt the custom of burial, sometimes with vigor. "Objectionable customs of the people such as burning corpses have been repeatedly prohibited, yet, as they still dare do this, the punishment must be heavy," wrote Huang Zhai-zhong, magistrate of Dading County in Guizhou during the Daoguan reign (1820–1850) (Huang 1849, quoted in Yang and Yang 2000, 66). State pressure and the massive influx of Han settlers caused most Yi communities on the plateau to abandon cremation during the Qianlong period (1735–1796) or shortly thereafter. In Dayao and surrounding regions, most of the peoples who called themselves Lipò and Lòlopò learned to bury their dead in a long, staggered process extending from the last part of the eighteenth through the end of the nineteenth century. In an ethnography of semi-mountainous Lianchi, just a few hours walk from Júzò, Yang Fuwang notes that old people can often point out the graveyards where the cremated remains of members of their lineages were buried. In the neighboring district of Renhe, Yang Fuwang was told that people burned their dead during the Yongzheng period (1722–1735) and began to bury them after their native chief was deposed (Yang 2008). Once they began to bury, Lipò and Lòlopò quickly began to erect tombs over the corpses, followed by inscribed tombstones. In Chuxiong Prefecture, in Wuding, Shuang-bai, and Yuanmo Counties, hundreds of tombstones inscribed in Yi scripts or a combination of Yi and Chinese have been found, dating from the late eighteenth and nineteenth centuries (Hua 1997).[6] The Lipò and Lòlopò of Dayao, Nanhua, and Yao'an Counties had no script for their language and inscribed stones only in Chinese. Their stones, although remarkable, have drawn no scholarly attention.

Traces of Fire

Li Ganxue led me along the path that ascends to Kàlìbò, Júzò's largest graveyard, to a place between two parallel banks of earth, about four feet high. "This is where old people say that they used to cremate the dead," he said.

> They carried the corpse up here on a stretcher with a bamboo mat on it. They built a wooden frame like a maize-drying rack, placed the corpse on top, and put a wooden cover over it. Everyone who came to help brought a stick of firewood, which they stacked beneath the rack. After the corpse was burned, they put some of the ashes in a small reddish bag, along with the jewelry the dead person wore, buried the bag, and placed a small square stone over it.

After both members of a couple had died, two stones were placed side by side. On the hillside below the tombs of many descent groups we found the rough,

6. Hua's survey found 420 stones inscribed with Yi scripts in a single graveyard in Wuding County; eighteen in Yuanmo County, and seven in Shiping County, with dates ranging from 1777 to 1938. These stones are substantial: the longest have over 600 characters (Hua 1997, 41).

FIGURE 1.1 Cremation stones below burial tombs (photo by author).

rectilinear stones, four to six inches high and three to four wide (see figure 1.1). No one can name these ancestors, yet many people know which stones belong to their descent group, and they clear the brush from them when they make offerings to the tombs of their buried ancestors.

Li Ganxue remembered tending as a child a cremation stone for his maternal great-great-grandfather, the last person in his mother's descent group to be cremated. His mother's own tombstone states that she was born in 1911.

Assuming about twenty-five years between generations, her great-grandfather would have been born around 1836 and, if he lived to the age of fifty, died around 1886. Others in Júzò confirm that it was around this time that cremation was finally abandoned, shortly after Li Zixue's Lòlopò-led rebellion was crushed in 1874. This was considerably later than in most places on the plateau. Yet, like the decades after the Qing abolished native hereditary chiefs, it too was a time when a disheartening loss of political autonomy followed closely upon an extended period of state violence.

Lòlopò funeral practices make few explicit references to cremation. Yet they contain many texts and gestures that might be read as belonging to an older system of thinking about bodies, both material and immaterial, as media for relations between living and dead. Funeral rituals combine two complex assemblages of images of how the dead might be situated in the phenomenal world. In one, dead couples sleep high in the sky, cradled together among the stars. In the other, dead couples live forever beneath the soil, tilling and herding in an underworld, subject to Chinese-speaking officials. Chapter 7 shows how these assemblages are developed in poetic language. Here I wish to introduce them by indicating a few elements of contemporary ritual practice that still refer indirectly to the history of cremation.

Among the procedures to be accomplished immediately after a dying person's "breath breaks" (cèts'ì), the most urgent is to appease the spirit of lightning, Shr̀mògù, said to strike from above at the moment of death and to send his servant Cánìshunì to shackle the soul and lead it away. This requires the services of a ritualist, or àpipò, skilled in speech to ghosts and spirits. The ritualist assembles an effigy beside the corpse, cuts a chicken's throat, spits water on the corpse's head, makes a speech, and sweeps the body and house with a fir branch, driving Shr̀mògù before him. He then walks to a deserted place on the mountain and builds another effigy to make manifest the spirit's salient attributes and intentions.

This effigy is a model, four to six inches high, of a maize-drying rack, an agricultural tool once common in these mountains (figure 1.2). Such a rack was constructed of four posts, nine to twelve feet high, planted in the ground. Each post was forked at the top; two beams were laid horizontally across the forks, and a number of poles were placed perpendicularly across the supporting beams. Maize was piled on the rack to dry, the rack's height preserving it from deer, livestock, and other thieves, and allowing the wind to circulate beneath it.

The ritualist also assembles a miniature ladder modeled after the tall ladders used to climb to the top of the rack. He then makes another speech, de-

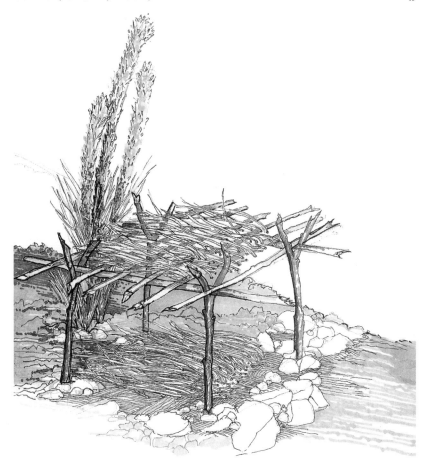

FIGURE 1.2 An effigy, or *nègu*, for Shr̀mògù, the lightening spirit in the form of a maize-drying rack echoing the shape of the world.

scribing Shr̀mògù's descent from the empty sky to the black clouds; to the yellow and white clouds; to the mists and mountaintops; to the firs, cedars, and pines; to the trees and brush, the rocks and pebbles, the river sands and weedy slopes; to the tiled roof of a house, the beams of a thatched house, the top of the wall, the hearth stones, the courtyard's head, the rice pounder's mouth, and into the bones and marrow of the dead person. The speech names the offerings, begs Shr̀mògù to release the dead soul, and asks Shr̀mògù to ascend along the same path. This speech contains a streamlined cosmology, a vision of the body's place in the world, inserted into house and courtyard, with the forested mountain slopes above, overhung by mists and clouds, and finally the sky. This is a world of substances connected by paths traveled by insubstantial beings. The effigy is an icon of this cosmos. The maize-drying rack models the world, described in mythology as square in shape with a sky supported by four great posts. The ladder is the path forged by the spirit's descent, materializing the ritualist's intentions to force it to ascend again.

Old people in Júzò who remembered stories their parents had told about cremation always mentioned the structure, similar to a maize-drying rack, that raised the corpse about six feet above the ground so firewood could be stacked beneath. In the 1940s, a similar structure was still used in some funerals. In an Emerging from the Courtyard ceremony, held two or three days after a death, kin and friends gathered to offer sacrifices of animals, grain, and alcohol. In most such vigils, the corpse was placed in a coffin on the ground at the center of the courtyard, while animals were killed at its feet and sacrifices offered at its head. In vigils for the wealthiest people, however, the coffin was raised on four sturdy posts and an arrangement of parallel beams to a height of at least six feet. The offerings were made beneath the coffin. This form of vigil, called *tsa̱te*, was undertaken only for a couple who had reached an old age, by sons and daughters who could afford to sacrifice at least one full-grown pig rather than the usual goats.

The long chant once performed during the tenth month explicitly linked the procedure of raising the corpse at *tsa̱te* to the souls of the dead couple swaddled together in blankets and cradled in the sky:

1.3	**tsa̱** bu **tsa̱** dà le	lifted coffin, lifted words
	n wú ǹ ni ŋæ **tsa̱** gɔ̀	you two cradled early and late
	tsa̱ hà **tsa̱** p'a ǹ p'u bò **tsa̱**	wrapped in quilts and cradled high
	mó pɔ̀ **tsa̱ te** le mà ma	a king's cradle too high to be seen
	mó pɔ̀ tsɨ wo **tsa̱** wo	a king's cradle for your love
	ni ní shr	
	tsɨ wo **tsa̱** wo ni chì ju̱	a king's nest to satisfy you
	tsɨ wo **tsa̱** wo ni lè tə	a king's nest to grasp in your hands
	tsɨ wo **tsa̱** wo ni ka̱ kò	a king's nest to take in your lap
	ni ka̱ kò yi mo	abundance returns to your lap

Here the specialized word *tsa̱* is used repeatedly to reference *tsa̱te*, the entire compound appearing in the fourth line. This speech was addressed to the two effigies that replaced the inhumed body of the deceased. One of these was an ancestral effigy (*nèts'ɨ*), a miniature icon of the dead couple bound together and cradled high in a "king's nest." This was a plaited platform of bamboo about six inches square supporting a figurine made of a straight pine twig bound with thread to a crotched chestnut twig (figure 1.3). An ancestral effigy

FIGURE 1.3 An ancestral effigy: a straight pine twig bound to a crotched chestnut twig with seven or nine turns of thread, lying on a bamboo bed and gazing up at a "flower" of chestnut leaves.

lived in a row of similar effigies in the upstream room of a house, high on the wall, supported by two sticks pounded into the mud bricks. Like the miniature ladder and maize-drying rack for Shr̀mògù, it was a streamlined icon of the cosmos, a material body for the dead, a bamboo bed cradling coupled ancestors in the squared-off sky of a house's cciling beams.

In offering speeches and effigies to spirits and ancestors, people in Júzò paired two forms of formal, bounded textuality—oral and material—to create contained icons of the worlds that the dead shared with the living. The intention was not as much to represent the cosmos as it was to act on it. Lòlopʼò textuality gathered powerful, animate nonhuman beings into iconic structures, then moved them along streamlined paths. Ancestral effigies gave the dead bodies and locations from which they could enter into proper relations with the living. Yet these locations were always provisional. All effigies were eventually destroyed so as not to give immaterial beings permanent footholds in the world of the senses. Ancestral effigies were no exception. They were moved down the wall as more people died, falling into lower ranks as they aged. After three generations an ancestral effigy was removed from the wall, placed on top of a coffin being carried out of a courtyard, and allowed to fall to the ground to be trampled underfoot, thus returning the forgotten ancestral soul to the undifferentiated animate substance of the world.

This principle of impermanence also applied to stone. The small square stones used to mark the remains of cremated bodies were a kind of effigy (*nègu*). Like ancestral effigies these stones made the souls of the dead material so that they might receive offerings from their descendants. Though many of these stones remained in place, the names attached to them were forgotten after three or four generations. Those that still stand are all nameless even though cremation was abandoned only in the late nineteenth century. Burying corpses beneath inscribed tombstones introduced a new way of connecting semiosis and substance, founded on new principles of remembrance, and supporting new forms of relations with the dead, materialized in corpses, stones, and texts.

Text (*và*) and Writing (*súvà*)

Two or three nights after a death, during the Emerging from the Courtyard vigil, kin, neighbors, and friends of the deceased exchange gifts, sing laments, and dance. As dawn breaks after this vigil, the corpse in its coffin is borne by kin out of the courtyard and up the mountain to the graveyard, followed by a long procession. After it arrives, sons and nephews dig a grave into the steep slope while others rest among the tombs. Once the hole is ready, the coffin is lowered, head pointing into the slope, feet pointing towards the mountains opposite, the precise angle determined by a geomancer. The coffin is covered in layers of quilts and blankets, buried with earth, then covered with stones to create a makeshift tomb, which suffices until kin can afford to build a permanent tomb of carved and mortared stone. A lament, called *shrtsìŋɔ*, "weeping for the dead," sung by a male ritualist, describes the scene:

1.4	wú nì bǫ lè bɔ	men like buffaloes' forelegs
	à bò pa yi kà lè t'a yi pę . . .	carry father to the gravesite . . .
	mò p'u tsæ̀ te do	ride out on your good white horse
	ŋa p'u vá te do tǫ pę	white bird soaring above
	tsɨ́ mo li lɔ	hoe on my shoulder
	lè lɔ jin cho də	shit basket in my hands
	ní he p'ò he jạ yi pę . . .	I build a house of earth . . .
	n dæ̀ ló he vè yi pę	live in this house of unworked stone
	n ti ní he vẹ̀ yi pę	live in this house of unmolded mud

FIGURE 1.4 Simple uninscribed tombstones (photo by author).

Later, after both members of a couple have died, their descendants will return to fashion the front of the tomb, carrying cut stones carved with sculptures that represent tales of filiality from Chinese history, legend, and myth. In present-day practice, these stones are shaped like an elaborate doorframe. Within the frame is installed a blank, flat stone called in Chinese, the language of the grave, a men 门, or door. Many in Júzò never inscribe this stone with text, an expensive and time-consuming enterprise. So, while many of the men in the valley's gravesites are fashioned of marble and inscribed, many more, carved from the local igneous stone, remain blank surfaces (figure 1.4). A few patrilineages bury their dead in sites where descent from the first Li 力 or Lisuo 力些 families who migrated to Júzò is demonstrated by their position directly beneath the giant tree, felled late in the Cultural Revolution, that formed the body of an apical ancestral spirit called Agàmisimo, the "great earth spirit behind the house." Those who use these sites adhere self-consciously to what are now seen as the authentic Lòlopò practices of using unpainted coffins and uninscribed stones.

These unwritten surfaces have correlates inside the house. The corner of a house that ancestral effigies occupy is a node in the mobile world of paths that the dead inhabit, linked to the site of the tomb. People speak of three souls of the dead, one residing with the ancestral effigies, one wandering the

FIGURE 1.5 A bed's-head spirit: a sheet of paper pasted to the wall, with a shelf below for offerings and a shelf above to protect from soot.

paths, one inhabiting the house of the tomb. In any house with ancestral effigies, another effigy is placed upstream of them in the same corner. This is the *gòwúdɛnè*, or "bed's-head spirit," which guards and protects the ancestral effigies (figure 1.5). A bed's-head spirit is a blank sheet of white paper tacked to the wall. A small shelf is placed below it to set offerings on; another shelf above protects it from falling soot; a "flower" is fashioned of twelve chestnut leaves tied to a twig and stuck into the wall beside it. This sheet of paper is where the spirit called the <u>cuiminggui</u> 催命鬼, or "fate-hastening ghost," writes the names of those about to die in invisible script. Yan Luo Wang 閻羅王 (locally pronounced Yàlɔ̀wù), king of the underworld, sends the <u>cuiminggui</u> to capture souls about to die. These are the underworld correlates of the lightning spirit Shr̀mògù and his servant Cánìshunì. The two pairs of spirits are associated with the two worlds the dead inhabit—the Chinese-speaking Yan Luo Wang and <u>cuiminggui</u> with graveyard and underworld, the Lòloŋo-speaking Shr̀mògù and Cánìshunì with the sky.

The idea of a blank stone that records the unwritten name of the dead, or a blank sheet of paper on which is written the fate of the living, is in keeping with a notion of textuality central to Lòlopò ritual practice. When resorting to healing ritual, people in Júzò brought a gift to a diviner, who would read a goat's scapula, the bones of a chicken's head, the surface of a bowl of grain, the ripples on a cup of tea or wine, or the weave of a length of cloth for traces of the being who had caused the illness. Most speeches to immaterial beings had passages devoted to listing the ways a diviner could read evidence of the being in text left on the world's surfaces:

1.5	su ŋo p'ǽ wú hɔ chì ni	we looked at the scapula
	p'ǽ dɔ̀ dǫ lɔ bɔ . . .	it appeared in the scapula's cracks . . .
	su ŋo mǽ t'è hɔ chì ni	we looked at the cloth
	mǽ mè dǫ lɔ bɔ	it appeared in the cloth's eyes
	su ŋo dò **kà** nè mi yi	we traveled to the world of ghosts
	dò t'è bǽ t'è dǫ	the cause of this pain appeared
	su ŋo dò **kà** cí mi yi	we journeyed to the world of spirits
	dò shɔ́ vǽ shɔ́ dǫ	the root of this illness appeared

The word *kà* in the fifth and seventh lines of this excerpt refers to Kàlìbò, the graveyard, the location of the underworld, where texts were written on blank tombstones for the ritualist to read. Lòlopò described this form of semiosis with the word *và*, consistently translating it as <u>wen</u> 文, used in a sense compatible with the explication of that word attributed to Jacques Gernet (1963): "It applies to the veins in stones and wood, to constellations, represented by the strokes connecting the stars to the tracks of birds and quadrupeds on the ground . . . to tattoos and even, for example, to the designs that decorate the turtle's shell" (quoted in Derrida 1976 [1967]; on the etymology of <u>wen</u>, see also Bol 1992, Bergeton 2013). *Và* was a trace on the surface of the world left by an agentive being, which could be read by those with skill. Writing (*súvà*) was a special instance of text, authored by living people rather than unseen beings. To write on stone was to shift the agency of textual practice from a reading ritualist to a writing descendant. And it was to tap into the power that the Chinese language represented for Lòlopò—the power of the state.

Writing Names

Júzò's graveyards were damaged extensively during the Smash the Four Olds campaign of 1966. Local activists plowed up the largest concentration of the small stones that marked cremated remains to make a maize field. Youthful activists sought out stones inscribed with old dates and smashed them, and people sometimes chiseled the dates off their ancestors' tombs in attempts, often vain, to protect them (figure 1.6). Unreadable fragments of inscribed

FIGURE 1.6 A smashed tombstone with dates chiseled off (photo by author).

stones can still be seen embedded in stone paths and the foundations of public buildings. The oldest surviving stones, some pieced together out of fragments, belong to the Wu descent group, whose forebears settled in Júzò in the
mid-seventeenth century at the same time as the first Lòlopò.

In the nineteenth century, the custom of inscribing eulogies for the deceased
was introduced on other Han stones. In the late 1820s, Gu Yuanzhang, his wife

née Jiang, and his brother Gu Yuanwei, also with a wife, settled in the valley, and acquired farmland. Gu Yuanzhang raised two sons, Gu Yuanwei four. After their fathers' deaths, the sons traveled to the regional center, Baiyanjing, and paid an elderly shengyuan, a successful candidate in the local-level imperial examinations, to memorialize their parents on stone. This was an effort to distinguish themselves from the dubiously Han Wu as much as from their Lòlopò neighbors. The scholar, Yang Bohe, seems to have delighted in his task. In contrast to the Wu, who employed only the most stilted of conventional formulas on their stones ("Tomb of the venerable Wu Xixian, who awaits an imperial title, conferred posthumously by his countrymen"),[7] Yang Bohe anointed the Gu stones with flowery but specific language. Indeed, his pride in his task seems to have tempted him to elevate his contribution above the goal of honoring the deceased. On Gu Yuanwei's tomb, for instance, Yang's name is on the first line, while the name of the deceased is nowhere to be found:

1.6 老大人之墓白鹽才儒學生員楊博和拜撰

Venerable father's tomb, respectfully composed by Yang Bohe, Confucian scholar and shengyuan from Baiyan [jing].

On Gu Yuanzhang's stone, Yang fulsomely praised both the deceased and his youngest son, the tomb's sponsor, before returning again to the subject of himself:

1.7　橠章名籍貿易於滇娶賢配江氏老孺人所生四皆豐衣足食季君尤賢教子讀書克光前烈母后佳城未奠擇吉建樹請志於余余處鄰居知公元德愛筆書之以垂永久

Named Yuanzhang, he came to Yunnan to trade. He took a virtuous woman of the Jiang for a wife, who bore four children, feeding and clothing them well. The youngest son, especially virtuous, taught and studied and sacrificed himself for the glory of his ancestors. After his father and mother were buried, he was unable to erect a tombstone [for a time]. He picked an auspicious day to create one and asked me to engrave it. I, who take my place among neighbors of the best morals, love to use my pen to write, so I have memorialized them forever.

Yang Bohe wrote his name on Jiang's stone as well, adding that he worshipped writing to his present age of eighty-two. As the Gu brothers worked to create themselves as their community's most civilized and literate family by memorializing their parents in writing cut into stone, they drew on sources of textual authority that extended far beyond the little valley they had adopted as their

7. "皇清伺贈乡谥吴老希贤大人之墓."

home—authority personified in this elderly exemplary representative of the rural Confucian elite and ratified through the examination system by the imperial state itself.

In the early twentieth century, a few other Han families also erected inscribed stones that foregrounded the situation of a tiny Han minority who saw themselves as struggling bearers of civilization among their goatskin-clad neighbors. These families were rare holdouts. Most Han migrants to this valley were quickly absorbed into the Lòlop'ò majority. Remembering one's ascendants—against the Lòlop'ò practice of forgetting them after three generations—was crucial for retaining Han identity, and stones served this purpose in the rough, poor homes of this valley far better than could paper. Lòlop'ò looked to the inscriptions on Han stones as models for their early tombstones, adopting many of their formal features, including many stock phrases used to introduce the names of the deceased and narrate their lives.

My surveys of Júzò's graveyards recovered dated stones belonging to Lòlop'ò descent groups from two periods: 1954 to 1958 and 1989 to 2012. If Lòlop'ò inscribed stones before the socialist era, these stones have not survived. In form, inscribed Lòlop'ò stones were of three types. Some listed only the names of the deceased and the bereaved. The deceased were nearly always a couple, and their names were embellished with elaborate formal introductory phrases and with dates of birth, death, and the stone's erection. Another type was divided into three vertical sections. On the right was inscribed a narrative of the life of the deceased; in the center were the names and dates of the deceased, and on the left were the names of the bereaved. A third type of tombstone expanded the surface area available for writing with three stones placed side by side. A biographical eulogy was inscribed on the right-hand stone; the names of the deceased and bereaved on the center stone; and filial, nostalgic, or revolutionary verse on the left-hand stone (figure 1.7).

Writing names required innovation. Most Lòlop'ò children received a birth name, used only in childhood.[8] At the age of seven or eight, a child was given a more formal Chinese name, a "school name," <u>xueming</u> 学名. In the early twentieth century, few girls were given Chinese names; after the socialist revolution, most were. After a married couple's first child was born, both parents took that child's birth name, adding the suffixes *p'ò* and *mo* for men and women respectively. They kept this name the rest of their lives, regardless of the fate of the child, using their formal Chinese names only on documents, if

---

8. Like other speakers of the closely related Central Ngwi languages (including Lisu), many Lòlop'ò used for personal names within their families a system of gendered terms indicating birth order, sufficient to differentiate any number of siblings. See Bradley (2007).

FIGURE 1.7 Tomb erected in 1991, with a biography of the deceased on the right-hand stone, the names and dates of the deceased and names of the bereaved on the center stone, and revolutionary verse on the left-hand stone (photo by author).

at all. As with Balinese teknonymy, described in Hildred and Clifford Geertz's (1964) classic study, this practice encouraged a degree of "genealogical amnesia" in keeping with the practice of forgetting ancestors after several generations. In addition, teknonymy focused social attention on childbearing couples as the centers of genealogical imagination—both members of a couple having essentially the same name—an emphasis reinforced by tombstones.

On stones, Lòlopò listed formal Chinese names when they were remembered and teknonyms when they were not. When not originally in Chinese, teknonyms were transliterated into Chinese characters with the suffixes p̲o̲ 颇 or m̲o̲ 么, 奵, or 嬷 added. In keeping with the tendency to refer to couples as bound together forever in the afterlife, teknonyms allowed them to be named on stones as though they were a single person, as in this example from 1998:

1.8

Teknonyms were often made more formal by being introduced with the Chinese-style surname followed by the character *jun* 君. The teknonym itself might or might not also include the surname. The first lines of a biographical narration on a stone erected in 2004 illustrate the complexity of naming:

1.9 罗公桂成乃起君起福生颇之次子也取名起发 . . . 成人后赘入罗府与罗君正福之么女

Luo Guicheng was Mr. Qi Qifushengpo's second son, named Qi Fa . . . As an adult, he married into the Luo household, with the woman Ms. Luo Zhengfuzhimo

The youth Qi Fa became Luo Guicheng after he married uxorilocally, then became Zhengfuzhipo (transliterated from Lòloŋo) on the birth of his first child. Luo Guicheng was used on his tomb, where his wife remained Luo Zhengfuzhimo. Many people chose not to use the teknonyms of female ascendants, naming them in the Han style merely with the surname of their family of birth, followed by *shi* 氏.

The Li, the majority in Júzò, chose between two characters to write their surname, often combining both on one stone: 力, meaning strength, bestowed upon the rebellious peoples of the Tiesuo Valley by Ming administrators, and the common Chinese surname 李. This choice appears to distinguish Chinese-language names from names transliterated from Lòloŋo. Thus, on the stone Li Fuzhong 李福忠 erected for his parents is inscribed "my father was the second born of Li Mingnai 力明叨," where Mingnai is a transliteration of a Lòloŋo given name. The same strategy is used for teknonyms. On the same stone, the deceased couple's names are recorded as Venerable Li 老李 and as Li Wangbaopo 力王保颇 and Li Wangbaomo 力王保奻, transliterations of Lòloŋo teknonyms. The daughters are listed as Li Yuanbaomo 力元保奻 and Li Xiangfumo 李想福奻, the last a Chinese-language birth name made into a teknonym with the addition of *mo* 奻. It was only the Li who employed this strategy. Those with other surnames wrote them with only one character.

The second essential task of every stone was to list the names of the bereaved, the *xiao* 孝. Early local Han stones sometimes listed the names of sons or grandsons and their wives after the name of the deceased. Lòlopò elaborated extravagantly, carving into stone a selected portion of the mutable universe of kinship performed funerals. As chapter 3 elaborates, people in Júzò divided the participants in all funeral events into three categories with distinct roles: *zòmæ*, *avə*, and *vedù*. The *zòmæ* were the deceased's married-out daughters and their family and friends; the *avə* were the deceased's affines and their friends, led by the deceased's brothers (if a woman) or brothers-in-law (if a man); the *vɛdù* were the deceased's sons and their friends. Most rituals had hundreds of participants, each of whom demonstrated allegiance with at least one of these groups. At every event, members of the daughters' group, or *zòmæ̀*, positioned themselves at the sides of the coffin, effigy, or tomb, the brothers-in-law's group, or *avə*, at its head, and the sons' group, or *vɛdù*, at its feet. At every ritual, the daughters' group made offerings first, the brothers-in-law's group went next, and the sons' group last (with many internal distinctions in each). Most participants had cross-cutting relations with *zòmæ̀*, *avə*, and *vɛdù*, and they chose their allegiance deliberately depending on their formal kinship relation to the deceased, their intimacy with a principal daughter, brother-in-law, or son (or one of his or her intimate kin or friends), or debts acquired at previous funerals. Thus, while patterns of seating and offering were formally prescribed, performance was flexible.

The limited surface area of a stone did not lend itself to writing names in the spatial order in which *zòmæ̀*, *avə*, and *vɛdù* usually arranged themselves. Instead, inscribers divided the space into vertical ranks for different classes of kin. An early example is a stone Li Fuzhong inscribed for his parents in 1958, listing thirty-eight bereaved. Sons and daughters are listed in the top rank, with the names of their wives and husbands in columns directly below them, so that each couple can be discerned. The sons' sons are listed in the third rank with their wives arranged below them in the fourth. The sons' daughters are on the fifth with their husbands in the sixth; the daughters' sons and daughters are in the seventh with their wives and husbands in the eighth. This tombstone includes the names of deceased and bereaved along with a biography on a single stone, so the space is limited. As more people divided inscriptions onto three stones in the 1990s and 2000s, the deceased man's (or woman's husband's) brothers' sons were listed on the same row as the deceased's own sons, including the brothers' sons' wives with the sons' wives on the next row, and the brothers' sons' sons and daughters, with their wives and husbands on further rows. This arrangement created ranks by generation and gender rather than by genealogical distance from the deceased, ranking brothers' sons the same as sons, brothers' daughters the same as daughters, and so on with spouses and grandchildren. All stones privileged spousal relations over relations of descent by making clear who was married to whom but not who was the child of whom. All, crucially, preserved the *zòmæ̀/vɛdù* distinction by separating children of sons from children of daughters. And all excluded the *avə* group. As brothers of the female member of a couple, *avə* and their children were not members of the descent group. They were protectors and supporters of their sister and her children and—since Lòlopò preferred bilateral cross-cousin marriage—the source of potential marriage partners. Finally, in distinction from funeral rituals, stones employed clear genealogical principles, excluding the hundreds who belonged to the *zòmæ* and *vedù* groups as extended kin, coresidents, friends, and neighbors.

Stone inscriptions preserved foundational features of the universe of kinship relations performed at funeral rituals while creating new ways of conceptualizing it. Inscriptions formally defined a select descent group, excluding all others. But they also employed new principles of inclusion. They listed the names of deceased descendants, usually without marking them, installing the living and the dead side by side. And they included the absent. Even more than most places in rural China, Júzò had emptied out by the 2010s. As the numbers of inscribed stones increased, those who remained in Júzò could find their names on many stones, as members of many descent groups. The surfaces of stone doors to tombs became the only places where a generation of brothers' sons and daughters with all their spouses, children and children's spouses, and children's children could be reconstituted and displayed in its full glory. In the past, people often spoke of the graveyard at Kàlìbò as a city of the dead, ruled by a Chinese-speaking bureaucracy, separated from the village of the living by a deep ravine. Now it became a place where an exclusive universe of patrilineal descent was redefined and reconstituted across the ever deeper ravines of death and absence.

Corpse, Stone, Door

In the autumn of 1992, Qi Ping erected inscribed stones for his parents who had both died in 1990, his unmarried elder brother who had died around 1970, and his sister's husband who had died in 1981. This event was the high point of his lifelong struggle to establish himself as his family's patriarch, over his elder brother Qi Long. Sometimes an elder brother might have taken the lead in erecting tombstones, but Qi Ping argued strenuously that he was better off than his brother; he had contributed more to his parents' funerals, and he had living children and grandchildren while his brother's only two children, both daughters, had died childless. His project caused much resentment in his brother's household.

Qi Ping had served as principal host, or *vedù*, in the funerals for all four of the deceased. At his parents' funerals, this was his right as the youngest son. At his elder brothers' funerals, he acted as a son to the childless dead. And he did the same for his sister's husband, to whom, since the latter had married into the Qi household, Qi Ping was in the formal position of a younger brother rather than a brother-in-law, or *avə*. Now, Qi Ping argued that it was only natural for him to continue the role of principal host, or *vedù*, as he planned for tombstones, despite his elder brother Qi Long's initial resistance.

In regard to the stones, Qi Ping's mother's brother Luo Guiyuan served as the principal brother-in-law, or *avə*, for Qi Ping's parents. Qi Ping's mother's sister's husband had married into his wife's household, and he acted as a second *avə*, or brother-in-law. Qi Ping's dead brother had been married to a deceased woman after his death; her brother acted as his principal *avə*. Qi Ping's living elder brother Qi Long acted as principal *avə* for their sister's dead husband. Qi Ping's living sister served as principal daughter, or *zòmæ̀*, for Qi Ping's parents, and her daughter served as *zòmæ̀* for both Qi Ping's childless elder brother and his sister's childless husband.[9] While Qi Ping took on most of the burden of planning the event, he could not have carried it out without the active support of all the principal *avə* and *zòmæ̀*.

As a schoolteacher and the most classically literate person in the valley, Qi Ping was often consulted by others to compose Chinese-language inscriptions for their tombs. He spent weeks writing out all text for the planned tombstones in a school notebook and repeatedly checking it with the three principal *avə*, translating it for them where necessary. He bought smooth marble stones in the county town, transported them to Júzò at considerable expense, hired a calligrapher to paint the text on the stones and a skilled carver to inscribe it, then invited the three *avə* to approve the finished inscriptions in keeping with their role as arbiters of ritual propriety. This was very likely the only occasion the stones would be read with any care (other, more casual, readings might occur at the yearly Climbing to the Grave ceremonies during the seventh lunar month, when the *zòmæ̀*, *avə*, and *vedù* groups would gather again to sacrifice to the stones).

On the day the stones were to be erected, all the kin and friends of the principal *zòmæ̀*, *avə*, and *vedù*, totaling more than eight hundred people, gathered in Qi Ping's courtyard to admire the stones. They were propped against the wall draped in red silk contributed by the *zòmæ̀*, who were responsible for clothing the dead. After much chaotic shouting of instructions, the nieces and nephews of all the deceased offered each stone two bottles of alcohol and some money and cigarettes.[10] Then the clothed stones were lifted carefully to the backs of the principal *avə*, who had once led deceased's coffins to the gravesite. Placing the stones on the bearers' backs had been a difficult choice. Another option would have been to seat the stones in litters in the style of

9. Chapter 3 explains in more detail how such decisions are made.

10. These were actually only the parallel nieces and nephews (*zòdu nedu*). The distinction between cross and parallel nieces and nephews and their roles is described further in chapter 3.

imperial officials. Yet Qi Ping worried that a stone might drop out of a litter on the rough path to the gravesite and break—an utter disaster. The stones, wrapped in silk and borne like dead bodies, were to be treated the same as corpses.

Bearing the stones, the *avǝ* walked the exact route along which Qi Ping's father had been borne two years previously, followed by the participants—first those allied with the *avǝ*, then those supporting the *vɛdù*, finally those with the *zòmǽ*. At the burial site, Luo Guiyuan, acting as principal *avǝ* for Qi Ping's parents, negotiated with the shanshen 山神, or mountain spirit, who guarded the portal to the underworld. Shanshen were local subordinates of Yan Luo Wang, king of the underworld, and like all spirits connected with the grave-yard they had no Lòloŋo name and understood only the Chinese language. Each descent group had its own shanshen, a small rock or stump (figure 1.8); decades before, most shanshen had been large old trees.

Luo Guiyuan killed a chicken, used its blood to paste a few feathers on the shanshen and made a brief speech in Chinese, offering the chicken, alcohol, and some rice. He then grasped a live chicken by its feet, swept each grave with it, and released it to flutter among the tombs, shouting, "dead enter, living de-part!" The *avǝ*'s supporters built the tombs, assembling the carved sandstone doorframes that had been prepared and placed nearby.

After being mortared in place, the stones were offered gifts. As *vɛdù*, Qi Ping killed a goat for each stone. His brother Qi Long killed a goat for his parents' stone (as secondary *vɛdù*) and one for his sister's husband's stone (as *avǝ*). The *avǝ* for Qi Ping's deceased brothers and sisters' husbands killed five goats in all. As principal *zòmǽ* for all the deceased, Qi Ping's sister and her daughter killed a goat for each stone. Each central offerant was supported by hundreds of others (as described in chapter 3). Later, the participants arranged themselves around the tombs, the *avǝ* group at the head of the tomb, the *vɛdù* at its foot, and the *zòmǽ* along the two sides, each person chewing chopped pieces of boiled goat meat and drinking a portion of alcohol served by daugh-ters of the *zòmǽ*.

These relations were also traced in other media. The men boiling the goat meat handed a scapula to each of the principal *avǝ*, who read the marks on their bone. In one method of divination, the fate of the sky was inscribed on the thin, broad upper portion of the triangular bone; the fates of the *vɛdù* family and its guests were inscribed in the middle of the triangle, on the left and right halves, respectively; the fates of the ancestors in their graves were at the bottom where the sides of the scapula came together in a point. Another method gave the broad upper portion of the triangle to all the guests, the

FIGURE 1.8 A "mountain spirit" or shanshen山神 (photo by author).

scapula's supporting left rib to the *avə*, and the bottom area near the point to the dead. Reading the scapula situated the dead in relation to the living within the phenomenal world they shared, placing the sky above, the living between, and the dead beneath. This was a world consistent with the buried corpse in its underworld house, subject to the cuiminggui and shanshen in the Chinese-speaking hierarchy of Yan Luo Wang but inconsistent with the image of the dead cradled in a sky nest, associated with the Loloŋo-speaking Shr̀mògù and Cánìshunì.

The ritualized erection of tombstones was new in Júzò in the early twentieth century. By the century's end it had been integrated into the inclusive structure of mortuary ritual, to be elaborated or simplified as context demanded. At the center was the inscribed stone, both door and corpse. As a door it was portal to an underworld house in the village of the dead. As corpse it was a *nègu*, a materialization of the dead being. Yet inscribing the door/corpse with text made it unlike any other *nègu*; it became a permanent body of the deceased, subject to potential readings in the future.

Inscribing Lives

Before the twentieth century, Lòlopʼò had no formal tradition of individualized biography (chapter 4 outlines the creation of one such tradition during the early twenty-first century). In several genres of lament and song, people in Júzò chronicled the lives of the deceased from birth through childhood, marriage, childbearing, and death. Yet laments were nearly identical for each decedent, rarely incorporating personal material beyond a name or two. Collectively, these forms of oral textuality inserted the life of the deceased into an expansive narrative of the history of creation. The long chant once sung during Tenth-Month Sacrifice opened by describing the creation of earth and sky, before moving on to the origins of plants, animals, and humans (as elaborated in chapter 6). In 1958, Li Fuzhong inscribed a stone, mentioned above, for his father, named only as "the venerable Li" (1879–1954), his mother Li Wangbaomo (1884–1919) and his stepmother Su Faxiemo (d. 1958). On this stone, in the position occupied in later stones by nostalgic or revolutionary verse, is a text that begins like an abbreviated translation of these songs of creation:

> 1.10 先有天地然后有万物先有父母然后始有兒女父母者为兒所虑不甚枚举为儿兒女者穷则呼天痛痒则呼为父母父母过去念养我骨肉...

> First there was Heaven and Earth, and then there were the ten thousand beings; first there were Father and Mother, and only then were there sons and daughters. Children do not have much concern for their [living] parents. Everyone raised as a son or daughter will cry to Heaven when in poverty and cry to parents when in pain. Only when our parents have passed away do we remember that they raised our flesh and bones. . . .

Laments detail the suffering parents endured raising their children, then speak of the happy circumstances the children were able to arrange for their parents at the end of their lives. The most common form of biographical inscription on stones combined the structures of lament and <u>suku</u>, "speaking bitterness," with which Chinese peasants of the 1950s learned to speak of their lives in relation to an approved narrative of the history of the nation.[11] As Li Fuzhong's inscription for his parents tells of the difficulty of life before Liberation, it narrates a tangled tale of family circumstances. Li Fuzhong's father married a virtuous woman from his village, who raised two boys and a girl:

1.11 欠百半抛夫丢儿乃夭没矣 . . . 孤儿血泪难堪言过三秋父娶对门大而村苏法邪嬷为我继母 . . . 随母及家眷丧女苏法邪因不能尽孝早亡殁迹灵魂嫁与比作伴继母后又育有一女嫁于耳田

Having reached only half her span of a hundred years, she abandoned her husband and cast off her children, dying at an early age. . . . The tears of blood versed by her orphaned children do not bear speaking about. After three autumns, my father married a proper match, Su Faxiemo of Da'er Village, to become my stepmother. . . . Following her mother into the household was her dearly remembered daughter, Su Faxie, who subsequently was unable to fulfill her filial obligations, dying early, [her line] extinguished. Her soul was married off to become the companion of a suitable partner. My stepmother later had another daughter, who was married off to Ertian Village.

The dead Su Faxie is listed among the bereaved, along with her husband, Xiaogou, "Little Dog," the name of the infant to whom she was married after her death.[12] The inscription transitions to the present, telling of the family's wellbeing and paying obeisance to the new apparatus of the party-state in the hamlet of Guiteng:

1.12 明日复明日往事不可复矣现在三代同堂桂藤方亦有公乡和公务职称者

Tomorrow repeats tomorrow, but the past can never be repeated. Now we are three generations under one roof, and Guiteng has township officials and public functionaries.

11. Hinton's (1967) incomparable ethnographic account of revolution in a village in Shanxi Province remains an indispensable source on rituals of "speaking bitterness." Apter and Saich (1994) give a historical account of how rituals of speaking in revolutionary ways were forged in Yan'an. Anagnost (1997, 18) usefully theorizes <u>suku</u> rituals as ways of making history speak in a palpably real way, which could then be inscribed as literature as revolutionary culture was fashioned. Hershatter (2011) gives an illuminating recent account of <u>suku</u> narratives, based on fieldwork with women who still remembered the early 1950s.

12. Parents of children who failed to thrive often exchanged their children's names with a rock, plant, or animal, so calling children the Lòloŋo equivalent of "little stone," "little bush," or "little dog" was not uncommon.

When Lòlopò began to inscribe stones again in the late 1980s, they found the old narrative structure of <u>suku</u> useful for organizing inscriptions for those born during the "old society." The stone Li Ganxue erected for his parents in 2000 is typical, drawing on tropes repeatedly used in earlier stones—wearing the stars and carrying the moon for poverty, diligent study for filiality—while also speaking of the difficulty of prerevolutionary life. The stone narrates the life of Li Ganxue's mother rather than his father, who died when he was a child:

1.13 自从小丧母 . . . 少年安父家境贫寒无房无地旧社会为人恩度日披星载月恋爱劳动 节省吃穿积攒薪金起房置地 . . . 膝下所生两男两女两女早夭折勤策全力抚育两儿 . . . 读诗书长大成才完婚极力扶育儿孙成长攻读诗书望子 . . . 精心抚育如愿以偿如今儿孙满堂四代同堂全家合欢和睦幸福共享乐年岁月难留九十寿终

Since she mourned her mother at a young age, . . . as a child she lived with her father. The family circumstances were lowly and poor; they did not have a house or land. . . . In the old society she relied on others' kindness to pass her days, wearing the stars and carrying the moon. She loved labor, economized on food and clothing, and saved her money to build a house and buy land. . . . Of children, she bore two boys and two girls. The two girls died prematurely, and she diligently spent all her strength nurturing her two sons. . . . We grew up reading the Classics and became men of substance; we married and did our best to raise children and grandchildren who grew up diligently studying the Classics and reading characters. We put our entire heart into raising our children, fulfilling her wishes in recompense. Now, children and grandchildren fill the house, four generations under one roof. The entire family rejoices in harmony, well disposed to one another and blessed. Together we have enjoyed many happy years. But the years and months cannot be halted, and she died at the age of ninety.

The inscription employs a simple classical grammar, used traditionally in Han areas to impart moral and auspicious sayings, blending the vocabulary of <u>suku</u> with another vocabulary about labor and frugality, rooted in works of communist morality. And of course the biography is extremely selective. In fact, Li Ganxue's elder brother never married, living in deep poverty with his mother until she died, while Li Ganxue raised a family of children and grandchildren separately. The fulsome descriptions of hardship in biographical eulogies are always about the suffering of the parents during the time before their children came of age, a structure that coincided happily with <u>suku</u> for Li Ganxue's mother's generation.

Many of the first stones inscribed after the long hiatus of the Great Leap Forward and the Cultural Revolution reached into the past to settle wandering souls uprooted by the chaotic political events of the century. A moving example is the simple stone Su Pingying inscribed in 1992, thirty-seven years after his cousin Su Haijun's death in 1955, a parallel cousin he called "younger brother" (*næmà*).

1.14 故人苏海钧原系吾父之弟苏公荣昌之第二之子青年时身强力壮勤劳诚实可敬很受人们的尊重家里一把得力的劳动能手只因旧社会一次强行征兵中被缚大气所伤病故民间传说阴曹地府孤魂难度经双方人说合与小村力英邪颇之次女力英能配为阴室为 . . . 唸故者特建佳城永垂不殁留表寸心.

My old friend Su Haijun was the second son of my father's younger brother, Su Rongchang. When he was young, he was strong and tough, and his industry and honesty were admirable. At home he was a capable and expert laborer. But, because in the old society his lungs were damaged when he was tied up during forcible conscription into the army, folk tradition has it that his lonely soul is suffering in the underworld. After the two parties reached an agreement, he received Li Yingneng, the second daughter of Liyingxiepo of Xiaocun, as his posthumous wife. . . . In memory of the deceased, we dedicate this auspicious compound, to endure forever, as a lasting display of our sentiments.

Li Yingneng, born a year after Su Haijun in 1924, died the same year as he, unmarried and childless. The wedding ceremony was held a during long-overdue Emerging from the Courtyard vigil attended by both families' kin, after which a handful of earth from Li Yingneng's grave was placed in a coffin and buried next to Su Haijun's grave. The tombstone was placed over both graves.

Other stones memorialized early enemies of the socialist state. In 1989, Luo Guiyuan erected a stone for his wife's father, into whose family he had married. His wife's father, Luo Guotian, the valley's powerful pre-Liberation militia captain, had been publicly executed as a "local tyrant and evil bully" in 1951. His wife, memorialized with him, died in 1960. Luo Guiyuan's project met with strong objections from his kin, and the first stone he inscribed was surreptitiously smashed before it was finished. Luo Guiyuan was no stranger to opposition, however—as Luo Guotian's heir he had suffered considerably during the Cultural Revolution—and he persisted, driven by a desire to put his father-in-law's ghost to rest and rehabilitate his descendants in the eyes of the community. Directly contradicting four decades of political education, the inscription praises Luo Guotian's contributions to the defense of his community:

1.15 時遇国难当头军閥混战各自称雄处处匪猖獗 . . . 鱼肉百姓处于水深火热之中而别无良策唯有组织江防队以作自卫慎防匪患严父出抵族官门户历任中队长之职多次与贯匪李自學斗智斗勇比高低又曾与丁海平部长和谈解百姓落难之虑严父中世从武得一手好枪法千米之外射飞鸟弹无虚发

At that time, the country was in imminent danger, as armies were mired in battle and bandits were everywhere. . . . Treated like cattle or vermin, the people felt as though the water had risen to their lips, as though they were singed by fire, and the best plan they could think of was to organize a river defense force to protect themselves and to defend against marauding bandits. My honored father left to lend support to the leaders of our nationality, and he repeatedly served as a squadron leader. Many times he matched wits and courage with the armed bandit Li Zixue to see who was stronger. He also once held talks with Minister Ding Haiping to alleviate the sorrow of the people in their distress. Although my father entered the military in middle age, he became a skilled marksman, who could shoot a flying bird at a thousand meters, every shot hitting its mark.

Luo Guiyuan insisted that his father-in-law had fought the nineteenth-century Lòlopò rebel Li Zixue, perhaps confusing him with an early twentieth-century bandit of a similar name. But Luo Guotian did defeat a bandit named Ding Haiping, who assaulted Júzò with a strong band; the reference to Ding as "Minister" (buzhang) is ironic. Luo Guiyuan told me the story of Luo Guotian's marksmanship several times, giving me the sense that as a youth this was what impressed him most about his father-in-law, before I saw it recorded (in perhaps an exaggerated fashion) on this stone. The stone lists fifty-three bereaved: Luo Guotian's brothers' sons and daughters and Luo Guiyuan's wife and sons and daughters, with their spouses, children, and children's children, reconstituting on stone a descent group much damaged by persecution during forty years of revolution.

These forms of biographical inscription—lament combined with speaking bitterness on the one hand and the rehabilitation of dead souls damaged by past wrongs on the other—both position the dead in relation to national history and state power. In part, this is a contingency of the periods of history in which the stones examined here were composed. During the revolutionary 1950s, all forms of writing paid obeisance to the ascendant state, as Li Fuzhong's stone for his parents does by mentioning the difficulty of the pre-Revolutionary period and praising the new local public officials. In the early reform era, erecting a tombstone was a foray into an arena the state had forbidden in the recent past. Inscribers chose from a range of strategies of appeasement and defiance, often combining both on one stone. The defiance on Su Haijun's stone was implicit: as a veteran of a military force that was not the People's Liberation Army, the wounded Su Haijun spent the last part of his life in a persecuted and neglected class, making a stone at the time of his death in 1955 unthinkable. The defiance inscribed on the stone for Luo Guiyuan's storied father-in-law was open, recognized, and controversial. Yet, whether in appeasement or opposition, all these narratives foregrounded the imagined state as a central addressee.

This is not to say that authors necessarily shaped their inscriptions for the eyes of readers who might be local officials or Party members. Stones were rarely read outside of a series of encounters centered on the process of writing and inscription, as when Qi Ping authored the text for the stones for his family in consultation with their *ava*, had others paint and inscribe it on the stone, had the *ava* approve the inscription, and invited his guests to admire it. Reading in all these contexts was oral, recitational, and communal, involving the active participation of the authors in interpreting and defending the text. To inscribe on stone in these contexts was to make claims about a world of relations among a deceased couple and living kin, present and departed. Yet, because stone inscription is permanent, it projected the text outside of this living community as well, to a potential universe of future readers. To inscribe on stone was to position the dead in history in relation to the future as well as the present. And the field in which this positioning took place was provided by the state, imagined as the master of history and history's central agent. The most elaborate tombs made room for direct reference to this field in the leftmost of three stones. A brief example of the conventional revolutionary verse that filled these left handed stones, from the otherwise defiant tomb for Luo Guotian, exemplifies the common style of praise for the socialist state:

1.16 蒋家王朝被推翻人民翻身做主人全家庆贺喜洋洋为民为利终日忙前程艰难无所惧

As the Jiang dynasty [of Chiang Kai-Shek] was toppled, the people freed themselves to become the masters, and everyone rejoiced with happiness, busying themselves continuously for the sake of the people, with no fear of future disaster.

In the other texts and gestures of funeral ritual, lives were situated in the local spaces of house and field, mountain and river, shady side and sunny side. They were situated in relation to kin and friends and to the cycle of suffering, labor, nurture of the young, and care of the old that dominated funeral exchange and lament. But when Lòlopò in Júzò abandoned cremation in the late nineteenth century, they developed a new set of tools for thinking about the relation of the dead to the world of the senses, tools that emphasized state authority over the dead. Writing on stone brought the state and the history of its efforts to reform ritual into the ways people narrated their ascendants' lives. In the mid-twentieth century, a reinvigorated state renewed its concern with ritual, banning all funerals for a few years and deeply curtailing many forms of ritual for several decades. When people began inscribing stones again, they could not but feel the redoubled weight of the socialist state's concern with the dead. Unlike other forms of *nègu*, stone inscriptions left permanent evidence of an author's attitude toward the problem of the relation of the dead to state power. As a result, these inscriptions positioned particular lives in the context of revolution and reform, giving new meaning to suffering, labor, nurture, and care.[13]

Conclusion: Kinship as Text

The long struggle between the imperial state and the Tibeto-Burman-speaking peoples of the Yunnan-Guizhou plateau over whether to burn or bury the dead was deeply consequential. In cremation, corpses were dematerialized with fire, materialized again in ancestral effigies or cremation stones, and dematerialized again when these *nègu* were deliberately destroyed or forgotten. In burial, corpses were preserved beneath the ground, made material in tomb-houses, then materialized more durably on inscribed stones. Lòlopò in Júzò preserved elements from both these assemblages in their funeral rituals. This gave them extraordinary flexibility as they selected among ephemeral or durable materializations of the dead to work on kinship among the living. They took ample advantage of this flexibility in the late twentieth and early twenty-first centuries as social relations among the living came to depend ever more heavily on ritualized relations with the dead. Although Lòlopò adopted writing into a field of textuality already constructed, writing on stone brought new properties to text. Stone inscriptions shifted the human agency involved in text from diviners' readings of traces of immaterial beings on the world's surfaces to the manipulation of text by people endowed with literary authority. Inscriptions also powerfully shaped the temporality of text, giving new durability to materializations of the dead. Among the consequences of this manipulation of time was the production of a specifically genealogical imagination. Inscriptions on stones created durable diagrams of relations based on narrowed principles of descent. And they employed new principles of inclusion as well, filling in descent groups with dead and absent kin.

---

13. In the twenty-first century, the Chinese state has broadened and intensified its centuries-long campaign to reform death ritual. Referring to a "war between the living and the dead" for agricultural land, many provinces have banned the practice of tomb building. These policies have forced most villagers in Yunnan to transport their corpses to crematoria in cities and carry the ashes back home. (Júzò, where tombs do not occupy land suitable for agriculture, is exempted from this policy for the time being.) We still know little about the local effects of this transformation.

As chapter 3 will show, funeral rituals wrap corpses in images of social relations by wrapping them in clothing, quilts, coffins, and the bodies of lamenters and dancers. Tombstones contributed to this process by diagramming the names of the dead couple's present and departed kin, reformulating this universe as a descent group and radically trimming it to fit the limited and organized surface of the stone. Inscription was another form of wrapping, reshaped by the "transmutation" (Severi 2014) or "transduction" (Keane 2013) involved in moving from one medium of representation to another. Images of the socialist state, appearing most prominently on the left-hand stone of the most elaborate tombs, might seem to be the outermost layer of this wrapping, a late addition. Yet chapter 2 will demonstrate that images of the state in other forms also appear at the core of dead bodies. At their center, corpses articulate singular but impersonal souls with forces that transcend the local social world. In these assemblages, images of state power, chiefly power, and the powers of the land's original inhabitants appear as transmutations of the forces of sky, waters, and the underworld.

2

A Life, a Soul, a Body

Luo Guifu died alone in her bed on April 11, 2011, at the age of sixty-two, following a brief illness. Luo Guifu was not her name, but it had to serve, since no one could remember her Chinese name, if she ever had one, and the birth name of her first child, long dead, had also been forgotten. It meant "the Luo Gui woman." It identified her as having married into a Luo household in the Gui generation, as Gui was the first syllable of her first husband's given name, shared by all his siblings and parallel cousins. It was not a proper way to refer to any living person, but it was sufficient after her death, when more attention was paid her than at any time during her difficult life.

Her neighbors all agreed on the difficulty (*shú*) of that life. In the days after the death, I sat with Qi Ping and his brother-in-law on the two low beds of Qi Ping's bedroom. Qi Ping's wife, Li Minzheng, busied herself in the courtyard as we talked, often stopping in the doorway to dispute a point or add another. Together, the three of them assembled a tangled narrative of the dead woman's life. She had married Luo Guiyan, moving from the village of her birth into his house, clustered with the houses of his brothers around a single courtyard. Her husband died five years after their marriage, leaving her with two small boys and a girl. One of the boys died of an infection resulting from an injection given him at the village clinic. The other wandered in and out of the valley as an adolescent. Several years after his final disappearance, his father's brothers held a funeral for him, placing his clothing in the coffin in lieu of a corpse. Her second husband was from the village of her birth. She moved in with him and gave birth to another boy. But he soon died, and she returned with her two children to the Luo courtyard. Luo Guiyan's brothers' families helped her survive for a time, then married her off to her third husband who was much younger and very poor and lived with his mother. She worked very

hard and gave her third husband's mother a proper funeral. He left her for another woman anyway, and she returned for a third time to the Luo courtyard.

Her son left for the army, and her daughter went to the county town to
work. She bought a small house with money her daughter sent home, where
she lived alone. Her fourth husband was her neighbor, who was raising two
children by himself after his wife left him for another man. She sold her house
and moved into his, with her ox, pig, and goats. Then her husband's eldest son
died upon blundering into a high-voltage line in the copper mine, and his
father was compensated with 180,000 yuan, an enormous windfall by local
standards. Tempted by this wealth, her fourth husband's former wife moved
back in and drove Luo Guifu out, keeping her livestock and property, leaving
her with nothing. Her refuge was the Luo courtyard once again. Her daughter hired a lawyer, who extracted about 25,000 yuan from her fourth husband,
keeping 20,000 and leaving her with 5,000, which helped the Luo family support her during her final two years.

In this telling, the life was a series of articulations and disarticulations of
affinal relations. Descent failed repeatedly, as the lives of children were truncated. A tale of a man's life, or a woman's more successfully lived, would have
lingered over the contours of descent—parents, children, grandchildren, inherited property, successes, disasters.[1] But in this tale, affinity repeatedly emerged
from the background when descent was not sufficient to give the life a shape.[2]
Her marriage to Luo Guiyan, reinforced by her periodic returns to his brothers' houses, proved the most stable, and it was the array of relations that this
alliance brought into existence that would be reprised, modeled, and severed
in the ritualized events that followed her death.

Nothing like what we might conventionally think of as a "self"—a center
of memory, consciousness, and personal identity—emerges from this series
of articulations and disarticulations. Some women in Júzò were mustering the
poetic resources to begin to ascribe such qualities to the lives of their most
intimate deceased (as in chapter 4), but none of these neighbors was intimate
with the dead widow. What persisted through these transformations? Not a
name. A little property survived a move or two only to be shed later. There
was a body, growing older, made through her parents' nurture and care and
remade repeatedly through labor, her own and others'. Such care and labor
are summed up in Lòloŋo poetics as difficulty itself: shú, suffering. Shú is the

---

1. An example is the tombstone inscribed by Zhang Wenxing, described in chapter 3.

2. Viveiros de Castro (2001, 2014, 2009) explores the implications of a similar ethnographic
situation, where a principle of affinity appears to subtend other forms of social relation, such as
descent (but see chapter 6).

substrate of this biography, the impersonal but singular substance of this life—
impersonal because it requires no personality, consciousness, or memory; singular because it is experienced uniquely by each being.

A powerful image of *shú*, invoked in lament, is the work of preparing and
weaving hemp to clothe both a dead corpse and a living family. Each step in
this process entails a wearing away of strength and flesh, as when one soaks
the stalks in the cold stream and peels the skin to be pounded into fibers:

2.1	lè vè hɔ̀ vɔ̀ mo do go	hands labor like iron bars
	lè ni hɔ̀ ka mo do go . . .	fingers work like steel needles . . .
	lo ŋá ts'ɨ̀ mo p'æ t'è zɨ do go	press the stalks with huge stones
	lo ŋá **shú** do go	suffer to move the stones
	lè mo sa p'à kə	three sides of your thumbs wear away
	lè ni sa tsɨ kə	three knuckles of your fingers wear away

The bodily strength and substance thus worn away is transferred to a dead
person through the medium of hemp in the same way that it is given in life
to those one feeds and clothes. In the tale her neighbors told of her, the substance of each of the series of alliances that defined her life became this: *shú*,
her difficulty, the gradual wearing away of her strength and flesh.

The Emerging from the Courtyard vigil and Dawn-to-dusk Sacrifice vigil
for the woman her neighbors were now calling Luo Guifu were crowded and
lively, even though few people admitted to caring about her very much. The
Luo brothers, in the role of hosts, took the unusual measure of killing a big
sow, anchoring their claim to center the world of relations that these vigils
would model and giving both vigils an air of extravagance. During the vigils,
a paired body for Luo Guifu and her first husband Luo Guiyan would be assembled out of many images of relations. Yet for the duration of these vigils, as
Luo Guifu lay between worlds, gradually accreting the layers of social partialities that would define her person in death, something else glimmered—
the quality her neighbors had recognized as they reprised her life. It was this
quality of suffering, as much as their obligations to the Luo brothers, that
drew her nieghbors to her funeral vigils. All I asked gave one reason for coming: "to help," and they all made clear that to help was also to suffer. Like the
eye-stinging smoke of the bonfires that thickened the air at both vigils, suffering subtended all the acts of exchange and expression of which her funeral
was composed, all the social partialities these acts brought into existence. It
was this that closed a circuit between their persons and hers as she lay on the
bed on which she had died and in her coffin. This chapter and the next attend
to the acts that shape a body for the dead out of mediating images of social

relations. Lending all these acts their force was this recognition of the singular but impersonal glimmer of suffering shared by living persons and one on her way towards death.

Bodies

In the late twentieth and early twenty-first centuries, the funeral events in which people in Júzò invested the most intensively were Emerging from the House (*hek'ǝdǫ*), in the day and evening two or three days after a death, Emerging from the Courtyard (*kukædǫ*), through the night and at dawn directly following Emerging from the House, and Dawn-to-Dusk Sacrifice (*nihèpi*), seven days (for a woman) or nine days (for a man) after the burial. The effects of the diverse series of "rules and procedures" mobilized during these events were deeply varied across several registers. In what might be called a sociological register, the corpse would accrete a core of relations with forces of the waters, sky, and earth, then be wrapped with layered images of human social relations. In an affective register, these procedures afforded opportunities to collectively fashion grief, both for the person who had just died and for others who died earlier. In an ethical register, repeated acts of giving created unities that cut across established relations of difference and taught an agonistic practice of relating sympathetically with dead others.

These sociological, affective, and ethical effects were, of course, inseparable in practice. All depended upon practices of assembling material bodies for the dead. To attend to how dead bodies are fashioned builds on the clear focus that the tradition of the anthropology of death has maintained on the corpse and its transformations, while running counter to that tradition's tendency to take dead bodies as given, problematic material entities left over after death, whose ritual manipulations provide a material anchor for grief and remembrance. This tradition began with Robert Hertz's (1960 [1907]) observation that death begins a period of transition marked by operations on the corpse and Arnold Van Gennep's (1960 [1908]) idea that transformations in social relations after death might be correlated with a corpse's movements over thresholds, a theme taken up in Victor Turner's splendid series of analyses of the threshold, the <u>limen</u> (especially Turner 1967, 1969, 1974, 1982). A vast and flourishing body of work continues to investigate transformations in social relations shaped by ritualized work on corpses. A prominent example is Thomas Laquer's (2015) monumental cultural history of corpses in the West, and some notable instances drawn from the anthropology of China are Watson and Rawski (1988), Ahern (1973), Ebrey (1991), Teiser (1988), and Chau (2005). However, another strand of scholarship refuses to consider dead bodies as the given vestiges of death. This work shows how dead bodies are fashioned with conscious deliberation, across a stunning variety of sites. Some of the most dazzling examples include the reliquaries of medieval Europe and Buddhist Asia (Geary 1991, Germano and Trainor 2004); the effigies that condensed one of the "two bodies" of the dead kings of France and England (Kantorowicz 1957); the carved Malanggan figurines of New Ireland, containers for dead souls wrapped in social "skin" (Küchler 1987, 1992, 1988; Wagner 1986); the vanishing *tau tau* effigies of the dead in Tana Toraja, Indonesia (Volkman 1990, Adams 2006); the mobile corpses of postsocialist Europe (Verdery 1999); and the charismatic embalmed bodies of Lenin (Tumarkin 1983), Mao (Wakeman 1988), and Dashi-Dordzho Itigelev, the final Khambo Lama of Russian Buryatia (Bernstein 2013).

In Júzò, to assemble bodies for the dead is to draw on the power of ritualized acts to selectively materialize elements of that enormous, variegated, manifold, and indeterminate ocean of sensation and affect that underlies the socially determined partialities of relation and identity. This is one way to speak of what Deleuze, drawing on Bergson, called the virtual: that ideal but nevertheless real "impersonal transcendental field" that opens up to all the immaterial potentialities that may be specified or concretized in thought or action (Deleuze 1989 [1969]). The formula "ideal but nevertheless real" also applies to dead persons. As souls, their individuality has disappeared. As souls, they are nothing but the impersonal and yet singular substance of suffering released from the "subjectivity and objectivity of what happens" (Deleuze 2001, 5). Yet as corpses, they are anchored in specific locations in the world of matter and affect. The death rituals of the late twentieth and early twenty-first centuries accrete specific material forms around these anchors to reinvest them with social partialities. Bodies, originally fashioned through relations of nurture and care, are recomposed formally as relations made visible in media like clothing, quilts, goats, and rice loaves.

While remaking bodies, death ritual specifies and organizes the immanent field of sensation and affect in which relations with the dead were fashioned. The semiotics of this effort draw on fundamental elements of experience—the riverside, the mountain slopes, the line dividing sun from shade, pine chestnut and bamboo, courtyard porch and rooms, and beds and fire pit. The poetics of death ritual, both verbal and material, are a doorway opening up into the virtual substratum of social life shared among beings without material existence and beings whose existence is given its grammar by the material world. To investigate this poetics is to locate the points where this stratum is solidified into the social, made determinate in exchange, reorganized into affective arcs of grief and memory, and narrated as mythologies of intensive bodies raised high, head to the west, feet in the stars.

The practical problem of how to materialize a fully social body for the dead is an instance of a more general orientation towards body and world that permeates nearly every aspect of life in Júzò and, with variations, many related places in West China and Inner Asia. Two anthropological idioms with problematic pasts, "fortune" and "animism," have recently been rehabilitated to describe variations of this orientation elsewhere in the region (Mazard 2016; Swancutt 2016, 2012; Willerslev 2013, 2007; Harvey 2014; Brightman, Grotti, and Ulturgasheva 2012; da Col and Humphrey 2012). I find niether idiom very useful to describe the problem in Júzò, where it appears, in the most general terms, as a process of actualization. Specific material things are fashioned with deliberate human intention to determine, specify, and individuate immaterial attributes of the world that otherwise remain undetermined, unspecified, and unindividuated. This process of actualization makes particular material things into handles or tools that may be used to manipulate a diverse variety of forces and affects.

This process can be observed with clarity in the many techniques Lòlopò use to affect unseen beings called *nè*, an inclusive term that may be imprecisely glossed as "ghosts and spirits." Every attempt to exert human will over unseen forces (such as a hailstorm or an ear infection) or over affects (such as the residue of anger from a quarrel or a chronic feeling of sadness) requires a process of divination that locates the origin of the force in a particular *nè*, a process of assembly that gathers the *nè* from the surrounding world into an avatar or effigy constructed for it, and a process of exchange that gives the *nè* food, drink, formal speech, and its own effigy in return for a negotiated outcome, usually that the *nè* depart. The general term for the avatar or effigy assembled to contain the *nè* during the exchange and negotiation is *nègu*, and of course there are *nègu* of many kinds, including *nègu* for the dead. But many other constructed things can also be construed as similar individuated material actualizations of unseen and indeterminate forces. A house usually contains several *nègu*—instantiations of ancestors; of beings that guard or guide ancestors; of beings that regulate the grain in the granary; of beings that provide warm companions for living souls; of beings that watch over the oxen and goats of the barn and the pigs of the sty; of beings that embody special skills such as carpentry, teaching, blacksmithing, or speaking to ghosts or spirits. Yet a house itself may also be understood as an effigy, its courtyard materializing all the relational forces that it contains. The earth too is an effigy, as we will see when we explore the speech to the dead that explicitly theorizes this form of actualization.

A dead body is the most complex of effigies, an analogue of the effigies of house and earth. We can illustrate some of the fundamental principles of actualization adopted in death ritual by looking first at a simpler technique, used to negotiate with unclean beings called *ts'ì* that invest a house with disaster or infertility. This technique, called *ts'ìcip'i*, is still performed once a year in many households, as well as when a domestic animal dies, a fire breaks out, or another disaster occurs that affects a household's productive capacity.[3]

Liyoŋcip'ò was an accomplished ritualist, well respected for his artful versions of *nèpi*, speeches to ghosts and spirits. He often performed *ts'ìcip'i* for kin and friends for the fee of a chicken and a small bag of grain. He demonstrated how to build the effigy for the *ts'ì* in the courtyard of a neighbor whose water buffalo had to be killed after falling from the path and breaking its leg. From a large bundle of materials he had gathered from the mountainside, he selected a pine branch, cut a three-forked twig, and made three slashes in its bark to be its eyes, nose, and ears. This was a *nèŋa*, a central component of many effigies—a form of "official," under whose eyes the rest of the effigy was assembled. Liyoŋcip'ò used his knife to fashion three groups of sticks that he planted in a row in the earthen floor of the courtyard. Each group consisted of an unbranched pine twig, another pine twig cut into a hook shape and carved with a crude face and ears, an identical twig of cedar, a three-forked pine twig stripped of its needles and carved with a face and ears, and a twig of cedar treated the same way. Faces and ears were included in all *nègu*; they gave the *nè* senses with which to accept and enjoy the offerings and hear the ritualist's words. Liyoŋcip'ò explained that the hook-shaped twig was a hoe and the naked, forked twig a pitchfork—weapons for use against the *ts'ì*. To each group he added a twig of chestnut, carved with a face, with some straw inserted into a notch on top for hair. In the first group, this chestnut twig had bark; in the second it had half its bark; in the third it was stripped of all its bark (figure 2.1). "The *ts'ì* is three," Liyoŋcip'ò explained, "the black *ts'ì* [with bark], the painted *ts'ì* [with half its bark], and the white *ts'ì* [without bark]."

With a needle and thread, Liyoŋcip'ò stitched together three pairs of chestnut leaves to form tiny bags. He sewed a bit of charcoal into one, a few grains of rice into another and some rice husks into the third. "The *ts'ì* is a thief," he said, "and very hungry. So hungry it will eat anything in your house—your rice, but also charcoal and husks. These are its stomachs." He placed a tiny mat of pine needles before each group of sticks, a scrap of hemp cloth on each mat, and one of the leaf stomachs on each piece of cloth. "The cloth is for all

---

3. Many Tibeto-Burman-speaking groups across the region practice cognate techniques. Rock and Janert (1965, vol. 7, pt. 2, 260–261) give the textual version of one such ritual, the Naxi *dtò ná*, carried out in a grand fashion near Lijiang in 1947. Rock (1947) shows photographs of this event.

FIGURE 2.1 Building an effigy, or *nègu*, for the *tsʼì*.

the unclean things in the household to stand on," he explained. "The *tsʼì* will wrap them up and take them away." After he slaughtered a chicken and offered the *tsʼì* meat, wine, and grain, he made a long speech to negotiate its exit from the household. Near the end of the speech, he used each of the hooked twigs to hoe open the corresponding little stomach, chanting,

2.2	á ní tsæ n̄ tsæ mó	is your heart good or bad?
	ní n̄ tsæ, chì zæ tsa pò pɛ	your heart is bad, a lifelong thief
	kʼó ne ní n̄ tsæ ni yɔ́ ni	your heart is bad, do you confess
	n̄ yɔ́	or not?
	ni ŋo kʼo kʼa tɔ́ tʼè kʼò zu	you've stolen from my grain
	ka n̄ te	basket
	ni yɔ́ ni n̄ yɔ́	do you confess or not?
	tʼa ká pi gɔ̀ hɔ	[I shall] dig and see!
	"a yí à lɔ"	"ay! ow!"
	æ mæ ni ŋo ne cì pæ̀	now watch me dig out
	cì tʼa ká pi tʼo	your stomach!

There is much to remark on in this little drama. It is a puppet theater, in which the puppets are real attributes of the world, materialized and assembled so as to be inserted into the aleatory flow of difference, like a stone placed deliberately in a stream. The theater assembles an audience as well as players—most centrally the indeterminate crowd of immaterial beings in which harm and good fortune originate, a representative of which, the *ts'i*, has taken the stage. This theater cannot be summed up with the concept of "performance" in the sense given in the anthropological literature (a sampling of efforts to define performance in anthropology includes Bauman and Briggs 1990, Fernandez 1986, Hymes 1981, Irvine 1996, Lemon 2001). The actors in this theater are immediately involved in the play of the world. Their actions repeat and refashion previous acts (remaking loss as theft) and reshape the future repetition of those acts (other losses and thefts). Our focal topic here, however, is how the material body of the *nè* is assembled. For this is a body closely analogous to, though in no way identical to, a human body.

What are this body's attributes? It is assembled mostly of things from the mountainside, along with some hemp and thread, in contrast to human bodies, which are largely made of matter from house and field, given in acts of care and nurture. The body is clearly a whole, materializing and individualizing a diffuse, immaterial being. But the body is also multiple, incorporating three differentiated *ts'i*—black, painted, and white—each fashioned of still others, every part given individual faces and ears. The *nèŋa*, official representative of the entire assembled body, incorporates multiplicity into its form. Its trunk forks into three branches and each branch into countless needles. This body is an assemblage of organs—eyes for seeing the offerings, ears for hearing the ritualist's words, stomachs for holding the stolen food. These organs are the means by which the *ts'i* acts, but they also track the intentions of the ritualist to appeal to the *ts'i* with offerings and compel it with words. Other organs even more directly materialize the ritualist's intentions, such as the little hoes and naked pitchforks he will use to expose the thief's nefarious heart. Organs that reveal the agency of the *ts'i* and organs that mark the intentions of the ritualist are mixed together: faces and ears for the *ts'i* are carved into the hoe and pitchfork. We can think of this artifact as Alfred Gell did a work of art—an index that catches various agents and patients up in a meshwork of intentionalities (Gell 1998).[4] Like a trap, this effigy reveals the intentions of both the hunter (ritualist) and victim (*ts'i*), but these intentions are given both a diagrammatic shape and a narrative form, the ritualist's aggression revealing and refashioning the thief's earlier predation on the household (Gell 1996).

The *ts'i* is an image of a relation between client, ritualist, and a force in the world that precipitates domestic disaster. Other persons are less directly

---

4. Specifically, this *nègu* appears to follow Gell's formula for volt sorcery—the form of magic in which a sorcerer makes an image of his victim and then does harm to the image in order to punish him (Gell 1998, 103). Gell's claim that volt sorcery is an instance of our general vulnerability as distributed persons to images of ourselves will also be pertinent below.

involved: the other members of the household with their varied intensities of interest in the matter, the water buffalo itself in the form of its ghost. Before this little ritual, this particular configuration of relations is undetermined and the force that causes the disaster unspecified. The body of the *ts'i* focuses these relations, brings them into determinate being, and gives them a specific character composed of the intentions of the persons involved, streamlined into the intention of the *ts'i* to steal from the household and the ritualist's intention to punish the *ts'i* on behalf of his client and drive it away. If this body has an interior, it is the three bits of matter stolen from the household, wrapped in leaf stomachs. Uncovering these stolen bits reveals the *ts'i*'s inner person, its thieving character. This assembled body thus correlates the two aspects of the personhood of the *ts'i*: its personhood as an aggregate of social relations and its personhood as internalized desires and intentions (Gell 1998, 147–149). That the innermost part is stolen indicates that this internalized person has a degree of independence from the network of social relations that wraps and surrounds it. The most complex effigies, which are always for those beings who are most like humans, always include a stolen animating bit, potentially freed by an act of theft from being entirely enmeshed in the endless partial exchanges of social personhood. In effigies for the most fearsome immaterial beings, the ghosts of people who have died badly, that stolen bit is a live parakeet or sparrow captured from the mountainside (Mueggler 2001). We will see that the bodies of the dead also have a central inner bit, vulnerable to theft.

While the effigy for the *ts'i* indexes only a few relations, a dead body is made of the images of many relations, each image ramifying until nearly every person in the community, alive or recently dead, is involved. The body becomes a *wrapped assemblage*, a complex core to which is added many layers, all images of particular instances of relatedness. The tension between these two parts of the corpse, its inner core and its outer wrappings, might be seen as reflecting the methodological tension to which Gell called attention: persons found to be composed of their immanent experience on the one hand, and persons understood as composed of the social relations that produce them on the other (Gell 1998).

Dying

"Love arises when death is near," said Àp'ìmà, who enjoyed talking about the proper conduct of death rituals of all kinds. Àp'ìmà, her nephew Li Lancong, and I were sitting in the little room where I lived in the elementary school, a good place to talk freely about these matters, as it was free from all the entanglements of human and nonhuman persons layered into any house, which often made it impossible to talk about ritual techniques inside any of a house's rooms. "To properly follow the rules and procedures," Àp'ìmà continued, "is to show your love." In the case of any serious illness, the best way to show love is to pursue all possible medical options: to take the loved one to the clinic, to spend money on medicines, to make sure she gets injections. Though medicine can treat a disease's symptoms, a diviner must be consulted to discover its root cause. For ailments that do not involve overt violence this search begins in the house, attending to those unseen forces with which one lives most intimately. "You try one thing, and if it doesn't work you try another," Àp'ìmà said. "You call on a diviner, speak to the big *nè*, see if the pain is relieved, call on the diviner again, and offer to the little ones." For instance, you might first kill a chicken or goat for the bed's-head spirit (*gàwúdɛnè*), which guards and protects the ancestral effigies. If this is not effective, you might offer to the ancestral effigies, taking each down from the wall, washing it, killing a chicken for it, and giving it a new "flower" of chestnut leaves. If the loved one still doesn't improve, you find other spirits to appease. "Orphans' verse" (*chřmèkò*) laments, sung in the first days after a death, often speak of a fruitless search for the cause of an illness, mentioning the little household spirits: the *jíts'a* who watches over the pigs, the *lósi* who guards the barn.

2.3	ŋo à bò no a do	my father was seriously ill
	ŋo à mo no a do	my mother was seriously ill
	jr dù à lí jr	where did the fault lie?
	dæ̀ dù à lí dæ̀	where did the blame sit?
	kə̀ kà cí mi chì	I invited a diviner from the spirit world
	pi kà nè mi chì	invited a shaman from the ghost world
	kæ pi kæ no no	the more I sacrificed the more they hurt
	kæ və̀ kæ no no	the more I offered the more they hurt
	á gà jí ts'a dæ̀ ŋa bɛ	they said the *jíts'a* behind the house was to blame
	mò shŕ là t'è tè do lu	I offered baskets of grain
	dò kæ cí t'è tè do lu	offered bowls of rice
	he wò ló si dæ̀ ŋa bɛ	they said the *lósi* under the rafters was to blame
	ŋo wò wú cæ k'à k'o lo tè do lu	I offered a cock with a golden cap
	wò chi cæ dà dò lu tè do lu	offered a cock with golden socks
	wò gə cæ gò hə́ lu tè do lu	offered a cock with golden feathers
	t'à yè p'u yi tè do lu	gave paper like silver flowers
	t'à yè cæ yi tè do lu	gave paper like golden flowers

"After you have given her all the medicine you can and made offerings to all the ghosts and spirits you can think of and she still doesn't get better," Àp'ìmà said, "you call her daughters who have married out to come back and speak to her; you call all her grandchildren to come sit for a while. You bring back all her favorite foods, and you have her children take turns holding her in their arms. When the father is dying, his sons hold him; when it is the mother, her daughters and daughters-in-law hold her." One dies properly only in an inner room of one's own house, surrounded by children and grandchildren, cradled in the arms of a son or a daughter.

As a parent lies dying, those who will be centrally responsible for her funeral, her sons and daughters and her brothers (or his wife's brothers), should be called together to discuss funeral plans in her presence. These are among the most serious and delicate discussions a family can have. The expense for some parties, particularly the daughters and their husbands, is potentially enormous, the obligation to show respect with as large a funeral as possible heavy, and the possibilities for lasting insult legion, particularly to the dying woman's brothers or dying man's brothers-in-law—the *avə*. Àp'ìmà explained,

> The eldest son's opinion holds the most weight, and he should be first to speak. He is the head of this family even though the youngest son will host the funeral. He should say to his dying parent, "We are going to give you a very large funeral if you permit." Then the dying parent's spouse can speak; he or she should support the son's opinion. The *avə* should speak next, and then the younger sons and the daughters should be asked their views. Each should discuss how much money they will be prepared to spend, the *avə* acting as a moderator and warning everyone that they should speak now so that they will have no further opinions after the funeral. They should discuss the daughters' responsibilities: the goats they should acquire, the cigarettes and alcohol they should buy, the clothing they must prepare. They should discuss whether to paint the coffin, whom to ask to play the gourd pipe or double-reed trumpet, all the hemp articles, and the very important question of firewood.

Any house has an upstream (*ɔwú*) and downstream (*ɔmæ*) axis, oriented to the flow of the stream below, and a perpendicular uphill and downhill axis, oriented towards the mountainside behind. A household's senior couple usually lives in the upstream room, in which two beds are placed parallel to each other, heads upstream, with a firepit in between. If this room is properly arranged, the man's bed is aligned against the inner, uphill wall, the woman's against the outer, downhill wall. A bed's-head spirit and ancestral effigies are placed high on the inner wall, above the man's bed (Mueggler 2001). Allowing anyone to die on this bed, Àp'ìmà said, would insult these spirits. A man who lays dying on his own bed should be moved across to the woman's bed immediately before his breath halts. This bed, positioned on the outer wall of the room, near the door to the porch and courtyard, is where any corpse should be prepared and a vigil kept until the body can be moved into the courtyard.

Few deaths are ideal, however, as Àp'ìmà was aware. As she spoke, the wind hissed outside, and she shivered a little over her tea. The wind, she said, is a ghost. When she was a child, whenever anyone died badly, everyone living nearby would seal all the gaps between the bricks of their houses with rags so the wind could not penetrate and sit inside the house for three days.

The sound of the wind brought some recent disasters to Àp'ìmà's mind. First, the beautiful roofed bridge that had guarded the end of the valley since the late Qing had burned down. It was rumored that some youths had set the fire to protest a birth-control crackdown, but the police had discovered nothing. And then there were two murders within days of each other. Both were brothers killing brothers over alleged affairs with each other's wives. Àp'ìmà was seventy-five, and she had never heard of a murder in Júzò before, aside from battles with bandits before Liberation and executions during the land reform campaign. She was certain these murders were linked to the burning of the bridge. Li Lancong, sitting with us, interrupted to describe his dream of the murderers with their hands tied behind their backs, the ropes running to a mountain peak to keep them from running away. In any case, Àp'ìmà broke in again, now that the bridge was gone, more disasters were sure to follow.

Anyone who dies outside their own house is already a wild ghost (chènè) and must not be brought indoors, Àp'ìmà continued. But the corpses of those who die outside their homes may be divided into different categories. Those who have lived and died well—apart from not dying at home—may be placed on the long porch that runs along the outside of the house within the courtyard. Those who have died of accidents or by suicide or murder are victims of wild ghosts and may not be laid directly on the porch. First, they must be placed in a coffin, then brought to an exorcism site where an exorcism should be performed and the coffin passed through an arch of willow branches, and only then might the corpse in its coffin be carried into the courtyard. Sometimes people make a temporary hole in the courtyard wall so the corpse might be brought in without entering the gate, as though it did not enter at all. Sometimes they take a wall of the house apart so the corpse might be brought into a room to be properly washed and clothed within, again as though it did not have to enter at all.

Bodies at the point of death or just beyond it are already subject to work that builds into them a path (jo) through the proximate world. A concrete instantiation of this path leads from the inner bed beneath the ancestral effigies to the outer bed, over the threshold onto the porch, into the courtyard, then out the courtyard gate, through the villages, and up to the mountain of graves. This path will eventually reverse directions as the soul is gathered from the mountain and brought back to be installed in the house in the form of an ancestral effigy. In its extended form, the path will lead out through dozens of towns in three counties before circling around to return to Júzò (chapter 6). The work of negotiating with the forces of house and courtyard as someone lies dying is as much about releasing the body from its attachments to the homely spaces of bed, hearth, porch, barn, and sty in preparation for this journey as it is about hoping that the patient will suddenly recover. The hushed discussions among kin that accompany every good death reassure the dying person that the many forms of work that will move her along her path will all be done with skill and attention.

A bad death truncates the route from ancestral effigies to gravesite and back. Bodies may be inserted onto this path at different points depending on the quality of the death—through a hole in the wall into the room, through the courtyard wall onto the porch, directly into the courtyard, or straight into the grave. The complex path making of exorcism builds another road for these bodies. This road circles through nearby villages, plunges into the Jinsha River, floats down to the cities of Wuhan, Nanjing, Shanghai, and Beijing, and disperses into sea and sky (Mueggler 1999, 2001). The road for those who die well is hoped eventually to bring them back in the form of life (zæ) and fertility for living descendants. The road for those who die badly is intended to forestall their return in the form of illness and death for descendants. These roads are closely related, each the reverse of the other, each often becoming the other.

Àp'ìmà was speaking in the early 1990s when her kin and neighbors were conducting exorcism after exorcism for the dead of the 1960s and 1970s, for whom it had not been possible to conduct proper funerals, and who were returning to afflict illness and death on descendants, who in their turn also became wild ghosts. By the 2010s every death was a bad death, every funeral cycle included an exorcism, and every return of life and health was mixed with a return of illness and death.

Souls

The work of making a body for the dead begins with the soul (yeho). Rather than imagining a soul to be the location of a self or a consciousness, we might begin by thinking of it as made of the singular but impersonal quality of suffering (shú), the substrate of every life, singular because every person experiences suffering uniquely, impersonal because suffering requires no personality, consciousness, or memory. Though a soul has no character, it always has a location and a trajectory of movement, and this enmeshes it in an ecology of relations with other unseen beings and forces. After a person ceases breathing, among the first tasks is to relocate the soul and begin to renegotiate these relations.

Around the time of the last breath, a small chick should be placed beneath the body to be crushed to death. The chick is charred in the fire and placed in a small basket at the corpse's head, a pair of chopsticks crossed between its wings. This chick is the only animal of the many killed after a death that is not a sacrifice. Its throat is not slit, and it is not offered to or consumed by any being. This is the "stolen chick" (*yetsa*), its small, charred form mimicking the uncanny otherness of the corpse and providing a receptacle for the displaced soul. It will accompany the corpse until burial. During the night vigil, the dead person's daughter will guard it, and the son of one of the *ava*—the deceased's brothers, if a woman, or brothers-in-law, if a man—will try to steal it, levying on the daughter a steep fine of ten to twenty jin of alcohol and much public scolding if he succeeds. While a human body makes the fate and personality of a living person visible in its physiognomy, the "stolen chick" reveals the dead soul as diminished and one-dimensional. The soul is not an essence: it is unstable and insubstantial and utterly dependent upon the daughter's grief-inspired vigilance.

Another measure taken shortly after death is to buy water from c_i, beings who guard the streams and springs and were the original owners of the land. This water will be used for many purposes, from boiling offerings to ladling into the mouth of the dead to provide sustenance for eternity. A relative of the dead who knows a little ritual language is sent to a spring or stream with a bucket. He leaves twelve coins by the water, burns a stick of incense, and speaks a few words before filling the bucket:

2.4	lɔ cị zò cị tsɨ mà	come little c_i and c_i officials
	a ye væ	I buy water
	zæ bɔ bɔ tɔ ve	that she may drink her fill for life
	ni jɔ jɔ tɔ ve	drink every single day
	he k'o bɔ bɔ tɔ ve	drink her fill each year
	mùi bɔ bɔ tɔ ve	so long as the sky exists
	mi jɔ jɔ tɔ ve	so long as the earth endures
	yi wú yi tsɨ mà ne tɔ ve	the finest water, the water of kings

C_i have cognates throughout the trans-Himalayan region. They still inhabit clusters of old trees around springs and streams in Júzò, trapping the souls of those who cut the trees, wash in the springs, or trample the undergrowth.

A *ci* might also be deployed against human enemies by stealing a bit of clothing or hair and burying it under a rock or fallen limb near a spring, with a brief speech asking the *ci* to seize the enemy's soul and feed it mud and leaves until it dies. One whose soul is thus imprisoned falls ill and gradually wastes away:

> You grow dizzy and your hair falls out; your legs lose their strength; you feel hot and then cold, and your skin turns yellow. When you sleep, you dream that you are in a tiny place, enclosed by trees and rocks. Even when you are awake, you have the sound of running water in your ears.

The remedy is to hire a ritualist to make a *nègu* for the *ci*, kill a cock for it, offer it some salt, rice, and alcohol, and make a speech. One such speech, from Liyoŋcipʼò, began by describing the *ci* and naming it as the cause of harm:

2.5	kʼù chǐ yi mó chǐ	spirit of swamps and springs
	sæ̀ se kɔ́ zò chǐ	spirit of thorns and brambles
	wo bó yi ŋa chǐ	spirit of toads and frogs
	tu và mè jé chǐ	spirit of tree ferns and sword ferns
	si̱ ka mè tʼè chǐ	spirit of tangled undergrowth
	ci̱ ce ci̱ tsì mà	great *ci*, great king *ci*
	ni nà ŋà lo̱ bɔ	it is you!

When a *ci* attacks and traps a human soul, it breaks the terms of an ancient peace treaty. Liyoŋcipʼò's speech outlined the history of this settlement in several hundred verses. Originally, humans and *ci* each agreed to mark out the lands they would inhabit. Humans marked land around trees, rocks, and meadows; *ci* marked slippery stones and pebbly pools. When the rains of the seventh month flooded the *ci* out of their lands, they begged for friendship, but the humans, now wise to the evil nature of *ci*, refused, and the two sides went to war. The humans crafted crossbows with stocks made of wild bamboo and bowstrings of tough vines; the *ci* fashioned crossbows with stocks made of hemp and bowstrings of grass. After winning the war with their superior weapons, the humans threatened to burn the *ci*, and the latter sued for peace, promising with evident sincerity never to attack humans. Any *ci* that attacks a living soul, Liyoŋcipʼò's speech argued, is in violation of this contract and must return the trapped soul.

"Soul" is a standard translation of the Chinese hun 魂, which Júzò residents use as an equivalent to the Lòloŋo term *yeho*. Both soul and hun pair an immaterial being with a material one, making each the other's analogue. Neither captures the sense that the word *yeho* gives of a distributed immaterial being that occupies the geographical surroundings of a body through time. A person is said to have three *yeho*: one hangs out in the house near the fire, another loiters in the graveyard, and the third follows the body about like a loyal dog. This distribution can be stretched over great distances, as when a child goes to work in the city, leaving a *yeho* in her parents' house, feeling the distance between body and soul as homesickness.

A *yeho* is susceptible to many forms of influence or harm from other beings. Liyoŋcipö's speech to the *ci* gave the sense that the soul, immobilized in the *ci's* thickets, caves, and pools, is further fragmented into constituent parts, each of which might be mistaken for a wild being:

2.6   ŋo bò mo ŋæ̀ mo zò ǹ ŋɔ   I'm no green fly or bumblebee
       mù̀ wò jé ne ba la zò ǹ ŋɔ   no hawk or eagle
           sɨ kò̀ ni t'à jæ   don't lock me in hollow trees
               sɨ ŋa ci tsɨ p'ò   hack open your trees
                   sɨ tsɨ p'ò kò lɔ   open your trees and let me return

       ŋo bù̀ zò jɔ pə zò ǹ ŋɔ   I'm no beetle or grasshopper
       wo bó yi lɔ́ zò ǹ ŋɔ   no toad or tadpole
           yi ká ni t'à jæ   don't drown me in springs
               yi ŋa yi tsɨ p'ò   open up your pools
                   yi dæ̀ yi tsɨ p'ò   strike open your pools

And so on with tigers and leopards, pheasants and grouse, yellow foxes and wild dogs, mice and rats.

Phenomenologically, a *yeho* is a round thing, small, watery, and insubstantial, like the boiled egg placed by the fire or the ring of pine needles floating in a bowl of water, with which live souls are materialized in funeral rituals to call them away from the dead, but also a fragmented thing, like bubbles in a stream:

2.7   yi tsú læ̀ mo tsú   bubbles rise in the water
       yi bù̀ læ̀ mo bù̀   the water bears bubbles
           læ̀ mo bù̀ kò lɔ   bear my bubbles back
               ŋæ̀ mo t'á he chi k'ɔ́ kò to our tiled house's upper room
                   cí mo lɔ̀ he chi k'ɔ́ kò to our shingled house's central room

The physical and mental health of a living person depends upon this mobile, distributed immaterial being—upon where a *yeho* is located in relation to the body and with what other beings, human and nonhuman, it is entangled. Funeral rituals deal with the problem of mobile dead souls, locating them within bodies, graves, and effigies, disentangling them from the souls of the living, and negotiating the obstacles and obligations with which they are confronted by other virtual beings. Death rituals surround the insubstantial cloud of bubbles of a dead soul with solid social flesh, modeling the relations out of which that body is made, by separating out the persons who make it. Buying water from the *cj* is crucial, all my consultants on funerals emphasized, for this water is used in nearly all of the exchanges that model relations in the dead body. This act acknowledges that human social relations are underlain by a substratum of relations with wild entities, beings whose powers extend beyond the human sphere into the landscape of rivers, forests, sky, and underworld.

The water is used to slake the corpse's thirst. The dead person's daughter (or her replacement) pours a ladle-ful over the corpse's head and, if she knows some ritual language, says a few words:

2.8 ni t̃ɛ̀ pu tṳ cæ lò gɔ̀	we have given a thousand <u>liang</u> of silver and gold
yi mo lɔ̀ lɔ̀ væ k̀ɔ lɔ gɔ̀ dǫ	to buy splashing flowing water
ni zò ni t̃ɛ̀ nɛ lu væ k̀ɔ lɔ gɛ̀ dǫ	your son has bought it for you
ni mùi zæ zæ ne tɔ yi	go drink as long as the heavens last
ni mi zæ zæ ne tɔ yi	go drink as long as the earth persists
ni t̃ɛ̀ hǽ zè də	that your thirst might be slaked

Another portion is ladled into a pot of water placed on the fire to boil. A laying hen is killed next to the corpse's head and boiled in the pot. This first sacrifice is *cèts'ɨ̀ mà tɨ̠*: *cèts'ɨ̀* is to cease breathing, *mà* is to judge, *tɨ̠* is a small offering. Àp'ìmà mentioned this offering in a lament she sang at her father's death:

2.9 p̀ɔ wú wò mo du dæ̀ tè do go	kill a flapping hen at father's head
du kó tè do go	scattering dust from her wings
ch̀ɹ də ch̀ɹ mi mæ	husk and boil rice
à bò p̀ɔ wú tè do go	offer it at father's head
lò tsó lò ts'o mo	a pot on the fire to boil the meat

Over the boiled hen, the person who has taken charge of the offering calls the dead person's attention to the fact of her death: "Your breath has broken now, you are dead now, we will give you a funeral now, know that you are dead!" Some funeral participants pointed out that a laying hen is also used to mark the beginning of life, in a child's naming ceremony. Àp'ìmà outlined the logic of this parallel: "For Han, Songzi Niangnang [The "Lady who Delivers Children," or the bodhisattva Guanyin] is in the sky; for Lòlop̀ɔ and Lòlomo,

Grandmother Wosomo is in the underworld. The dead person will carry the hen to Grandmother Wosomo to buy a child as a descendant. If you neglect this, you will never bear a civilized child."

As the hen is being killed and plucked, the youngest son (or his replacement), who will act as host (*vɛdù*), prepares thirty small rice loaves, each about three inches in diameter, giving three to each person who has come to support his mother's brother and saving the rest to be distributed later as rewards for various tasks performed. He prepares a pot of sticky rice for a first meal with the dead, placing one piece of pork on top if one member of a couple has died, two if both have died. Those who have gathered to support the daughters (*zòmæ̀*) and brothers-in-law (*avə*) offer cooked grain ornamented with pork fat in traveling bamboo rice boxes they have brought from home. The type of grain signals their degree of intimacy with the dead: the woman who will play the role of "central daughter" must offer sticky rice; other daughters may offer ordinary rice; others can offer other grains or even pieces of rice loaves. This grain is not eaten; it is cast into a basket placed at the corpse's head. Now that the person is formally dead, the daughters and their friends begin to sing "orphans' verse" (*chr̀mèkò*) lament. They will lament day and night, taking turns to rest, until the corpse is brought into the courtyard and then again until it emerges from the courtyard at dawn. More women arrive, each with a small bamboo box of cooked grain to cast into the basket at the corpse's head before she begins to lament.

Lightning, Sky, Underworld

Of all the immaterial beings a death brings into view, the most difficult and powerful is the god of lightning, Shr̀mògù, who claims the soul at the moment of death. Sacrificing to Shr̀mògù is a last-ditch effort to revive an ill person even after her apparent death and a first step in redressing claims that a host of immaterial beings will make upon her. Li Ganxue was not a ritualist, but he had a special relationship with Shr̀mògù, having been struck by lightning years before. He frequently made offerings to Shr̀mògù after the death of kin, first killing a chicken inside the house, then going to the mountain to construct the miniature maize-drying rack and ladder described in Chapter 1. His speech to the spirit appealed to it to depart to the sky and let the corpse live again:

2.10	ǽ mæ le lò kwé fù rɔ̀ pɛ le	I now speak of Luo Guifu
	mù̀ t'ù̀ ka ga ba	lightning has struck
	wú dɯ nọ ga be	her head is in pain
	chi vù̀ nọ ga be	her feet are in pain

le vùu noֳ ga be	her hands are in pain
chì gə chì chǐ noֳ ga be	her entire body is in pain
no ga t'á ǹ noֳ be	unbearable pain
wù ka bɯ ka ká lɔ be	her bones and marrow
	cry out

After buying water, announcing the death, and appeasing the spirit of
lightning, those gathered around the corpse begin to prepare it for its journey. A daughter (or her replacement) washes the corpse using water boiled
with a vine with antiseptic properties. She carves a wooden comb and combs
the corpse's hair straight up from its head, inverting the hairstyle of the living,
seven strokes for a woman, nine for a man. Dead men are dressed in old-style
black or blue silk robes buttoned down the sides and given silk hats of the
style once worn by local gentry. Dead women are dressed in embroidered
cotton shirts, trousers, aprons, and hats and adorned with silver earrings,
bracelets, and apron clasps. While daughters are primarily responsible for
clothing the dead, often the daughters' paternal aunts and female cousins also
contribute sets of clothing. Many corpses are bundled in ten or twelve layers
of cotton or silk. The orphans' verse laments performed during this vigil often
describe clothing the corpse:

2.11	jò kò mo cæ gɔ̀ tuֳ ga	give my bent father a bamboo cane
	wú p'uֳ sæ̀ hə yi tuֳ ga	his hair white as a flower
	à bò hɔ̀ yi mo cæ̀ gɔ̀ ka bə tuֳ ga	lay my withered father on a bamboo mat
	pɔ̀ wú nàn jin jù do go	place a cap from Nanjing on father's head
	pɔ̀ ŋə cin jin ní do go	tie a silken belt around father's waist
	sú pɔ̀ mæ nì p'à	shirts of red and sky blue
	bà lù mæ sa p'à	shirts of every color
	pɔ̀ gɔ̀ cí do go	wrap my father
	ǹ yì sa gò dֳə do goin so many layers the buttons won't close	in so many layers the buttons won't close
	ǹ dֳə sa chi k'à do go	what he can't wear pile on top
	bò pə mæ pə liֳ do go	cover him with cotton quilts and blankets
	hɔ̀ k'à tsa ló dֳə do go	lay him on straw mats and felt pads

While clothing a dead person is an expression of love and care, it also
places the dead in relation to the king of the underworld, Yan Luo Wang and
his bureaucracy of ghost officials, the Chinese-speaking analogs of Shr̀mògù

and his minions in the sky. This is a relationship of judgments and claims. A small cut is made in every item of silk or cotton clothing to spoil it so the underworld king will not requisition it for his own use. And the corpse is provided with ample hemp clothing to pay the taxes and fees that will be required. As one funeral participant put it succinctly, "The silk and cotton is to look good, the hemp is to follow the rules" (figure 2.2). The daughters should contribute a length of hemp cloth four <u>ke</u> (about five feet) long, two lengths if both members of a couple have died, to lay over the corpse. Once the corpse is placed in the coffin, each brother (if female) or brother-in-law (if male) should contribute a six-<u>ke</u> length of hemp to be wrapped around the corpse's waist. Envelopes of hemp cloth are placed over the corpse's shoes to pay the entrance fee at the underworld gate. The feet are tied together with strands of hemp, which are severed after the corpse is encoffined, so it will be able to walk. A hemp pillow, stuffed with unwashed hemp bast, is placed under the head. A small red piece of cotton cloth is stitched onto the pillow—a seal to show that the price for water has been paid. Silver coins are inserted in the mouth, one for each son. On the chest is placed a small, embroidered hemp wallet, filled with more silver and tied to a bamboo staff that helps the corpse frighten away robbers. The face is covered with a foot-square piece of white hemp lined with black cotton, called a "flyswatter," to protect the corpses from swarming bandit ghosts. The flyswatter is labeled with another seal of red cloth to show that the price for water has been paid.

All these hemp offerings serve as currency to pay taxes or bribes to the many officials the corpse will encounter on the path to the underworld: "It's like the paper money scattered along the path when you carry the coffin to the grave," one funeral participant said. "It is for the wild bandit ghosts and the ghost officials." Finally, the corpse is covered with a quilt; more quilts will be added when it is placed in the coffin and more still when the coffin is placed in the grave.

Àp'imà told me about a friend who had entered the door to the underworld during a long illness and reported what she had seen there after she recovered. The door was an ordinary tomb on the outside, but inside there was a path, clean and straight, lined with beautiful rows of fluttering flowers—the contraptions called "bird on a pine branch" (t'àyèɲatsì) that dangle from long bamboo poles over coffins and tombs to entertain the dead. At the path's far end, soldiers guarded a second door. These guards let her pass, saying nothing. But at a third door the guards asked, "Why have you come?" She replied, "I have come to live here." One guard stood over her while the other went to inform the official. The official was an old man, hatless, carrying a thick book. He looked through the book and said, "Your name is not here. You must go

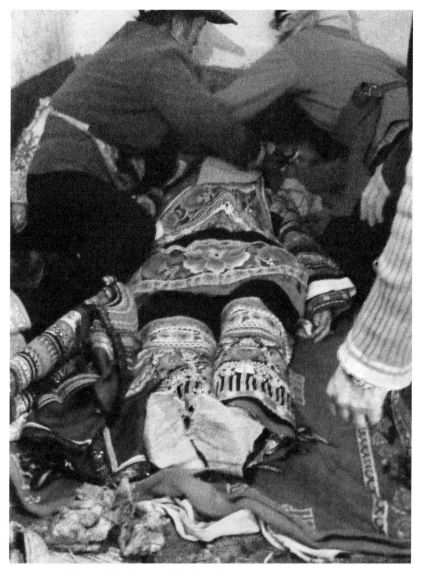

FIGURE 2.2 Clothing Lui Guifu's corpse (photo by author).

back." She wanted to stay, but the guards drove her off. As she stepped back through the door, she saw that her family had bought water; they were killing the hen to announce her death to her; some were crying, others were emptying grain into the basket at her head. She was certain, she told Àp'ìmà, that the old official was Mómi Yàlòwù, or Yan Luo Wang, king of the underworld. The place inside, she said, was spacious and clean.

Conclusion: An Inhuman Core

"Love arises when death is near," Àp'ìmà had said. As a person fades from life, death reveals to those crowded around the bed a virtual world beyond subjectivity, individuality, and human relation, a barely human world of impartial and impersonal experience in which we all also dwell despite ourselves. As a person dies, the living can recognize a direct connection to the fundamental quality of that field, the quality of suffering, *shú*, the shape of immanent life. Yet this field differentiates beyond suffering, to include every texture of immanent experience. The "rules and procedures" that guide the care of a loved one as she is dying and before her corpse emerges into the crowded, complex social arena of the courtyard sketch out the contours of this field. One by one, these procedures recognize claims made upon the dying person by the immaterial beings seen to populate this immanent world. Inside a house, such beings already have bodies that concentrate the elements of this field: hearth and bed in a bed's-head spirit and ancestral effigies, in the *lósi* and *jits'a* of the barn and sty. These beings are social beings of course, related to the dying person as his ancestors, his cattle and goats, his pigs and chickens. But they are also impersonal, merely immanent in most ways, their sociality thinned out to a few relational links. As their bodies of pine, chestnut, bamboo, paper, thread, fir, straw, and thorns attest, their substance is of the plane of experience, where the textures, scents, and noises of house and barn are dominant.

Souls are the parts of a person in most intimate contact with this field. Souls do not have social relations as such. They have relations of intensity and proximity to the hearth, gravesite, and living body; or to tangled forests, bubbling springs, and fern-covered rocks when trapped by the land's original owners; or to the road, mountains, and sky when lost and wandering; or to a bit of clothing, a pot of sticky rice, a ring of pine needles in a bowl of water, or an egg by the fire when called towards home. As people assemble a body for the dead, they begin with the soul, giving it a temporary home in the crushed and charred corpse of a chick. Unstable and ephemeral, the soul requires a loving daughter's sustained vigilance to keep it from being lost in the unruly unwinding of social relations that will take place in the courtyard.

Death requires a body open at its core to those elements of experience that subtend human social relations. Other parts of this core assemblage articulate with other elements of the world of immanent experience. Purchasing water from the c_i, the mourners bring in wild places set apart from human occupation long ago. Announcing the death with a flapping hen, they bring in the generative force of the underground and its secret links between death and new life. Vainly striving to ransom the life from the god of lightning, they recognize the claims of the sky. Placing silver in the corpse's mouth and giving it hemp shrouds and socks, a wallet with silver coins, a staff, and a fly-swatter, they distribute it along the perilous road to the underworld, clogged with bandit ghosts and guarded by soldiers of the underworld king. Some of these nonhuman forces condense historical experiences of conquest, echoing forms of power that operate arbitrarily, from a distance, following opaque logics, often using unknown languages. Their representational relation to prior inhabitants of the land (the ci), local chiefs (the lightning god), or imperial power (the underworld king) is inexact. But the sovereignty of these former enemies, chiefs, and rulers—their power over life and death—links them to realms that extend beyond merely human social relations into the forests, the sky, and the underground.

Gell notes that many images of divinities around the world are provided with a secret interior part, a homunculus or inner person that animates the idol from within, surrounded by the flesh of images of the external social relations in which the idol is enmeshed (Gell 1998, 126–154). His most exuberant example is a carving of the god A'a, or Tangaroa, from Rurutu in the Austral Isles. On the skin of its human-shaped body it sprouts many more carved bodies, imitating the shape of the whole god in fractal form. Inside, it once contained twenty-four tiny bodies of Rurutan gods. Gell comments that the god "images both the notion of personhood as the aggregate of external relations (the outcome of genealogy, fanning out in time and space) and at the same time the notion of personhood as the possession of an interior person, a homunculus, or, in this instance, an assemblage of homunculi" (Gell 1998, 139). Though such profligate fractality of form may be unique to Rurutan gods, the Buddhist and Taoist idols people from Júzò occasionally encountered as soul-trapping *bu* are also animated by secret internal parts. As Wei-Ping Lin (2015) shows, after carvers complete a wooden statue of a Taoist god, a ceremony is held to insert its inner parts. Into a cavity in the statue's back are placed ashes or talismans from the god's root temple as its spirit, a live hornet as its power, five precious metals as its organs or its grandeur, five grains to place it in relation to the seasons, and five colors of thread to give it command over camps of spirit soldiers. The eyes are then dotted to animate the statue's external form, and the image is bound to a village territory in a fire-walking ceremony. When the god thus assembled presides over ceremonies its social relations with humans accumulate and thicken as they encounter it face to face with their daily concerns.

Assembling a body for the dead out of a chick, water, a corpse, clothing, hemp, and rice offerings is analogous to these procedures that create images of gods. Yet this is not, as in Gell's idols, an inner person with individual character, desires, and intentions. The "stolen chick" is merely a soul, evanescent and without content. But, like the talismans in Taoist god statues, it is assembled with other materials that place it in relation to other elements and beings, fleshing it out with a fundamental cosmology of immanent experience: water, forest, earth, sky, weather. Yet even to assemble this core draws upon the most intimate relations the dead person had while alive, with sons, daughters, and siblings, each contributing their assigned hemp offerings to pay off the bureaucrats of the underworld, then wrapping the corpse in layers of clothing and quilts, images of love and care. As with Taoist god statues, these wrappings accumulate and thicken as time goes on. Once the corpse emerges into the courtyard, many more procedures will continue to wrap this bodily core in further layers until a full image of a complex social world is articulated.

3

Playing with Corpses

"A successful funeral should contain everything a life contains." I heard this principle repeated at every funeral I attended. If life consists of dramatic alternations between eloquent sadness and grotesque farce, I often thought with only a little irony, then Emerging from the Courtyard (*kukædǫ*) vigils succeed handsomely. Hundreds of people pack into a narrow courtyard to sit with the dead, weep for her, share heaps of food and alcohol with her, and dance around the coffin to protect her. Everyone who attends "comes to help," and to help means to endure: to sit up all night fighting off sleep, voicing grief, feeling the sting of smoke in your eyes, hearing the bleats of dying animals. A few vivid verses, repeated in almost every lament, spoke to the central role of the corpse in Emerging from the Courtyard vigils.

3.1   mæ̀ mi he ma chæ̀   cats give funerals to rats
        á nò zɨ ma ru   dogs give funerals to leopards
        p̀ò ma ru do go   we give a funeral to you, father

It is not that cats kill rats as hunting dogs once killed leopards, lamenters explained. It is that cats play with the corpses of rats, as dogs worry and fight over the corpses of leopards, and as the living play with corpses at funerals.

Daybreak, which signaled the time to bear the coffin to the graveyard, was for me an unsettling watershed in every night vigil. As the sky lightened at the funeral for Su Haicheng, a retired school principal and a Party member, the supporters of the dead man's *avə*, or brother-in-law, had been dancing around the coffin for hours—stomping vigorously to the tune of a gourd pipe, jostling the seated lamenters inside the circle, treading on unwary mourners seated on the outer edges. The master of ceremonies called a halt to the dance and

shouted for the hosts to bring out all the good things in the house. There was
a ham, a side of pork, canned fruit, packets of noodles, some cash, a whole
pineapple. These offerings were piled on a table, under which two men slept. A
drunken dancer took a hearty bite of the pineapple's prickly skin, cursed, and
cast the fruit away. Widows searched for edible pieces of meat in the basket at
the coffin's head, offerings given directly to the dead, not to be consumed by
humans. The master of ceremonies shoved one of the "thieves" toward the coffin and shouted for the other two. These three old widowers were supposed
to dance six final rounds around the coffin, but where were they? Eventually a
second was awakened, and the two old men stumbled around the coffin behind
the gourd-pipe player, calling for their third companion. The bearers bound
a pole to the coffin lengthwise with leather straps, tied shoulder poles to it with
hempen ropes, drenched the ropes with goat broth (the coffin was a horse, the
broth its water), and heaved the coffin up. One faced backwards, he was forc-
ibly turned around, the table of offerings was kicked over, and the coffin was
borne out the door.

It was all, every time, deeply shocking to my sense of ritual propriety honed
in childhood at weekly Catholic mass in the post–Vatican II secularizing style.
I surveyed a listless, shattered crowd, red-eyed from a night huddled in the
smoke, men asleep in the dirt, women with tears streaking the soot on their
faces, children owlish in the morning light girding themselves for a painful day
at school. The orderly assembly of living kin and concerned friends gathered to
send the dead off in the best possible style had disintegrated into a ragged and
dispirited collection of singular persons, each looking to carry off whatever he
could from the wrecked courtyard.

A "weeping song" (ɔchəŋə) lament sung during Dawn-to-Dusk Sacrifice
describes this scene more gently as it looks forward to the final meal served to
the guests to give them the strength to depart:

3.2 æ̀ t'ě t'ì kə sə	in a little while
hò pị̀ tsò tụ ŋæ	we will divide the meat to eat
rɔ̀ zɔ̀ cí ká pè	as lambs scatter at the scent of
	new grass
rɔ̀ mæ̀ rɔ̀ pè tụ ŋæ	they will all begin to scatter

At Su Haicheng's funeral I surveyed this scene with despair and alienation.
I could not help thinking that I had little in common with this disheveled
people, and that what they loved about life I did not love. Anticipating leaving the valley for what I vowed would be the last time, I even entertained for
a few seconds the possibility that they truly were as the township officials
directly responsible for their governance would have me believe: that in their

poverty, their frequent drunkenness, their stubborn clinging to a confusing jumble of habits and ideas, they were "backward" (<u>luohou</u>), an epithet hurled so frequently at "minority nationalities" that it would be trivial were it not deadly in its accumulated effects.

Only much later did it occur to me that similar feelings of alienation were likely widely experienced among the exhausted participants. Night vigils involved every participant in exchanges that meticulously crafted an image of a social whole, materialized in fractal fashion in the corpse, the coffin, the lamenters and dancers surrounding the coffin, and the crowd assembled within the courtyard walls.[1] The corpses, coffins, lamenters, dancers, and mourners of night vigils were concentrically layered—a wrapped assemblage. They were all analogues of each other, all simultaneously images of the social person of a dead couple and the sum of social relations in which that person was suspended (Strathern 1991). Each exchange reduplicated the social totality in the person of one living participant, revealing a relation with her person as among those that composed the person of the dead. But each exchange was also a partition, which cut the body of the dead couple out of the person of the participant. The process of making an image of a social totality divided each participant from that whole, placing her in relation to it as though across the rift, laboriously made, that separated the dead from the living. Feelings of alienation from a social collective were a natural result of this partition.[2]

This chapter traces these processes of assembly, partition, and analogy in the Emerging from the Courtyard night vigil. The other major funeral ceremonies—Dawn-To-Dusk Sacrifice, Tenth-Month Sacrifice, and Sleeping in the Forest—differ in many details, but these processes of assembly and partition are essentially the same in all. While the bodies of goats and rice loaves provide the media for these processes, the idiom of classificatory kinship provides their structure. For this reason, this chapter also describes the practice of preferred cross-cousin marriage that Lòlop'ò favored and the system of kinship terms that supported that practice. Kinship among Lòlop'ò can be said to

[marginal handwritten note: kinship provides a structure]

---

1. The metaphor of fractality has a robust lineage in anthropology, where it has been used to describe relations of social persons and social totalities as relations of analogy without scale (Wagner 1991, Strathern 1991, Mosko and Damon 2005).

2. These processes of composition and partition may seem to find analogues in the pairs of complementary oppositions that organize the lengthy tradition of scholarship on sacrifice—the "communion and piaculum" of Robertson Smith (1889), the "communion and expiation" of Hubert and Mauss (1964 [1899]), the "conjunction and disjunction" of de Heusch (1985), or the "integration and differentiation" of Jay (1992). However, this literature places such varied operations under each of the opposing terms that no agreement is possible on just what is being joined and what is being separated.

be essentially about the fabrication and destruction of bodies, as Viveiros de Castro (2009) said of the Amazon, with the twist that kinship among Lolopò begins with the assembly and partition of *dead* bodies. This work of assembling, disassembling, and ultimately destroying bodies for the dead is foundational: it creates the conditions for the generative production of living bodies. All bodies, living and dead, are assemblages of materialized social relations. Living bodies are made through generative relations of nurture and care; dead bodies are made through the ritualized modeling of relations. This modeling is the virtual ground out of which actual, particularized kin relations emerge. Viveiros de Castro made a similar point for indigenous peoples in the Amazon. "Classificatory kinship relations cannot be thought of as projections of 'real' ones; rather, the latter are special, that is particularized, reductions of the former" (Viveiros de Castro 2001, 25). A simple example in Júzò would be a series of small ceremonies at weddings, where children are taken by the hand around the courtyard and made to recite the classificatory term they will use to address each of their new affines—a simple matter in the case of the new bride's or groom's immediate descent group, more complicated in the case of their more extended kin. Because of the nature of kin terms in cross-cousin marriage systems, this often requires an adult to make a deliberate choice among equally viable alternatives. The choice determines the formal outlines of future relationships, including whom the child or the child's children might marry. Here, classificatory kinship, is being "reduced and particularized" to "real" kinship, as Viveiros de Castro put it. Yet this formula is incomplete; it works for only one side of the divide between the living and the dead. The work of fabricating a body for the dead "de-actualizes" (to use Viveiros de Castro's neologism) the particular relations out of which a living person, now dead, was composed in life, remaking them as classificatory relations. While all those involved begin as "real" kin to the living person, now dead, the relations modeled are progressively expanded and made less particular. For instance, the central classifications of daughter (*zòmæ̀*) and brother-in-law (*avə*) are repeatedly modeled in these exchanges, but those who occupy these classificatory slots are often substitutes for the "real" daughters or brothers-in-law—who may not actually exist. The same goes for a host of other classificatory relations, even the relation to the spouse with whom the dead soul will be united for eternity. In the final funeral rite of Sleeping in the Forest, once conducted by the dead couple's grandchildren or great-grandchildren decades after a death, the classificatory relations modeled did not change, but the people who acted as daughter or brother-in-law were several generations removed from the "real" daughter or brother-in-law, and the choice of possible persons who might occupy these slots was wide. Here, at the point where the relations between the living and the dead were about to disappear, "real" kinship had been progressively expanded and made less particular to become more purely classificatory kinship.

Work on the dead creates the conditions for kinship among the living. Procreation and bodily health among both humans and all other domestic beings, animal and plant, depend entirely upon the life substance channeled through filial relations with dead parents. But for this channel to work, bodies for the dead must be deliberately fabricated out of the relations in which the dead were suspended in life. This process begins with a core, made of images of relations with various nonhuman elements of the universe, described in the previous chapter. It continues with the processes of wrapping the core with images of social relations explored in this chapter.[3] At the same time, every act that adds an image of relation to those accumulated in the dead body simultaneously cuts the person of the living out of this model of a full, classificatory social universe. The grief of mourning—including feelings of loneliness and alienation—is a product of this work of assembly and partition; the grief of madness or possession (*tæ*) is an effect of this work having been done badly or gone wrong.

Hosts, Daughters, Brothers-in-law

Every funeral ritual is held not for one person but for a couple of spouses, and each couple is given a pair of Emerging from the Courtyard vigils and a pair of Dawn-to-Dusk Sacrifice vigils, one at the death of each. Verses performed during Tenth-Month Sacrifice couple spouses with the semantic pairs *chi* (early) and *lè* (late), and *p'u* (first) and *ne* (next), referring to the serial order of death, as they describe the spouses bound together in the sky:

3.3	tsa̱ chì shř na nè	ghosts cradled feet in the stars
	tsa̱ chi tsa̱ lè	early and late cradled
	n nɔ́ pi̱ tsa̱ gɔ̀	a pair cradled and offered to
	tsa̱ p'u tsa̱ ne	cradled first and cradled later
	n nɔ́ ní ŋa gɔ̀	your two hearts together

3. Assembling the dead body's core through negotiations with entities such as the god of thunder and the original inhabitants of the land, examined in chapter 2, appears to be about myth. Wrapping this core through the exchange of animal bodies, examined in this chapter, appears to be about sacrifice. Yet as Lambek points out, myth as sacred narrative and sacrifice as sacred action are both secular ideas, produced as analytical entities through processes of abstraction and isolation from their contexts (Lambek 2007, 21; see also Asad 2003). Among Lòlopò, as among Lambek's Sakalava, narrative is materialized in "sacrifice"; action is narrativized in "myth"; actions and narratives must be understood in relation to each other in order to be understood at all.

Who is to be coupled with whom at death is not always obvious. This is often the first issue to be worked out in planning for a funeral. In cases of serial marriage (as with the widow Luo), the dead person's first marriage is usually taken to constitute the couple, even when that requires some people to take part in several couples. In cases of polygamy, an occasional arrangement of the wealthiest families before Liberation, the man formed a separate couple with each of his wives or concubines. When a man or boy dies unmarried, an appropriate spouse can usually be found among the population of dead unmarried women and girls, and a wedding is conducted during the Emerging from the Courtyard vigil. When a woman or girl dies unmarried, her marriage often must wait until the funeral of an appropriate male partner. Parents hope to marry their dead children to suitable partners of the appropriate age at death and from good families.

Who is coupled with the dead person is crucially important, for it determines who will be the central groups of kin who conduct all funeral events for the dead couple. Every funeral requires cooperation among three groups, each of which has a central representative. First, the dead couple's household (the *vedù*, hosts), ideally represented by their youngest son. Second, the households of the dead couple's married-out daughters (the *zòmæ̀*, daughters), ideally represented by the most economically secure of the eldest or youngest married-out daughter. (This group also contains several other categories of kin, as we will see.) Third, the households of the dead man's wife's brothers or the dead woman's brothers (the *avə*, brothers-in-law), ideally represented by the eldest brother-in-law.

Each of these central groups, and the central representative of each group, might be replaced with others. The youngest son is the ideal representative of the host's group (*vedù*) because he usually stays in his parents' house, cares for them in old age, and inherits the house on their deaths, while parents help their elder sons build their own houses when they marry.[4] If the youngest son is dead or absent, the eldest son might take on the role of representative host; a middle son is recruited only if he is the only surviving son. When explaining this principle, people sometimes quoted the proverb, "walk on the left or walk on the right; if you walk down the middle, disaster will strike." If there are only daughters, a capable son-in-law or even an unmarried daughter who plans to inherit her parent's house might take on the role. In every case, who-

---

4. Cohen (1992, 370) calls this form of family division "serial division." While it is far from the most common pattern in rural China, it has been observed in a number of widely separated places, either as a response to socialism (Yan 1997) or, as in Júzò, as a longstanding custom (S. Huang 1992, 30; Harrell 1993; Selden 1993).

ever becomes the central host acquires the right to inherit the couple's house and remaining property. In cases where there is no obvious heir, who is to play the role of central host is an important decision, often strategized years in advance. Before land was collectivized in the 1950s, and after land contracted to households became inheritable in the 1980s, who represented the host's group could become a matter of deep contention.

The heaviest burdens of every funeral fall on daughters who have married out into other descent groups (*zòmæ*). With the active participation of their husbands, these daughters discuss who among them will be "central daughter" (*zòmæ kachi*). The most economically secure out of the eldest or youngest daughters should take on the role; a middle daughter might step up only if her eldest and youngest sisters are dead, absent, or destitute. If a couple has no married-out daughters, a substitute is sought first among households in relations of debt to the host household and then among other close kin and friends. In such cases, the host household usually agrees to repay the replacement daughter's entire contribution at later funerals. The central daughter's expenditure is emotional as well as material, for she takes the lead in the collective crafting of grief that is indispensible to Emerging from the Courtyard and Dawn-to-Dusk Sacrifice vigils. No substitute is likely to contribute as much materially or emotionally as an actual daughter, and to die without a married-out daughter is a serious misfortune.

The chief guests at every funeral are the brothers of the dead woman or of the dead man's wife (the *avə*), who choose from among themselves a "central brother-in-law" (*avə kachi*). If a man has married more than once, all his wives' brothers are *avə* at his funeral, but the central *avə* is a brother of his final wife. If no brothers are available, the woman's parallel cousins can serve as *avə*. This preserves the parallel relation of the *avə* to the dead woman and the cross relation of the *avə*'s children to the dead couple's children (which makes them potential marriage partners) (see figure 3.1). If a woman has no brothers and no parallel cousins, then another household has to be found to act as *avə*, usually one with to whom the host household owes debts acquired at earlier funerals. For an unmarried woman, any married brothers with their own households can act as *avə*; if there are none, a suitable substitute must be found. The need for an *avə* is an important reason that unmarried men and boys are married during night vigils; the parents or brothers of the dead bride become *avə* at this vigil and all the man's subsequent funerals. An affinal relationship established through marriage of the dead lasts only one generation, as there are no offspring to marry. While *avə* make some material contributions to funerals, their primary role is to assess the wealth and effort expended and to lodge complaints if the funeral is insufficient or badly

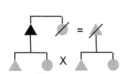 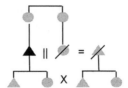 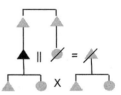

FIGURE 3.1 *Avə* substitutions preserve cross relations between the children of the *avə* and those of the dead. *Left*. The *avə* is the dead woman's brother; his children are in a cross (X) relation to the children of the deceased couple. *Center*. The *avə* is the dead woman's mother's sister's son. He is in a parallel (||) relation to the deceased couple, and his children remain in a cross (X) relation to theirs. *Right*. The *avə* is the dead woman's father's brother's son. He is in a parallel (||) relation to the deceased couple, and his children remain in a cross (X) relation to theirs.

conducted. An *avə* takes a stance of judicious watchfulness at his sister's funeral. His obligations are an extension of his duty to his sister during her life to see that her husband's family treats her well. Her children owe her a proper funeral, and his responsibility is to see that she receives it. At the same time, an *avə* is expected to show solicitude for his sister's children and aid them in their difficulty, and his gifts are offered in this spirit. An *avə* who is dissatisfied with the way a funeral is conducted or who harbors resentment at the way his dead sister has been treated by her husband's family may demand compensation. A seriously disgruntled *avə* might go so far as to sit on the coffin of his sister at dawn and refuse to let it be carried to the graveyard until the entire Emerging from the Courtyard vigil is performed a second time, putting his dead sister's children to enormous trouble and expense.

Hosts or *vɛdù*, daughters or *zòmὲ*, and brothers-in-law or *avə* are each joined by a crowd of others who have kinship relations and previous obligations to the principal participants. A daughter's kin and friends support her at funerals by bringing gifts: a live chicken, jugs of cane alcohol or bottles of beer, bags of grain or packages of noodles. Every participant household brings gifts for one or more of the principal descent groups. A single household might prepare twenty bags of grain, distributing one to each of the sons, one to each of the daughters, one to each of the brothers-in-law, and others to other central kin with whom they have significant relationships. All gifts have to be repaid at subsequent funerals by their initial recipients (rather than by the host family, the eventual recipient of most), producing a closely woven tissue of obligation that enmeshes every person in Júzò. While weddings also entail massive exchanges of gifts, the obligations from weddings and funerals are never mixed. One's presence is also an important contribution, and most participants choose one of the three central groups to support by sitting with them. Many households demonstrate their obligations to more than one group by splitting up, the men sitting with one group, the women and children with another, or by moving among the different groups.

The rules for composing the three central groups who will conduct a funeral begin already to construct an ideal image of a dead person. Fundamentally, this person is a couple, suspended in three separate categories of relation: (1) with the couple's own descendants, or sons, centering on the youngest son and heir (vedù); (2) with the couple's married-out daughters and their husbands and children (zòmæ); and (3) with the couple's affines, the brothers of the dead woman or brothers-in-law of the dead man (avə). This ideal image of the person of the dead couple is actualized in the selection of a person, alive or dead, to couple the dead person with; the selection of households to fill the central roles of vedù, zòmæ, and avə; and the selection of a representative for each group. For the rare dead person who has been married to only one spouse and who has an able youngest son, devoted married-out daughters, and respectable brothers-in-law, all these choices might remain uncomplicated. In most cases, the ideal is approached by degrees, and central households and persons are selected through discussion, negotiation, and compromise. In every case, those selected must find ways to muster resources and friends in order to carry out their roles appropriately. The person of the dead couple, beginning as an ideal image, begins to emerge into actual being through a collective labor of discussion and negotiation. This process of actualization grows more concrete and detailed during the processes of sacrifice and exchange at the center of every funeral ritual.

Cross-Cousin Marriage

The three central groups are hierarchically ranked. The daughters' group has heavy obligations to contribute gifts to the host's group; the host's group gives the brothers-in-law's group significant prestige in return for far less in material gifts. This hierarchy is clearly an effect of the brothers-in-law's group's status as wife givers to the host descent group and the daughters' group's status as wife takers from the host descent group. Most brothers stay involved in their married sisters' lives, demanding that their husbands treat them well and contributing to the naming ceremonies of their children, and sisters' sons look to their mothers' brothers as moral guides. Daughters look on their many gifts at their parents' funerals as returns for the care and labor lavished on them, but they repay this care as members of their husbands' descent groups. Their significant contributions to their parents' funerals might be construed as payments into their brothers' descent group for the gift of themselves as wives.

Work for the dead is organized through the idiom of kinship, which cannot be understood without reference to the architecture of kinship terminology in places where bilateral cross-cousin marriage is preferred, a topic in which my friends in Júzò showed avid interest (ignoring its current deeply unfashionable status in anthropology). Except for those belonging to a few Han descent groups, parents in Júzò encourage their children to marry their mother's brothers' children or father's sisters' children, seeing this as a way to wind the ties of family tighter. They find many ways to ignore the provision of the 1950 marriage law that forbids cousin marriage, and this form of marriage was common in the socialist and reform eras.[5] Yet while parents prefer cross-cousin marriage, they cannot prescribe it. Youths have considerable sexual freedom before marriage and a great deal of agency in choosing their marriage partners. In addition, wise parents know that if the married children of a sibling pair do not get along, they might destroy the peace and unity of several households. Still, marriage with actual cross cousins is not necessary to sustain a cross-cousin marriage system. Like other such systems, Júzò's system of kinship terminology divides *all* kin of one's generation into cross and parallel, allowing marriage with cross kin and proscribing marriage with parallel kin as tantamount to incest.

A preference for cross-cousin marriage is found among many Tibeto-Burman-speaking peoples in China's southwest (Wellens 2010, Ma 2013, Lu 1989, Chien 1999). Allied peoples in Burma and China were among those who provoked Levi-Strauss's famous analysis of the topic (Levi-Strauss 1969). The matrilateral variety of cross-cousin marriage has been observed among many Tibetan-speaking peoples in the Himalayas (Childs 2008, Levine 1988, Watkins 1996, Vinding 1998, Schuler 1987, Goldstein 1975). Even in Central Tibet and Amdo, where cousin marriage is frowned upon as incestuous and as violating Buddhist morality, there is linguistic evidence of a cross-cousin marriage rule in earlier times (Allen 1976, Fjeld 2008, Makley 2002, Lindskog 2000). Cousin marriage is widespread in Southern India and Sri Lanka, where it has been the subject of a great deal of discussion, most illuminatingly in Trautmann's classic, *Dravidian Kinship* (1981). As is well known, cross-cousin marriage rules are associated with and supported by a characteristic structure of kinship terminology, cut through by a distinction between cross and parallel. For Lòlopò, the categories that determine whom one might marry and those that guide people in their responsibilities at funerals intersect in kinship terminology. Table 3.1 arranges Lòlopò kinship terms in Trautmann's paradigmatic table, designed

5. On the effects of the marriage law in this region—rural Chuxiong Prefecture—see Diamant (2000).

TABLE 3.1 Lòlopò kinship terms arranged in Trautmann's (1981, 40) paradigmatic table.

		♂				♀	
		cross	parallel				cross
G²			àbo FF, SpMF MF, SpFF			àp'i FM, SpFM MM, SPMM	
G¹	e	avə mà MeB / ama pò FeZH / àbò və SpF	àbò vævæ̀ FeB MeZH	àbò F	àmo M	àmo vævæ̀ MeZ FeBW	a mà FeZ / anì mà MeBW / SpM
	y	avə tie MyB / amà pò FyZH	àbò tie FyB / aya pò MyZH			aya MyZ / àmo tie FyBW	a tie FyZ / ani tie MyBW
G⁰	e	hobə MBS FZS	àtạ eB e(FBS) e(MZS)	ego		àtsi eZ e(FBD) e(MZD)	fumo MBD FZD
	y		næmà yB y(FBS) y(MZS)			nεmo yZ y(FBD) y(MZD)	
G⁻¹		súvə ♂ZS ♀BS	zò S zòdu ♂BS ♀ZS			zòmæ̀ D zòmæ̀du ♂BD ♀ZD	chìmo súmo ♂ZD ♀BD
G⁻²			lípò SS DS			límo SD DD	

F=father, M=mother, B=brother, Z=sister, S=son, D=daughter, H=husband, W=wife,
Sp=spouse, e=elder, y=younger

to clarify the cross/parallel distinction around which such terminological systems are arranged (Trautmann 1981, 40).

Trautmann places parallel kin in the two central columns of his table and cross kin in the outer columns. He asks the reader to imaginatively transform the table into a cylinder by bending it until the male cross kin on the left are adjacent to the female cross kin on the right. The cylinder is now cut through perpendicularly by two of the central distinctions on which such terminological systems are built: between cross and parallel and between male and female. The third important distinction, between generations, is the cylinder's vertical dimension. The dimension of relative age, particularly important for Lòlopò, is subordinated to the dimension of generation.

The table makes it clear that the dimension of crossness applies only to the three medial generations—ego's generation, his parents' generation and his children's generation, here shown as G0, G1, and G–1. In ego's generation, all cousins are placed in one of two categories. All parallel cousins, the children of one's father's brothers or mother's sisters, are called by the same terms as siblings: *àta*, "older brother," *næmà*, "younger brother," *àtsi*, "older sister," and *nɛmo*, "younger sister." All cross cousins, the children of one's mother's brother or father's sister, with whom marriage is encouraged, are called by terms specific to cross cousins: *hobə* for men and *fumo* for women. When Lòlopò express a preference for cross-cousin marriage, they do not begin by talking about marriage with a mother's brother's daughter or father's sisters' son. Instead, the simplest expression of the rule is that *hobə* and *fumo* should marry, while *àta/næmà* and *àtsi/nɛmo* must not.

These terms, which distinguish cross from parallel, are extended laterally to all kin of ego's generation. For instance, to speak of the kintypes that English speakers call "second cousins," if I am male, my FMBDD is *àtsi/nɛmo* to me, thus parallel, as my father's MBD was *fumo* to him, a possible marriage partner, thus equivalent to my mother, making her daughter my sister, or *àtsi/nɛmo*. On the other hand, I, still male, find my MMBDD to be *fumo*, thus cross to me, as my mother's MBD, though *fumo* to her, was not a possible marriage partner, being of the same sex. So her daughter is not my sister, or *àtsi/nɛmo*: she can only be my *fumo*, making marriage with her possible. Equivalent reasoning might be applied to any of the thirty-two kintypes habitually called "second cousins" in English (Trautmann 1981, 48–49).

People in Júzò said that in principle one should be able to calculate a kin term to apply to anyone related to within seven generations—that is, nearly everyone whose family has lived in Júzò for several generations. In such calculations, all those of one's own generation (who may indeed be older than one's parents or younger than one's children) are either cross (the men *hobə* and the women *fumo*) or parallel (the men *àta* or *næmà* and the women *àtsi* or *nɛmo*, depending on whether they are older or younger than oneself). The rule that I have expressed as a preference for cross-cousin marriage thus operates more forcefully. While to marry inside Júzò, which nearly always means marrying one's *hobə* or *fumo*, is desirable, to marry the equivalent of one's sibling, one's *àtsi/nɛmo* or *àta/næmà*, is not possible, unless one can transform him or her into *hobə* or *fumo* by strategically calculating along another genealogical path.

The cross/parallel distinction carries into the ascending generation. In one's parent's generation, parallel kin are father's brothers and mother's sisters. Father's brothers are called by the same term as father, *àbò*, with a suffix of *vævæ̀* or *tiȩ* to mark the father's brothers as elder or younger. These suffixes are important for Lòlopò. For instance, though the most respectful term of address for father's brother is *àbò*, it is a horrible blunder to address him as *àbò* before outsiders to one's household, or to refer to him this way to others, for it implies that he has had sex with one's mother. He must be referred to as *àbò vævæ̀* or *àbò tie*. For occasions where more exact terms of reference are required, Lòlopò kinship terms allow one to distinguish among no fewer than twelve of father's brothers with six additional suffixes that may be applied after *vævæ̀* or *tiȩ* (*kævæ̀*, *alipò*, *avapò*, *akópò*, *achæpò*, and *kɔyǽ kɔyæ̀*, in that order). Thus the eldest of father's elder brothers is *àbò vævæ̀ kævæ̀*, the next eldest *àbò vævæ̀ alipò*, and so on, and likewise with his younger brothers. Mother's elder sisters' husbands are also addressed as *àbò* and referred to as *àbò vævæ̀*, but her younger sisters' husbands are *ayapò*. On the female side, mother's elder sisters are addressed as *àmo*, the same as mother, and referred to as *àmo vævæ̀*. Her younger sisters are *aya* (thus *ayapò* for their husbands, *pò* being a gender marker). Father's brothers' wives are also *àmo*, with *vævæ̀* or *tiȩ* added to mark them as wives of elder or younger brothers. These are all parents of those whom one must not marry. The age-ordering terms applied to father's brothers are rarely applied to mother's sisters. Terms that merge fathers with their brothers and mother's sisters' husbands on the one hand and mothers with their sisters and father's brothers' wives on the other are characteristic of systems associated with cross-cousin marriage; the Lòlopò system is a variation that cuts mothers' younger sisters and their husbands out of these mergings.

On the cross side, mother's brothers are *avə* (like wife's brothers), with *mà* or *tiȩ* marking them as older or younger than mother. Father's younger sisters' husbands are also *avə tiȩ* (the suffix referring to their wives' ages relative to father, not their own), but his elder sisters' husbands are a separate term, *amàpò*. Spouse's father is *àbò avə*. Father's elder sisters are *a mà* (thus *amàpò* for their husbands); his younger sisters are *a tiȩ*. Mother's elder and younger brothers' wives' are a slight variation, *ani mà* and *ani tiȩ* respectively. Spouse's mother is *àmo ani mà*. These are all parents of people one is encouraged to marry or has already married. Again, terms that merge mother's brothers with father's sisters' husbands and spouse's father on the one hand and father's sisters with mother's brothers' husbands on the other are characteristic of systems where cross-cousin marriage is established; the Lòlopò variation cuts father's elder sisters and their husbands out of these mergings.

The descending generation is also ordered by the cross/parallel distinction. All of a man's brothers' children and a woman's sisters' children, never

possible marriage partners for one's own children, are one category of niece
and nephew. One addresses the boys as *zò*, son, and refers to them as *zòdu*.
One addresses the girls as *zòmæ̀*, daughter, and refers to them as *nédu* (*né* is
a more formal term for daughter, used frequently in ritual language). On the
cross side, all of a man's sister's children and a woman's brother's children, desirable marriage partners for one's children, are a second category, *súvə* for the
boys and *chìmo súmo* for the girls (*chìmo* is an actual daughter-in-law, *chìmo
súmo* a potential daughter-in-law).

The cross/parallel distinction is neutralized in the grandparents' generation and above. In the grandparents' generation, all men are called *àbo* and all
women *àp'ì*, with suffixes often added to distinguish siblings by birth order.
Thus father's father's elder brothers are *àbo kævæ̀* and their wives *àp'ì kævæ̀*,
while his younger brothers are *àbo kæyæ* and their wives *àp'ì kæyæ*. These suffixes can be used to distinguish elder or younger siblings of any consanguineal
ascendants, and the six age-ordering suffixes used for father's brothers may
also be applied to groups of same-sex siblings or their wives or husbands. Men
of the third ascending generation are all called *abapʼò* and women *abəmo* and
men of the fourth *amàpʼò* and women *àmamo*. Often, more than one route develops with which to trace relations to those in ascending generations. Finally,
the cross/parallel distinction is also neutralized in the grandchildren's generation, all male grandchildren being called *lípó* and all females *límo*.

It is useful to note how different this is from the Han Chinese system of
kinship terms. Centrally, the Han system distinguishes between siblings and
cousins and between agnatic cousins (*tang*) and all other cousins (*biao*). And
it distinguishes rigorously between all levels of consanguines and all affines.
While the Lòlopʼò system is classificatory, in Morgan's (1870) terms, the Han
system is descriptive; "It incorporates more distant relatives not by including
them in categories defined with respect to closer ones but by creating new
terms on the basis of certain principles" (Harrell 1989, 191). While the Lòlopʼò
system clearly reflects the principles of bilateral cross-cousin marriage, the
Han system does not represent any prescriptive marriage practice other than
proscribing marriage with agnatic cousins, though Han have followed a variety of other specific marriage rules, in particular preferring the matrilateral
variety of cross-cousin marriage in some rural places (Hsu 1945, Qin 2001,
Cooper 1993, Cooper and Zhang 1993).

Bilateral cross-cousin marriage was the foundation for the system of funeral exchanges among the descent groups of host (*vɛdù*), daughters (*zomæ̀*),
and brothers-in-law (*avə*). Had Lòlopʼò practiced the matrilateral variation,
preferring men to marry their mothers' brothers' daughters while forbidding
them to marry their fathers' sisters' daughters, like many Tibetan-speaking and

some Tibeto-Burman-speaking peoples, the hierarchy of wife-giving and wife-taking descent groups that formed around each dead couple only to dissolve once that couple was finally put to rest would have stabilized. Descent group A would have repeatedly acted as wife-giving *avə* at the funerals of descent group B, while descent group B would have acted repeatedly as *zòmæ̀* at the funerals of descent group A. Leach famously outlined such an arrangement among Kachin, where, on the basis of preferred marriage with the mother's brother's daughter, wife-giving *mayu* patrilineages and wife-taking *dama* lineages formed stable relationships (Leach 1951). Wives flowing from *mayu* to *dama* and gifts returning from *dama* to *mayu* created a hierarchical social structure in which wives moved from chiefly to aristocratic and from aristocratic to commoner lineages, while wealth moved from commoner to aristocratic and from aristocratic to chiefly lineages. In Júzò, in contrast, bilateral cross-cousin marriage destabilized emergent hierarchies among local descent groups.

In a simple hypothetical case in Júzò, bilateral cross-cousin marriage would tend to create stable and equal relationships between two descent groups, with the children from descent group A marrying the children from descent group B through several generations. In such a case, if a man from descent group A acted as *avə* for his sister's husband in descent group B, his son's household, also from descent group A, would act as *zòmæ̀*. And when a man from descent group A died, his wife's brother in descent group B would act as *avə*, while the latter's son's household in descent group B would act as *zòmæ̀*. In descending generations, this pattern would repeat itself, descent group A acting as *avə* and *zòmæ̀* at funerals for descent group B and descent group B acting as *avə* and *zòmæ* at funerals for descent group A. Of course, this simple instance rarely occurred in reality. Marriage in Júzò established multiple relations among many descent groups rarely created reciprocal exchanges of wives between any two descent groups, and often allowed one group to act as wife giver to another for two or more generations. Nevertheless, preferring bilateral cross-cousin marriage ensured that the large quantity of gifts that flowed from married women's households to the households of their brothers did not, in the long term, stabilize hierarchies of wealth among local descent groups. While there were many sources of inequality in Júzò, the flow of gifts at funerals was not among them.

Opting Out

Some residents managed to use ethnicity and exogamous marriage to escape the valley-wide system of funeral exchange. The Zhang family, which distinguished itself from the valley's other Han descent groups by maintaining a Han identity more convincing to outsiders, provides an illuminating case study. Zhang Wenxing was the family's most prominent member in the 1930s and 1940s. Beginning with little, he developed a business in the salt trade, accumulated considerable landholdings, and became the community's township head (xiangzhang), the official representative of Long Yun's Yunnan government. In 1951, he was executed by the new socialist government as a landlord and counterrevolutionary, but not before he inscribed a tombstone in honor of his patrilineage. The inscription traced Zhang Wenxing's descent from Zhang Chengtao, who moved from nearby Lianchi 蓮池 with his wife, née Wu, in the Daoguan period (1820–1850). Zhang Chengtao's son Zhang Feng also married a Wu woman. The Wu patrilineage of Júzò, self-identified as Han, had resided there as long as any Lòlopò descent group, but it is likely that Zhang Feng and his father took their wives from a Han family in Lianchi. Zhang Feng's son Zhang Xueli took a wife née Yuan. As no Yuan resided in Júzò, she too was certainly from elsewhere, and probably from a Han family. Zhang Xueli's son Zhang Weimei was Zhang Wenxing's father:

3.4 勿寡言居合睦族处, 以和乡暨而得配吾母, 吾母内助有方, 曾赠得田地数亩.

not shy of speech, he lived together with the peaceful people of this place, even pairing with my mother of the same township. My mother, a proper wife, gifted him several mu of land.

That Zhang Wenxing would make a point of noting that his mother was a local supports the hypothesis that his other female ascendants were not. He failed to note his mother's name, but a generous betrothal gift of land, if not coerced, would be unheard of among Lòlopò families, who expected instead a complex and lengthy flow of animals and grain in return for a bride. Instead, she was probably from one of the two other prominent Han-surname groups in Júzò, the Wu or the Gu. Both the Wu and the Gu were better integrated into the Lòlopò community than the Zhang, but they both looked to the Zhang as exemplars of proper Han identity.

In Zhang Wenxing's generation, his descent group shed men. His eldest brother's first wife was a Fan, not a Júzò surname. The stone mentions an unspecified "abominable tragedy" that ended with this wife's death and the loss of all the family's land. "In order to put the family on a firm footing," the brother remarried uxorilocally into the Wu patrilineage. Zhang Wenxing's second brother also married out, into a Gu descent group, taking the ignominious surname Che 車 (meaning "cart") to signal that he was no longer a Zhang. This left Zhang Wenxing (who called himself Muxiao) and his third brother to care for their parents, "handsome and wise brothers, leaning on each other like beam upon girder," according to the inscription, until all three of his brothers died quickly in succession,

3.5 烏呼單存木肖一人, 时逢國難當中, 支持門戶, 不辭經商之苦, 不畏農汗之辛, 金積財 如水挑沙.

alas, leaving Muxiao alone in the midst of national calamity to sustain the household, making nothing of the hardship of trade, not fearing to suffer the sweat of farming, and accumulating gold like carrying sand in water.

Zhang Wenxing praised his wife for raising one of his dead brothers' sons, whom he adopted as heir. While he did not inscribe his wife's name or origin, others in Júzò recalled that she had been a Gu.

Thus, instead of marrying cross cousins, Zhang Wenxing's descent group took its wives from families outside of Júzò when possible and from local Han when not, with the possible exception of Zhang Wenxing's mother, exceptional in bringing a considerable gift of land. And the Zhang family turned to local Han families to marry off sons uxorilocally when the family experienced grave difficulties. Zhang Wenxing's stone did not mention the fate of the family's daughters, but other stones did. An undated stone for Wu Xixian, who passed away in 1766, lists two grandsons with their two wives, one from the Zhang descent group, the second from the Lòlopò Li. (His sons married women with Lòlopò names before the Zhangs arrived in the valley). A stone erected in 1832 for Yang Long, a Lòlopò woman who married into the Wu family and died in 1821, shows that two of her five sons took Zhang women as wives, the others marrying Lòlopò. On the other hand, I have discovered no Lòlopò stones showing marriages to Zhang women; they were no one's cross cousins. The strategy of taking wives from Han exempted the Zhangs from any obligations as *zòmœ* at Lòlopò funerals, a considerable drain on wealth for many Lòlopò. And their alliances with the Wu and Gu became useful when Zhang Wenxing's poverty-stricken brothers had to find households to accept them as heirs. Perhaps because of these strategies, Zhang Wenxing and his ascendants were reputed to be stingy and standoffish, keeping to themselves in their isolated compound near the valley's tail. "Zhang Wenxing was the only person in Júzò who ate rice all year round," one of his neighbors recalled. "If he ate pork today, he would eat chicken tomorrow and goat the next day, and he always ate alone." This reputation did much to seal the landlord's eventual fate.

Zhang Wenxing's inscription on his father's stone tells a story of exogamy and, when that was not possible, the next best thing: marriage into local descent groups struggling to retain a valued Han identity. As a counterexample, it illuminates the extent to which bilateral cross-cousin marriage made Júzò a largely endogamous place, where most people related to nearly all others as kin. Lòlopò had many ways of imagining the deplorable circumstances in which this endogamous standard was ruptured, as when Han of low morals, called Kúju (or Kújupò), were drawn to Júzò by the beauty of Lòlomo daughters. Here, for instance, is a fragment from a chant intended to drive away a spirit called Srkanè, who preyed on women who loved to dance and dress in embroidered clothing:

3.6	æ̀ mæ̀ né shɨ̀ rọ	seven beloved daughters
	shɨ̀ rọ k'o ka jɔ	seven loved ones over there
	chi bo và sè jɔ	sewing and embroidering
	væ cí væ ha jɔ	clowning and laughing
	k'o bò cæ̀ cæ jo	lively ones on that slope
	hé bò cæ̀ nì jo	noisy ones on this slope
	kú ju æ ve ŋò	Kúju greedy as wild dogs
	kú ju læ sì ji	Kúju laugh like fools
	kú tæ̀ læ mì ro	Kúju watch and drool

Júzò residents took many measures to make their little valley and its upland tributaries a whole. They reserved a large portion of the best land in the valley to fund a communal ritual and political system that reproduced a bounded territory into which outsiders were welcomed and feasted in order to be more precipitously hurried along on their way. They made yearly sacrifices to the original ancestors who had settled the valley, now construed as apical ancestors to all its inhabitants. They held a yearly feast, modeled on a wedding banquet, in which representatives of every household acted ritually as affines to a central couple, elected every year to deal with external representatives of the state and to care for the various manifestations of the apical ancestor scattered through the valley (Mueggler 2001, 2002). Encouraged to use the vocabulary of nation and nationality (minzu) to speak of community after the 1950s, Lòlopò in Júzò insisted that they were a singular nationality, distinct from all the other peoples the state called Yi, in particular the Lípò who surrounded them, the dangerous and uncivilized Mantsïpò (Nuosu) in mountains to the north, and the omnipresent immigrants, Kújupò (poor Han) and Cepò (rich Han).

The strong sense that *hobə* and *fumo* should marry was the foundation of all these efforts. It made Júzò into a place where one might hail anyone as kin and where if one had to use a proper name instead one was justified in treating the interlocutor with suspicion. The importance of kin terms in this process cannot be overemphasized. Kin terms made this social whole partible, dividing it into categories, making it comprehensible as an assemblage of parts that must be disassembled in a different way by each participant. The unique constellation of kin terms that partitioned one's social world was the primary medium for one's relations with this whole. The processes of sacrifice and exchange at funeral rituals reconstituted this whole by using kin terms to divide the social world of the deceased into its constituent parts and calling upon each participant to respond appropriately.

Ordering Relations

The central work of Emerging from the Courtyard and Dawn-to-Dusk Sacrifice rituals is a series of exchanges of goats, rice loaves, grain, and alcohol that involves every person in attendance. In Emerging from the Courtyard, this series of exchanges begins shortly after the corpse is placed in a coffin in the courtyard's center. A big bonfire is built for the host's group (*vedù*) at the coffin's foot, situated to the north; another is built for the daughters' group (*zòmæ*), at the coffin's side, and a third is built for the brothers-in-law's group (*avə*) at the coffin's head, situated to the south. Women from the daughters' group, along with their friends and supporters, take seats on makeshift benches placed on both sides of the coffin, to sing lament. A flat, rimmed winnowing basket, about three feet in diameter, is set up on a table at the coffin's head. This is where exchange will take place (figure 3.2).

At Emerging from the Courtyard, slaughter and exchange take four to six hours. Exchange at any one event is connected to exchange at many others, for every participant returns obligations formed at previous events, incurs debts to be repaid at future events, and puts others under obligations to be returned in the future. Funeral exchange, called *ji'íti* at every event, gives social relations material form and submits them to material operations. While the practical effect of *ji'íti* is to place relations with many others on the horizon of every participant, bringing others into calculations about the past and future, its indexical effect is to dissever bodies composed of many forms of relations into their component parts in the present. *Ji'íti* produces a body for the dead out of the entirety of relations in which the couple was suspended while alive, and it repeatedly reveals the intention to cut that body apart, as a butcher's knife parts the bones and sinews of a goat, in order to disentangle the dead from the living.

Sacrifice and exchange require the services of an energetic and knowledgeable master of ceremonies employed by the host, a "host's manager" (*vedù*

FIGURE 3.2 Distribution of the three central groups of kin and friends at the Emerging from the Courtyard vigil. The brothers-in-law's group (*avə*) gathers around a fire at the head of the coffin; the daughter's
group (*zòmæ̀*) sits on both sides of the coffin; the host's group (*vɛdù*) sits by a fire at the coffin's foot.

holo). In a spirit of formal parallelism, the other two groups also each choose
a "manager." As one funeral participant succinctly explained, "The host's manager is the busiest man, responsible for everything. The brothers-in-law's manager observes and helps judge if everything is done correctly. The daughters'
manager sits and drinks." Each group also chooses a "thief" (*tsapʼò*), preferably
a widower, near the end of his life, who likes to drink and has little fear left of
ghosts. The thieves wear hemp sashes around their waists, like the white belts
of policemen. At pivotal moments, they brandish pig-slaughtering knives and
whoop a "cry to heaven." Their task is to control the kinless ghosts (*sakʼá*) who
gather to eat the offerings. They are thieves because of their affinity with the
rapacious ghosts; they are police because it is their crude force that keeps those
ghosts in check.

On a pile of firewood near the host's fire, the master of ceremonies leads
the slaughter of the goats and chickens brought by the guests. Once a goat is
killed, gutted, and skinned or a chicken killed, eviscerated, and charred, the
master of ceremonies brings the animal to the coffin's head and touches it to
the winnowing basket, to pass its soul to the underworld, where the dead person will herd and nurture it. He then takes the animal back to the coffin's foot,
where it is butchered, chopped, and boiled, and its meat is marked with a combination of bamboo sticks to identify the person who gifted it. He immediately
returns the goat's pelt to the giver.

After all the animals are killed and butchered, exchange begins. Sacrifice and exchange take exactly the same order. Often this order is expressed simply. The daughters' group (zòmæ̀) is first; the brothers-in-law's group (avǝ) is second; the host's group (vɛdù) is last. In this formulation, the zòmæ̀ group contains six subgroups, which perform sacrifice and exchange in the following order: (1) The actual daughters or their substitutes. Their offerings can be construed as payments into the dead couple's descent group for the gift of themselves as wives. (2) The dead couple's parallel nieces and nephews. These are classificatory sons and daughters to the dead couple. In this subcategory, the dead man's brothers' daughters are central, as they are the closest kin to actual daughters. In essence, this category consists of substitute daughters supported by their siblings and parallel cousins. Like the actual daughter, these parallel nieces can be seen to be paying into the dead couple's descent group, which includes their own fathers, for the gift of themselves as wives. (3). The dead man's sisters. Their gifts to the dead couple can be construed as continuing to pay into their dead brother's descent group in a second generation for the gift of themselves as wives. (4) The children of the dead man's sisters, who are essentially aiding their mothers. (5) The dead man's father's sisters. They may be seen as continuing to pay into the dead couple's descent group for the gift of themselves as wives. (6) The grandchildren, except for the sons' sons, and including the daughters' children. In essence the grandchildren are all helping their mothers with their obligations. Put simply, all these subcategories represent descent groups in a wife-taking relations to the dead couple's descent group. This is why they are all said fundamentally to belong to the zòmæ̀, or daughters' group. The order in which these subgroups perform sacrifice and exchange begins with actual daughters (or their substitutes) and continues through categories of kin who are increasingly distant from the actual daughters in terms of generation and their cross or parallel relation to the dead couple.

Table 3.2 is a synopsis of this series, showing the generational relation of each central participant to the dead, the cross (X) or parallel (||) relation of the dead to each participant category, the cross or parallel relation of the dead couple's children to the corresponding generation of the participants' patriline (G^0 X/|| relation) and the cross or parallel relation of the dead's sons' children to the corresponding generation of the participants' patriline (G^{-1} X/|| relation).

The order of the series depends on the distance, generationally and laterally, from the actual daughters, the nodal zòmæ̀. Lateral distance is expressed in table 3.2 by relations of crossness through marriage, as it is in marriage calculations. Thus, category 2, the parallel cousins, are of the same generation as the nodal zòmæ̀ and close laterally since they are parallel to the daughter's

TABLE 3.2 Categories of *zòmæ* and their cross/parallel (X/||) relations with the dead couple, along with the cross/parallel relations of their children (G⁻¹) and grandchildren (G⁻²) with the corresponding generation of the dead couple's patrilineage.

Order of sacrifice and exchange	Relations of offerant to the dead couple	Kin terms by which offerant is addressed from point of view of dead couple	Generation of offerant in relation to the dead couple	Cross or parallel (X/||) relation of offerant to dead couple	Cross or parallel (X/||) relation of offerant's children to dead couple's children	Cross or parallel (X/||) relation of offerant's grandchildren to dead couple's grandchildren
1	D	*zòmæ*	G^{-1}	||	||	X
2	♂BS, ♂BD, ♀ZS , ♀ZD	*zòdu nédu*	G^{-1}	||	||	X, ||
3	♂Z	*àtsi nɛmo*	G^{0}	||	X	X
4	♂ZS, ♂ZD, (♀BS)	*chìmo súmo*	G^{-1}	X	X	X, ||
5	♂FZ	*amà atie*	G^{1}	X	X	X
6	SD, DS, DD	*lípó límo*	G^{-2}	0	X, ||	X, ||

generation, while some of their children will be cross to the daughter's children and others parallel to the daughter's children. Category 3, the dead man's sisters, are one generation removed from the daughter and further from her laterally, because their children are cross to the daughter and their sons' children cross to the daughter's children. Category 4, the dead man's sisters' sons and daughters, are the same generation as the daughter but quite far laterally, as they are cross to the dead couple and cross to the daughter. Category 5, the dead man's father's sisters, are even further. They are two generations removed from the daughter, and they, their children, and their children's children are cross to the dead, the dead's children, and the dead's children's children. Category 6, the grandchildren, are somewhat anomalous. Their position at the end of the series appears to stem from their generational distance from the dead.

After all the participants in the *zòmæ* categories perform their exchanges, it is the turn of the brothers-in-law (*avə*), beginning with the central brother-in-law and continuing with the others, eldest to youngest. Finally, it is the turn of the host (*vɛdù*) and his brothers. This fundamental order is materialized in space in several ways. When the corpse is carried out of the house and placed in the coffin, men of the *zòmæ* group support the sides; men from the *avə* group take the head, and men of the *vɛdù* group trail behind. As the corpse rests in the courtyard, the *zòmæ* group is positioned at its sides, the *avə* group at its head, the *vɛdù* group at its foot. At dawn, as the coffin is carried to the graveyard, men of the *zòmæ̀* take the sides, men of the *avə* take the head, and men of the *vɛdù* take the foot or trail behind.

These orientations are expressive of the shape of relations between each group and the dead couple. The *zòmæ̀* surround and support the dead couple. They wrap the corpse in fine clothing, swaddle it with hemp, feed it with rice, and water it with tears. The *avə* guide and guard the dead. They demand a fine funeral and judge its success; they lead the corpse along its road; they select the gravesite and approve the inscriptions on the tombstone. The *vɛdù* follow the

FIGURE 3.3 The brothers-in-law's dance. The coffin is wrapped first by lamenters from the daughters group (*zòmæ̀*), then by dancers from the brothers-in-law's group (*avə*), with all the members of the host's group (*vɛdù*) remaining outside the circle.

dead. They are the dead couple's heirs, receiving everything they leave behind. All kinship terms used in sacrifice and exchange are from the perspective of the dead couple, and from this perspective, the order *zòmc̀e, avə, vɛdu* is fundamentally concentric. It is materialized in concentric form deep into the night, after sacrifice and exchange are finally concluded. The *zòmc̀e* and their supporters continue to lament, holding their places on either side of the coffin; the *avə* and their supporters form a ring around them, linking hands to dance; the *vɛdù* and his supporters remain outside the circle in the courtyard (figure 3.3). The serial order of sacrifice and exchange replicates this concentric orientation in time.

The order of sacrifice and exchange shapes an image of the social relations out of which the dead couple are composed in life. This is an ideal image, not a snapshot of social relations at any particular moment. Yet, it is made real by degrees, as people determine to occupy each ideal category, reshaping the personhood of the dead couple. From the perspective of the performers, this imperfect realization, or actualization, of categorical kinship gives voice to the fluid stream of relations in which the corpse lies suspended. People often express this idea simply: "You can tell what kind of person the dead was by his funeral. You just watch who comes to offer goats, who comes to lament, who comes to help."

Goats and Loaves, Wholes and Halves

Every person named in the ideal order of sacrifice and exchange, or who substitutes for someone named in that order, brings a goat or chicken to sacrifice. Every such sacrifice precipitates a series of exchanges with a host of other people. This process of exchange is repeated twenty to fifty times at every Emerging from the Courtyard and Dawn-to-Dusk Sacrifice ritual, with crowds of people, mostly women, pressing around the winnowing basket at the head of the coffin to exchange pieces of goat, pieces of rice loaves, bags of grain, and jugs of alcohol (figure 3.4). As a bystander at many funeral events, I found these apparently very complex exchanges utterly bewildering until I absorbed two principles. First, I learned to take in a statement often repeated to me at funerals: "Everyone who brings a goat has to bring a big rice loaf too. And you can't bring a rice loaf unless you bring a goat." Second, I learned to think, as those I consulted on funerals consistently did, in terms of wholes and halves. The complex process of exchange may be decribed simply as an unfolding of these two principles. The parallel fates of goats and rice loaves is an expression of the cross-gendered nature of the dead couple and the world of relations that couple contains. Wholes and halves have to do with cutting each living person out of that world of relations.

FIGURE 3.4 Performing *ji'iti* exchange at the winnowing basket at the coffin's head (photo by author).

Every dead couple—and again, a dead person is always a couple even when one member of the couple is still alive—is made up of two gendered parts. Funerals repeatedly express the sense that the dead person is formally double, completing a person who died earlier or awaiting another death to be completed. For instance, at every opportunity, single things used in pivotal roles (cutting boards, pieces of fat on rice offerings, incense burners) are doubled when both members of a couple have died. Ancestral effigies materialize this double assemblage simply: a straight male-gendered pine twig bound with thread to a crotched female-gendered chestnut twig and placed on a woven bamboo bed. Graves also embody the double nature of the dead: a couple is always buried side by side, a tombstone for both is erected only after both have died, and inscriptions on tombstones usually use one name for both members of the couple.

Offerings of goats and rice loaves express this double cross-gendered character of the dead person. While goats and rice loaves are produced through multiple cross-gendered relations, they are retrospectively gendered at funerals. Men lead goats to funerals, sacrifice them and butcher them. Women make rice loaves, carry them to funerals, handle them and distribute them. Laments once sung by men detailed every step in birthing, herding, fattening, sacrificing, and butchering goats. Laments sung by women describe every step in growing and processing the rice used in rice loaves. (Rice loaves are made in several varieties; those that accompany sacrificial goats are dense, rounded masses of cooked, pounded rice, about a foot in diameter. At funerals, they are sliced and toasted over a fire to make a warm, tasty snack.)

As a prelude to each *ji'iti* exchange, the master of ceremonies makes a small distribution to the three "managers" and three "thieves." He pours out a bowl of alcohol, divides it into six bowls placed on the winnowing basket, and hands a bowl to each of these men. Usually, the master of ceremonies, needing all his faculties, pours his own bowl into a jug to save for later, but the others swallow theirs, the thieves whooping three times to announce the offering to the kinless ghosts. The managers belong to the world of the living; the thieves belong to the world of ghosts. The alcohol is divided evenly between the two.

In every *ji'iti* exchange, each central participant, representing her household, ideally offers a goat and a large rice loaf. If she cannot offer a goat, she offers a chicken and no rice loaf. The animal is partitioned and distributed; then the loaf is divided and distributed. These operations are strictly parallel. Because a rice loaf is a round, homogenous mass, divisible into equal parts, its partition and exchange complement and clarify the partition and exchange of the heterogeneous goat. Each *ji'iti* exchange involves several parallel distributions of goat and rice loaf.

First, the master of ceremonies slices off the entire bottom of the rice loaf and casts it into a basket at the head of the coffin. The contents of this basket are to be consumed directly by the dead, not eaten by the living like all other offerings. The master of ceremonies then casts the ears, tail, and half the neck and chest of the goat into the basket. The rice loaf offering clarifies the parallel offering of the goat. Like the entire bottom of the rice loaf, the ears, tail, and half the neck and chest are synecdoches—representative portions of the whole.

The soul of the goat was transferred to the dead when the whole slaughtered animal was touched to the winnowing basket. Now the whole body of the goat is given to the dead along with the whole rice loaf.

Second, the master of ceremonies slices the rice loaf in half and returns half to the person who offered it. The rice loaf remained unchanged in form after its bottom was sliced off and cast into the basket at the coffin's head—it remained whole. Now, half the whole rice loaf is returned to the giver. Of the goat, the master of ceremonies returns the liver, the heart, one leg, and one kidney. As the goat is strictly parallel to the rice loaf, these parts represent half of the whole goat.

Third, a representative of every household that has come in support of the giver (often up to twenty or thirty households) comes to the winnowing basket and empties a small bag of grain, a contribution from her household, into a large sack there, about the size and weight of a human body. The host household will boil part of this grain to serve to all the participants and keep the rest. In return, each supporter receives a slice of the half of the rice loaf that was not returned to the giver. The half of the goat's chest and neck that remains after half was cast into the basket at the coffin's head is divided among all the households that contributed to buying or raising the goat, as well as to each manager and each thief (or only to each thief if only one member of the couple has died). On the principle that goat and rice loaf are parallel, this half neck and chest appears as half of the whole goat, the half not returned to the giver in the form of pelt, liver, heart, leg, and kidney.

Fourth, women from every household that has contributed grain in support of the giver make rounds of the entire assembly, serving drink to each participant. These libations continue while the next exchange begins, so during the *ji'íti* for all those in the *zòmæ̀* categories—often three or four hours—a nearly continuous stream of women travels the courtyard pouring alcohol. Along with her goat and rice loaf, each central participant in one of the *zòmæ̀* categories brings several gallons of alcohol; her supporters bring more. Before the 1950s, these offerings were mainly of rice beer, a nourishing, slightly alcoholic drink prepared at home. After sales of hemp cloth brought Lòlop'ò cash income in the 1950s and 1960s, rice beer was gradually replaced by the potent grain or cane alcohol known as <u>baijiu</u>, bought in bulk. In the last decade, many participants have turned instead to more expensive (and far less potent) bottled beer. The *avə* do not offer alcohol with their *ji'íti*; the *vædù* usually offer only one round.

Fifth, after all twenty to fifty *ji'íti* exchanges are concluded, some of the grain and much of the remaining goat meat is boiled and served to the entire assembly.

TABLE 3.3 The parallel partition and distribution of rice loaves and goats at *ji'íti* exchange.

Rice loaf	Goat	Recipient
Whole (slice off the bottom)	**Whole** (ears, tail, and half the chest and neck)	**Dead couple** (basket at coffin's head)
Half	**Half** (pelt, liver, heart, one hind leg, one kidney)	Returned to **offerant**
Half (sliced)	**Half** (half of chest, half of neck)	Returned to **offerant's supporters**
Whole (grain, alcohol)	**Whole** (all remaining meat)	**Dead couple** (entire assembly eating on behalf of the dead)

When goats and rice loaves are considered as parallel, the apparently complex operations of *ji'íti* exchange become simple. First, the whole goat and rice loaf is given to the dead. Second, half of each is returned to the giver. *This half is returned by the dead*, funeral participants emphasized. Third, the half of each that is not returned to the giver is distributed to her supporters, along the lines of the relations that constitute her person, in exchange for bags of grain and gifts of alcohol. Finally, the entire goat and rice loaf is consumed by those assembled, eating on behalf of the dead (table 3.3).

In one of many sessions she spent explaining funeral ritual to me, Àp'ìmà, who was frequently consulted by people preparing to conduct funerals for their family members, summarized *ji'íti* exchange:

> The right half is yang; the left is yin. Yang is the world of people (*ts'ɔmi*); yin is the underworld (*mómi*). At one time, the dead couple was one family with the living. Now the dead people are ghosts in the underworld. The left half [of the goat] is the ghosts' half, from the underworld, brought back to you. This is the dead's gift to the living. The rice loaves are the same. One half is eaten by the dead, one half returned by the dead to the living. . . . All the meat and grain that is given to the crowd is for the dead, for the crowd is helping the dead eat. All that returns to particular people is for the living.

On the one hand, the dead accept the whole goat and whole rice loaf. They consume the goat and rice loaf, body and soul, with the mouths of the entire community of funeral participants, relations with whom form their person as an image of a social whole. On the other hand, the dead refuse half of each gift and the obligation for a particular continued relation with the giver that it entails. The bodies of goats and rice loaves are divided in half, one half consumed by the dead, one half eaten by the giver, a final meal shared between them, requiring no further return. It is as though the person of the giver is being cut out of this body with each partition of goat and rice loaf.

The single exception is the filial relation, the dead couple's relation to their heir, the *vedù*. In the *ji'íti* exchange for the *vedù*, at the very end of the sequence of exchanges, no part of either the goat or the rice loaf is returned to the giver. The entire goat (minus the parts cast into the basket at the head of the coffin) is placed in the pot to be consumed by the entire assembly; the entire rice loaf (again, minus the bottom slice placed in the basket) is placed in the bag of grain to be served to the assembly. The filial relation emerges out of the network of severed relations of alliance and affinity. The dead couple will be called upon repeatedly to make a return gift in the form of generative fertility for the *vedù* household and its descendants.

Wrapping, Affinity, Descent

Ji'íti exchanges compose a body for the dead through intensive processes that actualize an image of social relations retroactively construed to have composed the cross-gendered person of the dead couple in life. This image is concentric in form, expanding outward from the coffin's head, where goats and loaves are partitioned, to include every member of the assembly. It is differentiated by degree of generational and lateral distance, first from the dead couple and then from each nodal kin person. The dead body, an assemblage of social parts wrapped in layers of social skin, includes the entire gathering in the courtyard, which eats and drinks on behalf of the dead. In this regard, *ji'íti* exchanges repeat and further specify the operations begun before the corpse emerges from the house. There already, the dead body has been assembled, wrapped in layers of embroidered clothing, and swaddled in hemp. As in *ji'íti*, the daughters (*zomæ̀*) and their supporters begin this wrapping, and the brothers-in-law (*avə*) and sons (*vedù*) continue it. After emerging into the courtyard, the corpse is wrapped in layers of quilts and placed in a coffin so packed with cloth that it is opened several times for wrappings within to be rearranged or withdrawn before the lid will fit. Layers of human bodies then wrap the coffin, first the *zòmæ̀* and their allies who surround it to lament, and then the *avə* and their supporters who surround the lamenters to dance. *Ji'íti* exchange continues this assembling and wrapping process with other materials, adding pieces of each sacrificial body to the basket that is the corpse's mouth and returning other parts along the threads of relatedness that clothe and warm any body. Here is where the anatomical properties of animal bodies become useful: while various internal parts are distributed among managers, thieves, and each offerant's supporters, the pelt always returns to the offerant. Skins peeled from goat bodies at funerals wrap the living bodies that wrap the body of the dead, a final outer layer to this swaddled assemblage.

The composite gifts of goats and loaves are the cross-gendered motor of this assemblage. In every *ji'íti* exchange, sacrifices of rice loaves fill in a vast relational territory skipped over by animal sacrifices, taking each offerant as a node who gathers together many kin and friends to whom rice loaves are given in exchange for bags of grain. Animal bodies and rice bodies form an image of all the relations of affinity in which the dead person was embedded when alive. Relations of filial descent emerge from this background only through the repeated work of severing hundreds of relations of alliance.

Goats and rice loaves provide different perspectives on this image, emphasizing the emergence of descent on the one hand and the background of affinity on the other. This tension manifests with particular clarity in lament. Before the 1950s, lament during both Emerging from the Courtyard and Dawn-to-Dusk Sacrifice was often dialogical, men and women answering each other verse for verse, cooperating at the level of the whole to create a moving architectonic structure, while competing at the level of the verse along axes of both selection and combination. It was mostly women who revived lament in the late 1980s; few men remembered how to lament and fewer were willing to learn. Nevertheless, some qualities of men's laments were preserved in the genre called "weeping for the dead" (*shrtsïŋə*), performed at Dawn-to-Dusk Sacrifice by a hired male ritualist. Many laments used metaphors of gourd vines (*chì sæ̀*, the secure connections of descent) and balsam trees (*mə nɔ́*, the scattered fragrance of affinity) to reflect upon the relations revealed in sacrifice. In "weeping for the dead," sung only by male specialists, these relations were restricted and exclusive:

3.8 he nu du lɔ̀ — all these people
    ŋæ̀ chì sæ̀ jó mo lɔ mà gɔ́ — each strand of a tangled vine leads to
    do ŋà — the root
    ŋæ̀ chì sæ̀ jó ŋo ǹ ŋɔ ŋæ̀ . . . — those not on the vine are not here . . .
    chì sə k'ɔ́ shr gɔ̀ — a curly-horned billy goat
    chì mo k'ɔ́ p'e gɔ̀ — a flat-horned nanny goat
    k'ɔ́ p'e gɔ̀ tó ga mà — we give you that flat-horned goat

    ne mùu æ̀ ni lɔ̀ — this fine day
    kɔ́ kæ ni vè bæ — your entire family
    chì vè ni lí lɔ̀ — this family and its grandsons
    su lé ni t'è bɛ ǹ go — others have no claim

In contrast, the "weeping song" (*ɔchəŋə*) laments of women emphasize the multiplicity of alliances that are the ground from which descent must emerge. For instance, the following excerpt, which begins with the sacrifice of a goat, employs both the gourd-vine and balsam-tree metaphors to bring in all kin and neighbors, and it names the singer's maternal aunts and parallel cousins, who are not central participants in sacrifice, before naming her brothers, the product of descent.

3.9	à bò t̰ȅ chì ne mà tȅ do ga . . .	kill black goats to offer father . . .
	mə nɔ̰ pè vɯ̰̀ kɔ̀ go	call the scattered balsam trees back
	chì sæ̀ jo rú kɔ̀ go	call the gourd vine roots back
	mɔ̀ nɔ̰ pè t̰ȅ bo̰ do go	rely on the scattered balsam trees
	chì sæ̀ jo t̰ȅ bo̰ do go	rely on the gourd vine roots
	á gà yì zò bo̰ do go	rely on relatives from behind the house
	æ̀ jì ŋæ zò bo̰ do go	rely on neighbors from both sides
	mo cè né je bo̰ do go	rely on mother's sisters and their daughters
	kà jɔ mo zò bo̰ do go	rely on mother's sons

Like the two members of a couple whose deaths are both celebrated at the death of each, goats and rice loaves double and cross each other, allowing this singer to attribute the inclusive relations revealed by rice loaves to the sacrifice of "black goats." Many of the relations modeled in exchanges of slices of loaf for bags of grain are traced through friendship or coresidence rather than more formal categories of alliance. Put another way, they are analogous to the "fluid counterpoint that weaves around [the more] stable or centered mode" of filial descent, which Empson identifies in Buryat Mongol relatedness (2011, 18). Or, to transform the bone/flesh metaphor employed by many related Tibeto-Burman-speaking groups, if the modes of immanent experience assembled within the house are a corpse's organs, the emergent relations of descent would be its bones and the myriad relations of alliance its tendons and flesh. In any case, the body materialized by these operations is an actual dead body, rather than a virtual living one.

Cutting, Dancing, Emerging

After all *ji'ti* exchanges are finished, at perhaps four or five in the morning, an operation called "*avə* handover" (*avə lip̰'a*) formally severs the relation between the descent groups of host (*vedù*) and brothers-in-law (*avə*). A winnowing basket is positioned at the coffin's foot. Three sets of offerings from the host household are placed on it, each comprising one small rice loaf, one large rice loaf, and one goat's foreleg. A bowl of water and a bowl of lees, a by-product of making rice beer, are also placed on the basket. The central *avə* (the dead woman's youngest or eldest brother or his substitute) stands at the side of the winnowing basket closest to the coffin's foot; the *vedù* (the dead couple's youngest son or his substitute) stands on the opposite side. Men from both groups crowd around to watch. The *avə* lifts the bowl of water, the *vedu* lifts the bowl of lees, and they exchange, the *avə* passing his bowl over the top of the *vedu*'s. The *avə* drinks down his bowl of lees; the *vedù* pours out his bowl of water, and the surrounding men shout "*súà yeyé*" (which has no meaning other than to mark this performance). The master of ceremonies cuts the offerings up at the coffin's head; the *avə* distributes two sets of offerings to his supporters; the *vedù* distributes the third set to his.

These offerings are clearly another whole, the three sets being metonyms for the three central groups of offerants, the small and large rice loaves and goats' forelegs a synecdoche of the entire universe of goat and rice loaf offerings. The *vedù* takes only his own set, removing his descent group from this universe. The partition and distribution of the offerings extends this operation of deliberate severance to all the kin and friends brought together by the relation between *avə* and *vedù* descent groups. The ceremony is performed at the coffin's foot, the place of inheritance and descent. It clarifies or "obviates" descent, the *avə*, or wife givers, renouncing any debt to the descent group of their sister. In the future, however, when the actual mother's brother (acting here as *avə*) or his wife dies, his sister's son (acting here as *vedù*) and the latter's wife will attend the funeral in the position of *chìmo súmo*, sister's son, to the dead, obligated to participate in the fourth layer of the *zòmæ̀* category by slaughtering a small goat or chicken, paying again into the wife-giving descent group. In this way the relation, though severed here, reasserts itself to be severed again in the descending generation.

One of my consultants on funerals, Lichink'æpò, a man in his midfifties, elaborated on the "*avə* handover":

A verse describes this:

| je chì pe mæ̀ ts'ì | the harrow's rope has parted |
| à pá ts'ì du lò | our kinship is broken |

With the bowl of water the *avə* is saying, "Your mother, my sister, went to your house to raise you. Our relations are broken with her death, and we are now just ordinary neighbors." The orphan agrees by dumping the water out. With the bowl of lees, the orphan thanks the *avə* for his help in raising him. The *avə* must drink this bitter gift down to the last drop, even if he doesn't drink alcohol.

And relations with your *avə* do deteriorate after your mother's death. When she is alive her brother often comes to visit. He has very warm relations with her, and he treats you as his son, even though he doesn't actually help raise you. When you go to his house, he is nice to you, but his wife is not! You look on her as a bad person, and you are afraid of her. Once your mother is dead, he will visit a couple of times out of sympathy. But you are cold to him, because your mother is dead. As for his wife, you can forgive her when your mother is alive, but after her funeral you place his wife's faults on his head.

Fortunately for him, Lichink'æp'ò did not marry his mother's brother's daughter, so he was able to break off relations with his scary mother's brother's wife after his own mother's death. For those who do marry their actual cross cousins, relations with their *avə*, however problematic, continue in the form of relations with *chinjap'ò* and *chinjamo*, from the colloquial Chinese q̱injia, parent-in-law.

While the assembly's attention is focused on the winnowing basket at the coffin's foot for the *avə* handover, each of the three thieves steals a bowl of alcohol and a piece of meat from the winnowing basket at the coffin's head and consumes it on the spot. The thieves are agents of entropy and destruction. They serve as actualizations—effigies or *nègu*—for wild, kinless ghosts, manifesting those beings' intentions to destroy the offerings as well as the wishes of the assembly to protect the dead couple from their predations. Until the coffin actually emerges from the courtyard the three thieves will now be ascendant, the vigil dominated by their antics. Here, they mock the solemnity of the *avə* handover ceremony by stealing parallel sets of offerings, confirming the sense of general dissolution this formal severance provokes.

Their strength now bolstered by wine and meat, the thieves perform the "thieves' dance" (*tsa jə*). They wear hemp sashes around their waists and brandish long pig-slaughtering knives as they follow a gourd-pipe player around the coffin three circuits "towards the right hand" (counterclockwise), whooping "*uuu! uuu! uuu!*" "They cry out because the dead person isn't sure if she is dead or alive, and their cries remind her," said Lichink'æp'ò's wife Lichink'æmo, one of my most valued consultants on lament. They then discard their sashes and knives, emblems of their affinity with the ghost world, and dance three circuits "towards the left hand" (clockwise). One of the songs of the long speech once given at Tenth-Month Sacrifice, the "song of dancing beneath eagles' talons," devoted some verses to this dance:

3.10	à sà le bæ kɔ́ le bæ me do	who ripens the chestnuts?
	à sà le gu do sṵ?	who prepares the dance ground?
	və zò go do sṵ	the brother-in-law prepares the dance ground
	ní sɛ sa ja sɛ	dance three rounds backwards
	k'o nì le mó gu ŋɔ	this is the dance of ghosts
	wú sɛ le sa ja sɛ	dance three rounds forwards
	k'o nì bu gu ŋɔ	this is the dance of people

FIGURE 3.5 The brothers-in-law's dance (photo by author).

In the three reverse circuits, the thieves plunge into the ghost world to men-
ace and disperse predatory ghosts. In the forward circuits they return to the
world of people, where their task is to continue to guard the dead from the
ghost world's gathered inhabitants.

The "brothers-in-law's dance" (*avə gujə̀*) follows (figure 3.5). The *avə*'s male
supporters join the thieves, linking hands to form a full circle around the coffin and the lamenters clustered about it, stomping vigorously to the tune of the
gourd pipe, their glossy goatskin capes gleaming in the light of the great fires.
They continue to dance until daybreak, some occasionally leaving the circle
to rest while others replace them. Women representing the dead couple's sons
and grandsons give the thieves a half jin of alcohol each as their reward, serve
a bowl to each dancer, then continue around the courtyard to pour a bowl for
each participant. After this first round, women of the *zòmæ̀* group take over,
pouring round after round until dawn, being particularly generous to the
dancers. As dawn approaches, the circle of fifteen to twenty dancers grows unruly, jostling the lamenters on the inside, treading on resting participants on
the outside. Apparently, this dance dates only to 1930s, as Qi Ping, who was in
his mideighties in 2011, recalled

> Before that, it was only the three old widowers who danced. They were close
> to death themselves and not afraid. But gradually some other drunks joined

them to liven things up a bit and to get the reward of a bowl of alcohol now and then. Now it has become the "avə's dance," and men from the avə are expected to dance until dawn. It's hard work, so they deserve to drink.

Before the coffin departs, several meals are served, each a final meal with the dead. The master of ceremonies mixes goat intestines and blood into a large pan of rice and sets it out, along with the half rice loaf that was returned to the vɛdù during jì'ítị. The central daughter apportions this to the women who have been lamenting around the coffin all night. "This is to replenish their strength and courage so their souls will not follow the soul of the dead. It is the final gift from the dead," said Lichink'æmo. "You must accept it. If you don't want to eat it you can put it in your pocket to take home." Why blood and intestines? Lichink'æmo explained:

> A stupid person has short intestines. A wise person has long intestines. Stupid people are afraid of everything, so these intestines help them think and give them courage. As for the blood, it is for strength, as in this verse:

> | vɔ̀ ka bụ go gɔ̀ | fill the bones with marrow |
> | kə ka cè je gɔ̀ | fill the torso with breath |
> | ji ka sɨ je gɔ̀ | fill the skin with blood |

Any living body is an assemblage of parts made through nurture: marrow-filled bones, a breath-filled torso, and grain-filled intestines wrapped in blood-filled skin. The form of nurture this meal takes is appropriate to the women of the zòmæ̀ group who comprise most of the lamenters. They have made much use of their lengthy intestines, their cleverness and courage, in their offerings of verses and tears, and it is they who are primarily responsible for wrapping the body of the dead in the skin of hemp, cotton, and quilting.

A second meal is the heart, kidneys, and tongue of the goat sacrificed by the vɛdù household, offered to the dead at the head of the coffin, then brought in to the widow or widower who remains sequestered inside the house with friends of the same sex and generation who have also lost partners. These exta are "old people's meat," given to elders to reflect respect, intimacy, and a privileged inner position in a house and kin group. Just as the skin-nourishing blood conforms to the relation of the zòmæ̀ women to the dead, so do these organs conform to the relation of the widow or widower, holding out in the house's innermost room while waiting to join her spouse. Those who bring the meal do not hand it to the widow or widower, as would be polite, but place it on the threshold to avoid contact. Conscientious people continue to serve a bereaved spouse in this fashion for three years after her partner's death.

A third meal begins as the thieves accompany the dead in "drinking the

wine of officials." The master of ceremonies places three bowls of meat, three
bowls of alcohol, and three pairs of chopsticks on a sieve at the coffin's foot,
offering all to the dead with a paired verse:

| 3.11 | ni t̃ȅ tsɨ̀ ji mà ji ti̠ tú gɔ̀ | I give you the wine of great officials |
| | ni lɔ tsɨ̀ ji mà ji tɔ | come drink with these great officials |

Now cast as three great officials of the ghost world, the thieves devour the
meat and drink, sometimes aided by other inebriated men. This formally
commences a general feast in which the sacrificial meat, boiled and chopped,
is handed out to the participants, accompanied by boiled grain and more alcohol. This meal is construed as "helping the dead eat," as this is how the half
of every animal received by the dead is consumed. But for each person, it is a
final partition, a last meal with the dead.

After the feast, the thieves are summoned to dance three final rounds of
the coffin in reverse, "towards the right hand" and three more "towards the left
hand" Men of the *avə* and *zòmæ̀* groups lash poles to the coffin and lift it, over-
turning the cabinet and winnowing basket at the coffin's head and the benches
by its side as they head out the courtyard door. They are followed by a widow of
the *zòmæ̀* group carrying the "bird on a pine branch" contraption that has been
dangling from a long bamboo pole over the coffin. Trailing the coffin is a long
procession of adult mourners in the order *avə*, *zòmæ̀*, *vɛdù*, leaving the children
and old people behind in the courtyard (figure 3.6). A passage from "orphans'
verse" lament describes the scene:

3.12	wú ŋə̀ bó lè ba	men like buffalo's forelegs
	p̀ò ba chì de do yi pe	carry father out
	à bò ǹ chæ̀ chi sho̠ sɔ̀ tu̠ pe	father, walk out without moving your feet
	n vi̠ lɛ jà sɔ̀ tu̠ pe	walk clapping without moving your hands
	p'a pí ko p'ì pe	beat the dust from your apron
	p'a mo jà p'ì pe . . .	slap the dust from your coattails . . .
	mò p'u vá de do	ride your floating white horse
	mò wú jie də̠ tu pe	tie a rope to your horse's neck
	mò kə ho də̠ tu pe	tie a long pole to your horse's body
	mò chi pə̠ də tu pe	tie carrying poles to your horse's feet
	mò p'u tsæ̀ te do	ride your good white horse
	mùi lɔ ŋa p'u vá te do	a white bird floats in the sky

The *avə* has already consulted someone with geomantic skills as to the
proper location and orientation of the grave, beside the grave of a dead spouse,

FIGURE 3.6 Carrying the coffin. The brothers-in-law's group (*avə*) leads the coffin; men from the daughters' group (*zòmæ̀*) carry the coffin; the host and his supporters (*vɛdù*) trail behind.

man to the right woman to the left, in a lineage's plot, where its graves descend the mountainside by generational rank. The exhausted mourners sit in the morning sun while sons and parallel nephews of the deceased or their substitutes dig the grave and lower the coffin, head into the hillside, foot extending above the ground. Women of the six *zòmæ̀* subgroups pile blankets and quilts on top of the coffin before the orphaned son dumps the first handful of earth from his coattails into the grave. Others fill in the grave and pile rocks into a makeshift tomb, awaiting the time, perhaps years in the future, when a proper tomb might be built and a tombstone erected. Back in the courtyard a widow picks up the basket at the coffin's head, where offerings have been placed directly into the dead person's mouth. She dumps it into the road outside where it will be consumed by dogs: they too are "helping the dead eat." Other widows clean up the ashes of the great bonfires, throwing out all the wood that has been partly consumed as now belonging to the dead, carrying home any wood that remains. A "weeping for the dead" lament sums up:

3.13 à mo cì dù cì tsæ tó	mother, we have followed all the rules
p'i dù p'i tsæ tó	completed all the procedures
cì su cì du cì ga mó gɔ̀ mà	attended to all from beginning to end
n chì ma ne gɔ̀	given goats bigger than any ever seen
ní kə ní chì gə	given your body clothing
ni chì ní hɔ̀ gɔ̀	we give all to the mud
ni chì ní hɔ̀ p'à ye go	clothing and coffin become mud
ni sha ní zò gɔ̀	grind your teeth on the mud

Conclusion: Bodies

The fabrication of a dead body begins when a soul, singular and impersonal, is captured and placed in the charred corpse of a crushed chick. The body's core is assembled of the elements of experience—relations with the waters, the earth, the sky, and the underworld. This core is wrapped with images of social relations, which accumulate into the layered image of a whole social world. This whole is the social world from the perspective of the dead couple: the perfected image of the relations that composed that couple in life. From the perspective of a living participant, this world comes together so that her particular relationship with the dead couple may be cut out of it. She experiences this social whole as a rift, the return of half her gift, her last meal with the dead. From the perspective of the living person, work for the dead creates a formal and objectified image of a social world in the dead body, a world that is other to herself, divided from herself just as her goat and rice loaf are divided.

Sitting over a bowl of cane alcohol at Luo Guifu's night vigil in 2011, I tried to make sense of it all in stripped-down comparative terms. If in Euro-American traditions, we most frequently construe ourselves as individuals and our relations with others as external to ourselves, one result is that when people die—when their body as the medium of our relation with them disappears, throwing that relation into crisis—we react by striving to bring them back, to remember them. Freud's *Mourning and Melancholia* is the myth of this process, describing the way the work of remembering "resuscitates the existence of the lost other in the space of the psyche, replacing an actual absence with an imaginary presence" and enabling the mourner "to assess the value of the relationship and comprehend what he or she has lost in losing the others" (Clewell 2004, 44; Freud 1917). Where persons are construed as the sum of the relations that produce them, death creates a crisis of another kind, for relations with dead others remain among those that constitute one internally as a person. In Júzò, for living people to go on and for the dead to rest peacefully, relations with the dead must be deliberately cut out of the persons of the living and externalized in material bodies. Instead of the actual absences and imaginary presences of Freud's myth, people in Júzò work with virtual absences (the immaterial souls or intensive bodies of the dead) and actual presences (relations materialized in corpses, coffins, stones, and gatherings, the dead's extensive bodies). The dead are not resuscitated in the space of the psyche through the work of memory; they are actively and painstakingly purged from that space. Yet cutting a dead couple (one of whom may still be living) out of one's person is not easily accomplished: the dead tend to return repeatedly, making their living intimates ill, dropping them into harmful states of private grief, forcing on them unwanted forms of remembrance. This is why there is so much repetition in the ritualization of death—variations on the same exchanges made many times over the course of several years.

Kinship in Júzò is essentially about the assembly and partition of bodies. Goats are bodies, rice loaves are bodies, corpses are bodies: the corpse wrapped in clothing and quilts, the corpse wrapped in layers of lamenters and dancers, the corpse surrounded by the entire assembly of mourners. Each body is an analogue of the others, a whole produced by anatomical operations of partition. The division of these bodies makes them actual, approximating an ideal relation with a real instantiation—the category of zòmǽ realized in an actual daughter or her substitute, the category of avə with a brother-in-law or his substitute. This process of actualization rearranges the historical relations out of which a person was composed in life and remakes a partial person (a person without a daughter, a person without a spouse) into a whole person. From the perspective of the dead couple's heirs, the fabrication and partition of a dead parent's body forces the relation of descent to emerge from the background of alliance and affinity. It is through this relation that living bodies are produced, as the dead couple returns to its descendants the generative capacity to make children and grandchildren and produce food to nurture them. The work of assembling dead bodies creates the ground from which living kinship emerges. Chapter 4 looks more closely at descent, examining the central poetic form through which children image relations with their dead parents. In the present, laments are beginning to shape new forms of aspiration, regret, and shame among the living, transforming assumptions about what dead and living persons are.

4

Making the Dead Modern

When I asked Lichink'æmo to help me understand a lament I had recorded in Júzò in the spring of 2011, she gladly agreed. She and her husband, nearly eighty, were living with their son in the county town, a long way from the little valley where they had spent most of their lives. Even here, in their son's solid new three-story house, devoted to a flourishing business of banqueting police, the language of lament could bring harm if performed in the wrong context. For many reasons—this potential for harm, drunken police, curious grandchildren—we chose to walk to a park to transcribe and translate our recording.

As we sat with my recorder under the trees, people often stopped by to listen and comment. The old couple had a cheerful word for all who stopped to watch as we worked—tattered youths, shop employees, ladies who cleaned the park. When asked, the old couple patiently explained what we were doing. The onlookers' comments—awed, respectful, patronizing, suspicious, dismissive—revealed a gulf in sentiment and sensibility between these sounds and the forms of mourning with which they were more familiar. The recorder emitted long, wailing phrases in a language that none but my old friends could decipher. Our bystanders made it clear that to them this was emotion expressed in a backward and exotic mode, a remnant of the past from within dark mountains barely yet illuminated by the light of modernity. All who happened by belonged to the marginal populations of an unexceptional small town struggling unevenly towards prosperity. Yet all let us know that this tuneful weeping signaled a divide that distinguished them decisively from this pair of old farmers.

The shame and embarrassment provoked by this kind of reaction were among the reasons lament was in decline, Lichink'æmo told me. Like most of rural Yunnan, Júzò had changed enormously in the last two decades. While the valley had never been isolated, more people had recently been placed in contact with the Chinese-speaking majority in more intense ways than ever. The young women who migrated en masse to cities to find work brought urban sensibilities back on return visits. And those who had been moved to new villages on the dry plateau bordering the Jinsha River—a third of Júzò's households—often found others at their funerals, including other mountain people like Lisu and Nuosu, but also curious Han farmers and disapproving local and regional officials. All this contact with others had made Lòlopò increasingly self-conscious about lament, Lichink'æmo told me. It was like drunkenness at funerals, she said, and she quoted a passage of the lament we were working on:

4.1	à bò p̀ò me nə	O younger brother
	ni zò go zò yæ lò	your youngest son
	pæ pò t'à chì zò	swallows in the cliffs
	chí ga ŋa ne pe	stricken with grief
	sɔ́ ji dɔ ji yì bo	he got so drunk
	rɔ̀ wú lə tu lɔ	his grief rose up
	rɔ̀ k̀ò gə tu lɔ	his sorrow emerged

Drunkenness was an appropriate way for men to express grief at funerals, she explained. The aftermath of a day vigil, a Dawn-to-Dusk Sacrifice (*nihèpi*), was often an impressive chaos—men lying about in varied states of incapacity, some sharing space with the dogs who prowled about eating offerings. Drinking was one way for men to contribute to the collective fashioning of grief that women engaged through lament. But in town or in the diaspora villages, where others were watching, Lichink'æmo continued, public drunkenness was considered shameful. No one would sleep on the road after a funeral, grief or no grief. In a similar way, young people found weeping in public to be backward and embarrassing—not the kind of civilized behavior Lòlopò from Júzò preferred to display to their neighbors, Han and others.

Lament is tuneful poetic weeping in ritualized settings. Once common in many parts of the world, it has repeatedly been treated as incompatible with modernizing sensibilities that value forms of emotional expression marked by sincerity, authenticity, individuality, and privacy. Modernizers have often framed the emotion expressed in lament with a series of contrasts: it is scripted not authentic, ritualized not spontaneous, communal not individual, public not private (Wilce 2009). Scholarship on lament in Asia and Europe has shown how varieties of lament have succumbed to churchly opposition

(Bourke 1993, Tolbert 1994), Christian evangelizing (Feld 1995, Schieffelin 2002), Islamist rationalization (Wickett 2010, Wilce 1998), socialist transformation (Lee 2002, Holst-Warhaft 2000), and other institutionalized methods of introducing modernizing technologies for crafting internalized, authentic, spontaneous and sincere selves.

In China, funeral weeping (<u>kusang</u> 哭喪) and bridal lament (<u>kujia</u> 哭嫁) were once widespread. Laments performed in peripheral rural Hong Kong were a staple for the mid-twentieth-century English-language ethnography of China, at a time when, on the mainland, lament of all kinds had largely succumbed to early twentieth-century modernizing projects and sentiments (Blake 1978, 1979; Johnson 1988, 2003; Watson 1996). More recently, McLaren (2008a, b) has made detailed studies of bridal and funeral weeping in Nanhui, near Shanghai, actively performed in the 1920s and recorded and transcribed in the 1980s. On the eve of the socialist revolution, Lipʼò and Lòlopʼò in the mountains of Dayao, Yongren, and Yaoʼan Counties were among a few groups of speakers of about ninety-six Ngwi languages in Southwest China who still performed lament at funerals.[1] In Júzò, lament and other forms of extended poetic language were called *mèkòpe*, "speaking with metaphor." Women and men performed laments in several genres at every major funeral event not centered on tombstones. Lament was central to Emerging from the House, Emerging from the Courtyard, Third-Night Return, Dawn-to-Dusk Sacrifice, and Tenth-Month Sacrifice, and it was peripheral to Sleeping in the Forest. The vigilant suppression of ritualized poetic language in the 1960s and 1970s deeply harmed other forms of *mèkòpe*, such as wedding songs, lunar New Year's songs, and dialogical courting songs. These forms had mostly disappeared from Júzò by the 1990s. But funerals seemed inconceivable without lament. In the late 1980s, as funeral events were revived, women who had learned lament in the 1950s and earlier coached their daughters, nieces, and granddaughters at these events, teaching them how to construct the intricate, metaphor-laden lines of "orphans' verse" (*chr̀mèkò*) and "weeping songs" (*ɔchəŋə*).

In the early twenty-first century, lament had not disappeared, despite a new self-consciousness about public weeping, particularly in the villages on the dry plateau above the Jinsha River to which so many families had moved. Instead, lament was changing. Women from Júzò were adapting lament to align more closely with new expectations about what persons should be, what emotion is, and how emotion should be expressed. Women were using lament to make the dead into subjects more closely aligned with the modernizing sensibilities that

---

1. Li, Li, and Yang (2007) is an example of the small recent Chinese-language literature on the lament and epic poetry of Lipʼò and Lòlopʼò in present-day Dayao and Yongren Counties.

they found all around them. This chapter describes laments recorded in two periods: the early 1990s, after the reform era had gotten thoroughly under way, and 2011, after this little valley had come into far more intimate contact with the modernity-obsessed cultures of urban and semiurban China. Attitudes about ritual were quite different in these two periods. In the early 1990s, people were actively reviving forms of ritualized language and action that had been suppressed before the reform era. Their central concerns were authenticity and fidelity to the forms of the past, and lamenters strove to bring to their verse the richness and precision of poetic form thought to prevail before the socialist period. In 2011, people were less concerned with authenticity and more willing to transform ritual forms in response to the pressures of the present. The most respected lamenters were innovators—women who brought new images and metaphors into this very conservative art form while preserving its poetic power.

Two questions guide this exploration. The first is what do laments do? In the last twenty-five years, the most prominent scholarship on lament has treated its performance as rhetorical strategizing, in which mourners express grievances over social injustice, excoriate oppressors, or subtly compete with others for social status (Johnson 1988, Kligman 1988, Hertzfeld 1993, Briggs 1993). This scholarship honed a developing awareness of the role of poetic language in the micropolitics of social life, but it was also aptly criticized for missing the point of these poetic forms: the sadness and pain they seem to express. In response, some ethnographers have treated laments as therapeutic expressions of profoundly personal and internal states of pain, grief, or loss (Desjarlais 1993, Maschino 1992, Feld 1995, Gamliel 2014). Neither approach can adequately describe the ways that lamenters crafted grief in Júzò. The understanding of laments as primarily strategic rhetorical positioning requires individuals who are private, autonomous, competitive subjects. At its starkest, this is a vision of mourning in which, to quote philosopher Gillian Rose, "the self cannot experience truly transforming loss but plunders the world for the booty of its self-seeking interest" (1996, 37). Yet the understanding of lament as expressing profoundly personal states of grief and loss implicitly contains another version of the same vision, in which subjects ultimately rely on a private internal core or locus of the self, where affect takes place prior to being expressed (Mueggler 1998b). This understanding is ultimately an apology for lament on the grounds that it participates in what is so often claimed to be the key attribute of properly modern subjectivity—personal, internalized emotion expressed in a sincere and authentic fashion.

Before the twenty-first century, laments in Júzò did not work by expressing internalized emotions specific to the mourner. Instead, they worked on

fashioning proper forms of relations between the living and the dead. Laments
reveal what might be called the affective logic of these relations: grief was a
product, deliberately made, of that logic. In laments from the 1990s, this logic
was an economy of suffering (*shú*) that circulated between generations of parents and children. Laments from 2011 shifted emphasis to a logic of intimacy
(*ŋæ̀*) as the foundation for relations with the dead.

Because laments are about fashioning proper relations with the dead, my
second guiding question is: What kind of beings are the dead? The answer
to this question has also shifted. In the 1990s, lament helped craft the body
of the dead as analyzed in chapters 2 and 3, a wrapped assemblage ultimately
made to encompass all relations, intimate and distant, among kin, friends, and
neighbors. By 2011, while the ritualized "rules and procedures" that produced
dead bodies remained largely unchanged, some lamenters were addressing
more "modern" forms of dead beings with distinctive biographies shaped of
individualized memories and internalized emotions. Because the subjectivity
of the living was increasingly shaped by their relations with the dead, modern
dead helped make the living modern too.

Lives

Laments were always addressed to dead bodies. Close female kin of the dead
gathered around the corpse during Emerging from the House vigils to sing
orphans' verse (*chr̀mèkò*) as the body was being washed and dressed. Once the
corpse was encoffined in the courtyard, other kin, all of the various daughters
or *zòmæ̀* groups discussed in chapter 3, as well as unmarried daughters in the
host, or *vɛdù* group, sat on benches on either side, leaned their heads against
the coffin, and sang orphans' verse until daylight. Some stayed in courtyard
and house for the seven or nine days between the night and day vigils to continue to intermittently to sing orphans' verse, addressing the space where the
coffin had once lain. Other women of both *zòmæ̀* and *vɛdù* groups returned to
sing orphans' verse on the third night after the burial, sitting up all night with
the family as the dead soul revisited the house, the event called Third-Night
Return (*sahèlò*).

Laments of other genres were prominently performed in the Dawn-to-
Dusk Sacrifice vigil, held seven days (for a woman) or nine days (for a man)
after burial (figure 4.1). A paid male ritualist performed weeping for the dead
(*shrtsiŋə*) to formally begin the mourning at this event. Immediately after-
ward, women sitting on benches on both sides of the space where the coffin
had once lain began to sing weeping songs (*ɔchəŋə*), continuing until dusk. All
three genres—orphans' verse, weeping for the dead, and weeping songs—were

FIGURE 4.1 Lamenting around the empty space where the coffin once lay during Dawn-to-Dusk Sacrifice (photo by author).

also once performed during the funeral ceremonies of the tenth lunar month: Tenth-Month Sacrifice and Sleeping in the Forest. Outside these contexts, even if sung only in brief fragments, all three styles of lament were powerful signs of and inducements to madness, particularly the madness of overwhelming grief. During the socialist period, they were often used for this purpose—to mark oneself or another as mad (tæ) and not fully responsible for one's own actions (Mueggler 2001).

Singers distinguished these different genres by talking about what anthropologists have come to call "participant roles," after Erving Goffman (1979). Orphans' verse is sung in the voice of the orphan (an actual daughter or granddaughter of the deceased) by the orphan herself and by others on her behalf. The orphan is said to be directly addressing the dead, yet she makes her address largely with the words of others and often through others' mouths. Goffman's analytical roles of animator, author and principal better describe this situation than does the idea of a speaker.[2] As Keane writes, "One of the stakes in the precise distinction between author and animator is the degree of agency, authority

2. For illuminating discussions of Goffman's legacy in relation to the concept of participant roles, see Irvine (1996) and Levinson (1988).

and responsibility a performer is willing or permitted to assume" (Keane 2012). A performer of orphans' verse animates the words of a complex, many-voiced author. The words of lament are taken to be ancestral words, handed down from the distant past, yet performers also acknowledge that skilled lamenters often contribute much improvisational content. For Goffman, a principal was "someone whose position is established by the words that are spoken, someone whose beliefs have been told, someone who has committed himself to what the words say" (1979, 17). In orphans' verse, the orphan, real or imagined, is the principal. Ideally, the orphan laments beside other women singing on her behalf; in less ideal situations an actual orphan may be dead, absent, nonexistent, or incapable of lament. As for those who receive lament, the primary, ratified addressee of orphans' verse is the dead couple. Yet orphans' verse and other styles of lament also pull in a variety of unaddressed bystanders: primarily the other women on the lamenters' bench, who are learning and judging a lamenter's verses, but also other participants gathered on the porch or courtyard, who may be powerfully moved by the layered chorus of weeping voices.

At Emerging from the Courtyard vigils, lamenters competed with a chaotic soundscape—bellowed instructions of a master of ceremonies, the murmuring of participants preparing for their part in exchanges, the bleating of goats at the end of their lives. At the most lavish vigils, the screams of a terrified pig and the ear-wounding wail of double-reed trumpets (suona) drowned out all other sounds. Recording orphans' verse in context was thus very difficult. In the early 1990s, Lòlancemo, then in her midseventies, was known as one of the valley's most accomplished lamenters. She helped me make many recordings of orphans' verse, sitting with my machine on the lamenter's bench and attempting to isolate single voices. After many of our results proved unintelligible, Lòlancemo suggested that she perform in private the orphans' verse she had sung for her mother and taught to dozens of younger women. Since lamenting outside of the proper context was an incitement to madness, she would not weep; she would recite in an ordinary voice. We made the recording in my room, where I lived alone. Since I had known and loved none of her dead, Lòlancemo said, they would not harm me as they might her if she performed in her own home. Later, she sat with me day after day, sipping tea with red sugar as she helped me transcribe and translate.

The point of orphans' verse, Lòlancemo said, is to tell the story of the dead person's life in detail. A singer offers this life to the dead in song, just as she offers everything else—rice, meat, music, tears. Afterwards, one can sing of the funeral, offering that as well. Lòlancemo's lament began with verses about the poverty her dead mother suffered as a child and as a young married woman:

4.2	ts'i tí nì kò̱ lò tæ t'ù	when you were eleven or twelve
	ts'i nì sa kò̱ lò tæ t'ù	when you were twelve or thirteen
	à vò̱ à næ t'ù	when you were just a child
	à næ ye zò t'ù . . .	when you were but a chick . . .
	tsɨ ve chì vò̱ pe̱ tə lṵ	you wanted to make a family
	shú dù yi dæ ba	you married out to a poor place
	mì dù yi dæ ba . . .	married out to a hungry place . . .
	mṳ̀ ṇá tu mì zò	as hungry bats flap
	m mì lṵ ǹ jɔ	not a day without hunger
	lò bə lò shú zò	as a brindled bull calf bleats
	n shú lṵ ǹ jɔ	not a day without suffering

Of all the forms of parallelism these verses display, that which reappeared most often in laments was the semantic coupling of poverty or suffering (*shú*) with hunger (*mì*). This coupling appears twice in excerpt 4.2: the "poor place" (*shú dù*) and "hungry place" (*mì dù*) of the sixth and seventh lines, and the "not a day without hunger" (*m mì lṵ ǹ jɔ*), "not a day without suffering" (*n shú lṵ ǹ jɔ*) of the final quatrain.

The theme of poverty or suffering (*shú*) continued as the lament turned to the deceased's young married life:

4.3	jḭ lṵ jè ǹ jɔ	you herded no livestock
	kà dù mḭ ǹ jɔ	farmed no fields
	ló dù jǝ̱ ǹ jɔ	grazed no pastures
	mæ jḭ dɔ gò va ne shú	so poor your trousers ended at the knees
	mæ jù p'a ká bṳ̀ ne shú	so poor your shirt backs were in tatters
	pè̱ dò̱ né ho t'ù	you raised daughters like stinging leaves
	n shú cí ǹ je	so poor you had no straw
	n shú yi ǹ je	so poor you had no buckets
	p'a pí ló̱ zò pe̱	your aprons served as bags

Orphans' verse always began with the poverty of deceased parents and then described a turn from poverty to wealth. In laments of the 1990s, that reversal of fortune was Liberation, coinciding with the dead couple's children growing into adulthood.

4.4	à pà he chì po̱	in a little while
	zò ho zò væ̀ tṵ	your sons became men
	né ho hé mo tṵ	your daughters became women

yí kʼù lè mo kæ	as the bitter herb spread
kæ fáng lɔ chì næ	Liberation came
ló dù mi jǽ ci tụ lɔ	your pastures expanded
kà dù mi sho vǽ tụ lɔ	your fields widened

jí lu jè ja ka	you gained every kind of livestock
kà lu tso ja ka	gained every kind of grain
wú nì kʼə pẹ zò	like rings on the buffalo's horns
kà dù mo pẹ wo	your fields increased

As Gail Hershatter observes, "the use of the term 'Liberation' for the change of state authority in 1949, which quickly became part of the daily vocabulary in rural China, itself encoded a particular understanding of events. Citing Liberation as a signpost in one's life meant organizing one's own memories into a personal and collective narrative of emancipatory progress" (2011, 25). This organizing narrative merged orphans' verse with "speaking bitterness" (suku), the practice through which Chinese peasants learned to narrate their life circumstances in scripted relation to the time of the nation. Hershatter notes that the narrative conventions of speaking bitterness "have not disappeared from Chinese social life. They continue to pull on the memories and self-conceptions of those who once spoke bitterness or heard it spoken. Speaking bitterness has become the way that women of a certain age talk about their early lives and past selves" (2011, 34). Language from orphans' verse migrated into suku and vice versa between 1950 and 1958. However, orphans' verse turned the narrative form of speaking bitterness to its own ends. The fundamental narrative of all orphans' verse was the exchange of suffering/poverty (shú) between generations. The parents' suffering while raising their children in poverty was repaid in part by the children's suffering while caring for their parents in old age. Liberation was worked into the narrative as a turn of fate that enabled children to care properly for their parents in old age.

In her lament, Lòlancemo went on to describe her mother's illness, including the worried children's repeated calls on ritualists and diviners to search for a cause and cure. The diviners blamed the illness on the little household spirits such as the jíts'a, responsible for the flourishing of the pigs in the courtyard, and the lósi, guardian of the animals in the barn (as in excerpt 2.3). None of the cures they recommended had effect, and eventually,

4.5	wò jǽ wò hà hà yi ga	I grasped her but she slipped away
	wò dé wò hə̀ hə̀ yi ga	I hugged him but he wilted away
	ŋo pò̞ hə̀ yi ga	my father has withered
	ŋo mo hə̀ yi ga	my mother has died
	kæ lo fa ǹ jɔ	there is no hope left

Her lament tells of giving her dead father a cane, putting an official's cap on his head, tying a silken belt round his waist, clothing him in shirts of scarlet and sky blue, layer after layer until the buttons would not close, laying him on straw mats and felt pads, and covering him with cotton quilts and blankets.

Having sung of her mother's life and her parents' deaths, Lòlancemo moved seamlessly into a description of her mother's Emerging from the Courtyard vigil, describing the corpse crossing the threshold "like a hungry cock," the white horse of a coffin awaiting her and the black goats giving up their lives for her. She devoted a few verses to the lengthy and tumultuous process of *jì'ítí* exchange. "Call the gourd-vine roots back," she sang, "Rely on the scattered balsam trees."

4.6	á nò zì ma ru	dogs give funerals to leopards
	chì mo k'ə p̀è tè do go	offer a nanny with flat horns
	chì ka k̀è shɪ́ tè do go	a billy with curled horns
	ve né mà tè do go	an old black pig
	wò p'ə du d̀æ tè do go	a flapping cock
	wò mo tso ko̠ tè do go	a hen with dusty wings
	n tè cí ǹ je	don't keep back even a straw
	n tè yi ǹ je	don't keep back even water

More verses described the alcohol served after each exchange, as lines of women bearing jugs snaked around the courtyard.

4.7	ji wú ə̀ lə̀ ji	fine throat-burning wine
	ji jò cæ ne ji	delicious gold-bearing wine
	mí hè mà lú ji	lowland sorghum wine
	mi ho kò k'à ji	mountain buckwheat wine
	à bò tè do go	offer it all to father

Her description of the Emerging from the Courtyard vigil ended with the corpse riding its coffin/horse at dawn to the graveyard, where its attendants covered it with mud. She concluded her lament with an appeal to fortune and fertility: a wish that planting and herding go well, that the barn fill with black pigs and the corral with black goats, that the granary be stuffed with rice, that the sons and daughters be blessed with a sea of wealth.

What kind of beings are the dead? It is easy enough, and often fruitful, to understand the dead as absences around which exchanges among the living are organized: corpses and their repetitions as media for the reorganization and reaffirmation of social relations among the living. Rupert Stasch puts this well, speaking of a similar context: "[R]elations with the dead . . . throw into relief how the copresence of living persons is not self-evident and seamless but is composed of concrete semiotic media of contact" (2009, 210). Yet these laments cast the dead in another light as well. Though lamenters insisted that orphans' verse should contain a detailed description of everything the dead person experienced in life so as to offer it in death, laments actually described lives only briefly and formally, emptying the life of social particularity and anchoring it to a series of well-worn tropes. The substrate of all such narratives was *shù*, suffering or poverty, recognized as the impersonal but singular substance of every life. Suffering extends parent-child relations beyond immediate, personal, and particular exchanges of care or nurture toward a more impersonal relation through time, in which parents give suffering to the children when they are young and children return suffering to the parents after their deaths. As beings that consume their descendants' suffering, the dead are more than absent media for exchanges among the living. They are social beings who sense and experience. The ritual efficacy of laments depends upon their capacity to sharpen the senses of the dead so that they might take in all that is being offered to them: grain, wine, meat, and lives, but also the sights and sounds of the night vigil. Other styles of lament thicken these connections between the exchange of the singular yet impersonal experience of suffering and the experiential being of the dead.

Dawn-to-Dusk Sacrifice

Though laments are always addressed to dead bodies, these bodies are never singular. Even in Emerging from the Courtyard, where the many operations that divided goat and rice loaf bodies produces a whole, centered on the wrapped assemblage of the corpse, the soul inhabits a different body. The soul stays a little to the side, in the tiny charred corpse of the "soul's chick," which the central daughter watches anxiously, lest it be stolen by robbers from the *avə*'s group. As the corpse is carried to the graveyard, the soul follows tentatively, a little behind the procession, eventually settling like a flying fox into a pine tree somewhere on the mountainside.

Before Dawn-to-Dusk Sacrifice can be performed seven or nine days after the corpse is buried, the soul has to be retrieved from the mountain. The morning of this event, the youngest orphaned son or his replacement walks with the principal *avə* to the graveyard. On the mountainside above, the *avə* selects a small pine sapling and shoots a crossbow bolt into it (or sticks the bolt into its roots). He offers the sapling a pot of sticky rice with a piece of pork fat (two if both in the couple are dead) and half a jin of alcohol, and he says a few words entreating the soul to come live in a corner of the house under the tile roof. He directs the orphaned son to pull the sapling up by its roots, wrap it in hemp cloth, and carry it to the grave. There, the *avə* takes a piece of chestnut wood, about three inches long, and carves it into the shape of a head and crotch. He had carefully marked the tree from which this wood had come before cutting it. He carves the figurine so that its head is oriented upward in the same direction as the wood was in the tree, and he wounds the side that faced east in the tree with a slash of his knife. He places the east side of the chestnut figurine against the west side of the pine figurine, the two knife slashes meeting, the pine lying in the chestnut's crotch. He binds the figurines together with colored thread, seven turns if only the wife has died, nine if only the husband has died. If both have died, he simply rebinds the existing effigy, carried from the house to the grave, with nine turns of new thread. He weaves a bamboo platform with seven or nine warp strands and places the figurines on it, pine on top of chestnut. He ties twelve chestnut twigs with leaves together to form a "flower" for the dead souls to gaze up at, like the "bird on a pine branch" that dangles over coffin and grave. After another offering, the effigy is wrapped in cloth, placed in a wooden bowl with rice, and carried down to the house. There, an *àpi̠pò* chants while the orphaned son's wife (or sister, if he is unmarried) chooses a place on the wall downstream of the bed's-head spirit and upstream of the older ancestral effigies, and places the effigy there. A verse from "weeping for the dead" lament touches on this recovery of the lost soul:

4.8	à mo wú dù yi kə zò	mother, like a precious urn of silver
	gò ja pe kò lɔ	we have brought you back
	cí gò dú tú ka mà	placed you beneath the beam
	cí kæ go gò tú ga mà	prepared your place on the wall
	nè mi k'à dɔ gò	your place in the ghost world

Though the lament and exchange of Dawn-to-Dusk Sacrifice may not begin until this body for the dead is in place, the focus of this vigil's action is the absent form of the corpse that once lay in the courtyard's center. Benches are placed on either side of the space where the coffin had been, in the same positions as during Emerging from the Courtyard. A basket is placed at the space's head to receive offerings given directly to the dead. Also at the head is placed a table with a winnowing basket, a length of hemp cloth, a ji̠n of alcohol, and a little money. The central daughter digs a shallow hole where the corpse's head was and scratches a shallow trough down the length of the space to serve as its intestines. She positions herself on the bench on the side away from the house, at the end nearest the head of the space, with a ladle and a bucket of water mixed with some of the water bought from the *ci̠*. Other women join her on the benches. These are not restricted to the various *zòmæ̀* groups, as at Emerging from the Courtyard—any woman, no matter how distant her relation with the dead, may lament. Bonfires are built, and the *avɔ, zòmæ̀,* and *vɛdù* groups

FIGURE 4.2 Distribution of the three central groups of kin and friends at the Dawn-to-Dusk Sacrifice vigil. The brothers-in-law's group (*avə*) gathers around a fire at the head of the empty space where the coffin once lay; the daughter's group (*zòmæ̀*) sits on both sides of the empty space; the host's group (*vɛdù*) sits by a fire at the foot of the empty space.

and their allies position themselves at the head, sides, and feet of the absent corpse, just as at Emerging from the Courtyard. Men busy themselves killing goats and chickens in preparation for the *jì'ítí* exchange, which takes the same form as at Emerging from the Courtyard.

Thus, sacrifice, exchange, and lament are directed at the absent corpse, even as the soul is displaced to that other body, the ancestral effigy, hiding within the house. It is as though the soul (*yɛho*) becomes another name for the private, partial body that will become increasingly circumscribed by the transactions of descent, while the space of absent corpse and coffin form the fully social body, available to every mourner, through which an image of a whole social world is articulated. The scene of mourning in the courtyard—involving every member of the *vɛdù*, *zòmæ̀*, and *avə* groups and their friends and allies—is offered whole to the dead in weeping for the dead (*shrtsiŋə*) lament, performed by a skilled male mourner for the fee of hemp, cash, and alcohol that had been placed on the table. This mourner performs his lament crouching at the tail of the empty space, while the women on the benches on either side wait to begin their own laments. Weeping for the dead lament changed little between the early 1990s and 2011, perhaps because there were only a handful of elderly male performers of this style. The same man, Yang Fuzhong, performed at nearly every event I attended in both periods. The gender difference seemed to isolate the poetry of weeping for the dead from the circuits of transmission along which verses sung by women traveled. The women who ordinarily worked with me on laments declined to help to translate and transcribe weeping for the dead laments without saying why. Their husbands, however, confidently declared that their wives were afraid, as this was a matter for men.

Weeping for the dead laments explicitly offer the scene in the courtyard to the dead. Yang Fuzhong's lament began by asserting that this is the auspicious day and hour for the sacrifice. It described the search for the soul on the mountain and the soul's installation beneath the beam. The lament mentioned the goats being slaughtered and boiled into fragrant broth, the rice loaves being divided, the knife wiped with a chunk of fat. It reported on the details of the scene—the table and benches, the basket at the absent corpse's head, the ladle and bucket of water. The water had been bought from the flowing river, for tens of <u>yuan</u>, for thousands of <u>yuan</u>, the lament claimed, "costly water that will not cloud for ten years." This water would flow into the dead person's mouth with the daughter's tears:

4.9	à mo me gɔ̀ ne te lɔ	mother, all eyes pity your daughter
	à mo yi gɔ̀ yi bu bæ	mother, she spoons pails of water
	yi lu cé lɔ bæ	spoons clear clean water
	à mo yi dɔ̀ gɔ̀ bu jɔ	mother, a sea of water flows
	yi ji yi bu jɔ	clear water overflowing
	cí mi jɔ dù yi	flowing to the spirit world
	à mo kæ pe ŋa bi lɔ̀	mother, her tears fill the courtyard

As the male mourner sings, women preparing to lament empty small, square bamboo traveling rice baskets packed with cooked rice and one or two pieces of fat, depending on the number of dead, into the basket at the head of the space where the corpse had once lain. (By the 2010s, packets of manufactured noodles replaced traveling rice baskets for many offerants.) These offerings are to be directly consumed by the dead. Immediately after the professional male mourner concludes his lament, the central daughter begins ladling water from the bucket into the shallow hole that marks the absent corpse's head. The water flows from the hole through the shallow trough scraped into the earth—the absent corpse's digestive tract—gradually muddying the lower part of the courtyard. The central daughter weeps as she ladles, and other lamenters join her: "Once you see her weeping and ladling water, your own eyes begin to weep," one lamenter told me. Women continue to lament through the remainder of the day as participants crowd around the head of the empty space to conduct *jì'ítì* exchange. The day ends at dusk, when a ritualist goes to the courtyard door to call back the souls of the living that have gone wandering with the dead soul during this seven- or nine-day period of intensive grief.

Suffering

The *ɔchəŋə*, or weeping songs, performed at Dawn-to-Dusk Sacrifice all begin with addresses to the absent corpse. The principal of these addresses is not the orphan, as in orphans' verse; the principal is the singer herself, expressing her sorrow in solidarity with the orphan in her own voice. Here, too, are bystanders, constructed in the verse itself, and not only among the living. Weeping songs serve as vehicles for offerings of tears, cloth, food, and alcohol to be passed to the focal dead of the vigil and then on to other dead, the singer's own intimates, usually her parents or siblings.

Here, invoking the intersubjective play of gesture and glance in which one person acknowledges the hunger of another, so familiar to everyone in Júzò in the 1990s, a lamenter pleads with the focal dead of the vigil, her elder sister's husband's father, to pass rice and meat on to her father's sister's son and his wife, now dead for several years:

4.10	chì bùi æ mæ bo dú mà	now you carry this rice to them
	su tsò dù me lə t'à hɔ nɔ̪	no need to watch them chew it
	su də dù le nɔ̪ t'à hɔ nɔ̪	no need to watch them grab for it
	k'o nì bɛ le gò lɔ mà	tell them all this:
	hò nà hò kǽ lɔ du̪	we brought extra meat
	chì k'ò chì cí kǽ lɔ du̪	we brought extra rice
	mo cæ gò ti̪ zò	sit on your golden bamboo mats
	yì væ su p'ò chì cè tsò	elder sister's father, eat a mouthful
	du̪ lè a lù chì chè jú lɔ mà	feed a mouthful to father's sister's son
	a lù lù mo chì chè jú lɔ mà	feed a mouthful to father's sister's son's wife

After an initial address to the focal dead, every weeping song performance moves through such transitional verses to address more intimate kin. Yet in some ways these intimate dead remain less than fully ratified participants in this exchange of gifts and song. They receive no offerings directly; their food and drink is channeled through the focal dead of the day vigil. They often appear in verse as tentative presences, looking on at the feast from the ditch behind the house, where refuse is thrown, afraid to show themselves and receive food:

4.11   a mo dɛ̀ jì wú lɔ ŋo   mother clutching your cane's head
          sɔ̀ li a gà lɔ tú hɛ́ nì dɔ̀   I think of you stepping behind the house
          sɔ̀ li hə wò lɔ tú hɛ́ nì dɔ̀   I think of you standing there in the ditch

The participant roles of the recipients of weeping songs are thus complex. The dead are subject to social hierarchies, the focal dead couple being the fully ratified participants in the feast, the others relying on their generosity. To this may be added the varied roles of living listeners: performers of weeping song laments always sing in concert with other lamenters also asking the focal deceased to pass gifts on to their own dead kin, creating a soundscape structured by many competing hierarchies of intimacy and distance. In contrast, the roles involved in "speaking" in weeping songs are relatively simple. Animator and principal are the same, as the singer voices her own grief rather than fashioning grief for others. Grief is individualized, each singer framing hers in relation to her own dead kin. Even authorship is less ancestral and more personal, as singers craft verses to fit the social circumstances of their own sorrow. It is perhaps for this reason that weeping songs have lent themselves to transformation, as lamenters have shaped new forms of grief that are more individual, more personal, and more spontaneous than the participation frameworks of the other styles allow.

My consultants on lament and I found that weeping songs were far easier than orphans' verse to record in situ, due to the absence of dancers, gourd-pipe players, and (usually) double-reed trumpet players, and we made many recordings. In 1993, Lichink'æmo, a skilled lamenter herself, sat next to Li Lanmei, whose laments she admired, to record Li Lanmei's weeping song at a day vigil for her elder sister's mother-in-law. Li Lanmei's own mother had died recently, so her lament asked her sister's mother-in-law to pass gifts on to her own mother. Later Lichink'æmo helped transcribe and translate the lament, consulting with Li Lanmei on more troublesome verses.

In the early 1990s, the central theme of weeping songs was the labor required to produce gifts for the recent dead to pass on to those who had died earlier. Laments focused on two offerings: hemp cloth and rice. During the early twentieth century, women in Júzò had achieved a modicum of prosperity by spending nearly all their working time in hemp cloth production. The state set high hemp procurement prices in 1950, and these prices rose steadily in relation to the prices of rice and cotton cloth between 1950 and 1979. During the first wave of market reforms in 1979, the state abandoned price supports for hemp. Grain bag manufacturers then turned to cheaper synthetic fibers, and people in Júzò abruptly abandoned hemp cloth production for the market (Mueggler 1998b). By the 1990s, hemp cloth was made only for funerals.

Li Lanmei's lament meditated on the difference between the value of hemp, determined by the suffering invested in the labor of its production, and its price, determined by mysterious entities in Beijing and the underworld. She described each step in the long process of planting and harvesting hemp, extracting its fibers, spinning the fibers into thread, and weaving the thread into cloth. She told of bearing manure up the mountain in back baskets, spreading it on the steep slopes, and plowing the fields. She sang of winnowing and sieving the seed, scooping it into bags, bearing it up the mountain, sowing, weeding, and cutting grass from the field margins, harvesting the stalks, separating them into male and female, stacking them in the fields to dry, bearing them down to the house, sinking them in the river, and pressing them under huge rocks:

4.12	lo ŋá shú do go	rocks so cruelly hard to move!
	lè mo sa p'à kə	three sides of your thumbs wear away
	lè ni sa tsɨ kə	three knuckles of your fingers wear away
	je chɨ̀ ni tə tə	clenching wet and cold
	k'o nì shò le mæ	such hard-won cloth!
	su mo gɔ̀ do go	to give to you, mother

She described grasping the stalks with sore thumbs, peeling them with aching fingers, washing the skins with sore toes, bearing them back to the house to dry, separating them into lengths, making a mortar out of stone and a pounder out of logs, and pounding the skins into a tangled mass of fiber. She sang of making a spinning wheel of yellow wood and a spindle out of palm leaf to spin the spliced fibers; then of making a loom of hardwood posts, beams of pine, and a frame, heddles and comb of bamboo; then of stringing the warp and weaving with painful hands and iron fingers.[3]

The second central topic of weeping songs was rice, with which every woman in the valley had abundant experience. In describing the labor of growing rice, Li Lanmei's lament emphasized that the relations that produce grain are relations of mutual suffering that pair household members of the same gender and different generations: fathers with sons, mothers with daughters, daughters-in-law with mothers-in-law, and (in other excerpts) grandmothers with granddaughters.

---

3. Selections from a weeping song, or ɔchəŋə, lament, describing the process of making hemp cloth are given in Mueggler (1998b).

4.13   pʼò jo zò jo shú mæ̀ ŋæ   father and son suffer together
        mo jo né jo shú mæ̀ ŋæ   mother and daughter suffer together
            chɨ̀ kà su mo tɪ gɔ̀ do go   to make grain to give mother

        chì bɨ̀ lí mi hɔ̀ do go   bear manure to spread on the fields
            mò cæ kʼa má tsɔ̀ do go   use a bamboo manure basket
            kʼò ji bæ wú tsɔ̀ do go   use a leather carrying strap

        mi ká lò mò tsæ̀ do go   lead down a plow ox
        lò chè pʼú tʼú bɨ̀ do go   bear down an iron-tongued plowshare
        sɨ́ go lò li vé do go   hand down the frame and yoke
        lò jæ̀ lò pu pɔ̰ do go   carry down a harness of braided vines

        né chɨ̀ lí shɨ́ pɔ̰ do go   the orphaned daughter carries rice
                                         seed
        mo jo né jo pɔ̰ do go   mother and daughter carry together
        chì jo mo jo pɔ̰ do go   daughter-in-law and mother[-in-law]
                                         carry together

The language of lament intertwines formal and semantic parallelism. Roman Jakobson's influential view of parallelism as the foundation of the "poetic function" has been summed up simply: verbal art "takes the form of placing naturally equivalent linguistic elements in equivalent positions or, put another way, of using equivalent positions as settings for equivalent phonic and/or semantic elements" (Levin 1962, 30). Though Jakobson focused his demonstrations of parallelism on morphological features like meter and rhyme, he also noticed that such parallelism is often shaped by semantic content, commenting, for instance, that "rhyme necessarily involves a semantic relationship between rhyming units" (Jakobson 1987 [1960], 81). Others have applied Jakobson's insights to forms of poetic speech where semantic equivalence receives far more emphasis than in Western-language poetics (Fox 2006). Semantic parallelism uses the meanings of words to poetic ends. It has been, in different eras, an exceptionally important feature of Chinese-language writing, both in verse and prose (see especially Liu 1962; Owen 1977, 1985; Cheng 1982; Graham 1986; Plaks 1990; McCraw 2006).

In Lòloŋo verse, semantic parallelism often takes the form of semantic couplets: verses that, in Mannheim's useful definition, "set pairs of word stems into identical morphological and syntactic environments, expressing the inherent semantic connectedness of the stems" (1998, 248). The first two lines of excerpt 4.13 above are an example:

4.13a   pʼò jo zò jo shú mæ̀ ŋæ   father and son suffer together
         mo jo né jo shú mæ̀ ŋæ   mother and daughter suffer together

These verses are identical except for the paired-up (and pared-down) kinship terms *pò* and *zò*, *mo* and *né*. Each couple is placed into a single verse; the morphological and syntactic pairing between verses reinforces the coupling within each verse. In this way, dyadic relationships are doubled, parallel and cross: fathers with sons, but fathers also with mothers; mothers with daughters, but daughters also with sons; and a relationship is established between the two pairs to make a parallel-cross quartet. Each term is also marked or unmarked in relation to its dyadic other, expressing a hierarchy where the unmarked term is seen as dominant in relation to the subordinate marked term. Drawing on Jakobson's insight that "language is hierarchical at all levels of organization," Mannheim (1998) shows that Quechua semantic couplets pair word stems that are marked and unmarked relative to each other, arranged so that the unmarked term usually precedes the marked. Greenberg (2005 [1966], 1990 [1980], 1988) applied markedness theory to kinship terms, attempting to identify universals. After comparing markedness in kin terms across many languages, Greenberg claimed that hierarchies held universally in two categories: genealogical closeness and generational distance. Lineal relations are unmarked against collateral relations (e.g., sibling as against cousin); consanguineal is unmarked as against affinal (mother as against mother-in-law); male is unmarked as against female; older is unmarked as against younger; each ascending generation is unmarked in relation to the corresponding descending generation (grandmother as against granddaughter); and the closer a generation is to ego, the less marked it is. "Two basic factors are evidently at work: seniority and genealogical remoteness from ego" (Greenberg 1990 [1980], 319). The semantic couplets of weeping songs most frequently hierarchize kin terms as Greenberg would predict, placing the unmarked before the marked term: in excerpt 4.13a, father before son, and mother before daughter, but also the unmarked male pair before the marked female pair.

Greenberg argued that such hierarchies are residual in linguistic codes, reflecting cognitive hierarchies. In any case, these hierarchies made natural sense to Lòlopʼò, who repeatedly ranked people by gender, generation, and lineal status as against affinal status across many domains: seating patterns, sleeping places, food distribution. Indeed, poetic language might be understood as a way to formally diagram relations that are performed with more variation and less formality in other domains. Yet all such formalities are effective in verbal art only to the extent that they produce regularities that might then be broken or manipulated. Reversing ordinary hierarchies of kinship terms to create tension or emphasis was a deliberate feature of the art of lament. Take the final couplet of excerpt 4.13, where Li Lanmei makes a reversal in the familiar generational order, placing daughter-in-law before mother-in-law.

4.13b   mo jo né jo pǫ do go   mother and daughter carry together
        chì jo mo jo pǫ do go   daughter-in-law and mother[-in-law] carry together

Li Lanmei was at the stage of life where she had a mother-in-law but was not yet a mother-in-law herself. Though she did not live with her husband's aging parents, she visited them frequently to bring them presents and cook for them. While she lamented as an orphaned daughter (*né chř*), the terms in her lament that best described her own roles in labor and life were mother (*mo*) and daughter-in-law (*chì*). In this couplet she perhaps found it natural to place both first, pairing them at the cost of the customary parallel of mother and mother-in-law.

In excerpt 4.13 (and in many other passages in this lament) hierarchically ordered semantic couplets containing kinship terms frame other verses that describe acts of labor. Each verse pairs a specific task, such as bearing, spreading, using, leading, handling, and carrying, with materials and implements: manure, baskets, straps, lead ropes, plowshares, plow-frames, yokes, and harnesses. The insistent parallelism of weeping songs also assembles tools (scoops and urns, winnows and sieves), products (seed and chaff), and body parts (hands and feet, left hands and right hands):

4.14   mò cæ k'à də wừ mæ̀ ŋæ   weave a golden bamboo urn
       mò cæ jé le wừ mæ̀ ŋæ   weave a golden bamboo scoop
       sí cæ á gə rù mæ̀ ŋæ   carve a yellow wooden ladle

       cí mo ŋə̀ he t'e   in the pine-shingled barn
         lí shŕ k'ə̀ tò kò   scoop up the rice seeds
         lí k'ə̀ dæ kæ t'ə   scoop them into the courtyard
           mò cæ jo mo jù mæ̀ ŋæ   prepare a golden bamboo winnow
           mò cæ o je jù mæ̀ ŋæ   prepare a golden bamboo sieve

       chì jo mo jo o do go   daughter-in-law and mother winnow
                                        together
       mo jo ne jo o do go   mother and daughter winnow together
         ji va ji va va do go   shake and shake to sieve
         te ko te ko o do go   toss and toss to winnow

In the 1990s and before, to grieve with weeping songs was to decompose in tuneful poetry the offerings of hemp and rice passed to the dead. Grieving broke these gifts down into the social relations of labor that had produced them, then broke those relations down into relations between body parts and implements, which it further decomposed into materials (bamboo, leather, wood, and stone). Finally, grieving dissolved these relations among body parts and the tools of labor into the singular but impersonal substance of suffering.

The form of labor in cultivating rice most evocative to people in Júzò was uprooting the seedlings from their warm, crowded, fertile beds and transplanting them into the mud of wider paddies, paralleled metaphorically in many contexts with the act of giving birth. Women transplanted, stooping and backing up in rows; while men plowed, harrowed, fertilized, and irrigated. Cultivating rice could be accomplished only in groups. Women found ways to work communally through each of the successive transformations of economic organization in the twentieth century, groups of related women transplanting rice seedlings together on each other's fields for the entire season in exchange for others' labor on their own. In describing transplanting, Li Lanmei's lament expressed regret that she did not better care for her mother when her mother was alive.

4.15	lɔ né bùɪ tæ læ	as worms burrow by the riverside
	tæ nà lí ho chi	transplant in the fourth month
	pɔ̀ jo zɔ̀ jo kà do go	father and son farm together
	mo jo ne jo kà do go	mother and daughter farm together
	mi tæ ní tí kò lo chɪ̀	back up planting seedlings
	su mo ti̱ gɔ̀ do go	to offer to mother
	á gà sæ̀ jó tsɨ	pears growing behind the house
	su mi chɪ̀ su mo jó ǹ lò lu̱ bɔ	we orphans did not feed mother enough ripe pears
	né chɪ̀ su mo jó ǹ lò lu̱ bɔ	this orphaned daughter did not feed mother enough
	zɔ̀ chɪ̀ su mo jó ǹ lò lu̱ bɔ	this orphaned son didn't feed mother enough
	n chí nò ǹ go	we cannot rest without sadness
	n jò jɔ ǹ go	we cannot live without regret
	ro lè lí p'æ shú do go	the right hand painfully ties the seedlings
	væ̀ lè lí tsa shú do go	the left hand painfully gathers the bundles
	lí p'æ lí wo lè	once the seedlings are tied
	p'ì jo lí jo bùɪ	grandmothers and granddaughters bear together
	mo jo ne jo bɯ	mothers and daughters bear together
	mo jo chì jo bɯ	mothers[-in-law] and daughters-in-law bear together

Weeping songs in the 1990s used strings of semantic couplets to bind kinship, affect, and labor closely together. Lamenters sometimes used these pairings to make correlations between particular kin and particular acts or affects. Here

Li Lanmei pairs the orphaned daughter with sadness and the orphaned son with regret. She correlates acts of the right hand, associated in both verbal and spatial organization with hierarchically superior kin, with grandmothers as against granddaughters, mothers as against daughters, and mothers-in-law as against daughters-in-law, but also with the orphaned daughter as against the orphaned son.

Mannheim (1998) suggests that the sequential ordering of pairs of words in semantic couplets reflects their cognitive hierarchy in a situation where the lexicon is characterized by a variety of different organizing principles in different domains. The domain of kinship terms, for instance, might ordinarily be organized along quite different principles than the lexical domain of affect or the domain of technical talk about labor—definitely true in daily life among Lòlop'ò. Weeping songs gained expressive power in the art of crossing these domains with similar hierarchical principles in the service of establishing a tightly organized context for the production of grief. This was the circuit of suffering—parents gave suffering to children when they were young through acts of nurture and care; children returned suffering to their parents in old age. The latter was an impossible task; the debt could be repaid only after the parents' deaths, through the suffering of labor transformed into the substance of offerings to the dead. The pain (*shú*) of laboring together was the sole antidote to inevitable regret. Grief (*wúla*, *kòga*, but also *shú*) was another name for the portion of this circuit in which suffering was returned to the dead. With weeping songs, lamenters fashioned grief in a public setting by using the resources of verbal art to make the economy of suffering as vivid as possible.

Intimacy

Dawn-to-Dusk Sacrifice changed little in form between 1993 and 2011. Yet lament was changing quickly. The fine lamenters of Lòlancemo's and Li Lanmei's generation had all passed away. Of those who remained in Júzò, Lichink'æmo said in 2011, perhaps her cousin Luo Meixiu was the most accomplished. She had learned lament from Lòlancemo, who had also been one of Li Lanmei's teachers, but she had much to weep about lately, and her laments had become more refined and creative. Lichink'æmo took me to Luo Meixiu's house on the morning a day vigil was to be held for Luo Guifu, the widow who died alone without family or name in chapter 2. Luo Meixiu was in the courtyard chopping feed for her water buffalo, while her teenage son, visiting home from the county town, sat on the porch sewing up a shoe. "You can't just cry in your house or while you are working," she said cheerfully. "A funeral is really the only time you can cry without harm. Of course I'll go and cry. I lost my own mother two years ago, and I still feel very bad. I still have to cry. To you this is a backward custom, but to us, well. . . ."

"It is the literature of the Yi people," Lichink'æmo interrupted firmly in Chinese, echoing a phrase crafted by urban Yi intellectuals to give legitimacy to the arts of *mèkòbɛ*, or spoken verse. Luo Meixiu was happy enough to let us record her lament if we could be discreet. We arranged for her teenage daughter, also visiting home from the city, to sit next to her mother and record her song with my iPhone. When I attempted to show the daughter the phone's recording app, she responded with a scalding look. Luo Meixiu laughed. "Oh, she understands technology!"

On the lamenters' bench, Luo Meixiu began by addressing the focal dead of the funeral, her nephew's wife. After death, she sang, the soul hid in the forest, numb with anger like a mouth numbed by Sichuan pepper. Her children found her there and bore her back in the form of a pine sapling to carve into an ancestral effigy. Her son brought her water to drink, as the water in the underworld is foul with leaves; her daughter brought rice, as rice in the underworld is clotted with worms.

"Actually, no one cared about that pitiful old woman," Lichink'æmo said as she helped me transcribe. "She died with no one to tend her." Her first husband had died long ago; her second husband divorced her; her sons abandoned her; her daughter moved away. Luo Meixiu would have attended her nephew's wife's funeral in any case, Lichink'æmo went on, but she had little reason to grieve for the old widow. "Take a mouthful of rice," Luo Meixiu sang, "and pass a mouthful on to Mother." She established claims on the dead widow on behalf of her mother by repeatedly invoking an intimacy of place—the deceased and her mother had been neighbors in life, so they must be friends in the underworld:

4.16	ce pò dué tsɨ zò	as Han write paired phrases
	jɔ dù yì dué də lu ŋæ̀	your houses were paired on the same path
	bə̀ tsɨ rɔ ló mo	as cicadas chant
	ló dù chù ju də lu̧ ŋæ̀	you herded along the same roads
	tsɨ sɻ̍ tsɨ və kà	hemp seeds and hollow stalks
	kà dù t'ì vá də lu̧ ŋæ̀	you planted the same ground
	hè yi mó mi yi	you have dropped into the underworld
	ma lè tú jr ŋæ̀	you must see each other there
	a lù su mo lɔ̀	O nephew's wife

It was not only her mother that she came to mourn, however. She mentioned her little brother, her father-in-law, her sister's son, and her sister's husband, all of whom had died within the last two or three years. With each, she evoked a scene of intimacy with the dead widow: here she mourns her father-in-law.

4.17	a lù su mo t'è	think, nephew's wife,
	ŋǽ mi jǫ t'ù lę	of when you were in our world
	ŋǽ mò nɔ́ t'ì pè ŋǽ	seedlings around one tiled house
	chì sæ̀ t'i ju ŋǽ	vines around one gourd
	t'à nɔ̀ chì bɔ́ ŋǽ . . .	a many-branched pine tree . . .
	a lù su mo ni	O nephew's wife
	ne lu t'ɔ̀ gɔ̀ lɔ	give some to him
	ne lu pe gɔ̀ lɔ	give him my speech

It was as though the circuits along which gifts and grief might flow between various dead were opened up by the lingering effects of friendship and proximity in life, rather than formal relations of kinship as in the past. Lichink'æmo commented,

Each of these deaths brought further hardship, and perhaps that is what she is weeping about here. She had to kill a goat for each funeral, and goats are expensive now—500 to 600 yuan. And because they were such close relatives, she had to bring a big one, plus alcohol, candy and cigarettes. When her father-in-law died, the whole burden fell on her, because her husband is a drunk and his elder brother is an idiot.

Only twice in Luo Meixiu's lengthy lament did she employ the kin-ordering semantic couplets that were a staple of the weeping songs of the 1990s. Both instances simply paired father and mother in coupled verses: gone were the deftly ordered cross-parallel quartets that correlated kinship terms with acts of labor and expressions of affect. She made repeated invocations of her nephew's wife, her own mother, and other intimate dead, as well as referring to herself repeatedly as "your orphaned daughter." These addresses are consistent in style with those used in the laments of the 1990s. But nearly every other kinship term was used to refer to a specific relative, living or dead, in a specific context: I count forty-nine instances in this lament, referring to twenty-nine separate people in all. Excerpt 4.1 above, about her dead younger brother and his drunken youngest son, is one example. Here is another, about the children of the focal dead:

4.18	ni zò ho zò væ̀ lɔ̀	your first son
	rɔ̀ vú lə ga be	his heart aches
	rɔ̀ k'ò gə ga be	he is truly in pain
	zò ho zò ba lɔ̀	your third son
	wò t'ɔ̀ be ǹ kɔ́ to dù	his hands no longer have strength

a lù su mo lò	O nephew's wife
ni né go né tí lò	your only daughter
fu li cé mi yi	married out to Han lands

Apart from direct addresses to the dead, such personalized references to kin were absent in lament from the 1990s. In those laments, kinship was public and categorical, a matter of ordering varied participants into stereotyped hierarchies, rather than private and personalized, drawing directly on the singer's knowledge of specific persons.

Luo Meixiu did not launch into descriptions of mutual suffering in labor after she had established relations between her nephew's wife and her more intimate dead. Instead, she sang a detailed story of her mother's life. Thematically, this was more like chr̀mèkò, orphans' verse, than the ɔchəŋɔ, or weeping songs, we were familiar with. But the orphans' verse of the 1990s narrated the shape of a life—it could be any life—moving from deep poverty in youth to expanding pastures and increasing herds in middle age, and then to the tragedies of illness and death. In contrast, Luo Meixu presented specific scenes from her mother's life, beginning with her love of earrings as a girl:

4.19   à mo ts'i tí nì k'o lo   mother, at eleven or twelve
        ts'i nì sa k'o lo   at twelve or thirteen
            nó p'u nó ŋà zò   white and black millet
            p'u nó ŋə̀ də lu pe̯ ŋæ̀   they say you loved earrings
            p'u nó ŋə̀ na lu pe̯ ŋæ̀   you could afford no earrings they say

        ts'i tí nì k'ò lɔ   at eleven or twelve years
            wò mo ló tsə lu pe̯ ŋæ̀   they say you herded goats on the mountain
            lɔ né kà tsə lu pe̯ ŋæ̀   you labored by the river side they say
                ni dɔ̀ ne lu t'ə də lu ŋæ̀   you used to say this

        ni p'ò jí nè lu ŋa pe̯ sə̣   they say your father parted early
        ni p'ò jí cæ lu ŋa pe̯ sə̣   your father died young they say
            ni p'ò nó ŋə̀ tə ŋa pe̯ ŋæ̀   they say you longed for a father

And she repeatedly used metaphors for intimacy in speaking of her mother—not merely the spatial intimacy of good neighbors, as when singing of relations among the dead, but of affective intimacy as well:

4.20   à mo ŋæ̀ mi jɔ t'ù le   mother, when you were in our world
            ŋæ̀ nì mo lò sə̣   we two, mother and daughter
            ye fu à lə zò   held the eggs tightly
            à lə t'ə lè tə   you spoke clearly
                ŋæ̀ dɔ̀ væ̀ ǹ jɔ lè   you never scolded me

        à mo la né bùi næ næ   mother we were like paired water bugs

The orphans' verse of the past often made reference to Liberation as the point where fortunes turned, fields expanded, and granaries filled. This was not appropriate for Luo Meixiu's mother's generation, which did not live through Liberation. Instead, Luo Meixiu used the phrase, "government policies improved," referring to the rural tax liberalization of the early 2000s. Yet this was not the paean to stuffed granaries and fertile herds of earlier orphans' verse. Fire, as in the first line of this excerpt, is a common metaphor for pain.

4.21	pæ pò à tó mà	fire on the mountainside
	ŋo mà ǹ jɔ sǫ	I too have no luck
	ŋo jɔ lṵ ǹ go	I have no skills
	p'à lṵ ǹ go	no learning at all
	æ mæ jen ts'ə̀ tsæ ka lḛ	now government policies have improved
	chì lu à mo jǫ m mæ	not in time to give mother good food
	tsæ lu à mo cí m mæ	not in time to give mother clothing
	ni shú bǜ pæ mǽ ts'i yi ga	the belt of your suffering has broken
	ni shú vé tà kǽ t'ə tṵ lɔ	the strap of your back basket has parted
	p'a pí p'a dɔ chì	your shirt front is wet
	p'a dɔ lè té chì	your shirt tail is wet
	chì su rɔ̀ t'ì tsò	we are all orphans

Perhaps Luo Meixiu's most moving verses were a direct, detailed portrait of her mother in her last days.

4.22	à mo bə́ nɔ̀ cæ ne k'u	mother, you lay like a coiled boa
	tḭ nà kɔ̀ lò bə	you sat like a horned owl
	bə́ le bə́ le ǹ do ga ne pḛ	you lay but could not sleep
	tḭ le tḭ le ǹ do ga ne pḛ	you sat but could not sit still
	ni dɔ̀ ne lu t'ə	this is what you said
	à mo lè tsí wú gə̀ ŋo	mother, you used your elbow as a pillow
	chi tsí k'à dɔ ŋo	you drew your knees up in the blanket
	à mo ŋæ mi jɔ t'ù lɔ̀	mother, when you were in our world
	né chì né te lɔ̀ sə kɔ̀	when this daughter returned
	à mo lə də t'ù	to visit mother
	chi no wú ǹ tse ŋa pḛ	you said, "my feet hurt up to my head"
	wú chæ ne mó də	"massage my head"
	ci chæ̰ ṇe ṃó də	"massage my feet"

Reorienting the temporal economy of suffering established in laments from the 1990s, Luo Meixiu's lament presents suffering not as mutually fashioned by cross-generational pairs and quartets of kin but as personal and internal, experienced by the singer as a lonely sorrow, voiced to uncaring mountains and rivers:

4.23   à mo ŋo shú dɔ̀ t'ə kɔ́ ǹ sa   mother, my suffering is too much to speak of

        ŋo shú dɔ̀ wò mo t'ə   I speak my suffering to the mountains
          wò mo t'à bɯ̀ lɯ̀ sɛ lɯ̀   the wind in the mountain pines replies
          wò mo mɯ̀ he p'ì yi ga   the mountain winds blow my words away

        shú dɔ̀ lɔ né t'ə   I tell my suffering to the river
          lɔ né yi væ̀ p'ì yi ga   the river carries my words away
          lɔ né yi væ̀ lə lə   the river only babbles
          lɔ né yi væ̀ sa sa   the river only gurgles

Orphans' verse had provided a formal framework with which to understand any life as a movement from hardship in youth to ease in old age, and to understand grief as the effort to stem regret by repaying the dead with suffering. Luo Meixiu's lament turned this formula inside out, speaking of specific scenes from her mother's life and death, claiming that the turn to prosperity had come too late to ease her mother's suffering, and displaying her own grief as flowing from lost intimacy with her mother. Intimacy replaced suffering as the central affective logic of this lament. Here, the dead were composed of specific memories, explicitly voiced. Luo Meixiu's mother was owed not the suffering of communally laboring kin but the sincere heartbreak (*wúlə*) of a daughter personally attempting to come to terms with her loss.

   This revaluing of intimacy is hardly surprising in a context where every family in Júzò has scattered. Voicing regret about not being able to care well enough for her mother when she was ill, Luo Meixiu complained that she could receive no help from her two sisters, as one suffered on the mountainside (having married out to a Lipò community) and the other suffered by the riverside (having moved to the county town to find work). And she mentioned her own children:

4.24   ni p'è dɔ̀ lí zò lɔ   your grandchildren, like pine grubs
          ro lè chì jɔ tụ hɔ̀ pẹ   their right hands search for food
          væ̀ lè lò jɔ tụ hɔ̀ pẹ   their left hands search for drink
          ve kò à mo jú du gù   to bring back to you mother

Luo Meixiu's children were currently looking for work in the city and were unable to offer their mother anything for their grandmother's care or funeral. Luo Meixiu's husband too lived in the county town, leaving her alone to bear the burden of the recent deaths that had befallen her. This diaspora was reflected

in the pervasive sense of loneliness that haunts her lament, so different from
the emphasis on collective suffering of earlier weeping songs:

4.25	t'à da lí vɔ́ zò	siskins in the pine trees
	kæ lu pe̱ kæ ǹ sa gá . . .	I know nothing else to say . . .
	ŋo me à mo ma ǹ kɔ́	my eyes cannot see mother
	à mo ni me ŋo t'è ma	mother, can your eyes
		see me?

The scattering of her family brought home to Luo Meixiu some part of that
ensemble of conditions and aspirations that are conventionally identified as
"modern." Her husband and children were undergoing forced tutelage in what
is required of modern immigrant subjects in Chinese cities. Largely severed
from their kin, they drifted through cities as free agents, hoping to sell their
unskilled labor for enough to live. Their skin of darker color and bodily habitus made them immediately identifiable as "peasants" (nongmin); their ac-
cents identified them as "minorities" (shaoshu minzu) ranking at the bottom
of the hierarchy of "quality" (suzhi) so important in urban China.[4] Her children were learning to strive to abandon the forms of speech, emotion, and
bodily habitus that marked their origins. In sum, they were learning humiliation, a sensibility central to modernization in many settings: the conviction
of their low worth and the worthlessness of their culture. Luo Meixiu's initial
response to my interest in her lament had been to frame it with this sensibility:
"To you, this is a backward custom . . ."

Though lament itself may be a humiliating reminder of "backwardness"
(luohou), the verses of Luo Meixiu's lament show a striking familiarity with
the shifting core collection of attributes required of "modern" subjects. The
dead addressed in her lament display many of these attributes. Their lives
are described not as transformations of conventional assemblages of social
relations but as the lives of individualized beings recalled in specific memories. The lamenter, defined through her relations with the dead, also displays
items from this collection. Her grief is individual rather than communal; it
is more internalized and more private than in laments of the 1990s, and it
springs spontaneously into being rather than being deliberately fashioned.
Though this sorrow is brought to a public, ritualized setting, it is expressed
there as a deeply personal form of affect, rather than being produced there

4. The literature on the effects of discourses and practices of "quality" (suzhi) on peasant
migrants and minorities in urban China is large. For an introduction, see Anagnost (2004), Kipnis (2006, 2011), Lin (2007, 2011), Barabantseva (2009), Sun (2009), Day (2013), and Lin (2013).

only through the collective labor of kin. As a result, this grief carries some of
the trappings of sincerity and authenticity that are the gold standard for "modern" emotion—the standard against which lament in so many places has been
judged, often in humiliating fashion, to belong to backward or primitive forms
of emotional life (Robbins 2005, Sahlins 1992).

Conclusion: The Modern Dead

Like many rural people across China, particularly the poor and minorities,
people in Júzò live under immense time pressure. In many ways they have
repeatedly been told that they exist in another time, a backward time, and
they must strive without cease to come forward into the present. The message
comes from every direction—from state agencies, from Han neighbors, from
urban elites, from returning migrants. In Júzò, though it has taken widely dif-
fering forms over the last half century, this message has nevertheless been incessant. The women who are refashioning lament in Júzò are groping towards
new ways of being persons in a context where their once-insular home has
exploded outward, subjecting them to the corrosive gazes of many different
outsiders, all avid for some version of modernity and frequently condemna-
tory of phenomena that appear to be modernity's opposites. From their parents and grandparents these women inherited effective ritual technologies for
constructing subjectivity, centered on creating proper relations with the dead.
They rescued many of these technologies from sixty years of consistent deni-
gration and inconsistent suppression or prohibition. Lament was among the
most flexible and powerful of these technologies, and in the twenty-first century, they used lament to experiment with new forms of personhood while retaining as the horizon for all forms of subjectivity their relations with the dead.

The ways women grieved in the early reform era show evidence of being
deeply influenced by the conditions of the socialist period: by the midcentury
euphoria, quickly deflated, about the possibilities created by Liberation; by the
forms of collective labor in which "mothers and daughters, fathers and sons,
grandmothers and granddaughters" worked side by side; by high and steadily
increasing state hemp procurement prices, which catastrophically deflated as
the reform era began; by ideologies that named labor as the only legitimate
source of wealth; by the household registration system that kept rural people
at home and in mutual contact, allowing them the sense that the entire social
world might assemble in a single courtyard. In this sense, lament and the dead
were already modern in the 1990s, though in a very different mode. Twenty-
first-century transformations have been merely another in a series of responses
to successive, if inconsistent, efforts to modernize the people of this valley.

In many ways, this is a familiar story. A great deal of scholarship has shown that the production of sincere, authentic, internal affect is a common effect of "modernizing" aspirations and projects in China and beyond (some fine recent examples are Rofel 2007, Keane 2007, Moore 2011, Lempert 2012). It is not remarkable that such globally familiar forms of subjectivity might emerge through efforts to fashion proper relations with the dead. In his classic longue durée history of death in the West, *The Hour of Our Death* (1982), Philippe Ariès proposed that the shape of individuated personhood usually identified as the core of modern forms of subjectivity began to take shape in elite experiences with death in the eleventh century. Rich, educated, and powerful people, seeking to assert their wills in new ways, began to replace past forms of relations between self and other with a sense of individual identity and personal destiny. The notion of the immortal soul became a foundation for the experience of centering one's person on individual identity. One imagined one's own immortal soul chiefly by elaborating, in collective, ritualized settings, the shapes of the souls of dead others. Ariès writes, "The individual insisted on assembling the molecules of his own biography, but only the spark of death enabled him to fuse them into a whole" (Ariès 1982, 605). I read Ariès' unique insight here to be that what we take as "modern" forms of subjectivity have depended from the start on ritualized relations with the dead. Women in Júzò find themselves under pressure to craft forms of personhood that are indirect descendants, along a long and tortured path, of the forms Ariès explored. It is hardly surprising that some of these women should find a resource for this work in tuneful poetic conversations with their dead.

PART II

5

Songs for Dead Parents

I know very little of Li Bicong's life. Everything I do know is about his relation to a great heap of verses of which he was a lifelong servant and the final custodian, and which he sold to me for a few hundred <u>yuan</u> shortly before he died. He was born around 1926 in Chezò, "little village," Júzò's largest. As a youth he apprenticed as an *àpǐpǒ*, literally "man who speaks," with his mother's brother, learning techniques for communicating with unseen beings. By the early 1950s he had mastered two very long speeches, which he frequently performed at the large ceremonies called Tenth-Month Sacrifice (*ts'ǐho nèpi*), held during the first tenth lunar month following a death, and Sleeping in the Forest (*likádùhè*) held the same month several decades after a death.

I began to hear about these verses shortly after I first became acquainted with Júzò. In the context of reviving old forms of poetic language, they were the topic of many nostalgic recollections about lost treasures. Each contained seventy-two "songs" and took eight hours to perform, I was told. The songs were about the origins of the world, of all the beasts, birds, and insects, and of every kind of invisible being. They were about the secrets of life and death. "Han have the story of how Pangu 盤古 created the earth and sky," said Liyoŋcipǒ, whose erudite versions of *nèpi* I admired. "But it is only a few paragraphs, and even then they forget some of the characters when they read it. The great chants told of the creation of everything and every being, in ancient and beautiful language."

This chapter sketches the twentieth-century history of these two chants, tells of the ethically fraught circumstances in which I acquired a recording of them, and outlines a method for exploring them. This history is a story of suppression, displacement, and difficult reemergence. It was conditioned by perhaps the most important characteristic of these speeches: that the agency of their authorship and vocalization was distributed. The chants were authored by ancestral lineages of àpipò, beginning with the first shaman, Pimæneli, the hero of their songs. And they were voiced by an agency that was and was not the àpipò's own. The verses were not so much learned by as lent to the few talented àpipò who mastered them; they were lent by a tutelary spirit, a pinè, a "ghost of speech." My most valued consultant on these matters, Àp'ìmà, explained:

> The àpipò was a great official to the dead, but if the ghost of speech wasn't present and comfortable, the àpipò wouldn't remember. It was as though the ritualist were possessed: the ghost of speech sat on his head and spoke for him. . . . If you had such a ghost you had to perform the great chant at least once a year at Tenth-Month Sacrifice or Sleeping in the Forest, or you would fall ill or go mad. Some àpipò went around to the houses of the brothers-in-law of those who had died that year, begging to be hired to perform the chant. Even those who could not speak well had to speak, so they would hire a teacher to sit nearby and help them.

It was thus not only authorship of the speeches that was collective and ambiguous. Their animation too was not entirely the performance of the àpipò who spoke them. Àpìmà was speaking with hindsight, for the central feature of the stories she and others would tell about the two great chants was the harm that tutelary spirits, ghosts of speech, visited upon àpipò who were forbidden to perform after 1957. This shaped conditions under which, instead of simply being forgotten, the speeches survived in a displaced and concealed mode, as àpipò covertly enunciated them for their tutelary spirits in attempts to deflect pain, illness, and madness.

These features—language that is collectively authored, where "there are no possibilities for an individuated enunciation that would belong to this or that 'master' and that could be separated from a collective enunciation," and language that is deterritorialized, displaced, driven underground, and thus "appropriate for strange and minor uses" are two of the characteristics of a minor literature that Deleuze and Guattari list in their book on that topic, an incandescent reading of Kafka (1986 [1975], 16–17). These features are joined by a third: everything in such literatures is political. In major literatures, Deleuze and Guattari note, individual concerns, like the family, join with no less individual concerns. But the "cramped space" of minor literatures "forces each individual intrigue to connect immediately to politics. The individual concern thus becomes all the more necessary, indispensable, magnified, because a whole other story is vibrating within it" (1968 [1975], 17). One of the other stories vibrating within the verses of these two chants is the history of attacks on ritual language and its speakers in the context of socialist transformation. In the decades that followed these attacks, a direct connection emerged between the physical and psychic pain that discredited *àpipò* experienced and these histories of suppression, persecution, and loss. My acquisition of a recording of the two great chants was conditioned by these direct, if subterranean, links between the politicized suppression of speech in the past and physical and psychic pain in the present.

Yet the language of these two chants was political in another way as well. In addition to sketching out the late history of this verbal art, this chapter starts to outline a method for approaching it as a direct attempt to imagine and describe a world of subjugated others, who must be controlled, forced to live, and put to work by means of a bureaucratic machine. This method will be expanded and elaborated in the following chapters as I work through the songs of the two chants. Yet imagine and describe are not quite the right words: I will argue that, in addition, these long intricate, repetitive speeches work to *construct* a world for dead others and install dead bodies in that world. The stance the speeches take towards the dead others is ethically complex. While they subject the dead to bureaucratic authority in the interests of the living, the world they fashion also gives the dead potential routes of escape, possibilities for evading an endless round of life and life and dissolving into something else. If I am inclined to think of the great chants of Tenth-Month Sacrifice and Sleeping in the Forest as a form of "minor literature" in Deleuze and Guattari's terms, it is not only to highlight the ways the recent history of their suppression and loss directly linked the intimate bodily concerns of their former enunciators to political events. It is also to point out that they were an attempt to investigate, with a degree of empathy, or even compassion, the lives and worlds of that most intimate of "minorities" whose political subjugation was necessary for the living, but who could nevertheless, by means of a "minor" language, be heard with a sympathetic ear.

Vacating the Tenth Month

In the early 1950s, only six or seven *àpipò* in Júzò had mastered the great *nèpi* performed at Tenth-Month Sacrifice and Sleeping in the Forest. Each possessed several treasured tools: a bell with a clawed handle, a wide-brimmed felt hat, a staff with a pair of eagles' talons bound to it with strips of red, yellow, and black cloth. The difficult passage that introduced every song in both speeches mentioned the shaman's bell and hat, using a single homonym, *chè* to indicate the bell's ring, the shaman's song, the way the felt hat hangs on his head, and the spirits to which the song is addressed. The repeated chime of this word echoes the bell's sound as it carries the shaman's speech over earth and sky.

5.1 chì **chæ̀** ni lɔ sa	come hear my bell echo
ni lɔ sa yí sè	hear my bell ring
shɼ eɼ lò k'o̧ **chæ̀**	I hang my twelve felt hats
chæ̀ lò so p̀ò ni	you male ghosts of the house
chæ̀ mæ̀ shɼ mæ̀ mæ̀ lè	you female ghosts of grain
shɼ mo ni	and seed

Other passages mentioned the severed talons of the shaman's great adversary the eagle, who stoops upon the living as upon a crowd of chicks in a courtyard, seizing one to carry off. Bell and talons gave the shaman's song the bite and carrying power to overcome the speech of ghosts.

5.2 nè cè pi̧ cè t'ȩ lè lɔ	compare a ghost's voice to a shaman's voice
pi̧ cè ju̧ cè ŋɔ	a shaman's voice is a bell's voice
nè cè k'a le t'ȩ	a ghost's voice no matter how sharp
ju̧ cè lɔ ǹ t'ȩ	is not so sharp as a bell's voice
lɔ ǹ t'ȩ lo ŋɔ	not nearly so sharp
nè chi pi̧ chi t'ȩ le lɔ	compare a ghost's claws to a shaman's claws
ŋo pi̧ chi jé chi ŋɔ	my shaman's claws are eagle's talons
ni nè chi k'a li t'ȩ	your ghost's talons no matter how sharp
ŋo jé chi lɔ ǹ t'ȩ	are not so sharp as my eagle's talons

By the time I first visited Júzò, the sense of shamanic power that rings through these passages was a thing of the past. Walking on red-hot plowshares, dealing death to enemies with secret witchcraft, capturing the ci, inhabitants of springs and swamps and the original owners of the land, and leading them away dripping frogs and toads: all this had been deemed the worst elements of a superstitious past when ritualists scandalously took advantage of the people's honest naïveté. Even in the relatively relaxed political atmosphere of the 1990s and 2000s, ritual practices that drew on any form of charismatic personal power were subject to censure. Local officials reluctantly allowed the *àpipò* who remained to carry on with their chanting and healing to a limited extent, largely because of the efforts of urban Yi elites to redefine them as the "intellectuals of the Yi people" and the inheritors of the precious cultural tradition of "primitive religion."[1] These ritualists were careful to claim no per-

---

1. These efforts, which made my own ethnographic work possible, were spearheaded by Liu Yaohan, who identified as Lolopo from Yao'an County and who became a founder and long-

sonal powers other than the capacity to remember the words of particular *nèpi* and the formulae for building the associated *nègu*. The longest and most difficult *nèpi* of which any claimed mastery was the speech for "wild ghosts" (*chènè*), which took about a half hour to recite, and only a few could perform and understand even that (Mueggler 2001).

In contrast to these humble technicians, those who had mastered the great chants (*pimo*, "great speakers") were, when possessed by their tutelary spirits, creators of worlds and vanquishers of death. Their ritual speech (*pi*) brought a world into being, with beasts, birds, and insects. Their breath (*cè*) made the world as a series of series, a list of lists, and remade human bodies as one series among many, parallel to series of animals, birds, human kinds, omens, ghosts, and places. Their speech (*bɛ*) ascended to the heavens along the steps of these series; it battled the bringers of death; it touched a dead body part by part, bringing it back to life entire. Their songs (*chæ*) traversed a world beyond this world in a quest to overpower death.

The masters of the great chant gained considerable honor and some wealth for their accomplishment. Júzò's central valley had only three sites for Tenth-Month Sacrifice: large flat empty terraces elevated above the valley on land unsuitable for farming. The two largest villages, Chemo and Chezò, shared one site just below their main graveyard; Chemo had another site of its own, and a third site served the smaller villages of the valley's opposite side. Sleeping in the Forest was held in a grove of huge old trees next to the largest Tenth-Month Sacrifice site: the entire valley and surrounding hamlets shared this grove. Tenth-Month Sacrifice was carried out during the daylight, Sleeping in the Forest at night, and during the tenth lunar month, when the harvest was in and most people did little but prepare for and attend funeral rituals, these sites were filled with crowds of hundreds nearly every day and night. The masters of the great chants were in high demand, chanting one or the other speech nearly every day of the month, sometimes twice. Their fee for both rituals was the same: an entire goat minus its forelegs and skin, along with everything they could eat and drink during their day or night of work. They spent the month speaking and eating, and they accumulated enough meat to last through the winter and beyond.

The final Sleeping in the Forest ceremony was held in 1949. The tenth lunar month fell in late November and early December that year, and in January 1950, representatives of the People's Liberation Army declared Júzò liberated.

time director of the ethnographically oriented Chuxiong Yi Culture Research Institute. See Liu (1980a, 1985), Liu and Lu (1986), Liu (2007, 1980, 2002), and Chen, Lu, and Liu (1984). For a discussion of related issues among the Yao during the same time period, see Litzinger (2000).

Since this ritual could be held several decades after a death, whenever the deceased's descendants could gather enough resources, it was easily put off for less complex times. The new township government, centered in Chezò, announced that there was no longer any need for Sleeping in the Forest; Tenth-Month Sacrifice would suffice. The timing of the latter was far more urgent. If the deceased's descendants did not have the resources to perform the ritual during the year of a death, it might be postponed to the next year, after an àpìpò performed a briefer temporary rite as a placeholder. But even then the family was likely to be plagued by bad health, poor crops, and sickly animals, and this would get worse every year that the full ritual was delayed.

In the first few years after Liberation, local leaders made concerted efforts to discourage Tenth-Month Sacrifice. When a typhus epidemic swept the region in 1953, Yang Lixin, the county's deputy chief and a Júzò native, chose to build the valley's first medical clinic on the most visible of the three sites for the ritual, shared by Chezò and Chemo. It was the first deliberately staged confrontation between a new world imbued with the morally laden disciplines of civilization, sanitation, and health and an older world where disease was the effect of relations between material and immaterial beings. Yet all three sites were as busy as ever for four more years. Tenth-Month Sacrifice rituals were staged in 1956 and 1957, after all Júzò's villages had been united into a single high-level agricultural producers' cooperative. The ceremony was abandoned along with Emerging from the House, Emerging from the Courtyard, and Dawn-to-Dusk Sacrifice in 1958 as the Great Leap Forward gathered momentum.

The autumn of 1958 began a time of extreme hardship for the àpìpò who had mastered the two great chants. Though they had no clients, most continued to perform the chants for their tutelary spirits at least once during the tenth month. Officials who descended from the county town "to look and record" confiscated the treasured bells and eagle-claw staffs. Some àpìpò were caught sacrificing for their tutelary spirits after falling ill. "In Jɔjɔmò, Li Huoxing went mad after they took away his bell," Àp'ìmà recalled, and she named others who fell ill and died after the effigies for their tutelary spirits were destroyed. The chief of one of the commune's two management districts ordered the arrest of the two most eminent àpìpò, the brothers Qi Dezhong and Qi Deyi. The brothers were forced to labor building an addition to the medical clinic that stood on the Tenth-Month Sacrifice site for Chezò and Chemo. Qi Dezhong died of exhaustion and malnutrition, and Qi Deyi completed the task alone. For the next two decades, he was the repeated target of struggle sessions in which he was beaten, humiliated, and denounced as an evil purveyor of superstition. "While I was building that clinic I forgot the great chant, he told me in 1993. "I don't remember it, don't ask me to sing it, no one remembers it now."

Li Bicong escaped most of this. In the early 1950s, he left Júzò's central valley with his wife to establish a home high in the mountains. Before Liberation, many families in Júzò kept rough seasonal houses in the mountains, where some household members resided during the summer, herding goats and farming potatoes, buckwheat, and hemp. At collectivization, these lands were assigned to production teams centered in the valley, and some people gradually made seasonal houses into permanent homes. Though living conditions were bad, work points were worth more than in the valley, more grain was distributed, and work was less tightly managed. The steep, shady gullies were ideal for growing hemp, which the production teams distributed to mountain households to process and weave, and which could be kept by households and sold at a good price to state procurers between 1960 and 1981. The waves of political activism, social tension, and selective persecution that overtook the villages during this period rarely reached into these high, sparse settlements. In the early 1980s, the residents of these settlements were invited to return to the valley to participate in the distribution of collective land to households, but most refused, asking instead that the dry land around their houses be distributed to them. Many hoped to live on hemp cloth production and timber harvesting, but the introduction of synthetic-fiber grain bags in 1981 made the former profitless, and progressively tighter laws against timber harvesting made the latter illegal and increasingly dangerous.

In the 1990s, Li Bicong still lived with his wife in a small house that stood alone on a wooded hillside in a hamlet now named Daomaidi. Four or five other houses were scattered below, belonging to Li Bicong's sons and a few others. Each household had some fields of potatoes and buckwheat and a herd of goats. Above the hamlet stood a huge old pine tree surrounded by a low fence of rocks, stained with the blood of sheep sacrificed during the new year. This was a *misi*, the material body of a founding ancestor, responsible for the health and wellbeing of its descendants below, a covert replacement for the great *misi* of Júzò, which had fallen to the axes of activists early in the Cultural Revolution. *Misi* had once towered behind every mountain village in this region. Many still stand, evidence of secret histories of deeply consequential relations between people and their ancestors, their spirit familiars, and the ghosts of loved ones who have died badly or not been properly mourned (figure 5.1). Beset by chronic illness, Li Bicong sacrificed covertly to the *misi*, and he set up an effigy for his tutelary spirit inside his house. He quietly performed the great chant for this effigy once a year for more than thirty years, warding off his chronic illness.

FIGURE 5.1 A *misi* (photo by author).

Similar troubles were common in Júzò. Political campaigns during the socialist period and development campaigns in the reform era inserted themselves into histories of relations between people and immaterial beings, forbidding exchange and negotiation. Difficult relations with dead forebears or other beings, which in earlier times might have been released with a speech and a sacrifice, stretched out instead over decades, expressing themselves in daily routines of illness and mental instability. The effects of these campaigns were inherited: as those affected died, they too became ghosts who inflicted their own descendants with further illness or pain. These effects are still being felt, now distributed more widely in a situation of generalized social fragmentation, when all deaths are bad deaths and all dead become wild ghosts.

Series and Histories

For nearly two years I was told repeatedly that the great chants of Tenth-Month Sacrifice and Sleeping in the Forest were lost. The few masters of these chants who had survived the socialist era had fallen silent or gone mad. I accepted this situation with equanimity despite my friends' nostalgic hyperbole: after all, I reasoned, people could say anything about texts no one would ever hear again. As I was preparing to leave Júzò for what I thought would be the last time, Lichink'æpò, my stubborn, reliable self-appointed research assistant, in his fifties, insisted that I walk with him to the hamlet of Daomaidi. His wife Lichink'æmo had just returned from a trip selling cloth and embroidery thread to women in high-mountain hamlets, where she had encountered a cousin for the first time in decades, the cousin who had married Li Bicong. She told Lichink'æmo that her husband still performed the great chants in private for his tutelary spirit.

We arrived in Daomaidi late in the evening. Li Bicong's wife gave us a narrow bed to share in her barn where we slept head to foot so as to fit. In the morning, Lichink'æpò sat with the old àpipò over the tea we had brought and negotiated. Li Bicong said that he and his wife had both given up superstition long ago. His wife didn't want him to perform the nèpi because it made him sick, as his tutelary spirit didn't like it. He had not performed it in more than fifty years, and he doubted he could remember more than a verse or two. Lichink'æpò offered him three hundred <u>yuan</u>. At the time this seemed like a great deal, though I now look back on this exchange and the petty transfers that followed with shame and regret. The àpipò folded the bills, tucked them behind the beam above his cooking fire, and told us to wait until the next day. In the morning, however, he refused to speak. His wife had told him to ask for more money, he said, as he would require medicine after speaking. Lichink'æpò balked. I was groggy and disheartened: the bed had been but a hard board, Lichink'æpò's feet none too clean, the rats industrious. Enough pandering to this wretched old man, I thought. I placed the two bottles of cane alcohol I had brought as a gift at the ritualist's feet, told Lichink'æpò to give him the money, and began preparing my bag for the walk back to Júzò. Li Bicong quickly tucked the bottles into a bag. "Or else my wife will take them away," he explained. "Come with me." He walked outside, let the goats out of their corral, shooed them up the hillside, and sat down under a tree. "Turn that on," he said, gesturing to my small tape recorder:

æ ni shr ni	long ago
mùʊ bə mi bə	the heavens took form, the earth took form
mùʊ go mi go	the heavens emerged, the earth emerged

> In the old society, poverty was everywhere, hunger was everywhere. People ate wild plants, drank only water, and had only soup of pickled vegetables to eat with their grain. To be a person you must first bear poverty and only then gradually grow rich. In the past, because of government policies, everyone below heaven was hungry. Now that government policies are good, no matter whether inside China or outside, all over the earth all have food and drink and can plan efficiently. Heaven cares for all. No one is poor, no one dies of hunger or thirst, no one fights or quarrels, everyone is cheerful and satisfied.

This was not the Tenth-Month Sacrifice chant. It was a history of the world, already familiar to us. Like the tombstones of the 1950s it began with the emergence of heaven and earth, using the language of *mèkòbɛ*, poetic speech. Like the speaking-bitterness narratives of the early socialist period, it described the "old society" as a place of deep hunger and poverty. Like lament, it split the time after Liberation into two eras: before and after a change in "government policies" that brought wealth and happiness—the change marked sometimes by contracting land to households and market reforms, sometimes by tax liberalization policies decades later. This was an echo of official history, now the background against which all other narratives of time and descent took shape. Its official nature was marked by the language of speaking bitterness, by the agreement worked out in the 1980s and 1990s to speak of the socialist era in terms of mistaken government policies, and by the blindly optimistic concluding sentences. With the precipitous fall in hemp prices and the ban on timber cutting, these deeply impoverished settlements were hardly experiencing a time when "everyone is cheerful and satisfied."

The form of this little history, however, is significant. It contains two temporal series. The first series is double: sky (*mu*) and earth (*mi*), on the one hand, and heaven or the spirit of heaven (tianshen) and government policies (guoajia zhengce), on the other hand, their difference marked by the switch from Lòloŋo to Chinese. The second is the chronological series of a life (*zæ*), proceeding from poverty in youth to wealth in old age. This second series parallels the first: the change in government policies that brings wealth and happiness. As we saw in chapters 1 and 4, a similar correlation is at the center of all the narratives about death and historical time, from tombstones to speaking bitterness to lament. It is the task of poetic language to reconcile the history of the cosmos, of Liberation, and of socialist and postsocialist campaigns with the course of life and the event of death. This correlation is the present

antidote to the paths of time and descent trod by wild ghosts, disgruntled tutelary spirits, and deracinated *misi*, the secret paths of blood and pain that exiled
Li Bicong to this high mountain place. The verses of Tenth-Month Sacrifice
came together long before Li Bicong's history of the world was negotiated and
consolidated, and they would not perform this particular correlation. Still, this
little history contains the seeds of a picture of world, person, body, life, and
death as composed of correlated series that would eventually center my understanding of Tenth-Month Sacrifice.

Li Bicong glanced up with what I was beginning to recognize as his habitually wary expression. "Turn that on," he said again, poking at my already
spinning recorder. "Now I'll tell a story."

mi nè tsì mà Yan Luo Wang (閻羅王)	Yan Luo Wang, king of the ghosts of the earth
á mǜ nè tsì mà Guanyin Laomu (觀音老母)	Mother Guanyin, queen of the ghosts of the sky

We don't know what day we will die or when we will fall ill. We want only to
eat, drink, farm, herd, and labor: we don't understand death or illness, but Yan
Luo Wang keeps track of all this. And Guanyin provides children and justice
from heaven.

Sipping from one of the bottles of cane alcohol I had given him, Li Bicong
spent the rest of the afternoon telling stories that elaborated on these points.
Once Yan Luo Wang confused the soul of a man of 126 years with that of a man
of 20. Unable to tell which was which, he let the old one live long past his time.
The underworld king consulted an *àpipò* who told him, "tomorrow afternoon,
the old one will carry leafy branches to his buckwheat field. On his way home
he will cross the river. Wait at the crossing and boil a stone in a clay pot. Wait
at the crossing and wash a piece of charcoal. Then you will understand what
you want to know." Yan Luo Wang did as the *àpipò* instructed. Many people
passed him, bearing loads on back frames, saying nothing. Finally, an old man
asked him, "What are you doing?" "I'm boiling this stone until it's soft," the
king of the underworld answered. "I'm washing this charcoal until it's white."
"Ah," said the old man. "In all my 126 years I've never seen a stone boiled until
soft nor charcoal washed until white." Before he had gone three steps further
his breath ceased: Yan Luo Wang had taken him back.

Li Bicong told the story of the flood, which a brother and sister survived in
a gourd, after which Guanyin instructed them to have sex and repopulate the
world. They were ashamed, but they covered the sister's vagina with a leaf and
went at it, "that heaven and earth might emerge, that people and tigers might
emerge" (*mù go mi go, bu go lò go*). The leaf broke, the sister got pregnant, she

bore a chunk of meat, they sliced it up on a cutting board, and where they
tossed each slice a person sprang into being.[2] "Everyone on earth has his difficulties," Li Bicong said.

> To be an official isn't so wonderful, to be a deaf-mute isn't so harsh. Both must
> live, both must eat. All over the earth the lives and deaths of all people are gov-
> erned by Yan Luo Wang, king of the underworld. People come from the earth
> and return to the earth. On this earth, you become a person for a lifetime, you
> sit in the sun for a bit, then it's over.

He told the story of how General Yonŋliwánli invented the flute. The general was leading a great army in a desperate war. On a day like today, with
sunshine and a breeze, as the armies were resting, the general went to a bamboo grove to sit in the shade. The wind blew, the bamboo stalks rattled. It
was as though the world had just been created (kaitian pidi 開天闢地), and
all was at peace. He cut a bamboo stalk, and it made music as the wind blew
across it. He cut a hole and blew into it, and the sound was better. He cut five
more holes, and the sound became very sad. He went back to camp and commanded his soldiers, "prepare your bedding and bags; this evening we will
fight a battle." So they prepared their bags and bedding, but at midnight the
general played his flute, and every soldier in both armies thought of his children, his wife, and his parents; every heart was stricken with grief. Each soldier picked up his bags and walked home, peace settled over the world, and
Yonŋliwánli became emperor and held all state power.

Here Lichink'æpò interrupted. Why was his cousin putting us off with stories? "À lə lə bɛ," "slowly, slowly," Li Bicong replied. He pulled a flute out of his
bag and played it for a while. Soon enough, stubborn, annoying Lichink'æpò
interrupted with more arguments. I was enjoying the flute, making the best of
a bad situation, and I couldn't help but imagine my friend's face on the mule
in Li Bicong's story of the flood, who declares to Guanyin, bringer of life, "My
mouth is a fire tongs, my feet are shovels; I'll pinch you, I'll dig at you!"

"À lə lə bɛ": more precisely, bɛ is to speak, and à lə lə is what you say when
you are gradually working your way into a task or a journey. We both believed Li Bicong was prevaricating, putting off the task of voicing the words
that had lodged with him for more than forty years, making him ill, shaping
his life's course. Now I think he was testing his voice, traveling slowly into a

---

2. This story is told in Mueggler (2001, 73–74). For a historical introduction to flood stories
as a regional phenomenon, see Lewis (2006).

world brought into being by his speech, beginning to sketch out that world's contours. He was making his way into the territory that the opening verses of his *nèpi* would cover again at the extreme rapid-fire pace of ritual speech. "Yan Luo Wang, king of the ghosts of the earth; Mother Guanyin, queen of the ghosts of the sky." Male king and female queen, earth and sky, underworld and world of people: these are the differential couples at the foundations of the world the *nèpi* would build of parallel poetic verses. The practical work of the *nèpi*, its work in service of the living, would be to coordinate these oppositions, so that the power of death might become the generative potential of life.

Li Bicong's stories elaborated some of this world's elements. Yan Luo Wang is the authority who records and enforces the specific quantity of life allowed each person. But the underworld king's authority is not total. When he forgets, or when he fails to inscribe, he must consult a shaman, a separate power, orthogonal to Yan Luo Wang's own. The shaman too brings death but he does it with words. And his words take a certain form: parallels, oppositions, correlations, transformations—a stone boiled till soft, charcoal washed till white. Another theme is outlined in the story of the flood: consanguinity is transformed into affinity so the world might be repopulated—the final, secret verses of the Tenth-Month Sacrifice chant will defy the incest taboo in favor of generalized fecundity. The story of General Yoŋliwanli's flute brings the problem of organized violence into this world, along with its source, the historical state. Here Li Bicong practiced some more ritualized code switching. Yoŋliwanli is in the form of a Lòloŋo name, but the sounds seem to combine the period names of two of China's most famous rulers, Yongle of the Qing and Wanli of the Ming. Li Bicong used the Chinese formula <u>kaitian pidi</u> to express the sense that the world has just taken form. The act of genesis, summed up in the parallel Lòloŋo phrase *mù ts'i mi ts'i kà,* would be the topic of the first songs of the *nèpi*. And there is the flute itself, embodying the transformative power of sound at the very center of the long chant.

After Lichink'æp'ò's last interruption, my tape recording cuts off: I have pushed the pause button on this tiresome conversation. When the recording begins again, Lichink'æp'ò has been victorious. "Tenth-Month Sacrifice," he announces in an officious voice. Then Li Bicong, quite drunk, chants the first, difficult verses of the *nèpi*:

5.3   à gə   Oh!
          á sa le te do yi   I have come out
              te lò vǽ sa yi   chaff in my dangling bag
              cá wo jẹ sə yi   cattle on my lead rope

dɔ̀ wò t'à lo yi   the rabbit hops below the branch
dɔ̀ p'æ hə lo yi   the weasel creeps above
    shú lɔ mùi zò sa   heaven's son, I stand guard with my
                                                crossbow
    nè mi tsɨ̀ zò tsǽ mo sè   ghost-world officials crouch beneath
                                                pear trees

Later we spent weeks struggling with this passage, consulting all we had come to know as experts in poetic language. The drunken slurring of Li Bicong's voice was not an issue, as he would chant these verses nearly a hundred times: they announce every song in both chants. Rendered in a spooky, quavering tone, they belong unmistakably to these *nèpi* and no others, for which they set the stage with their "high coefficient of weirdness" to invoke Malinowski's playful phrase (1965, 218). Their difficulty lay in their arcane vocabulary and compressed form, which allowed several possible meanings to be attached to each brief word. In addition, Li Bicong always chanted these verses so rapidly that many sounds, particularly the initials /t/, /t'/, /d/, /l/, /p/, /p'/ and /b/ were difficult to distinguish from one another. We made half a dozen tentative translations into ordinary speech based on our friends' speculations. Finally Dolecipò, the most reclusive of our consultants, who had shown himself master of the most arcane of the briefer *nèpi* we had studied, gave us the sense that I have rendered above, made convincing by its precise parallelism, as well as by his attitude, contrasting with those of our other friends, of knowing exactly what he was about. As was often the case, our decision to fix particular sounds depended in part on our translation. Among the qualities that give the most artful of *nèpi* their force, a quality that ordinary language rarely possesses in segments extending beyond a phrase or two, is the ambiguity of passages that may be heard in several ways at once, sometimes with extraordinary precision. Any transcription and translation that fixes sounds and settles on a single meaning, as ours all do, dampens that explosive polysemy.

These verses compactly announce the shaman's presence, evoke his power, and prefigure the world in which this power will take effect. "Chaff in my dangling bag" describes a skin bag swinging from the *àpipò*'s staff like a bull's testicles swinging from its crotch. This was echoed in the next, paired line by the specialized word *cá wo*. I have rendered *cá wo* "cattle" as it seems to reference the sacrificial goats while also clearly evoking the ox sacrificed by a deaf-mute to form the earth in the chant's first song. This verse plays with a differential parallel: the world-forming deaf-mute and the shaman who brings the world of the *nèpi* into being with his voice. A central, troubled feature of this world is rendered in the next semantic couplet: "The rabbit hops below the branch, the weasel creeps above." *Dǝ wo* more literally means "the shady side" to *dǝ pìæ* "the sunny side," usually referring to the two slopes of a river valley, but we made the slopes into a branch for the rabbit (*tʼà lo*) and weasel (*hǝ lo*) to travel under and over. The line between sunshine and shade snaking through the world is an analogue of the line between the world of people (*tsʼɔ mi*) and the world of ghosts (*nè mi*) or the yangjian 陽間 and the yinjian 陰間—one of the two borderlines that cleave the *nèpi* and structure the negotiations it performs between clearly visible and shadowy beings. The second borderline, between sky and earth, is figured in the final semantic couplet: "I stand guard with my crossbow, ghost world officials sit beneath apple-pear trees." The crossbow, one of the *àpipʼò*'s essential implements, appears frequently in the chant in the story of the shaman who grasps a golden bow with his right hand and plucks the silver string with his left to shoot the eagle, bringer of death, from the sky. These verses reverse the sky/earth opposition of this story to make the *àpipʼò*, standing guard with his bow, a "son of heaven" (*mù zò*) while the ghost-world officials sit beneath the apple-pear tree (*tsæ mo*), the species in which the eagle nests, flapping his wings over the dead souls he has carried there.

A Purchase

As I settled down next to Lichinkʼæpʼòʼs unwashed feet for yet another night, I held out little hope for anything more of Li Bicong. I knew several so-called *àpipʼò* of his kind: foolish old windbags who, when plied with alcohol, would incoherently mime a few verses of poetic language to impress visitors. I had been down this road early in my fieldwork, and it was humiliating to find myself here again so late in the day. Still, I liked his skill with the flute. Lichinkʼæpʼò, perhaps kept awake by my own quite horrible feet, was thinking along much the same lines. He scolded me for wasting my money. "The old buffoon just wants to get drunk. Maybe he remembers a little of the *nèpi*—that bit he chanted sounded like something—but probably not. Tomorrow he will be ill with a headache, and he will send us away. You are a big spender, but that doesn't work with rascals like him."

In the morning the fine sunshine had given way to fog. We intercepted Li Bicong as he trudged wearily up the hill after his goats, looking unwell. He had vanquished one of the bottles I had given him; the other was not in evidence. We learned later that his wife had confiscated it as predicted. He squatted under the same tree and motioned us to sit. "Let's get started," he said, grimacing. I thumbed my recorder and he launched into a rapid stream of five-syllable lines, each passing by in less than a second, followed closely by the next. He didn't pause until I had to turn over the tape at the thirty-minute mark. After two hours Lichink'æp'ò went down to the house and brought back a jar of tea, which we all shared. Now and then Li Bicong would slow for a story or an explanation. But mostly he chanted at a breakneck pace, for more than four hours. The next day he started in again, this time on the Sleeping in the Forest chant. This performance was slower, since the chant had a more leisurely cadence and most lines had two extra syllables inserted at their center. When we said goodbye the morning after, I gave Li Bicong the last two hundred yuan I carried, braving Lichink'æp'ò's emphatic disapproving glare. He tucked it into the hollow behind the beam without saying a word.

I delayed my departure from Júzò for two months. Lichink'æp'ò and I spent nearly every day huddled with one àpip'ò or another in my little room in Júzò's elementary school, playing each rapid verse repeatedly, transcribing it, then working out a translation into ordinary Lòloŋo, usually clarified with Chinese, from which I constructed an English approximation. Parts of the chant, particularly the introductory and concluding segments of each song, were demanding, but our consultants understood most of the rest easily enough. The chief difficulty was length. The male ritualists, who came expecting libations, lasted only an hour or two into each session. But Àp'ìmà stuck, always alert and cheerful, returning each day for nothing more than cup after cup of green tea with red sugar. She clearly delighted in the chant's language, some of which she remembered from childhood when she spent the tenth lunar month sitting close to àpip'ò, listening. Often a verse would send her off into a story or explanation, very welcome breaks. Lichink'æp'ò, reliable to a fault, was indefatigable, and without his steady, good-natured labor we would never have finished. But he was also hopelessly pedantic, and his lengthy commentaries, usually covering ground I knew quite well, contrasted with Àp'ìmà's compact and witty stories. Others stopped by to listen or pitch in, particularly Lichink'æp'ò's poetically skilled spouse Lichink'æmo, the erudite ritualist Liyoŋcip'ò, and small hordes of schoolchildren, clustering like bees around the candy I always had on hand for the woman they all called Abómo, Great-Grandmother. The room was tiny, with two small beds, a schoolchild's desk, and one chair. But my friends vetoed my suggestion that we take the work elsewhere. Repeating the chants in any of their homes might bring disaster, and it was best that the knowledge of what we were doing be kept to a few. Here the schoolteachers could monitor who came and went, and they knew how to explain my projects to visiting officials—not everyone did. I made a trip to the county town to buy two mini tape recorders like mine, made two copies of the recordings, and gave Lichink'æp'ò and Àp'ìmà each a set of tapes and a machine to play them on.

My last month in Júzò that visit was the tenth lunar month. Lichink'æp'ò's encounter with the chants had been no less intense than mine, and he talked of them incessantly to Lichink'æmo, whose work as a traveling tinker drew on an expansive network of contacts in high villages across the region. While no one in Júzò had done Tenth-Month Sacrifice since 1957, she told him, some small places in the mountains, where the people were merely rough Lìpò (even if they *called* themselves civilized Lòlopò), had borrowed the practice from Júzò long ago and now revived it. A few hours walk away in Wòdɔwò, an old *àpipò* was leading a performance of the ritual again, and she knew a family for which it was being done this year, since a girl from Júzò had married one of their sons.

Lichink'æpò and I walked up to Wòdɔwò on the appointed day. It was a high-mountain place with scattered houses surrounded by dry fields of beans, maize, buckwheat, and potatoes. More than a hundred people attended the lively ceremony. The *àpipò*, at least eighty years old, chanted from dawn to dusk with some extended periods of rest. He didn't want us to record him, and I was almost grateful at the time, as there were some challenging dialect differences. (Of course I feel differently now.) But we sat through all the proceedings, and Lichink'æpò used his new recorder to interview some knowledgeable "old people." Later, we sat with Àp'ìmà, who had attended more Tenth-Month Sacrifice ceremonies than she could count. She took us through every step of the process, comparing the "rules and procedures" we reported to those once followed in Júzò. In essence these consisted in exchanges of goats and rice loaves very similar to those of Emerging from the Courtyard and Dawn-to-Dusk Sacrifice, paired with very different procedures for building a material body. It was as though the layers of social clothing that wrapped the core of the dead person were merely renewed, despite previous efforts to sever particular relations, while the corporeal core itself was becoming lighter, growing up from the ground like a grove of trees or a blade of grass—resurrecting.

I returned to Júzò for the first time seven years later. "We heard that you had died in a terrible automobile accident," Lichink'æpò complained with some indignation, for I had not written. Having appointed himself warden of my health years before, he immediately walked up the mountain to gather medicinal plants to boil into a bitter stew. My hepatitis-ridden liver was better, he said, but my hair was still the color of infertile mud: it should be black and glossy as a goat's pelt. Àp'ìmà asked if I had written my book about death ritual. I had written about the valley's former rotating headmanship system instead, I confessed, a topic in which she had little interest. We sat in the graveyard for three afternoons while she once again talked me carefully through each step of every major funeral occasion. "I suppose you lost your notebooks from years ago," she said kindly. "Write all this down and arrange it, and you will finally have your book." I asked Lichink'æp'ò about Li Bicong. "He died about two years after you left," he said. He paused for a long time. "People say that you paid him a lot of money for that chant and took it away. Some people say that perhaps his tutelary spirit didn't like that." Horrified, I said nothing. "Too bad you didn't write that book," he said after another long silence.

I didn't see Àp'ìmà again: she died in 2004 at the age of ninety-four. I was not present for her funerals, which I trust were crowded and noisy, with meticulous attention to procedure. The old *àpipò* who had revived Tenth-Month Sacrifice at Wòdɔwò also died, and the ritual seemed to have died with him. No one could say if it was practiced anywhere else. Lichink'æp'ò and Lichink'æmo took advantage of the resettlement plan that transferred many of Júzò's households to Yongren County's arid lowlands. I visited them in 2012 in their tiny new village home, where they had pocked the courtyard with young fruit trees, and they took me to their son's large, modern house in the county town. Together, we went up to Júzò, where we spent a few weeks attending funerals and walking about chatting with old friends. We reminded each other of the two great chants we had recorded so many years before. "If there are any treasures from that place, those two *nèpi* are the greatest," Lichink'æp'ò said, repeating a formula used so often by people who assumed the verses they were talking about had been lost forever. He had not played his tapes of the great chants for years. "I need to work on them. I need to arrange them," he said. I knew exactly what he meant.

A Method

I sat on Li Bicong's pile of verses for many years. It held little interest for me. It was huge, unwieldy, difficult, and repetitive. And it seemed to belong entirely to a time before the energizing dynamic between socialist action and ritual form that fascinated me had emerged. A select few verses made their way into a publication or two, but mostly the chants sat on a shelf as a pile of tapes and notebooks. After Àp'ìmà's death, the knowledge that Lichink'æp'ò and I were now sole custodians of these verses troubled me. Yet the obligation this placed me under did not seem to be one that could ever properly be released. I knew enough about *nèpi* to understand that these verses were nothing without a living speaker and a dead person to speak to. Perhaps a speaker might emerge? I had the recordings digitalized and scrubbed of wind noise, and I distributed compact discs to several *àpipò* in Júzò. But on subsequent visits I found that those old ritualists had passed away, and the recordings had disappeared, probably burned with other personal effects in the ceremony to send away wild ghosts. Perhaps if I placed the recordings and a full transcription on a website, some younger Lòloŋo-speaking person might take an interest? I eventually found time between other tasks to work on the *nèpi*. I cut the recordings into tens of thousands of lines and retranscribed each line, cleaning up the errors and inconsistencies in our original transcriptions. I worked through my notes and made new translations. I made tables of place names, plant names, spirit names, correlations, oppositions.

I spent hundreds of hours at this without knowing quite why. I felt compelled to engage with this pair of *nèpi*, to use or describe it in some way, even though the context for its proper use had long since disappeared. My first instinct was do with it what I had done with other smaller artifacts of ritual language from Júzò, mining it for insights into a shared way of seeing the world, using it as ethnographic and historical evidence of a common cultural milieu. I soon discovered many problems with this. The *nèpi*, in its two iterations, was unique. While a few verses had made their way into lament, most were very different in language and theme from any lament we had explored. On some levels their imagery of death resonated with the rich world of images that surrounded death in the late twentieth and early twenty-first centuries. But much of this imagery was very far from anything people in Júzò were still familiar with. In addition, the chants were hardly a shared resource. Even in the early 1950s when they were performed several times a day during the tenth month, they were the province of a learned few—a few *àpipʼò*, a few apprentices, a few interested men and women who sometimes sat nearby to see if they could extract some sense from the rapid flow of verse. I had no evidence that most people had known much about these *nèpi* at all, apart from the general idea that they were a capacious repository of knowledge about the things of the world and their origins. As I watched the *àpipʼò* work during Tenth-Month Sacrifice in the outlying village of Wòdɔwò, it became clear that his focal audience was not among the living and that it mattered little if any living person understood a word.

These difficulties in imagining that these *nèpi* might serve as evidence of a shared mode of engaging with a common world forced to awareness some things I had known about *nèpi* in general for a long time but had found convenient to ignore. While most *nèpi* tell stories and describe immaterial beings, they are primarily a kind of perlocutionary speech, intended to act rather than represent (Austin 1962). The foremost tasks of any *nèpi* are to construct in verse a materialization of a virtual being, to negotiate a contract with that being, and to transfer to its possession offerings that fulfill one side of that contract. In this light, a *nèpi* is merely an extension in verse of its accompanying *nègu* (chapter 2). A *nègu* locates the being in time and space, places it face to face with its living interlocutor, and it gives it bodily attributes such as eyes, ears, hands, and aprons that it can use to take possession of offerings. Like any body, a *nègu* is an assemblage of materialized social relations. But as a body intentionally constructed to serve a finite set of exchanges, it brings to light particular relations and emphasizes definite intentions of agents on either side of the exchange. The verses of the *nèpi* enliven this materialization, giving it moral, affective, and historical layers. These verses make explicit the relations the *nègu* reveals, and they place its assumed intentions in dialog with those of a ritualist and his clients. *Nègu* and *nèpi*, body and speech, neither effective without the other, are two halves of a material/semiotic whole, a local world that encompasses human and nonhuman beings.[3]

This is all to say that to use a *nèpi* as ethnographic or historical evidence of a shared mode of engaging with a common cultural world is to deliberately misconstrue what this form of speech is. Fortunately, the *nèpi* for Tenth-Month Sacrifice and Sleeping in the Forest repeatedly declare exactly what they are. In the introduction to each song of both chants, the *àpip'ò* tells the dead about the song to come. Before the first and longest song, which brings earth and sky into being, he sings:

5.4	ni p'ì shr p'ò shr mǜ wo ga	your grandfather's and grandmother's deaths have the sky
	bǜ shr bo̱ shr mi wo ga	great-grandfather's and grandmother's deaths have the earth
	ni shr mǜ ǹ wo	your death has no sky
	ni shr mi ǹ wo	your death has no earth
	ŋo ni mǜ mo mi k'à̱ chæ̀	I shall sing the sky and earth to you

Introducing the second song, which speaks of the rules that guide death ritual and the seeds from which mountainside forests spring, the *àpp'ò* uses the same verses, slightly modified.

5.5	ni p'ì shr p'ò shr dà wo ga	your grandfather's and grandmother's deaths have been spoken
	bǜ shr bo̱ shr mí wo ga	great-grandfather's and grandmother's deaths have been named
	ni shr dà ǹ wo	your death has not been spoken
	ni shr mí ǹ wo	your death has not been named
	ŋo ni ci̱ shŕ lò p'e chæ̀	I shall sing rules and seeds to you

3. For a comparative case with many similar attributes, see the discussion of Naxi dongba texts in Mueggler (2011b).

Each subsequent song is introduced in the same way: "I shall sing human creation to you," "I shall sing the emergence of fowl to you," "I shall sing discussions [of death] to you." The *nèpi* do not present themselves as describing the creation of the world and the emergence of its beings. They present themselves as using song to bring a world into being around the death of a couple, a world that the ancestors of the dead have already gained but that the dead will lack until the *àpipö*'s chanted intervention.

In this way, this pair of *nèpi* seem to demand a method that will show how they fashioned and elaborated a singular world rather than represented or reflected a shared world. A method that will take them, in effect, as a massive construction project, showing how, verse by verse, series by series, song by song, they assembled a world for their dead listeners to inhabit and threw bridges across to that world from the assembly of living beings gathered on the hillside. That this was a virtual world made in speech for unseen listeners did not make it imaginary. Like any localized world created by any of the host of smaller *nèpi*, it was fashioned of relations and intentions, actualized in exchanges of gifts and words as well as in material forms that crop up in the world of people in the form of bodies for the dead: the ancestral effigy made of pine, chestnut, and bamboo, the great *bu* effigy for Tenth-Month Sacrifice assembled of pine and chestnut saplings, bamboo stalks, crossbow bolts, brine shrimp, and a dead squirrel and wrapped in cotton and hemp cloth and layers of embroidered clothing, with a live blade of grass uprooted from the grave placed in its heart. These were the extensive forms (extensive because extended in space) of the dead body in the world fashioned by the *nèpi*, appearing in the world of the living as the foci of exchange. The dead's intensive bodies (intensive because their forms depended upon the degree of investment by the living) were bound together, spouse with spouse, swaddled in monkey skins and abandoned in a monkey's nest, clothed in silks and laid in an eagle's nest with piles of snake's blood and green bottle fly maggots, wrapped in quilts and discarded through the door of the underworld to face Yan Luo Wang, with eyes like millstones and arms like iron bars.[4]

---

4. While I use the traditional vocabulary of body and soul in places, the division between material and immaterial that it presupposes fails to hold in these two *nèpi*. The material bodies of the *nègu* are ritually enlivened by souls; the immaterial souls of the *nèpi* have many bodily properties: they are not similar to the singular yet impersonal souls (*yeho*) described in chapter 2. To replace this vocabulary, I have (somewhat playfully) imported the couplet extensive/intensive from Deleuze and Guattari (1987 [1980]). Delanda (2002) gives a cogent account of extensivity and intensivity as properties of difference in Deleuze, particularly in regard to the biological sciences.

In the chapters that follow I describe the two *nèpi* as they build a world for the dead to inhabit, trace the several possible fates of the dead in their intensive bodies, and delineate the origins and powers of the dead in their extensive bodies. Several ethical and methodological problems complicate this effort. I have tried to show already how my transaction with Li Bicong was conditioned by a long history of intimate violence: the threat of socialist persecution that forced the young ritualist and his family to flee their home in the early 1950s, the decades of hardship and illness he suffered as a result of being forbidden to perform the verses in their proper context, the poverty that forced him to accept our meager payment as an inducement to chant into our tape recorder, and the illness precipitated by this performance, which may have led to his death. Several forms of representational violence have also been involved. In context the verses were a rapid flow of sound chanted in a repetitive wavering melody, the sounds of each line building on sounds that precede and follow it. Our procedure of slowing the flow down, taking lines one by one, fixing a chain of phonetic values for each, and producing a gloss for each line in ordinary Lòloŋo, Chinese, and English produced another object whose relation to the verses Li Bicong may have chanted before his flight from Júzò is merely hypothetical. In context the *nèpi* were conversations between their enunciator and a dead audience, with a few bystanders listening in. To present the transcriptions and glosses produced from our recordings in the form of a publication for an English-reading audience, whose dead take quite different forms, distances each inscribed line yet further from a hypothetical contextualized vocal origin. All this may seem too obvious to recount, but making it explicit, even if in this perfunctory way, seems to be among the obligations I incurred when I recorded these verses.

Beyond the distorting procedures of recording, transcribing, translating, and inscribing, many further issues of presentation remain. How might these *nèpi*, even thus transformed, be presented with an eye to accuracy and comprehensiveness? A full transcription and translation would prove utterly inadequate. In the first place it would be unreadable. We have no established habits to guide an encounter with such a text, since we no longer construct linguistic objects, written or spoken, in any form analogous to that of these *nèpi*. To take only the most obvious issue, how might you read full transcriptions and glosses of the opening and concluding segments of each of the *nèpi*'s songs, repeated with some variation nearly a hundred times? The only possible answer is that you could not read them: you could only look them over the first two or three times they are presented and skip all subsequent iterations. Yet this repetition is the vital frame or mold (*kà ca*) of the *nèpi* from which various series emerge to constitute the world and its beings. The repetition must be described, and a mere full transcription and translation is not an adequate description. It is obvious that this descriptive effort must engage actively with what, to borrow Strathern's words, is the "technical problem" that anthropology faces: "how to create an awareness of different social worlds when all at one's disposal is terms which belong to one's own" (Strathern 1990, 91). To seek the principles of construction that animate the world of these *nèpi* is to replicate this problem at a second level. For we must begin with the assumption that these are *not* the same principles that found the social world of human beings, the *ts'ɔmi*, or "world of people." Much like anthropology, the *nèpi* were staged engagements in which intellectuals created, through texts, social worlds of difference, worlds of others. And the *nèpi* were reflexive about the terms of this engagement. Among their topics, resolutely pursued, was the question of how the world of people and the world of dead others intersected, how the boundaries that divided them could be traversed. The dead have no mouths; how can we hear them? What is their language? How can we know how they live, how their bodies, seen and unseen, are made, what are their fates? In many ways the *nèpi* are skilled attempts to engage the dead in conversation, to observe their interactions, to divine their intentions, to somehow piece inadequate fragments of insight together into a comprehensive account of their worlds and lives, echoing the foundational problem of anthropology. My task is to describe the world the *nèpi* fashioned as a world of encounter between speaking *àpipʼò* and dead others while hoping to catch some glimpses of who those others are ultimately found to be.

Two Procedures

Li Bicong's performance of Tenth-Month Sacrifice is made of forty-eight sections that, following the vocabulary of the *nèpi*, I will call songs (*chæ̀*). Eleven songs are unique to this *nèpi*, not shared with Sleeping in the Forest. The latter has forty-seven songs, ten belonging to it alone. Thus, there are fifty-eight unique songs, considerably short of the seventy-two each chant was reputed to have. Thirty-seven of these are shared, though often one version or the other is longer or more elaborate. After he sang the *nèpi*, Li Bicong rehearsed the songs' titles for us (also included in each song) and made it clear that the final six songs he had performed were out of order: they were to be performed at particular times during the ritual, while clearing a space and constructing an effigy for the dead. Beyond this division, the *nèpi* seems to fall naturally into three parts, which overlap to a degree. The first, to which chapter 6 is devoted, constructs the world. The second, the topic of chapter 7, shapes the intensive, immaterial bodies of the dead. The third, described in chapter 8, theorizes their extensive, material bodies.

In describing the *nèpi* I follow two contrived procedures, which both break down at specific points during my presentation. First, I endeavor to take the songs in the order of their performance (which sometimes varies between the two versions), and I mention the title of every song and quote from most. In chapters 6 and 8, where I follow this procedure with only a few exceptions, it has forced me to confront songs that interfere with my readings and sometimes to abandon or modify particular analytic efforts. In chapter 7, about the architecture of intensive bodies, this procedure turns out to be inappropriate. This middle section of the two *nèpi* is built of four sets of songs that are rigorously parallel to each other. These sets are distributed through the flow of songs with other songs intervening between them. My presentation follows the order of parallel sets rather than the order of performance.

Second, I endeavor to show the process by which the *nèpi* constructs a world, assembles an architecture for souls, and theorizes the construction of bodies, without making many statements about how this material illuminates a world that Júzò residents might be assumed to share with the interlocutors in this event: the *àpipò* and the dead. When I do bring in ethnographic material from outside the world of the *nepi*, it is to advance my interpretation of the text, rather than vice versa. And this material is of a similar order as the *nèpi*: stories and statements intended to shed light on particular songs. Admittedly this already blurs my artificial boundary between the world of the *nèpi* and what lies outside it. Still, even if unevenly maintained, this boundary forces me to attempt to understand the world of the dead almost entirely as presented in the *nèpi*. I see this as an effort to take the dead on their own terms, for the terms of the *nèpi* are the only ones they have in this context. While the chants are practically oriented, intended to extract from the dead what the living need, they are also sympathetic dialogs. As the *nèpi* repeatedly state, the dead have ears to hear speeches, eyes to see gifts, and aprons to gather offerings, but they have no mouths with which to speak. They speak only through others' mouths—usually a very bad thing: the madness of the possessed. Yet the *àpipò*'s tutelary spirit, who is arguably the agent of his speech, is a comrade of the dead, hailing from their own land, convening with them in the "fine places of the spirit world, the gathering places of the ghost world." While in the repeated opening and closing verses of each song, the *àpipò* speaks on his own behalf and on behalf of the living, the middle verses come from the land of the dead and may be seen as speech in which the dead have a part.

This procedure of bounding the *nèpi* in order to listen more closely to what the dead may have to say in it reaches its limit in my presentation of the third part of the chant in chapter 8. This part is largely concerned with the origin and construction of the two extensive bodies of the dead: the ancestral effigy and the great *bu* to which the *àpip̀ò* directs most of his speech. This is where the content of the songs intersects with the world of the living in the most concrete way, as ritual participants move the ancestral effigy from its home to the ritual ground and back and gather the dead soul from the mountainside in the form of materials for constructing the *bu*. This intersection gives me the opportunity to briefly outline the course of ritual action in Tenth-Month Sacrifice and Sleeping in the Forest. The focus of this outline is the movement of the two extensive bodies of the dead, rather than exchanges, laments, and other kinds of ritual action, which mostly repeat themes already explored in previous chapters. The intent, again, is to keep the dead, now in their material form, at the center of description.

Conclusion: A Politics of the Other

In 2012, I walked by myself up to Daomaidi, straying off the fading path several times. My friends had warned me that I would find nothing there. The entire hamlet had accepted the government's offer of roads, water, and electricity, abandoned their houses and land, and scattered to several new villages in the lowlands. The houses were but piles of mud bricks and old wooden shingles, for their timbers had been hauled down the mountain to be reused. After searching for a while, I found the courtyard where Li Bicong had lived with his wife. I knew it was his because of the great pine tree that still stood directly above it on the mountainside surrounded by a ring of stones: the *misi* the *àpip̀ò* had set up in the late 1950s to watch over his house and those of his sons, to protect them from harm and to preserve him from the periodic bouts of pain that afflicted him, brought on by the huge store of words he had been given and, for decades, forbidden to speak.

I have suggested these words were a burden to Li Bicong, their final enunciator: that the socialist politics of iconoclasm that forbade him to enunciate these verses in context forced them inside him, as it were, making him ill and eventually killing him. But it is also likely that the chants were an important resource for him, for the politics of the other they outline, while despotic at its core, is also abundantly creative. As chapter 7 will show, squeezed between the building blocks of a regime that makes deliberate, instrumental use of dead others are possibilities for creativity, power, flight, and escape. Li Bicong effected an escape of his own, reaffirming his power to speak, though covertly, by leaving Júzò for a new mountain home under the shadow of his *misi*, his ancestral progenitor. It is possible that the political vision outlined in these chants, absorbed through years of repetition and elaboration and performed every year in his exile for his tutelary spirit, also sustained him, affirming possibilities for developing the personal powers he needed to build a new life and fight off the physical and mental illnesses that destroyed his peers. Political relations with the dead found and sustain politics among the living: there is no politics that is not also a politics for the dead.

6

Earth Work

The first part of Li Bicong's performance of the *nèpi̠*, or great chant, for Tenth-Month Sacrifice and Sleeping in the Forest, comprising twelve songs, is about the genesis of the world and the possibility of human persons. Within the framework of nearly identical introductory and concluding segments, the songs begin with first principles. The smallest unit of matter is a single active relation: earth reflects sky, sky reflects earth. But even this atom is not self-contained. Its activity cannot even be named without bringing in other creatures in other relations: the eagle, the sky's organ of sight, looks at the earth; the serpent, the eyes of the earth, looks at the sky; and both eagle and serpent are agents of death. The force of every active relation generates further relations until an ordered series is produced. The activity of series is always to come into an ordering relation with further series, and this activity multiplies until a world of creatures, powers, and acts is delineated along two axes. A vertical axis extends from sky to earth, along which pain and death descend. A horizontal axis extends along the earth's surface, along which political and historical geography come into being. At the intersection of these two axes is the human person—the dead person.

The songs are deliberately ordered. Li Bicong made this clear when, after his performance, he listed the names of songs in order, the scaffolding of the *nèpi̠* that is memorized as a first step in learning the chant. This serial order unfolds in the space and time of the world the *nèpi̠* fashions. In space, it produces vertical and horizontal axes that are the posts and beams that support this world of creatures, powers, and acts. In time, it creates causal series, songs that set conditions out of which subsequent acts may emerge. The way lament speaks of agricultural labor provides a precise analog. Once manure is

spread, the fields may be plowed; once plowed, they may be harrowed; once
harrowed, they may be flooded; once paddies are flooded, rice seed may be
sowed; and so on. The *nèpi* creates similar chains. Once sky and earth are fashioned, they may be connected with a vertical axis. Once earth and sky relate
to each other, there can be sacrifice. Once sacrifice is possible, it can be used
to bring features of the earth into being, including rocks, cliffs, rivers, and
markets. Once these spatial foundations for social relations are in place, then
the rules for negotiated exchange between material and immaterial beings
may be sowed. Once the rules and procedures of ritual action are cultivated,
human persons can emerge. Once persons emerge, human bodies can come
into being. Once bodies exist, then the earth's horizontal dimension—its
human geography, embedded with human histories—takes shape. This is a
deeply simplified account, for every movement requires series of beings acting upon and organizing further series. Yet it is the serial order of the arc of
genesis that I wish to emphasize as we begin, an order that may be schema-
tized still further: difference ⇒ affinity ⇒ persons ⇒ bodies ⇒ geographies.

Frames

Each song of the Tenth-Month Sacrifice and Sleeping in the Forest *nèpi* begins
and ends with segments that are mostly though not entirely identical. If we
think of the repetitive verses of these chants as building a world as one might
build a house, then these introductory and concluding segments are like the
intricate cross-tied structure of posts, beams, struts, and purlins that one raises
to support the mud-brick walls and tile-and-girder roof in the tailiang framing
system that still guides construction of all houses in Júzò (Knapp 1990). These
conventional frames perform the foundational work common to all *nèpi*. They
call up a relation between particular living bodies and an immaterial being;
they concentrate that being's senses on a set of offerings (including the relational process of creating and presenting offerings); they demand the proper
return for these offerings; and they dissolve or release the focus on the relation
in question. Since these were funeral *nèpi*, the relation was between a dead couple and various living kin and friends; the offerings were goats, rice loaves, water, tears, and words, and the proper return was growth and fertility for living
beings. As argued in chapter 3, funeral participants used exchange to create a
formal image of all the social relations assumed to compose the dead person
in life, within the rectilinear form of the courtyard. The introductory and concluding segments of these songs work over this familiar ground once again.
But the verses they frame turn this rectilinear form inside out to open into a
world beyond the domestic frame of social relations among living beings—the

world of earth and sky; animals, birds, and insects; arrows, words, and forces. The primary task of the verses within these frames is to line up beings in series and put them in motion, so they might affect other beings and series of beings. This world, the world of the *nèpi*, is only accessible *from within* this relation that frames each song of the *nèpi*, the relation of the living with the dead and all it entails.

Let's look briefly at this framework. We have seen much of the introductory segment already. The introduction to each song begins with excerpt 5.3, where the *àpipò* declares his presence, calls attention to the bag of chaff swinging from his staff like a bull's testicles, and evokes the world arrayed before him: shady side and sunny side, the heavens of which he is the son, the ghost officials squatting beneath earthly trees. Then, in verses present in Sleeping in the Forest but absent from Tenth-Month Sacrifice, the *àpipò* describes the harm that has come to living descendants as a result of their neglect of the dead. (Sleeping in the Forest was often prompted by illness or absence of flourishing in a grandchild's household, signs that this final offering could no longer be put off.)

6.1	mùu ne chì ni pọ	harm floats in the sky
	mùu ne pọ lɔ bɔ	harm drops from the sky
	mi ne chì ni tọ	omens lie on the earth
	mi ne tọ lɔ bɔ . . .	omens roll from the earth . . .
	à sà chì wú chì ka t'e	to his entire head
	chì kə chì ní t'e	his torso and heart
	pọ jo rɔ chì væ̀	harm comes to his family
	jo do rɔ̀ chì kạ	centers on his room
	lò mò rɔ̀ chì he	on the ox of his house
	he sɔ́ rɔ̀ chì tsọ	his house has tilted
	pọ sɔ́ rɔ̀ chì væ̀	his hive has split

The *àpipò* then addresses the dead couple by their birth names, with which no one has hailed them since childhood, pleading with them not to be angry at this necessary insolence. He announces the name of the song he is about to sing (as in excerpts 5.4 and 5.5), and he invokes his bell and felt hat (excerpt 5.2). He describes the scene around him, with kin gathered to give the dead their gifts of grain and meat, in much the same terms as the laments of the 1990s, considered in chapter 4, even using some of the same language, evidence of mutual borrowing. The introduction ends with verses that assure the dead that all preparations for this funeral have been made. Years, months, and days have been counted to ascertain the auspicious day, grain and drink have been bought; wine and rice have been prepared; nothing has been borrowed or rented.

6.2	no shó ni lɔ tsɔ̀	you suffered pain
	no shó tsˀì kə̀ gə̀	we gave you medicine for your pain
	shr shó ni lɔ tsɔ̀	you suffered death
	shr shó ma ru gə̀	we give you a funeral for your death
	nɛ́ jɔ vi tˀè pˀi ga	we've spent a sea of wealth
	hæ tˀè tu̧ tsɔ̀ bò tˀè gə̀	driven away thousands of strange things
	nó jɔ sə tu̧ gə̀ jo mo	thousands more block your road

The concluding segment, chanted at a scathing pace, begins with verses that offer the song just sung to the dead. The conclusion parallels the introduction to an extent, framing each song in a-b-a form as a chiasmus, including verses that provide a counterpoint to the verses in excerpts 5.4 and 5.5, which announce the song to come.[1] Thus the conclusion to the first song, "song of sky and earth," *mùi mo mi kà chæ*, begins:

6.3	mùi wo mi wo ni ní shr	sky and earth for your heart's content
	mùi wo mi wo ni chì ju̧	sky and earth for your satisfaction
	mùi wo mi wo ni lè tǫ	sky and earth to grasp in your hands
	mùi wo mi wo ni ka̧ kˀò	sky and earth to take in your lap
	ni ka̧ kˀò yi mò	abundance returns to your lap

Like the parallel verses in the introduction of the song, these are modified in each song to reflect its title: "rules and seeds for your heart's content," and so on. The rest of the conclusion drives home this point: songs are what is being offered, and to the greatest extent possible. Other offerings are not even mentioned, beyond some generic references in the introduction, such to a "sea of wealth." The *nèpi* builds and offers a world, but it is in the words of the songs that the world has being. The rest of the repeated concluding segment characterizes this offering of sound with reference to the different capacities for sensation of the living and the dead:

| 6.4 | che dæ bǫ sa tsa | threshed rice straw on drying frames |
| | sa pˀə ŋò tsa gə̀ | three stacks on five frames |

·

1. On chiasmus, see especially Mary Douglas's (2007) illuminating discussion of "ring composition" and David McCraw's (2006) beautiful essay on chiasmus in old Chinese literature.

shì ho jo me mə	blind to the road in the seventh month
jɔ sụ me m mə	the living are not blind
jɔ́ ho jo nó bà	deaf to the road on the final month
jɔ sụ nó m bà	the living are not deaf
mó me mó mo yi	walk open eyed to the underworld
mó mo m mo mà	grow old forever there
wò vǽ ni lɔ sa nó	as my bell peals for you

Rice was once threshed by pairs of workers swinging flails in relentless contra-puntal rhythm. After threshing, the naked straw was bound into bundles and hung on frames similar to, but smaller than, the maize-drying racks mentioned in chapter 1.[2] Skillful farmers made the straw beautiful by making all their bundles equal in size and spacing them evenly, like words grouped in rhythmical lines of even lengths. The song specifies "five frames" because five is the preferred number of syllables in a line of verse. Poetic language encounters the problem of the dull senses of virtual beings, contrasting with the clear senses of the living. Only with aesthetic virtuosity rendered with indefatigable repetition can verse open the eyes and ears of the dead.

6.5	ǽ mǽ yè cạ	pitiful women untangling hemp
	bə lu dà ŋa gɔ̀	I offer you this reasonable speech
	thə lu dà ŋə gɔ̀	I paste this speech onto you
	ni p'à p'o ní t'à ŋǽ	don't turn your face back
	jr p'o lè t'à mì	don't wave as you go
	pe kə̣ wò vǽ ga	I have spoken with great skill
	t'ə kə̣ lo ci ga	discussed at great length
	ti a ló dɔ̀ ga gɔ̀	sat until my tongue has worn out
	t'ə lu nẹ ga gɔ̀	spoken with great depth
	ni gə gə sa sa yi[3]	now you go happily on

And then finally the name of the song once again:

6.6	mừ mo mi k'à chǽ	I've sung of sky and earth

The work of smoothing the mass of fibers produced by soaking and pounding hemp stalks is like the work of speaking, arranging one's words to form a smooth, ordered flow. It is the task of poetic speech to make the world as

---

2. Electrical threshers, used with gasoline powered generators, were introduced in the late 1980s.

3. While excerpts 6.4 and 6.5 are included in nearly every song, their verses do not always take the order presented here.

vivid and convincing as possible for the dead, whose ears are stopped with wax
and eyes are nearly blind. It is as Hume famously said of all the objects of the
world, "The belief or assent, which always attends the memory and senses, is
nothing but the vivacity of those perceptions they present; and that this alone
distinguishes them from the imagination" (1888 [1738], 86).

Songs of Genesis: Series

In the first song, the "song of sky and earth," *mù mo mi kà chæ̀*, the primordial
acts are seeing (*hɔ*) and looking (*ma*). Seeing brings into being the axis on
which sky and earth will hang. This seeing is not located in the dull senses of
the dead nor the bright senses of the living but in primordial forces animated
by serpent and eagle.

6.7   cæ ne rɔ̀ à le   that boa, he
      je nà mi lɔ je   lies coiled in fields
      ja̱ k'ù ti̱ t'è je   slithers into dry canals
          wú ǹ chæ̀ ǹ do   cannot but raise his head
          wú chæ̀ mù lɔ hɔ   raises his head to see the sky
            mù lɔ mù po̱ ma   looks at the sky's form
               sa po̱ kə po̱ ma ti̱ yi   three times, nine times, he
                                    looks and creeps on

    æ̀ jé rɔ̀ à le   that eagle, he
      vá nà mù lɔ vá   circles in the sky
      vá lɔ t'à mo ŋə mo wú t'è nò circles over the tips of pines and cedars
          wú ǹ chæ̀ ǹ do   cannot but raise his head
          wú chæ̀ mi lɔ hɔ   raises his head to see the earth
            mi lɔ mi po̱ ma   looks at the earth's form
            mi po̱ shɨ̀ po̱ ma   looks at its form seven times
              shɨ̀ po̱ ma te yi   looks seven times and
                                 soars on

Serpent and eagle are images of impending death. Those who study omens
know that to run head on upon a boa (*cæ ne*, literally "black snake"), or to
come upon one boa entangled with another, is to know that a death will occur soon in one's own household. Àp'ìmà took note of the line "three times,
nine times, he looks and creeps on" as especially evocative, calling to mind
the image of a boa cleaving a clump of ferns as it slithers through, a certain
omen of death. The syllable *po̱* repeated in the final two lines of the first stanza
and the final three lines of the second stanza, which I have translated both as
"form" and as a marker for the number of times that boa and eagle look, is also

the word for harm brought by an omen (as in excerpt 6.1). Thus, an alternate translation for the line that struck Àp'ìmà might be "three harms, nine harms, he looks and creeps on," where *pǫ*, harm, is an actual cause of death. Serpent and eagle index the two ultimate destinations of the dead, the underworld and the sky. In them, the earth and sky reflect each other in a world shot through with looking and seeing.

Genesis is about beings, powers, and acts. First, measuring:

6.8	mùù lə sụ ǹ jɔ	no one to measure the sky
	bùù hɔ̀ mùù lə sụ	flying ants measured the sky
	mi lə sụ ǹ jɔ	no one to measure the earth
	chà wò mi lə sụ	dragonflies measured the earth

And then the varied processes of making:

6.9	a ts'a mùù k'a ca?	what was the sky's mold?
	ná chì mùù k'a ca	a spiderweb was the sky's mold
	a ts'a mùù nà cho?	what patched the sky?
	tị pu mùù nà cho	white clouds patched the sky
	a ts'a mùù gɔ̀ vὲ?	what stitched the sky?
	t'ὲ ce mùù gɔ̀ vὲ	pine needles stitched the sky
	a ts'a mùù gɔ̀ jẹ?	what was the sky's thread?
	ná chì mùù gɔ̀ jẹ	spiderwebs were the sky's thread
	a ts'a mi nà cho?	what patched the earth?
	chì sὲ mi nà cho	gourd vines patched the earth
	a ts'a mi gɔ̀ jẹ?	what was the earth's thread?
	jẹ và mi gɔ̀ jẹ	vines were the earth's thread
	a ts'a mi gɔ̀ vὲ?	what were the earth's needles?
	lò cí mi gɔ̀ vὲ	thistles were the earth's needles
	mi nà mi wo ga	thus the earth was patched

Already, the principles for the world's construction begin to emerge. A series of beings (dragonflies, spiderwebs, clouds, pine needles, vines), a series of acts (measuring, molding, patching, stitching). Another series of beings (flying ants, gourd vines, vines, thistles), the same series of acts. An insistent parataxis, where each being is merely a name, placed beside other names, granted a glimmer of existence as a negatively defined place in a relational series (as in the structuralisms of Saussure and Levi-Strauss). Yet no series stands alone: each becomes a series only in articulation with others, and through this articulation each being gains a certain power or capacity. And the whole series is structured internally and externally in this articulation, sets of beings taking form only as correlated with structured sets of acts and vice versa. Finally, the two series are coordinated with a third series (earth and sky), which emerges into being through their initial articulation.

Who does the making? Men and women, actualizing capacities that typify their genders:

6.10   à sà mù̀ pẹ sụ   who made the sky?
         chò p'ò mù̀ pẹ sụ   six men made the sky
      à sà mi pẹ sụ   who made the earth?
         chò mo mi pẹ sụ   six women made the earth

      zò pẹ zò nị vằ   the sons had reckless hearts
         mà sụ sú và tị   the elders sat and wrote
         yæ sụ sú bo tị   the youngsters sat and drew
         tsú tsɨ hò chằ tị   sat with a table full of meat

      zò pẹ zò nị vằ   the sons had reckless hearts
         zò ní vằ jr mo   blame their reckless hearts
            mù̀ pẹ mù̀ yæ wo   they made the sky too small

      né pẹ né nị yæ   the daughters had timid hearts
         k'a má tɔ chɨ̀ mo   back baskets wet with sweat
         pæ p'ì wú tæ mo   head straps worn ragged
            nạ chì wò jù mo lu pẹ   noses running with snot
             mi pẹ mi vằ wo   they made the earth too big

Since the women worked too hard and the men did not work hard enough, the sky was too small to fit over the earth. They all thought about what to do, the men by discussing, the women by laboring. They sent three pairs of anteaters to dig back the earth's head, three pairs of boas to tug back the earth's tendons, three pairs of antelope to roll back the earth's corners, and three pairs of ants to nibble back the earth's length. Now the sky fit the earth, though the sky was split by lightning and the earth was fissured by earthquakes and crumpled into mountains, leaving no peace in the sky and no place to lie down on the earth.

The agency of this emergent, recursive self-organization is thoroughly dispersed. It is the generative friction of men and women that powers the process of genesis. But again it is a series (six) of men correlated with a series (six, again) of women (twelve is the universe's foundational number and basis of all astrological calculation). These series are not agents so much as different affects that actualize differential capacities—the recklessness (nị vằ, big hearts) that gives rise to laziness, writing, and discussion; the timidity (nị yằ, small hearts) that gives rise to diligence, sweat, and suffering. The energy of these differences creates another series of beings (anteaters, boas, antelope, ants) articulated with another series of acts (digging, tugging, rolling, nibbling) and with yet another series comprising the body of the earth (head, tendons, corners, length). If these series (and there will be many more) amount to a system of classification, this system is founded on, as Deleuze put it in a lecture on Spinoza, "what a body can do" rather than Aristotelian concepts of genus and species. "A body must be defined as the ensemble of relations that compose it," Deleuze added, "or, *what amounts to exactly the same thing*, by its power to be affected" (2014 [1978]). Anteaters, boas, antelope, and ants become a kind through their power to act on the matter of the emergent earth. Such powers to affect and to be affected are the relations that compose these beings: series articulated with other series. As for the series men and women, the differences between what a male body can do (sit, write, discuss) and what a female body can do (labor, sweat, suffer) crumples the earth and splits the sky, leaving no space to lie down below and no peace above. Still, because these initial series are made up of men and women, it might appear that earth and sky are brought into this friction-filled generative correspondence by a primordial principle of affinity, of negotiated alliances between groups.

One ethnographic analogue might appear to be the "grand unified theory" that Viveiros de Castro has offered as an abstract description of kinship in the Amazon (2001). Viveiros de Castro's theory is concerned with the play between what is given and what is made, on the principle that "no province of human experience is (given as) entirely constructed; something must be (construed as) given" (2001, 19). Viveiros de Castro's argument begins with the principle that in Amazonia affinal relations hierarchically encompass consanguineal relations; affinity is the generic, unmarked, given form of relation, to the specific, marked, constructed form of consanguinity. This is why relations with others in Amazonia are always expressed in the idiom of affinity. "Guests and friends as much as foreigners and enemies, political allies or clients as much as trade partners or ritual associates, animals as much as spirits, all these kinds of beings bathe, so to speak, in affinity. They are conceived either as generic affines or as marked versions—sometimes inversions—of affines" (2001, 23). Kinship is made by "extruding" actual affinity out of the relational field of potential affinity—actual marriage out of potential relatedness—and the marked, specific form of consanguinity is made to appear out of these actual affinal relations.

Does the generative friction between male and female bodies that sparks genesis bespeak a relational field structured by the principle of affinity, as the virtual, given background out of which every actual, constructed form of relation—in particular the consanguineal relations necessary to the production of kinship—may then be made to emerge? Consider a parallel story of genesis, the story of the flood to which chapter 5 made glancing reference. A brother and sister hide in a gourd together to survive the great flood that wipes the earth clean. Grandmother Wosomo (Guanyin) tells them to farm grain and raise sons and daughters, but they are ashamed. So they begin the work of correlation, articulating their capacities in series with the capacities of other bodies. He rolls the top of the millstone (*nip'ə*) down that slope, she the bottom of the millstone (*nimo*) down this slope, and they roll together, top over bottom; he rolls the sieve down that slope, she the winnowing basket down this slope, and they roll together, sieve over winnowing basket. Then they cover her vagina with a leaf and play around. The leaf breaks, and they become husband and wife. After a three-year gestation, she gives birth to a chunk of meat, which they slice up and scatter about; each slice lands on an animal or plant, which becomes a person. Here, affinity appears to be "extruded" from a prior consanguinity, through the work of producing difference, in accordance with a bilateral cross-cousin marriage system, which transforms cross-sibling relations in one generation into affinal relations in the next. In light of this story, it makes as much sense to consider the six men and six women who create sky and earth as consanguines, cross-siblings, and potential affines who may be transformed into actual affines through the nurturing work of consanguinity.

In the world for the dead made in these verses, neither a potential affinity nor its logical opposite forms a background of relationality out of which actual relations, including the work of producing kin, might emerge. These stories are about series and the correlation of series: bodies, capacities, acts. Men are correlated with reckless hearts, writing and discussion, and the sky, women with timid hearts, sweat and suffering, and the earth, a brother with that slope, the top of the millstone, and the sieve, a sister with this slope, the bottom of the millstone, and the winnowing basket: these correlations create the series manwoman, brother-sister, husband-wife. The friction of one upon the other, man upon woman, sky upon earth, millstone upon millstone, sieve upon winnowing basket is what generates worlds and beings. No "principle" such as affinity is a given ground out of which all other relations emerge; the only given is difference: the work of correlation and motion transforms difference into being. After all, sky and earth begin not with the series six men, six women, to which we have been attending, but with the series flying ant, dragonfly, spider web, white cloud, pine needle, gourd vine, thistle. What is given is simply the infinite "pluralism of wild or untamed differences" that persists alongside all the simplifications and limitations of the manifest world (Deleuze 1994 [1968], 50).

A second creation story in the "song of sky and earth" is about sacrifice, butchery, and distribution. It begins with a deaf-mute (*à bà*) who raises "three pairs of white cattle, three pairs of black cattle, brindled cattle with colored faces and mouths, red cattle out front grazing up to the mountain peaks." He attempts to call the cattle (*lò*) to him but he has nothing with which to call them:[4]

6.11	a tsʼa lò nó du	with what did he call the cattle?
	tsʼò kʼa lò nó du	he called the cattle with salt
	tsʼò dù tsʼò pʼu ma	saw white salt at Tsʼòdù
	rɔ ló ŋa tsʼò ma	saw salt while herding sheep
	ní kæ tsʼò kʼa ma	saw salt flakes in the mud

Of course, salt once had enormous significance in the region. Tsʼòdù, literally "salt place," was the Lòloŋo name for Yanfeng 鹽豐, the administrative center of the region until the socialist period. The Ming state established a regular local government at Yanfeng to preserve the state salt monopoly at the important salt-well complex of Baiyanjing 白鹽井 (Guo 1968 [1922]). While most highland people in surrounding counties were governed indirectly through native hereditary chiefs, the Tiesuo Valley and its surrounding mountains lay within the pale of this local administration, which extended its direct governance over the valley after its residents were defeated militarily in 1573 (Ma 2014). Older people remembered their fathers telling stories of hiring on as muleteers to haul salt, in large cakes, from Tsʼòdù to the nearby centers of Dayao and Yongding.

The story of the deaf-mute finding salt at Tsʼòdù, a variation on the story of the origins of salt told in the introduction to this book, resonates with an anecdote recorded in the Ming dynasty, *Brief Account of Yunnan* (<u>Dianlue</u> 滇略), about the origins of the wells at Baiyanjing, reflecting a very old folk tale of wide regional distribution:

The stone ram is one <u>li</u> east of Yao'an. During the time of the Meng clan, Mr. Dong Ting's beloved daughter once herded goats there. A ram licked the earth, and when she tried to run it off it wouldn't go. She dug into the earth and discovered a salt spring, naming it White Sheep Well (Baiyangjing 白羊井). They built a temple to the goddess there and a bridge. The well was said to

---

4. In our transcription sessions, the noun *lò*, used in ordinary language to mean tiger, occasioned much discussion. Many people not familiar with ritual language, Àpʼìmà explained, might make the mistake of thinking that *lò* always means tiger, as it does in many places in this *nèpi*. And this popular story of creation is sometimes told in ordinary language as the sacrifice of a tiger. Yet the context makes it clear that in the *nèpi*, the sacrificial victim, is an ox—or rather a bovine of unspecified sex—not a monochrome water buffalo (*áà*), but an ox of the dry fields, which come in many colors.

belong to the stone sheep, the ram that licked the earth. Later it was given to
the temple to the goddess. That well is White Salt Well (Baiyanjing 白鹽井).
(Xie 1972 [1567–1624], <u>juan</u> 10, p. 10)[5]

Having found brine, the deaf-mute could not render it into salt. He searched
along three rivers for a salt maker; he called, panting, through three cities,
visiting officials and kings; he called, panting, through three hamlets, visiting
farmers and herders; he called on those with great ability and on those with
no more ability than the dogs of flying ants (aphids); he called on thieves and
robbers; he called through three valleys; and he finally found a salt maker
to boil the brine. He used a cow's dewlap as a bag to hold the salt; he used a
leather strap to tie the bag; and he carried the salt home. He found a rhododendron tree (*memo si*) behind his house; he made pans of its trunk, bowls
of its heart, and spoons of its branches to set out the salt. He sat on his bed,
hemp strands between his toes, and made a rope, twisting with his right hand
while wrapping with his left. He set out rope snares around the roots of the
rhododendron tree. An ox approached but saw the rope and ran off; it turned
back and approached again. The ox stretched out its head, and a snare caught
its head; it moved its torso forward, and a snare caught its torso; it stepped
forward, and a snare caught its feet. Having caught the ox, the deaf-mute
had nothing with which to kill it. He borrowed a king's golden hammer, an
official's silver hammer, a shaman's wooden hammer, but he could not kill
the ox with these. He came back and made a club of pine; he made a club of
cedar, and he beat the ox to death. He made a cushion of ferns, and he used a
chopping knife from the ghost world (*nèmi*) and a killing knife from the spirit
world (*cími*) to butcher the ox:

6.12	ṁ bə lò hò ts'i nì bə	twelve portions of meat remained
	ṁ bə lò wú je	the ox's head remained
	lò wú mi wú lò	the head became the earth
	ṁ bə lò me je	the ox's eyes remained
	lò me kæ me lò	the eyes became the stars
	ṁ bə lò cè je	the ox's breath remained
	lò cè mi cè lò	the breath became the earth's wind
	ṁ bə lò sə̀ je	the ox's teeth remained
	lò sə̀ vé ji lò	the teeth became the cliffs
	ṁ bə lò lo je	the ox's saliva remained
	lò lo sá me lò	the saliva became the pine pitch

5. 羝羊石在姚安東一里許昔蒙氏時洞庭君愛女於此牧羊有羝餂土驅之不去掘地遂得
鹵泉名曰白羊井人即其地立聖母祠及開橋頭井得石羊云即餂土之羝後歸於聖母祠其井
即白鹽井也.

m bə lò ji je	the ox's skin remained
lò ji mi ji lò	the skin became the earth's skin
m̀ bə lò bùɨ je	the ox's fat remained
lò bùɨ mi bùɨ lò	the fat became the earth's fat
m̀ bə lò wu je	the ox's intestines remained
lò wu na shɨ́ lò	the intestines became the vines
m̀ bə lò ní je	the ox's heart remained
lò ní mi ní lò	the heart became the earth's heart
m̀ bə lò bə̀ je	the ox's hooves remained
lò bə̀ ló mo lò	the hooves became the rocks
ló mo lò do̱ ga	changed into the stones
m̀ bə lò sɨ̀ je	the ox's blood remained
lò sɨ̀ né yi lò	the blood became the rivers
m̀ bə lò mæ je	the ox's tail remained
lò mæ shɨ̀ na lò	the tail became the seven stars [the Big Dipper]
shɨ̀ na lò do̱ ga	changed into the seven stars
m̀ bə lò və̀ ts'i nì ts'ɨ́	twelve bones remained
cho tsí mùɨ lɔ do̱	six propped up the sky
cho tsí mi lɔ do̱	six supported the earth
mùɨ tə̀ hɔ yí ne	he saw the sky
mùɨ tə̀ mùɨ sa zhɔ	thunder and lightning
mi li hɔ yí ne	he saw the earth
mi li mi lì zhɔ	earthquakes and fissures

In general, anthropology has understood sacrifice as establishing or managing particular forms of (social) relations between humans and immaterial beings (gods, spirits, ancestors, ghosts). The deaf-mute's sacrifice of the ox, however, is prior to social relations. For all his calling along rivers and through cities, the deaf-mute is less a social being than merely a bearer of an intention to sacrifice. From this intention emerges series after series. Sacrifice is the series of relations among these series, defining a world of creatures and powers as varied as criminals and spoons, all structured by the series ox, salt, rope, rhododendron, hammer, knife, club. None of the series, not even the series of places where salt is found nor the series of kinds of people (officials, kings, farmers, shamans, etc.), involve the deaf-mute in any form of specifically social relation; they are merely among the beings and powers brought together to compose sacrifice. This sacrifice is not a gift or exchange, not from anyone or for anyone; it is the virtual *form* of sacrifice, which comes into being prior to actual instances of sacrifice that place persons in relation.

Butchered and distributed, the ox's body becomes a series that brings into being a corresponding world series. In his study of literary lists in the West, Umberto Eco notes that the list form tends to swing between a "poetics of 'everything included' and a poetics of 'etcetera,'" a sense of comprehensiveness quickly giving way to a sense of terminal incompleteness, giving lists a unique capacity to collect the world and gesture towards the infinite (2009, 7, 49). Before the sacrifice, as a virtual body, the world is potentially infinite, just as the living ox is composed of an infinity of unseen relations that make it live and move. Therefore, both may be covered with the briefest of lists, earth and sky for the world, and head, torso, and feet for the ox—each member of which contains an infinity of possible relations, a poetics of etcetera. Yet when the ox is killed and butchered, and rendered into an actual partitioned dead body, the list becomes comprehensive. Though it may not include every organ, the possibilities are strictly limited, a poetics of everything included, with a sense of terminal incompleteness giving way to a sense of comprehensiveness. Sacrifice places this comprehensive series in relation, part for part, with the series of the world, determining and structuring it. The creative act of killing and distribution transforms the virtual, infinite relations of a living body into actual, manifest relations between body parts. The virtual world (earth and sky) is brought into actual being (stars, wind, cliffs, and pine pitch) in exactly the same way that the body for the dead is brought into being by exchange, dismembered goat and rice loaf bodies matched part for part with relations that compose the dead human body. The world is made in the same way that dead bodies are made. The deaf-mute did not change into stone after he discovered salt, as did the ram in the *Brief Account of Yunnan* and the old man in the story told in the introduction. Instead, his analogue became stone—the virtual body of the world, immobilized as a dead body, an effigy.

Having distributed the ox's organs to create the world, the deaf-mute turned to distributing the ox's meat, of which twelve portions remained. Two portions became gathering places in the ghost and spirit worlds:

6.13   lò hò ts'i nì bə   of twelve portions of meat
           chì bə tə yí ne   he took one portion
              nè mi hò yí ne   and gave it to the ghost world
                 ŋǽ bò lò dọ bɔ   to become the field of ghosts

        lò hò ts'i nì bə   of twelve portions of meat
           chì bə tə yí ne   he took one portion
              cí mi ho yí ne   and gave it to the underworld
                 tị chɔ̀ lò dọ ga   to become the hall of spirits

The deaf-mute distributed the other portions across the earth to become those centers of exchange and negotiation that bring together varied series of goods and peoples, the markets:

6.14	lò hò ts'i nì bə	of twelve portions of meat
	chì bə tə yí ne	he took one portion
	ts'ò dù ho yí ne	and gave it to Tsʼòdù
	tsʼò ji lò dǫ ga	to become the salt market
	lò hò ts'i nì bə	of twelve portions of meat
	chì bə tə yí ne	he took one portion
	væ chò ho yí ne	and gave it to the buyers
	cæ ji lò dǫ ga	to become the gold market
	lò hò ts'i nì bə	of twelve portions of meat
	chì bə tə yí ne	he took one portion
	vè lí ho yí ne	and gave it to Vèlí
	vè ji lò dǫ ga	to become the pig market

And so on, to make twenty-two markets, including markets for pigs, chickens, horses, dogs, wine, crossbows, and water. This list of markets includes twelve named places that can be found on a present-day map of the region.

If killing the ox and distributing its organs creates the landscape of stars, cliffs, stones, and rivers—the landscape of immanent experience—distributing the meat creates the economic and political landscape that will eventually give rise to humans. The song makes it clear that the meat is not distributed to preexisting markets; its distribution brings the markets into being. The word for market used here, *ji*, is the short form of the fuller *vòji væji*, where *vò* is to sell and *væ* is to buy. *Ji* is clearly a cognate of the Chinese jie街 (pronounced gai in local Yunnan Chinese), which refers to a market street or periodic market. In other words, *ji* is a specific place where things are bought and sold in a face-to-face context. The root verb *lò* in the lines glossed "to become the salt market," "to become the gold market," and so on, means more precisely "to transform into," and the construction used, *lò dǫ ga*, gives a forceful sense of transformation and emergence. The markets spring into being out of the distributed portions of meat.

This economic and political landscape includes the specific places in the ghost world and spirit world where humans and unseen beings meet to negotiate contracts, together with the markets where humans exchange with humans. This landscape is quite narrowly delimited, extending west to the center of early twentieth-century local governance at Tsʼòdù/Yanfeng 鹽豐 and northeast to the closest city, Làjà/Dukou 度口, now a major industrial center. It includes the villages of Vèli/Yueli 月理 and T'esò/Tiesuo 鐵鎖, from which the Lip'ò ancestors of Júzò's Lòlopò migrated, as well as other, nearer villages and market towns. Most of these places have majority Lipò/Lipo populations, and all are within a few days walk; they are places to which most men of any experience would have traveled in the early twentieth century. The landscape that sacrifice creates contrasts with a much wider region explored in later songs. It is the catchment area within which, when exogamy proved necessary, one found daughters-in-law or sent excess sons.

Thus the sacrifice of the ox created the preconditions for human life and kinship. The deaf-mute's long labor of making salt, making a rope, snaring the ox, finding a hammer, killing the ox, finding a knife, and butchering the ox transformed the series of the living ox (head, torso, tail), with its multitude of unseen virtual relations, into the series of organs and portions. The deaf-mute distributed the organs to become the parts of the world, transforming the virtual world (sky, earth) into the actual world of immanent experience, an effigy whose every part embodied a relation or intention. He then distributed the portions of meat to create the conditions for social relations mediated by things. Markets embody the *form* of mediated social relations, just as the sacrifice of the ox is but the form of sacrifice; markets are prior to actual social relations in the same way the form of sacrifice is prior to actual instances of sacrifice. As an intentional act, sacrifice is a complex coordination of many different series, which must be articulated in order to fashion the world as an effigy and lay down the conditions for affinal relations. The next song shapes a further precondition for the emergence of human persons—the rules of ritual.

Song of Rules and Seeds: Ritual Origins

The "song of rules and seeds," *cì shŕ lò p̀e chœ*, establishes the origin of the rules and procedures of ritual action. The song begins, after the introductory frame, with the excerpt quoted in the introduction (0.3): "Who made these rules? A woman of seventy made these rules. Who made such fine rules? The little yellow mouse of the underworld made these fine rules."[6] *Cì*, which I gloss as "rules," condenses the phrase, *cìpe mope*, rules and procedures, used to refer to the sequences of effective action with which the conditions for communication and exchange with unseen beings are established. In Júzò, as in many Tibeto-Burman-speaking places on the Yunnan-Guizhou plateau,

---

6. Some *àpịpò* say that the "little yellow mouse of the underworld," *he mó cœ*, is the name of the wife of the younger brother of the king of the underworld, Mómi Yàlòwù or Yang Luo Wang.

speech about ritual action is elaborate, systematic, and highly reflexive.[7] However, not everyone is capable of such speech. Behind the scenes at every funeral ritual are elderly women seen as the ultimate authorities on the rules of
complex rites, directing the small acts that fall below the threshold of attention of the over-busy master of ceremonies, such as dressing the corpse or
preparing the correct numbers of small and large rice loaves. In every line of
excerpt 0.3, *cì*, or "rules" is followed by *shŕ*, "seeds," creating a compound that
combines both meanings. The seeds are of trees. Rules and seeds spread out
over the surface of the earth, the raw material out of which the actual bodies
of immaterial beings are fashioned. Both originate with the woman of seventy, who sows seeds in ranks and files over the slopes and valleys:

6.15	lí ho ŋò ho lɔ	in the fourth and fifth months
	cé ho sa tsà lɔ	three thunderstorms a day
	væ̀ lè sa tə shr	her left hand sowed three rows
	t'à mo ŋə mo sa je nə̀	three columns of pines and cedars grew
	rò lè sa tə shr	her right hand sowed three rows
	tsə mo ní mo sa je nè	three columns of coconut and poplar grew
	wò mo sa je shr	three columns up the mountainsides
	t'à mo ŋə mo sa je nə̀	three columns of pines and cedars
	bæ læ sa je shr	three columns over the plains
	bæ shi tsæ̀ mo sa je nə̀	three columns of Yunnan pear and apple-pear
	lɔ né sa je shr	three columns by the river
	tsə mo ní mo sa je nè	three columns of coconut and poplar
	hè lɔ sa je shr	three columns in the lowlands
	tè mo cá mo sa je nə̀	three columns of pigeon trees and barberry

The series of tree kinds (reminiscent of Chaucer's famous tree list in *The Ro-
maunt of the Rose*) is correlated with the series of geographical features. On
the mountaintops are the most social of trees, pines and cedars, which form
the material bodies of the most sympathetic and benign immaterial beings.
Descending into the valleys and along the rivers are less common trees, such
as coconut and poplar, used to mark the attributes and intentions of some less
benign beings. In the lowlands are Yunnan pear and apple-pear, which form
important parts of the bodies of the most fearsome beings of all, wild ghosts

---

7. Keane (1995) notes that the capacity for elaborate self-reflexive speech about ritual action seems to be characteristic of some places and nearly absent in others. Tomlinson (2004)
and Goodman (2003) reflect on some of the methodological consequences of such self-reflexive
eloquence among their informants, in relation to Bourdieu's foundational analysis of the production of ethnographic objects (Bourdieu 1977).

(*chènè*). Elsewhere in the *nèpi,* trees form a path from sky to earth on which death or harm descends. Here, they make the sky accessible to rules from the earth:

6.16	lí ho ŋò ho lɔ	in the fourth and fifth months
	cé ho sa tsà lɔ	three thunderstorms a day
	cé ho tsì shř tsi̱	seventy kinds of rain
	p'ì næ̀ mùɨ gò tæ	the rules apply to the sky
	na lè shì wù tæ	the spider spins up to the seven stars
	cí nɔ̀ na wo tsə	grass grows up the vines

In this song, rules—which are limiting determinate abstractions by nature—are materialized as generative seeds, clothing the earth with trees, pushing up from the earth to form bridges with the sky. In the final verse of the segment, the series of earth-handling beings from the "song of sky and earth" is deployed to form other bridges, down into the earth towards the underworld, and across the river from the shady side to the sunny side:

6.17	t'à k'æ̀ sa tsə p'ɔ̀	she sent three pairs of anteaters
	chì ŋɔ̀ ni thu bɔ̀	to dig a single tunnel
	cæ ne sa tsə p'ɔ̀	sent three pairs of boas
	ji gɔ̀ ǹ ŋə te	to swim across the river

The rules of ritual come into existence as articulating forms, linking sky with earth, world with underworld, this side with that side. Ritual rules are the seeds of trees, generative protobodies distributed in their millions over the earth, awaiting human intentional action to become effigies, the material bodies of ghosts and spirits.

Songs of Emergence: Humans and Chickens

The "song of sky and earth" and the "song of rules and seeds" create the conditions for human persons: earth, sky, sacrifice, the landscape of mediated relations, ritual form. Only after this foundation is built do humans come into existence. In the "song of human emergence," *bu go chæ̀,* humans appear not as singular beings but as a series of kinds, matched with characteristic acts or abilities. Actual valued human persons—pigeons or Lòlo—take form only at the end of the series, as those who "take the trouble to become people." The witty series of human kinds is worth quoting in its entirety, as it will become an important building block of the *nèpi:*

6.18	mo shr k̓o bò ka̱	hillsides choked with dead bamboo
	ka̱ p̓ò sa tsə go	three pairs of stubborn folk emerged
	bu go bu ǹ lò	people had not emerged
	chì dæ̀ chì pa ye̱	halting at every step
	pa ye̱ sa tsə go	three pairs of Dai emerged
	bu go bu ǹ lò	people had not emerged
	chì je p̓a lè ce̱	coats dangling, hands clasped
	ce p̓ò sa tsə go	three pairs of town Han emerged
	bu go bu ǹ lò	people had not emerged
	á nò wù kə lə fù	coax a dog with a bone
	fù p̓ò sa tsə go	three pairs of beggars emerged
	bu go bu ǹ lò	people had not emerged
	jè jí á chì kɔ	billy goats graze
	kú ju sa tsə go	three pairs of Han bumpkins emerged
	bu go bu ǹ lò	people had not emerged
	tè pi̱ tè jò go	crook-legged pigeons emerged
	tè mo sa tsə go	three pairs of pigeons emerged
	tè pi̱ tè lò lo	these pigeons, these Lòlo
	lò lo sa tsə go	three pairs of Lòlo emerged
	bu go nì pú lò	father and son emerged
	bu go te t̓è thə̀	took the trouble to become people
	bu go sa p̓ò lò	father and two sons emerged
	bu go te t̓è ha̱	stood as people in the river fields

The term for people used here, *bu*, distinguishes valued human persons from other living beings. (The alternative word for people is *ts'ɔ*, which distinguishes living humans from ghosts and spirits.) Like many series to come, this one takes apophatic form, arriving at a negative definition of valued human persons through elimination.[8] These characterizations are determined in part by the poetic form of this series, common in lament but confined in this *nèpi* to the series of human kinds. This form is similar to the chained verse of medieval popular French and English poetry or, closer to hand, the style of linked patronymics in which a father made the final syllable of his name the first syllable of his son's, once common among many Tibeto-Burman peoples in Yunnan

---

8. An illuminating comparison is Carol Anne Duffy's (2007) poems for children, "The Birds, the Fish and the Insects" and "The Fruits, the Vegetables, the Flowers and the Trees," analyzed by Debbie Pullinger (2014).

(Luo 1945).[9] In the variation in excerpt 6.18, the final one or two syllables of a couplet's first line are repeated as the first syllable or two of the second: "*mo shr k'o bò ka̱, ka̱ p'ò sa tsə go,* hillsides choked with bamboo, three pairs of stubborn folk emerged," the repeated sounds punctuating and emphasizing the names of the human kinds.

While some of these genera may appear to be ethnonyms (*Baye,* Dai) and others social categories (*Fùp'ò,* beggars), they are all actually of the same order. *Kap'ò,* stubborn folk, live in certain villages in lowland Yongren County and pass on their *Kap'ò* status to their progeny, and *Fùp'ò,* beggars, are drifting landless migrants from Sichuan. They are both human kinds in the same way as *Cep'ò,* urban Han. My interlocutors had excellent fun with this passage, miming the weary pace of lowland Dai climbing a steep mountain grade, pouring scorn on unmannered *Kúju,* rural Han of low morals, and ridiculing the arrogant swagger of citified *Cep'ò,* urban Han who walk with hands clasped behind their backs and jackets draped over their shoulders, sleeves dangling free. Human kinds are matched not only with characteristics but also implicitly with geographical locations. The series touches on various local populations on Júzò's periphery before coming to settle in the valley's center, father and son standing in the riverside fields like the beautiful and peaceable pairs of green imperial pigeons (*Ducula aenea*) that alight on paddy borders and terrace walls, cooing their low, ringing song (MacKinnon 2000, 137).

With the next song, parallelism extends for the first time beyond the levels of line and verse to place two songs in close relation. The parallel is announced in the songs' titles, *bu go chœ,* "song of human emergence," and *wo go chœ,* "song of the emergence of fowl," and carried through the defining series of these songs. The "song of the emergence of fowl" presents an apophatic list of birds: "three pairs of collared crows and black crows emerged, but they were not chickens; three pairs of green pigeons emerged, but they were not chickens; three pairs of geese emerged, but they were not chickens." Seriality and analogy intersect between the two songs. Valued human persons are

---

9. Luo Changpei's seminal article noted that the incidence of linked patronymics in the house of the Nanzhao rulers as well as in the Tibeto-Burman-speaking groups known as Naxi, Moso, Lolo, Akha, and Woni, strong evidence that the Nanzhao had not been a Tai state, as many Western scholars had argued, but had been ruled instead by Tibeto-Burman speakers (see Lloyd 2003 for a discussion). Luo also shows that the Gao 高 lineage of north central Yunnan—appointed native hereditary rulers of Yao'an Fu by the Qing—used linked patronymics (Luo 1945, 362–363). While ordinary speakers of the Central Ngwi languages of Lisu and Lipo (of which Lòloŋò spoken in Júzò is a dialect) are unlikely ever to have used such a system, my informants in the late twentieth century were familiar with linked patronymics as a custom of formerly aristocratic families of the region.

distinguished from Han, and domestic chickens from crows in series; human
persons and chickens are identified analogically across series.

After chickens emerge they differentiate, bringing into being another series:

6.19	wò go à lí go	where do chickens emerge?
	wò go kæ ka go	chickens emerge as a courtyard emerges
	wò go kæ t'è hǫ	chickens emerge standing in the courtyard
	wò tị dù m ma	no place for the hen to sit
	kæ ka mo t'è tị	it sits in the great courtyard
	he wú he mæ tị	it sits at the house's head and tail
	wò hǫ dù m ma	no place for the hen to stand
	dò jo bò t'è hǫ	it stands beside the path
	wò fu dù m ma	no place for the hen to lay
	tsa lè mo t'è fu	it lays in the barn loft
	pá p'u mo t'è fu	it lays in the white straw
	k'a má jè t'è fu	it lays in the back basket
	wò fu n ts'i t'i	it lays for twenty-one days
	wò mɔ́ n ts'i ni	it sits for twenty-two days
	wò je dù m ma	no place to cage the chicks
	pɔ́ t'u mo t'è t'è	cage them in a shit basket
	k'a má tsì t'è t'è	cage them a back basket
	wò zò tụ je ga	they drag their wings
	wò zò tụ k'à ga	their wings go bald

Through the generative and nurturing activities of chickens, the basket-strewn
courtyard and the surrounding domestic space of barn and paths emerge as
the great gathering place of humans, animals, and spirits. The busy lives of
chickens have finally cleared a place in the world for the activity of death. The
generative activity and enclosed domesticity of chickens make them analogous to valued human persons in many ways. But the courtyard is the stage
for this analogy, and death is its idiom. The courtyard is the place into which,
in later songs, the eagle will stoop again and again to snatch up a chick from
among the crowd, defining the arc of human death.

Songs of Discussion, Illness, and Death

In the *nèpi*, as in life, discussion (*tsɛ gu*) is the way kin show love and solicitude
for a dying person. To gather around a sickbed and negotiate carefully and
soberly the serious matters of who should contribute what to a dying loved

one's care and funerals is perhaps the most important way one displays, at a moment of deep crisis, the qualities of a true human person. These are often extremely contentious matters, especially among brothers, for while the brother who will act as *vedù* will inherit his parents' house and remaining land, the others also deserve a share of inheritance, a matter that may well have been left unresolved until the bedside discussion. Whether brothers continue as friends or become lifelong enemies, with all the innumerable consequences for relations among other kin, may well depend on the quality of discussion at a parent's deathbed. The "song of discussions," *tsɛ gu chæ*, brings two pairs of series to bear. The first is a series of beings paired with the places they inhabit:

6.20	mʉ̀ wú mʉ̀ tsɛ gu	discussions in the great sky
	ti p'u lɛ zò tsɛ ǹ gu	little and big clouds don't discuss
	mi wú mi tsɛ gu	discussions on the good earth
	ní p'u ní cæ tsɛ ǹ gu	white and yellow mud don't discuss
	yi wú yi tsɛ gu	discussions in the rivers
	yi shŕ yi ja tsɛ ǹ gu	whirlpools don't discuss
	ní wú ní tsɛ gu	discussions among the wild animals
	t'à lo hə lo tsɛ ǹ gu	rabbit and weasel don't discuss
	ŋa wú ŋa tsɛ gu	discussions among the bright birds
	mʉ̀ ŋa mʉ̀ he tsɛ ǹ gu	bats don't discuss
	bʉ̀ wú bʉ̀ tsɛ gu	discussions among the bugs
	bɯ t'ù tsɛ ǹ gu	mud larvae don't discuss

The second is the series of human kinds introduced in the "song of human emergence," including two not mentioned there:

6.21	mo shr á lè ve	dead bamboo in their hands
	ve pǒ tsɛ ǹ gu	procrastinators don't discuss
	kò dæ kò li̠ li̠	buckwheat threshing rods
	li pǒ tsɛ ǹ gu	Lipǒ don't discuss

Those who discuss are "those green pigeons, those Lòlo, father and sons, father and two sons." Illness is treated much the same. While the "song of discussions" begins by considering the possibility of murmuring negotiations among clouds and mud, the "song of illness," *no pe̠ chæ*, moves immediately to the series of human kinds before settling on those green pigeons, those Lòlo. Thus:

6.22	chì je p'a lè ce̠	coats dangling, hands clasped
	ce pǒ sa tsə no	three pairs of Han fell ill
	ni no ni ǹ ja̠	this was not your illness

And so on through the series. Yet illness does not stop with Lòlo fathers and sons. The song mentions the measures taken to curb illness and then the way, like an infected wound, it penetrates to the body's core:

6.23	no me 'e le le	you cried out when it hurt
	n no 'e le le	groaned when it did not hurt
	ŋò ho kǽ mæ̀ zò	fire grass in the fifth month
	tsì go pạ go tị go sa ni hɔ	we washed it, dressed it, waited three days
	tsì go pạ go tị go mo ǹ do	washed it, dressed it, no result
	nè mi á t'ò lɔ̀	chopping knife from the ghost world
	cí mi á t'ò sha	killing knife from the spirit world
	tsì go pạ go tị go sa ni no	we washed it, dressed it, waited three days
	tsì go pạ go tị go mo ǹ do	washed it, dressed it, no result
	ni ní no ní dɔ̀	the pain penetrated to your heart
	ni me no me ve	the pain carried to your eyes
	no me ve dọ ga	right to your eyes

Illness introduces an embryonic body series: heart, eyes. Yet the body comes into being only as an extension of other series: the series of sky, earth, river animals, birds, and bugs through which discussions make their way and the series of human kinds, with their implicit geography, through which discussions and illness proceed. It is as though first there are kinds and then only bodies: a body is the effect, the materialization in flesh, of the pain that courses through the series of kinds, settles onto green pigeons standing in the river fields, and then moves into their hearts and eyes.

The third of these three parallel songs is the "song of death," *shr pẹ chœ̀*. It is brief and simple, deploying only the series of human kinds—"halting at every step, three pairs of Dai died, not your companions in death"—until reaching "those green pigeons, those Lòlo, father and son, your companions in death." We might remember that each song ends with the same concluding lines, offering up the song to the dead: these three songs give the person's own discussions, illness, and death to him. The movement in all three songs is concentric. Discussions, illness, and death move inward towards a specific person and then into the interior of a body, becoming more concrete as they move. The songs offer not the idea of death but the specific social relations of *a* death. Inside the frame of these offerings, death has opened up a window through which to consider how a world might come into being. Later songs will widen this window, moving from the concentrated relations of *a* death to the impersonal idea of death as a force and a law.

Songs of Signs and Sealed Rooms

Lichink'æp'ò was a student of omens (*lot₂*). He spent many hours over many years teaching me how to observe courtyards, fields, and paths for signs of impending difficulty. One encounters omens with eyes and ears, and while these senses are one's own, the effects follow lines of established social relations. One sees and recognizes an omen, and as a result someone connected to one by kinship or residence, intimate or distant, will fall seriously ill or die. Omens are made by the actions and orientations of plants and animals in relation to my sight and hearing, as though an impending death opens up a subterranean network of correspondence among the world's beings. Yet the energy of omens travels slowly along this network. One does not stumble over a boa, fall from the path and die. Instead, the effect is more like a snake bite, the poison of which takes time to work. This is why the proper response to an omen is never to attempt to thwart death. It is to go home and begin preparations for a funeral—one's own, perhaps, but more likely that of another, someone close.

The "song of signs and omens," *lo yì t₂ yì chœ*, begins with an apophatic list of omens pertaining to nonhuman begins:

6.24	bɔ̀ hò á lí zò	dogs of flying ants
	lí zò sa tsə go	three pairs of puppies
	lí zò ŋo m bɛ	I speak not of puppies
	lí zò t₂ zò ŋo m bɛ	I speak not of dogs' omens

The signs that do pertain are more intimate: strange eddies in the currents of fertility and growth that flow through house, courtyard and field:

6.25	ni chi mo zò sa lu	your nanny bore three kids
	ŋɔ̀ mo zò nì lu	the cow bore two calves
	rɔ̀ mo zò nì lu	the ewe bore two lambs
	ho zò shɨ̀ lu	the little sow bore seven piglets
	vè jæ zò l̲i lu	the big sow bore four piglets
	sɨ k'ə wò p'ə lu	the cock crowed before midnight
	wò mo fu nò lu	the hen laid soft eggs
	wò p'ə bɛ ka̲ lu	the cock crowed half his call
	wò zò chæ̀ chæ̀ lu	the chicks stuck to the hen's breast

tsì shŕ zo che lu	the hemp stalks formed circles
he wò na̠ chi lu	spiderwebs under the eaves
jí sha jo chi lu	spiderwebs where the pigs are killed
lo yì to̠ tsí go	thus signs and omens formed

In a world where idea and affect are separate, omens would merely represent. Generated by some unseen agent (perhaps ancestors) in order to communicate with the living, they would merely portend coming death. In this world, however, omens are both ideas and affects. Omens are not generated by any transcendent agent; they are active beings in the world. And since the power of omens to represent is also a power to act, their communication of death brings death, which is why in excerpt 6.1, harm (*po̠*) and omens (*t̠o̠*) are parallel. In the world of the *nèpi*, all ideas are affects to some degree, and it is to that degree that they have the force of sense: to portend death is to bring death.

If death opens up subterranean paths along which the power to affect and be affected travels among the world's beings, death by violence, accident, suicide, or childbirth turns this power up full throttle until it saturates every being and act. Until the 1950s, people in Júzò stayed inside their houses for three days after hearing of a bad death anywhere in the valley. They barred the door to the courtyard, shut the wooden panels that ran along the fronts of their houses, filled the gaps between the boards with straw, and sealed the thresholds with lines of ash. Close kin were told to shoot three crossbow bolts out of the barn window and turn the millstone on the porch backwards three times. Elderly people told me about sitting in their sealed houses in the dark as children, hearing the howl of the wind outside, and knowing that this was the sound of *chènè*, the being produced by a violent death. In the days following such a death, nearly everything one encountered outside one's own courtyard could portend a death. Kin of the dead followed a series of proscriptions to avoid such omens. Women did not spin, weave, wash clothing, or use the pounder or millstone. Men did not cut wood with a knife or axe. Those in the dead person's household did not have sex. In the weeks that followed, particular acts were proscribed on particular zodiacal days: setting forth on a journey on the day of the dog, weaving on the day of the snake, washing on the day of the rabbit, and so on.

After the "song of signs and omens," the "song of sleeping in a sealed room," *he i'ù zo iso chìè*, sketched out the trajectory of the harm brought by ghosts of those who died badly. That harm is quick and violent, shooting like a bolt of lightning from the sky:

6.26   mù̀ ni lí wò pa   shoots from heaven's four sides
        mé ne lí p'æ tà   strikes the earth's four corners
        mé ne lí p'æ pa   shoots from the earth's four corners
        t'à mo ŋə mo wú t'è̀ tà   strikes the pines and cedars
        t'à mo ŋə mo wú t'è̀ pa   shoots from the pines and cedars
        bæ chr tsǽ mo wú t'è̀ tà   strikes the Yunnan pear and
                                                   apple-pear trees

The series continues, exactly parallel, through coconut and poplar trees, mulberry trees, barberry and pigeon trees, pine forests, grassy mountainsides, streams, rocky slopes, riversides, black rocks, a tiled roof, the roof beams, the wall of the granary, and the bamboo bed mat. Then the harm

6.27   mo cæ ŋə̀ t'è̀ pa   shoots from the bamboo bed mat
        à gə̀ rɔ̀ wú lɔ jɔ lụ ne   settles in the head of the beloved
        à gə̀ rɔ̀ kə lɔ chi lɔ wú lɔ   comes to the torso and feet of the
                                                   beloved
        ji lɔ lè̀ lɔ jɔ lụ ne   settles in his skin and his hands
        ni nà ŋa lo pe   it is thus you!

In the "song of sky and earth," earth and sky were consistently parallel, reflecting and opposing each other. In the "song of rules and trees," trees, vines, and grasses provided a support for the rules of ritual to climb from earth to sky, but this action was restricted and tentative. In the songs of discussion, illness, and death and now especially in the "song of sleeping in a sealed room," the world gains a pronounced vertical axis. In the latter song, series from previous songs (the series of trees, the series of mountains, rivers, and stones) are joined with new series (a house series, a body series) into a lengthy chain. Each subseries is organized by a vertical principle, trees that grow on mountains above those that grow in valleys, rocky slopes above black river rocks. The house is also clearly vertical: roof tiles, roof beams, granary wall, bamboo bed mat. And the body's complex verticality is reaffirmed: head, torso, feet, then outward to skin and hands. How is the body inserted into this upright cosmos? On the one hand, body parts belong to the same lengthy chain of series to which trees and rocks belong. They are characterized by their relations of contiguity in this chain: below the roof beam and next to other body parts. On the other hand, body parts have a different capacity to be affected than other links in the chain. Grassy slopes, black rocks, and roof beams are conduits for harm, which hits them and shoots on. Body parts stop the harm, which settles in them. In this way the body series reveals a different class of being than the tree or house series. In relation to a vertical cosmos, where earth and sky are joined, human bodies are defined by their capacity to be harmed: to suffer illness and death as a result of the energies that travel along relational links from being to being.

Road Songs

At death a lightning bolt strikes from above, forging the creatures of earth and sky into a chain of vertical series that terminate in the body. Brought into this world by illness and death, the body is a hinge between these vertical series and various horizontal series that move outward over the earth's surface, generating more creatures with more characteristic powers. Following the "song of the sealed room," the "song of driving off bugs and beasts," *bùu kà zò kà chæ̀*, evokes the stomping dance in which the brother-in-law's thief leads male kin around the coffin or effigy, trampling the ground and whooping to scatter all the beings that might come to feed on the dead body. This act of driving away (*kà*) generates a new series of beings that begins in the sky and moves down into the mud and water:

6.28	mùu wò jé ne pa la sa tsə jɔ	three pairs of hawks and eagles
	ŋo ni bùu n̊ kà	I drive these bugs for you
	ŋo ni zò n̊ kà	I drive these beasts for you
	chí p'ə lo p'ə sa tsə jɔ	three pairs of musk deer and muntjac
	ŋo ni bə̀ n̊ kà	I drive these bugs for you
	ŋo ni zò n̊ kà	I drive these beasts for you
	dɔ̀ mo ví mo sa tsə jɔ	three pairs of foxes and squirrels
	ŋo ni bùu n̊ kà	I drive these bugs for you
	ŋo ni zò n̊ kà	I drive these beasts for you

And on through rabbits and weasels; tigers and leopards; bats, rats, and mud larvae; coiled gray boas; white and black fish; and minnows and brine shrimp. This is the first appearance of a series that, in various arrangements, will be repeated throughout this part of the *nèpi*, swinging far towards Eco's "poetics of everything included," a litany of all the beasts, birds, and insects in the world. Next, the "song of stepping along the road," *kò t'ò chæ̀*, repeats this series, enchaining it with two others, a sky series and the series of human kinds, as it forges a network of paths across the earth's surface.

6.29	mùu wò mi mo ho mo chì k'o t'ò	sky and earth step along their road
	tì p'u lə zò chì k'o t'ò	mists and clouds step along their road
	mùu wò ho mo kǽ mo chì k'o t'ò	all the sky's stars step along their road
	cá nì shu nì chì k'o t'ò	Cánìshunì steps along his road
	zì mo lò mo chì k'o t'ò	leopards and tigers step along their road

dɔ̀ mo ví mo chì k̓o t̓ò	foxes and squirrels step along their road
vè pǫ və ŋɔ̌ chì k̓o t̓ò	bears and boars step along their road
chi p̓ə lo p̓ə chì k̓o t̓ò	musk deer and muntjac step along their road
t̓à lò hə lò chì k̓o t̓ò	rabbits and weasels step along their road
k̓o t̓ò k̓o mo lò	that is not your road
k̓o t̓ò k̓o mo wo	do not step over there
m bə là k̓o t̓ò	a road remains

A parallel segment follows, listing grackles and blackbirds, black crows and collared crows, pigeons and green pigeons, jays and magpies, geese and cranes, fish and shrimp. Then a segment about small crawling beasts and insects: coiled gray boas, white and black fish, minnows and brine shrimp, black-tailed dragonflies, mud larvae and water bugs. These several enchained series offer an elegant and comprehensive system of classification founded on two principles. First, the place beings occupy when ordered by a vertical world series: sky, trees, underbrush, ground, mud, water. Second, the beings' characteristic size and activity. Thus bears are paired with boars because they root about in the earth, rabbits are paired with weasels because they slink silently through the underbrush, and geese are paired with cranes because they are large and fly quickly past overhead. Each pairing is a generic rather than a specific classification: the grackle and blackbird genus includes all medium-sized birds that perch in trees, show off, and make a lot of noise; the coiled gray boa series includes all snakes that travel human paths; and so on.

Next, the song moves through the series of human kinds: "coax a dog with a bone, beggars step along their road, that is not your road, don't step over there." Now that we find this series in close conjunction with the series of beasts, birds, fish, and insects, we might note that it does not offer a category of the human separate from the notion of valued human persons, or Lòlo. The series is a grouping of kinds that are not Lòlo, distinguished from other series of kinds only by its characteristic poetic form. The vertical principle of these series does not define any kind of moral hierarchy. The only such difference drawn is the difference between valued human persons and all other beings, whether clouds, bears, or beggars. The series of human kinds ends, as always, with "those green pigeons, those Lòlo," and then:

6.30	kǝ ts'i pò mà bɛ	a ninety-year-old man speaks
	kǝ ts'i mo mà bɛ	a seventy-year-old woman speaks
	k̓o nì chì k̓o t̓ò	that is your road
	k̓o t̓ò k̓o wo ga	step along that road
	sa k̓á t̓ò mà kạ	do not step after ghosts of ridges
	sa bɔ̀ t̓ò mà kạ	do not step after ghosts of gullies

Innumerable pathways fill the world, along which all its multitude of beings step, scattering away from the corpse at the courtyard's center. But there is only one road for the dead person, and that is the road forged by the speech of elderly men and women.

The culminating song of this part of the *nèpi* is the "song of the sky and earth road," *mù ts'ì mi ts'ì chæ*. This song is the speech of elderly men and women that makes a road for the dead:

6.31	ŋo mù ts'ì mi ts'ì kà	I shall point out the sky and earth road
	ŋo mù ts'ì mi ts'ì chæ	I shall sing of the sky and earth road
	ni nà mù jo chɔ	you follow the sky road
	ŋo nà mù jo kà	I shall point out the sky road
	ni nà mi jo chɔ	you follow the earth road
	ŋo nà mi jo kà	I shall point out the earth road

I have glossed the verb *kà*, repeated three times in these six lines, as "point out," while in the "song of driving off bugs and beasts" I rendered it as "drive." Paired here with *chæ*, to sing, and *chɔ*, to follow, it gives the sense of guiding the dead along the road with a degree of compulsory force. The song traces four circuits of toponyms: roads that first skirt the sparse outer horizons of Júzò residents' experience, then move inwards to the places where that experience has accumulated most thickly. Most of these toponyms can be located on present-day maps of the three contiguous counties of Dayao, Yongren, and Yao'an, where most people living in the mountains speak Lipo, the Ngwi language of which Lòloŋò is a dialect. The *nèpi* uses the Lòloŋo versions of many of these place names, and the Chinese versions, transliterated into Lòloŋo sounds, of some. In order to emphasize that these are real places, my translation gives the names in Chinese, the language of maps, wherever possible. The first circuit begins:

6.32	yò an pá tsì san shï san kæ chì	we've heard of thirty-three markets in
	mi jo	the Yao'an basin 姚安壩子
	chì kæ sa kæ chì mi jo	of the first and third markets
	bɔ t'à hɔ yin kæ chì mi jo	of Yun Street 雲街 behind Baita 白塔
	lò lì mo k'u sin chò chì mi jo	of the Kongxian Bridge 孔仙橋 at Lòlìmo

In the early twentieth century, the towns of the Yao'an basin defined the southernmost border of the Lipo-language catchment area (Lietard 1913). From the Yao'an basin, the road stretched north to the market town of Dayao, which became a county center in the 1950s. At the summit of a hill a kilometer west of the town center was a brick pagoda shaped like a bell's clapper, the Qingchuita 磬椎塔, known locally as the Baita 白塔, White Tower. The tower was built during the Tang dynasty in the first half of the ninth century by the

architect Weichi Gongtao 尉遲恭韜, who also built towers in Kunming and
Dali. Weichi Gongtao's towers contained bricks printed with dhāraṇī in an
ancient form of Sanskrit; they are evidence of vibrant links between Yunnan
and Myanmar nurtured by the Nanzhao Kingdom (Liu 1845, juan 13, p. 7;
Liebenthal 1947; Howard 1997; Sen 2004). The main road in the early twentieth century proceeded north to Yanfeng and then west towards Dali. At
the western border of Yanfeng County, the road crossed a gorge at the fork
of two rivers, the Sanchahe三岔河 and the Yipaojiang 一泡江. There, during the Qing dynasty, a bridge spanned the gorge, linking the counties of
Yanfeng, Binchuan 賓川, and Xiangyun 祥云. The bridge was built in 1729,
rebuilt after a flood in 1821, and destroyed again in an 1875 flood, with only its
foundations remaining. It was called Kongxian Bridge 孔仙橋, Bridge of the
Confucian Immortal, as funds for its renovation were raised by a Confucian
scholar collecting alms (Guo 1968 [1922], 137). The first circuit continues,

6.33 shà yè a chì mi jo — heard of Xiangyun 祥云
    tsò dù bò wú bò mæ chì mi jo — of the upper and lower slopes of Yanfeng 鹽豐
    tá yò bò wú bò mæ chì mi jo — of the upper and lower slopes of Dayao 大要
    jé ne mo lo ko jò ká tə jò chì mi jo — of Zhenamo 者納么, Lukouchang 魯口場, and Kátəjò
    jò mo ŋá te chì mi jo — of Dacun Xiang 大村鄉
    vè li kə la ló la chì mi jo — of Yueli 月利, Kəla, and Luola 倮拉
    bà la chì mi jo — of Bala巴拉
    wan pè yì ji tí chì mi jo — of Yìjití in Wanbie 湾碧

After crossing the gorge into Xiangyun County, the road circles back
through Yanfeng and Dayao Counties. Zhenamo in Liuzuo 六苴 Township,
Lukouchang in Longjie 龍街 District, and Dacun Xiang, a former township
center now in Guihua 桂花 Township, were all Lipò villages of about 150 to
200 households. They formed an arc from south to north, roughly circling
Júzò on the western side. This arc then extends north through Yueli 月利,
a small Lipò village of only about 50 households in the mountains of Santai
三台 Township, from which the first ancestors are said to have immigrated to
Júzò. The arc then circles east to Luola 倮拉, Bala 巴拉, and Yìjití: Lipò villages of 100, 300, and 350 households respectively in Wanbie 湾碧 Township
of present-day Yongren 永仁 County, to the northeast of Júzò.[10] In sum, this

10. My sources for place names and population numbers in this paragraph and the next two
are county place-name gazetteers (Yongren Xian Renmin Zhengfu 1992, Dayao Xian Renmin
Zhengfu 1993).

circuit begins with famed centers that once linked this region in historical and
literary imagination to a larger world to the west, circles through the regional
centers of governance, then works through an arc of small mountainous Lip'ò
villages, surrounding the valley of Júzò, before ending with a passage we have
already quoted in the introduction (excerpt 0.4): "We've heard of such a land,
officials live there, kings live there, land where fathers cannot eat salt, land
where mothers cannot swallow salt . . . foothills stand by the river, stand and
mark the land, the land is marked and owned, all that land is owned."

A second circuit begins again with the land of kings, in Dali, the former
seat of the Nanzhao and Dali Kingdoms. It moves immediately to continue
the spiral begun in the first circuit, working through mixed Han and Lip'ò
villages in the low mountains and dry foothills to the north and east of Júzò,
which descend gradually toward the Jinsha River. The villages of Mùk'ò and
Yéjimæ near Bagai 八改, Baizhidi 白西地, Jŕmochemo/Xinfangzi 新房子,
Jɔwújɔmæ/Dazhimo 大直么, the Zhonghe 中和 Plateau, and Niupengzi
牛棚子 are along the road from Júzò to the township center of Zhonghe and
clustered around that center. Ŋómələ/Wanma 万馬, Tsɔpe, and Yizi 迤資 follow the Zhonghe River from there down toward the Jinsha River. Ganshuzi
干樹子 and Yongxing 永興 are further to the east, in lowland Yongxing 永興
Township. From there, the road circles back to Jene/Zhina 支那 and Dagamo
大嘎么 in Zhonghe Township before moving west again into Dayao County:
Mukala 木卡拉 in Liuzuo Township and Yibola 衣博拉 in Tanhua 曇花 Township, just over a high ridge to the west of Júzò, and then Tsɔ̀tə/Weidi 維的, to
the east again in Yongren County.

After the chorus, "all that land is marked and owned," a third circuit moves
south through Zhenamo 者納么 and Liuzuo 六苴 in Dayao County and then
back through a cluster of villages in Nijiu 宜就 Township of Yongren County,
only a few hours walk east and south from Júzò: Jixinketu 基心克土, Aduo-
suo 阿朵所, Huoba 火把, Waipula 外普拉, Nijiu 宜就, Dishenzuo 地仕苴,
Laohushan 老虎山, Mumahe 木馬河, and Takeshu 他可樹. Then it is closer
in still, to villages in and around Menghu 猛虎 Township, into which many
daughters from Júzò have married: Lianchi 連池, Yikedi 义可的, Jɔ̀mojɔ̀zò/
Yipalazha 迤帕拉乍, Kæmo/Gemo 格么, and Kæzò/Gezu 格租. Here, the
resolution is fine; the villages are only a few minutes' walk apart. Finally, a
brief fourth circuit works down through the lowlands towards the Jinsha
River and Sichuan: Lòchò/Yongren 永仁, the county town to which Júzò became subject in the 1950s, Kámi and Véjə (without Chinese language equivalents) just beyond Yongren, Datie 大鐵, referring to the Yunnan-Sichuan
railroad, built in the 1950s, prosperous lowland Renhe 仁和, near the Jinsha,

then Hemenkou 河门口 near Dukou 渡口, and then the giant city of Dukou, now Panzhihua 攀枝花, itself. Finally,

6.34 kò lɔ rɔ̀ mi jú zò come back to this land of Júzò
vè kà vè ló mi land to drive and herd pigs
te ka mò go mi riverside lands where oxen plow
te cí mò go mi long riverbeds where oxen plow
là là jó do mi where grain springs from furrows

m bæ jà bæ mi land where corn hangs heavy before harvesting
n tí jà che mi ... where rice falls without threshing
tsɔ̀ kʼo yé sa je where hens peck at the pestle
tsò tí ye sa mi where cocks eat from the mortar

shɨ̀ tsʼi ho dà hɔ̀ seventy-year-old women stand in the fields
mo dɔ̀ mo jo kɔ mothers and daughters harvest together
mo ta ta væ̀ hɔ̀ old people stand on the field margins

The policies of the socialist period produced an intense localization in this region, as in most of rural China. In the early twentieth century, many men and some women from Júzò made their living on the roads. Some were conscripted into warlord armies in Yunnan and Sichuan and died far from home. Others hired on as porters or muleteers to haul bricks of salt from Tsɔ̀dù/Yanfeng into Sichuan or thick braids of opium from Sichuan into Yunnan. The new socialist government shut down markets for salt and opium, nationalizing the former and demolishing the latter. Land reform and collectivization tied farmers to the land, and all opportunities for peasants to engage in long-distance trade disappeared. While many men spent periods of several months working on reservoirs and other waterworks during the Great Leap Forward, most of this time was spent in labor camps rather than in travel. After the Great Leap Forward, household registration policies severely restricted movement away from the land until the reform era. By the time young people began to move away from Júzò to find work in the last decade of the twentieth century, a new system of motor roads, following the nodal hierarchy of socialist administrative centers—provincial capital, prefectural capital, county town, township, administrative village—had replaced the old networks of mountain paths. Most youths initially moved directly down these roads in their search for work—to the township center of Zhonghe, the county town of Yongren, then either the prefectural and provincial centers of Chuxiong and Kunming, or the border city of Panzhihua and the Sichuan basin.

The "song of the earth and sky road" traces an older geography oriented towards the mountainous west. As I puzzled over these lists of Lòloŋo toponyms and Chinese toponyms spoken with Lòloŋo sounds, I found that only elderly men could give me any help—men who had once found work in caravans of muleteers hauling salt and opium. The roads traced in this song might be compared to those of two other genres of road song. The first genre of road song is a chant performed in the early twentieth century for Agàmisimo, a collective ancestral spirit responsible for the health of Júzò's central valley. This was the *nepi* that Li Bicong performed yearly for the *misi* that he set up behind the mountain house to which he fled to avoid violence and persecution in Júzò. It tours mountain places in a somewhat tighter circle than in the "song of the sky and earth road" before settling into the favored, fertile valley of Júzò (Mueggler 2001, 134–139). The second genre of road song is included in the *nèpi* to exorcise wild ghosts, performed in secret during the socialist era, and then openly in the reform era. In segments called "driving over earth and sky" and "driving to market," this *nèpi* sends ghosts in an outward spiral around local mountain villages with Lipʼò populations, then down to the port of Dukou on the Jinsha River from whence the ghosts are told to ride the river as their steed to the cities of Chongqing, Nanjing, Shanghai, and finally Beijing, where the kings and queens of wild ghosts lived (Mueggler 2001, 228–235). The chant was clearly shaped by the geographical imagination of the socialist period, during which it attained intense importance as a reaction to local violence brought by the policies of the socialist state. The "song of the sky and earth road" has the same general shape as this chant for wild ghosts, until it reaches the port of Dukou, where it draws back from the great river flowing east and returns to Júzò.

The vertical movement of harm (*po̱*) joins sky and earth, the space in between filled with an infinite variety of creatures, a movement that ends in the body of the dead. Then a horizontal movement of driving and guiding (*kà*) spreads out from the dead body, the hinge between the world's two axes. The difference between vertical and horizontal is human intention. The vertical axis is created by inhuman powers, forces that "shoot from heaven's four sides" and link the abnormal births of animals to human deaths. The horizontal axis is the product of ritualized action intended to drive away creatures that might prey upon the dead and to guide the dead soul along its path. Driving (*kà*) compels the varied series of creatures along innumerable pathways spreading out over the earth's surface. Guiding (also *kà*) gives this surface a human geography and a human history. This geography is politically and economically complex. It begins with icons of historical connection to the west—the ancient White Tower of Dayao town, the Bridge of the Confucian Immortal that made passage west possible. It takes in the fraught administrative centers where salt was strictly controlled by the state authority that administered the wells at Baiyanjing. It works its way through the Lìpò villages of the Tiesuo Valley region from which the Lòlopò ancestors fled to Júzò. It skirts the villages downstream through which one travels to reach the great cities to the east and south, and it finally turns back to Júzò's fertile little valley, where all needs can already be met. Here, the relations involved in becoming dead are not simply immediate, concrete, and personal. Nor is death merely a cosmological circuit of gifts of goats, grain, rice loaves, and suffering exchanged for the gift of generative power. Here, death involves actual earthly geographies, with all their political striations and histories of movement, settlement, and ownership. The *nèpi* brings the historical imagination of a regional geography into the process it outlines for becoming dead: the toponyms of this geography are among the layered series that constitute the dead being and bestow upon it the power to destroy or amplify the lives of the living.

Conclusion: The World Effigy

The twelve songs that begin the *nèpi* for Tenth-Month Sacrifice and Sleeping in the Forest bring a world into being. I have noted where the body, subject to harm and death, first appears in this world, joining its vertical and horizontal dimensions. Yet this world as a whole may also be considered an analogue of the dead body. The world is made with operations analogous to those that fashion a dead body, which render the infinite, indeterminate relations of a living body limited and determinate. This is made clear in the "song of earth and sky," which outlines in many series the relations through which an ox is raised, captured, killed, and butchered, relations that already draw in each of the earth's elements, from the mountains that the oxen graze to the worlds of ghosts and spirits from which the deaf-mute borrows his butcher's knife. These are virtual relations, that is to say they are presocial: they come into being before the possibility for determinate, mediated social relations has been defined. The actual world is made through sacrifice and distribution, matching the dissevered body parts of the ox to the parts of the world, shaping the world as an effigy, each part manifesting a particular relation or intention. The difference that sacrifice generates creates the world as a ground for mediated social relations, as twelve portions of meat are distributed to become twelve markets, setting up the foundational conditions for the emergence of human persons and human bodies. Later songs follow the forces that travel through this world effigy, through relational chains that traverse sky and earth: the logic of the active harm of omens. Still later, the earth effigy is layered with the effects of actual social relations, in the histories and geographies evoked by songs of driving and guiding.

The vertical and horizontal axes of this world effigy correspond to the phases of making a dead body traced in chapters 2 and 3, where a body was defined as the ensemble of relations that compose it—amounting, this chapter argues, to exactly the same thing as its power to be affected (Deleuze 2014 [1978]). Chapter 2 examined processes that acknowledge the powers of the various nonhuman forces of sky, earth, courtyard, and house to affect the dead body, layering into that body elements of the immanent experience of the surrounding world. The *nèpi* operates in a similar way on the world body, composing the world of series after series of beings, powers, and acts along a vertical axis from sky to earth, sedimenting it with every possible expression of immanent experience. Chapter 3 looked at the complex processes that wrap the dead body with images of actual socal relations. The *nèpi* performs a less particularized version of these processes as it traces repeated circuits of toponyms along the earth's surface on a horizontal dimension, wrapping the world effigy with geographical images replete with implicit histories of actual social relations. These songs of genesis trace the emergence of the world as an actual body, each song determining conditions from which the next might emerge. The arc of genesis proceeds from an essential difference to a generalized affinity, to the more specific emergence of persons, to their materialization in bodies, and finally to their involvement in geography and history. Though I have presented these songs as being about the genesis of a world effigy, they must also be heard as profound expressions of thought about the genesis of living human persons, of which dead bodies are an essential determinant.

7

Soul Work

At the intersection of the vertical and horizontal series that form the earth, a body has emerged. Yet this is less a true body than a dimensionless point of inflection. It defines no particular person(s); it has no intensive shape and no material form. In essence, it is nothing but the point at which pain from above settles and stops, and the point from which beasts and paths radiate across the earth's surface. Without this hinge between vertical and horizontal, the earth itself would be one-dimensional. From this intersection, the earth unfolds as an actual body, with depth and extension, composed of series related to series. If the earth is a body, an effigy, this point of inflection relates to that body in the same way a bed's-head spirit (*gɔwúdɛnɛ̀*) relates to the house that contains it. A bed's-head spirit is a sheet of paper on which the underworld king writes the names and fates of dead and living in invisible ink. It is tacked to the wall in the upstream corner of the inner wall of a house's upstream room, with a platform below for offerings and a platform above to protect it from soot (figure 7.1). A bed's-head spirit materializes the principle of ancestry without being the spirit of any particular ancestor. It resides above the head of the bed of the household's senior man, from whence it guards and protects the ancestral effigies that descend the wall downstream of it, defining the house's vertical (or filial) dimension. Across from the bed's-head spirit, above the bed of the senior woman, along the house's horizontal (or affinal) dimension, is the spirit that guards and protects the granary. Other beings unfold from this hinge as well, giving depth to the house's various spaces—in the attic, the barn, and the courtyard. Each of these spirits indexes specific human and nonhuman inhabitants, intentions, and qualities. The featureless, dimensionless body of the bed's-head spirit fuses them into a differential

FIGURE 7.1 A bed's-head spirit and ancestral effigies above the man's bed in a house's upstream room.

whole, a house with spaces that differ from and communicate with each other (Mueggler 2001, 78–92).

Below the bed's-head spirit, extending from the crease it produces, the ancestral effigies fold into complex dimensionality—a couple, lifted up, bound together with colored thread, supported on a bed woven by a brother-in-law, gazing up at a flower in the sky. The intensive bodies of the dead, described in the great chant for Tenth-Month Sacrifice and Sleeping in the Forest, are strict analogues of these ancestral effigies. As the chant explores these intensive bodies, it too accumulates a new dimensionality, new orders of organization. While series correlated with series remain the basic building materials for the *nèpi*, after the first twelve songs of genesis, few new series are added. Instead, the series introduced in those early songs are linked into long chains of series, from which new capacities emerge—to receive gifts, to make contracts, to live according to the law, to discuss with reason, and so on. At the same time, new narrative lines emerge from chains of series, and these narratives begin to fold one on the other. Instead of series correlated with series, or terms matched with terms, songs are correlated with songs, and verses are paralleled with verses. As soon as one song emerges as parallel with a previous song, groups of songs reveal themselves as parallel to other groups of songs, along both horizontal and vertical axes, so that each song correlates with two others, forming a set of three, and this set parallels three more sets of three. The effect was disorienting and exhilarating for me and my collaborators in transcription and translation. One song, outlining a coherent scenario, appears as a nearly word-for-word repetition of a previous song until a difference emerges of a single repeated syllable, or even a single phoneme—*mò* becoming *mó* for instance. This difference, which first appears as an inconsequential variation of sound, repeats across many verses until, quite suddenly, a familiar scene shifts to become a new and strange one. Because the parallels between songs and sets of songs are in two dimensions, this effect occurs again and again, the relentless repetition of songs and verses unfolding into what appears as an infinite process of differential recombination. Yet even this is too straightforward a description, since the tightly structured song sets are broken up by other songs, not structured into sets. Some of these intermediary songs tell of preparations to be made to the ritual ground, others spin out narratives orthogonal to those of the song sets.

Thus, as the *nèpi* begins to assemble dead souls, the simple progression of series creased at a single point of inflection evolves into a structure of many folds or planes along three dimensions, traversed by orthogonal lines of force. This is the shape of the dead couple's intensive bodies: assembled along several planes at once, each plane correlated with the others through the device of parallel verses, this matrix distorted by swooping lines of flight that disorganize and recombine the planes. Three forms of power are involved: the negative freedom of souls abandoned in the forest, the despotic power of the underworld to force the return of life for life, and the aleatory power of a shaman in alliance with death. Since these forces come to bear on the dead soul, directing the details of its assembly, we can understand these intensive bodies as dead subjects—subjected to powers of mutually contradictory origins. And because the subjectivity of the living depends on relations with the dead, we can see this complex, shifting, multivalent, variously affected dead subject as a sketch of possibilities that living subjects may also share.

The Soul Engine

This middle portion of the *nèpi* consists of twenty-one songs that investigate the fates of the intensive bodies of the dead. Twelve of the songs are structured into four parallel sets; ten intermediary songs are interspersed among these sets. The sets are composed of closely related images and narratives, rather than beings and acts. The songs in these sets are discrete, repetitive, and organized, built to be aligned with other songs along two axes, much like the mud bricks that are laid in horizontal courses (*tə̣*), built up into vertical wythes (*je*) between supporting wooden posts when a house is built. This parallel and opposed set of terms, *tə̣* and *je*, is important throughout the *nèpị*, to the point that it might be seen as a principle of construction.

For instance, this pair of terms shows up in the "song of rules and seeds," described in chapter 6, when the seventy-year-old woman sows the seeds that clothe the mountainsides in trees.

7.1	vǽ lè sa **tə̣** shr	her left hand sowed three rows
	t'à mo ŋə mo sa **je** nə̀	three columns of pines and cedars grew
	rò lè sa **tə̣** shr	her right hand sowed three rows
	tsə mo ní mo sa **je** nè	three columns of coconut and poplar grew

The term for rows, *tə̣*, is used in couplets that describe the structure the underworld:

| 7.2 | shr̀ ho le mo tə̀ **tə̣** | layered bamboo of the seventh month |
| | mó mi k'o chì **tə̣** | one layer in the underworld |

The underworld is layered like the gravesite, with rows of graves across the hillside containing family members of the same generation, and columns up the mountainside with older generations above younger. For this reason, the "life portion" *zæ t'ù*, described in this middle part of the chant, is sometimes referred to as a "life layer" *zæ tə̣*. It is the layer of life that one generation lives and then returns.

| 7.3 | ts'ì k'ò **zæ tə̣** dù m ma | where are you to return your life layer? |

In lament, the opposition between *je* and *tə̣* is sometimes also used to distinguish agnatic from affinal descendants:

| 7.4 | sa **je** lí zò jɔ | three columns of grandchildren are here |
| | sa **tə̣** lí zò jɔ | three rows of grandchildren are here |

The children of sons accumulate in columns, *je*, remaining in the house and lineage; the children of daughters accumulate in rows, *tə̣*, spreading out to other houses and other lineages.

We might use the same terminology to describe the interrelation between the parallel sets of songs in this part of the *nèpị*. Table 7.1 arranges the titles of these twelve songs into rows and columns, each row or column comprising a set, and gives each song a number to show where it appears chronologically in this part of the chant.

TABLE 7.1 Song sets as columns (*je*) and rows (*ta*).

	Monkey Songs (*mò*)	Underworld Songs (*mó*)	Eagle Songs (*jé*)	Life Songs (*zæ*)
Cradling Songs (*tsa*)	2. Song of cradling monkey like a king, *mò tsì ché tsa chæ*	11. Song of cradling high with kings, *mó ju ja tsa chæ*	16. Song of the eagle cradled like a king, *jé tsì jé tsa chæ*	5. Song of life discussions, *zæ dà chæ*
Clothing Songs (*væ t'ù*)	3. Song of the monkey's portion, *mò wo væ t'ù chæ*	12. Song of the underworld portion, *mó wo væ t'ù chæ*	17. Song of the eagle's portion, *jé wo væ t'ù chæ*	6. Song of a life portion, *zæ t'ù chæ*
			19. Song of generations of ancestors, *tsí zò tsí sa chæ*	
			20. Song of the binding cloth and eagles' talons, *jé wò ka bæ chæ*	
Return Songs (*ts'ì kò*)	4. Song of monkey's life returned, *mò wò ts'ì kò chæ*	13. Song of return from the underworld, *mó wò ts'ì kò chæ*	21. Song of the eagle's life returned, *jé wò ts'ì kò chæ*	7. Song of life returned, *zæ p'i chæ*
			22. Song of dancing beneath eagles' talons, *jé t'ò gu t'ò chæ*	
	Soul's movement ————————————————————————>			

The columns, or vertical sets of songs (*je*) give the dead's intensive body a vertical structure (it is up high, looking down) and describe a movement of lift, descent, and return. In the monkey set, the soul lives swaddled together with its spouse in a monkey's nest, wrapped in monkey skins, looking down upon wild animals sleeping or dying in their own nests. In the underworld set, the soul is briefly lifted up into a king's cradle to see the goats and pigs being sacrificed for it before it steps into the tomb to live forever underground, wrapped in quilts and blankets, subject to the underworld king. In the eagle set, the soul is snatched from life by an eagle and taken up to die in the eagle's nest to live there forever in piles of snake blood and blue bottle fly maggots.

Three songs in each column are parallel to three songs in the other two, forming three rows or horizontal sets, *ta*. The cradling set describes how souls are lifted to nest and sky, where they can look down and see but not be seen. The clothing set specifies the ways souls are wrapped: in monkey skins, in quilts and blankets, and in silks. And the return set calls upon souls to return to life as powers of generative fertility. Within each horizontal set, the songs are formally and often strictly parallel. The song titles vary by only one or two syllables. The most important of these syllables are *mò*, which marks the monkey set, *mó*, which marks the underworld set, and *jé*, which marks the eagle set. Many lines are repeated across the songs of a set, and other lines differ only by one of these three syllables. Within each vertical set, the songs describe the same vertical line of movement for the soul: lifting up to a cradle, swaddling in clothes, and return to life. This line of movement is described in a more abstract way in a fourth columnar set of three songs, the life set. This set is thematically rather than formally parallel to the monkey, underworld, and eagle sets.

Three distinct fates of the soul are given in the monkey (*mò*), underworld (*mó*), and eagle (*jé*) sets of songs. The crucial distinction has to do with the soul's contractual relation with the living, mediated by specific forms of authority over life and death. In the monkey set, the soul is subject to no authority and has no contractual relation with the living. It is like a child abandoned in the forest, swaddled in monkey skins, looking down on sacrifices made for it by wild dogs. In the underworld set, the soul is subject to the bureaucratic authority of the underworld king, and it is bound into an iron-clad contract with the living. The soul is swaddled in quilts prepared by daughters-in-law, and it gazes down on sacrifices of pigs and goats. In the eagle set, the soul is subject to the authority of the shaman, and it has an ambiguous personal relation with the living. The soul is clothed in silks but given no sacrifices, even by wild animals. Through these distinctions, the monkey, underworld, and eagle songs describe a second—horizontal—line of movement of the dead soul, from a wild state of nonrelation to a domesticated state of relation mediated by bureaucratic authority, and finally to an ambivalent state of unmediated and personal relation/nonrelation, under the charismatic power of the death-killing, life-renewing shaman. This horizontal movement is a clear reflection within the chant of the historical transformation from cremation to burial, but this reflection is refracted into fragments with different moral and affective coloring. The power of the shaman over life and death, reflected in the eagle set, upsets any one-to-one correspondence between history and song, any final acceptance of, or resistance to, the underworld order of bureaucratic authority.

While distinct, the three fates of the soul converge at the end of their vertical movement, in the return set. The titles of the songs in this set and their placement at different locations in the chant are their only real distinction: all are basically the same song, describing the return of life from the underworld. Though each vertical trajectory ends in return, it is only the bureaucratic

TABLE 7.2 Placement of intermediary songs in relation to the structured song sets.

Tenth-Month Sacrifice	Sleeping in the Forest
1. Song of green pigeons, tè pi̱ chæ̀	
2, 3, 4. Monkey set	1, 2, 3. Monkey set
5, 6, 7. Life set	4, 5, 6. Life set
	7. Song of shaman and ghost, pi̱ p'ò nè p'ò chæ̀
	8. Song of the funerals that drive you away, ma ru ma kà chæ̀
	9. Making the temporary offering, və chæ̀ ve chæ̀ pe̱
8, 9, 10. Underworld set	10, 11, 12 Underworld set
	13. Song of the courtyard, kæ dù chæ̀
11. Song of underworld tigers, mó lɔ lò væ chæ̀	**14. Song of underworld tigers, mó lɔ lò væ chæ̀**
12, 13. Eagle set	15. Eagle set
14. Song of the hunt, ni k'a zò lí chæ̀	
15, 16, 17, 18. Eagle set	16, 17, 18 Eagle set
	19. Song of green pigeons, tè pi̱ chæ̀

Bold font indicates intermediary songs about the series of exemplary beings.

Italic font indicates intermediary songs about preparing the ritual ground.

Normal font indicates the four vertical sets.

authority of the underworld king enforcing the contract between living and dead that makes the return of life possible. Shamanic authority does not compel a return of life; it creates a return *to* life, a far more ambivalent state, the state of the soul materialized in an unburned corpse or an effigy.

Distributed among the songs of the monkey (*mò*), underworld (*mó*), and eagle (*jé*) sets are intermediary songs, many of which appear in one chant or the other but not both. Three of these intermediary songs—the "song of the funeral that drives you away," *ma ru ma kà chæ*, the song called "making the temporary offering," *və chæ̀ ve chæ̀ pe̱*, and the "song of the courtyard," *kæ dù chæ̀*—are intended to ratify that certain vital ritual tasks have been accomplished. They belong to a *preparation set* that extends into the third part of the chant. The others are narrative songs about a series of powerful and iconic beings: green pigeon (*tè pi̱*), eagle (*jé*), shaman (*pi̱*), tiger (*lò*), and river deer (*chi p'ə*)—the *series of exemplary beings*. Table 7.2 shows the distribution of these intermediary songs in relation to the structured monkey, underworld, and eagle sets in the middle portion of both chants.

The monkey, underworld, and eagle sets work out the effects on the dead's intensive bodies of the implacable logic of life and death described more abstractly in the life set. In this logic, the soul is lifted and immobilized, or buried and immobilized, then forced to return as life. The series of exemplary beings, distributed through these static blocks, create less predictable lines of movement in other dimensions. The eagle traverses all boundaries between the vertical sets of songs and the songs of exemplary beings. Swooping from the sky to the courtyard, then to its high nest in the forest, the eagle draws green pigeon and shaman into an areal narrative of death, disrupting the circular engine of burial and rebirth worked out with such repetitive insistence in the vertical sets of songs. Tiger and river deer shape more lines of movement, descending into the grave and springing out of the grave into earth and sky, though these lines are quickly truncated, and the songs become cautionary statements about the impossibility of escape.

This architecture—structured blocks traversed by lines of movement that disrupt and attempt to escape—is the blueprint of the differential engine beating in the heart of this massive construction project. The difference that powers this engine is the asymmetry between the two central themes of funeral ritual. On the one hand, relations among the living are actualized in processes that wrap dead and living together into circuits of exchange: suffering passed to the dead, new life to the living. On the other hand, this practical, contractual relation with the dead must ultimately be dissolved. The question the *nèpi* repeatedly confronts is, how might the contract established under the binding authority of the underworld king finally be vacated? This is not merely a question about the souls or intensive bodies of the dead. It is ultimately a question about all social relations.

Songs of Life

Having assembled the song titles into a preliminary sketch of this engine of souls, we may now break this plan down to describe each working part. Following the twelve songs of genesis and preceding the twenty-one songs of this middle section of the chant are two songs that further specify the distinction between Lòlo and all other beings. The "song of receiving a portion," *kæ shǫ chæ*, chains together many of the series of beings created in the songs of genesis to form a single series named "all below the sky down to the maggots"—first the sky series (clouds, mists, thunder, lightning, and Cánishunì, god of thunder), then the beast series (leopards and tigers, flying foxes and flying squirrels, boars and bears, and rabbits), and finally the bird series (grackles and blackbirds, collared crows and black crows, snow pigeons and green pigeons, magpies and jays, hemp-washing kingfishers, and bats). All these beings receive a portion, which they all

7.5   kæ shǫ kæ mà wo   receive and do not accept
        kæ shǫ kæ mà lò   receive and it is not enough
        n lò ŋæ̌ kæ shǫ   not enough, and they take ours

After the bird series, the chain arrives at Lòlo, who "receive and accept, receive
and it is enough." Unlike all other beings, Lòlo are capable of acknowledging
the receipt of their portion as what they are due—capable, that is, of negotiating binding contracts, of following the law. The "song of ranked generations,"
tsɨ tsɔ chǜ, moves again through the same list, appending the series of fish and
shrimp and the series of bees and bumblebees. Though all these beings are
ranked into generations (*tsɨ tsɔ̰*), their generations are unacceptable or insufficient (*tsɨ mà wo*). By contrast,

7.6   lò lo tsɨ tsɔ̰ sṵ   Lòlo are ranked by generation
        tsɨ tsɔ̰ nì pó lò   generations of father and son
        tsɨ tsɔ̰ tɨ̰ tʼè tʼe   ranked generations established here
        tsɨ tsɔ̰ tɨ̰ tʼè hɔ̀   ranked generations standing here

These distinctions are about what makes human persons. The capacity to
negotiate contracts is the ability to produce affinal relations; the capacity to
recognize generational ranking is the ability to make consanguineal relations.
These are crucial preliminaries for the life set of songs (placed in both chants
directly after the monkey set). The three songs of this set are simple. They each
work through the sky series, beast series, bird series, and insect series to show
the logic of life (*zæ*) that moves through all beings on earth. The "song of life
words," *zæ dà chǜ*, is about the discussions or words (*dà*) about life. Discussions about life move through every being:

7.7   mi dà le mǜ tę yi   words ascend from earth to sky
        mɯ dà le mi je lɔ   words descend from sky to earth
        tí pʼu lə zò le rɔ̀ zæ dà   white clouds and mists discuss life
        mǜ gù cá shu rɔ̀ zæ dà   thunder and lightning discuss life

        mǜ wò pi mo ho mo rɔ̀ zæ dà   all below the sky down to the
                                            maggots discuss life
        mǜ wò kæ mo rɔ̀ zæ dà   all the sky's stars discuss life
        zæ dà rɔ̀ zæ ǹ tsɨ   their discussions have no logic
        zæ dà zæ ǹ lò   their discussions are not enough

In contrast, among "those green pigeons, those Lòlo, fathers and sons discuss
life, seventy-year-old women and ninety-year-old men discuss the funeral,
they discuss it around and behind the house, they discuss it at the house's
sides. Their discussions have logic, their discussions are sufficient." The logic of

life is fashioned in discussions among bereaved kin, and it belongs exclusively to Lòlo.

But what is life? The next song, the "song of a life portion," *zæ t'ù chæ̀*, answers this question in a beautifully simple fashion, exactly following the chained series of the first song in the life set. Life is a portion (*t'ù*), a quantity, measured out to each creature on earth. Clouds, beasts, birds, and insects all have life portions, but

7.8	zæ t'ù zæ mà tsɨ	their life portions have no logic
	zæ t'ù zæ mà lò	their life portions are not enough

T'ù indicates a quantity of wealth. It will be used again in the vertical sets of songs to describe the wealth given to dead souls in the form of clothing and quilts. Only the life portions of Lòlo have logic; only their life portions are sufficient. Finally, the fourth song of the life set is the "song of life returned," *zæ p'i chæ̀*, exactly parallel to the first two songs. All creatures return lives, but the lives they return have no logic; they are not enough. Only Lòlo return lives with logic, lives that are sufficient.

Life has no place in the songs of genesis. The world's coordinates take shape vertically around death striking from the sky and horizontally around the dead being made to walk the earth's geography. It is not until the "song of ranked generations," *tsɨ tsə chæ̀*, preparing for the life set, that life (*zæ*) has its first mention, as the topic of the contract between living and dead. In the early songs of genesis, death is personal and specific, always the death of the one being mourned or his parents and grandparents, a particular event rather than an abstract force. Life, in contrast, begins as an abstraction. It is utterly impersonal; it has no specificity, only quantity. Though all beings share life, only the life of Lòlo is subject to laws and segmented into specified and immutable quantities. Life is discarded (*p'i*) through the door of the underworld and returned (*p'i*) through that same door. The life portion thus established is utterly arbitrary, yet it is enforced by the iron hand of bureaucratic authority, which records the quantity of each portion in writing, executes its end when that quantity is used up, and requires the return of that exact quantity.

Cradling Songs

Life invades and occupies the world for the dead, binding living and dead together in an endless round of exchange, measured in the life portion and regulated by the underworld bureaucracy. In the monkey, underworld, and eagle sets, the logic of words (*dà*) from the life set is transformed into the first obligation to the dead: lifting and cradling. The logic of apportioning (*t'ù*) becomes the second obligation: swaddling and clothing. And the logic of return (*p'i*) is repeated, compelling exchange, drawing all obligations together under the law of the underworld.

The first song in the monkey set, the "song of cradling monkey like a king," *mò tsì ché tsa chœ*, reveals the dead couple nesting together high in the sky:

7.9	tsa chì shr̀ na nè	ghosts cradled feet in the stars
	tsa chi tsa lè	early and late cradled
	n nɔ́ pi tsa gɔ̀	a pair cradled and sacrificed to
	tsa p'u tsa ne	cradled first and cradled later
	n nɔ́ ní ŋa gɔ̀	your two hearts together
	tsa ha tsa p'a nì p'u bò	early and late both sides cradled together
	nì p'u bò tsa gɔ̀	two sides cradled together

"Early and late" and "cradled first and cradled later" refer to the two members of the dead couple, one who has necessarily died before the other. These verses are built around the specialized word *tsa*, suggestive of lifting and cradling. The song then specifies,

7.10	mò mo **tsa te** mà ma ma	monkeys hang their nests out of sight
	chi p'ə **tsa te** ma	the nests of river deer can be seen
	lo p'ə wú ju ma	the pillows of muntjac can be seen
	dò be ma je ma	wild dogs can be seen clawing cattle
	ma je ma mo gɔ̀	clawing cattle as a sacrifice

| | mò p'ò tsì wo tsa wo ni ní shr | a monkey king's nest for your heart's content |

Here, *tsa* becomes *tsa te*, the name of the ceremony, once performed mainly for the wealthy, in which the coffin was raised up on posts at least six feet above the courtyard so animals could be slaughtered below. This song sketches out the fundamental structure of the dead's intensive body: raised up high, seeing without being seen, and anterior to any relation between the dead and their living descendants (since the sacrifices here are not from devoted sons and daughters but from wild animals killing each other).

"Monkeys are like people, in many ways," Àp'ìmà said while we were transcribing this song. She told a story about a child left to play on its carrying cloth while its parents went out to find food. When the parents did not return, the child ate fruit from a thistle growing beside its cloth. The parents still did not return, so the child wandered about eating wild fruits. After six months, the parents finally returned, but the child would not come to them. They chased it from tree to tree, but it grasped the branches with its feet, climbing up, never to descend, the first monkey. "Monkeys were once people," she concluded, "which is why we do not eat monkey meat." Before the socialist era, children who died before growing their first teeth also nested in trees: they were wrapped in their carrying cloths and placed high in the crook of a tree branch rather than being cremated or buried, for they would have no obligatory entanglements with their living kin.

The parallel song in the underworld set, the "song of cradling high with kings," *mó ju ja tsa chæ*, repeats and transforms the "song of cradling monkey like a king," beginning with a description of the funeral offerings: "We rented silver fields, sowed silver grain by the river, transplanted sticky rice on the shady side, transplanted short-grained rice on the sunny side. Fire cane bloomed in the eight month, pine needles yellowed in the ninth month, rain fell all summer, the sun shone all fall. We trapped insects in baskets, grasped weeds in our hands. We counted the years to choose the month, counted the months to choose the day. Your daughter brought out all she had, your orphaned son led out cattle, those who had silver brought it, we gave you the road to walk out happily." The song shares some of these verses with the "song of cradling monkey like a king." It transforms other verses by altering a single phoneme, replacing *mò*, monkey with *mó*, underworld.

7.11	mó p'ò **tsa te** le mà ma ma	your cradle hung out of sight in the underworld
	bo no **tsa te** ma	listen and see from your high cradle
	chì shə le te do ma	see the goats come out
	vè gò le mà je ma	see the sacrificial pig bound up
	vè cho le wú ju ma	see the pig's head laid down
	mó p'ò tsɨ wo tsa wo ni ní shr	an underworld king's nest for your heart's content

Here, *tsa te* does not refer figuratively to raising the dead up in a tree; it refers literally to the ceremony of raising the coffin above the courtyard so the coffin's inhabitants might look down upon the slaughter of goats and pigs by devoted daughters and sons.

The parallel song in the eagle set is the "song of the eagle cradled like a king," *jé tsɨ jé tsa chæ*. This song tells the story, repeated with variations many times in the *nèpi*, of how the great shaman Pịmænelì killed the son of the eagle, bringer of death. In the fifth, sixth, and seventh lines of excerpt 7.12 below, the meter changes abruptly when the eagle's son stoops over the garden fence to grab a chick. The regularly paced seven-syllable lines of the song are transformed into extremely rapid nine- and twelve-syllable lines, the words blurring together in

a swooping cadence. (I quote from the Sleeping in the Forest version, where the
syllables *à le* are inserted into the center of each line).

7.12   à sà à le zò mè ne   whose son was hungry?
            æ̀ jé à le zò mè ne   the eagle's son was hungry
        à sà à le zò tsa do   whose son was a criminal?
            æ̀ jé à le zò tsa do   the eagle's son was a criminal

        he bò và mi à le k'a wò lɔ   came to the garden fence on this slope
        wò lò ye le vù t'à mo à le ji chæ̀ yi   grabbed a chick by the neck and
                                                        carried it off
            k'o bò t'à chì à le ji ka də̀   plunged into the pine forest on
                                                        that slope

        pi mæ̀ à le ne lì rɔ   Pimæ̀nelì, he
            ro vè à le p'u je t'ù   took the arrow in his right hand
            væ lè à le æ mo nà   grasped the bamboo bow in his
                                                        left hand

                æ̀ jé à le pa je lɔ   shot that eagle down
                æ̀ jé à le kæ̀ k'o lɔ   brought that eagle back

        jé p'ò à le rɔ pɛ le   the eagle said
            n hə à le tsɨ nó ŋə̀   "please don't bury this king
        jé p'ò à le tsɨ nó ŋə̀   this eagle wants to be a king
        jé p'ò tsa̱ nó ŋə̀   this eagle wants to be cradled"

In verses that repeat or parallel those of the other cradling songs, the eagle is
cradled head to the west, facing east, feet in the stars. Eagle and shaman are
cradled together, he who died first and he who died later, two sides mixed together, two hearts together. Like the spouses cradled together in the monkey's
nest, the eagle looks down to see only wild animals dying in their nests, rather
than goats and pigs sacrificed by sons and daughters.

7.13   jé p'ò tsa̱ pi̱ à le mà ma jɔ   eagle and shaman cradled together
                                                        unseen
        vè po̱ ve ŋə́ à le mà je̱ ma tsa̱ te̱ ma   see descendants of boars and
                                                        bears cradled
            chi p'ə à le wu rù ma   see the river deer snared
            ve ŋə́ à le te to ma   see the bears come out
            lo p'ə à le mà je̱ ma   see the descendants of muntjac
                                                        slaughtered

        jé p'ò tsɨ wo à le ni ní shr   an eagle king for your heart's content

As Àp'ìmà, Lichink'æp'ò, and the latter's elder brother Li Guoshan and I worked
on transcribing this song, we argued over the first line of this excerpt. *Pi̱* indi-

cates poetic ritual speech accompanied by animal sacrifices. So I heard the line as saying that the eagle was both cradled (*tsa*) and sacrificed to (*pi*). As parallelism is often the key to understanding these verses, I sought a parallel in the line, repeated in the other two cradling songs, *ǹ nǎ pi tsa gә*, which clearly means "we gave the pair of you sacrifices [or speeches] and a cradle" (excerpt 7.9). But my collaborators all insisted that *pi* in the first line of excerpt 7.13 must be heard as the first syllable of the shaman Pịmæ̀nelì's name. The idea that the bringer of death and death's executioner should be cradled in the same nest upset my developing sense of the *nèpi* as consistently working against death, towards the return of life. I understood only that Pịmæ̀nelì, of whom the chanting *àpipʼò* is the avatar, kills death to enable life's return. Yet my consultants insisted that eagle and shaman, death and death's killer, are cradled in the same nest like spouses bound together. Later songs would bear out their deeper understanding.

Swadding Songs

This movement, from paired souls with no human relations in the monkey's nest to paired souls embedded in contractual relations with their descendants in the raised coffin, and finally to death and the end of death raised high together in the eagle's nest, is repeated and developed in the songs about swaddling and clothing. The "song of monkey's portion," *mò wò vǽ tʼù chæ̀*, describes carrying live monkeys back from the forest and butchering them to clothe the dead. The actors in this song are anonymous body parts and functionaries—necks, shoulders, hands, and butchers—rather than sons and daughters.

7.14	chì mo tẹ li ti	carry one on the neck
	mò mo tẹ li kạ	bear a monkey on the shoulders
	mò mo mæ kʼò lɔ	bring a female monkey back
	tụ va kʼà na mo	lay it on a bed of ferns
	lò cí á tʼù mo	use spear-grass as a knife
	hò kạ hò le cè	a butcher cuts the meat
	lè cè à le lɔ le hò	nimble hands divide the meat
	mò ji chì ho nì tsɨ jụ	one hundred twenty monkey skins
	nì ho sa tsɨ p̀è	two hundred thirty half skins
	mò ji ve kʼò lɔ	carry monkey skins back
	mò pʼò hà wo ga	receive the bedding of monkeys
	mò pʼò pʼà wo ga	receive the clothing of monkeys

In the present, clothing the dead is given enormous emphasis. The several layers of embroidered clothing, often prepared in anticipation of death and worn only in the coffin, the special trousers and shirts for men, the hemp wraps, the quilts and blankets crammed so tightly into the coffin that it cannot be closed, the further layers of quilts placed on top of the coffin in the grave— all this is expressive of daughters' grief and their devoted attempts to repay their dead parents for their gifts of nurture and care. Here, Àp'ìmà's suggestion, prompted by the monkey set, that monkeys are like abandoned children, gives the eerie sense that the skins for wrapping the dead are made not from the worn substance of mourners' fingers and hands but from the bodies of children abandoned in the forest. The intensive bodies in the monkey's nest are abandoned souls, bare and presocial.

A few songs later, in the underworld set, the "song of the underworld portion," *mó wò vǽ t'ù chæ̀*, repeats most of the "song of monkey's portion" while in several passages making small emendations of sound that create large transformations of sense.

7.15	chè mo tẹ li ho	daughter-in-law carries all out
	mó mo tẹ li kà	carries all to the gravesite
	mó mo t'à mo mæ kò lɔ	brings one back to the underworld
	vǽ hò le vǽ hò mo	the left hand does the left hand's work
	vǽ hò le rò hò mo	the left hand does the right hand's work
	mó ji chì ho ni ts'i jụ	one hundred twenty quilts to the underworld
	nì ho sa ts'i p'e	two hundred thirty half quilts
	mó p'ò hà wo ga	receive quilts in the underworld
	mó p'ò p'a wo ga	receive blankets in the underworld

The song fully recuperates the sense that clothing is a materialization of the relations of nurture and care out of which a dead body is composed. Yet, as with the cradling songs, this set of songs does not stop with this image of paired souls swaddled in quilts, resting in the underworld, accepting gifts from the living. In the eagle set, five songs later, the "song of the eagle's portion," *jé wò vǽ t'ù chæ̀*, picks up the theme of clothing again. This song, appearing only in the Sleeping in the Forest version, is a labor narrative of the kind performed so often in lament. In some detail, it outlines the process of producing silk cloth.

7.16	bùि t'ù à le rɔ à lè	the silkworm, that one
	bə sì à le sa ho chi	in the second and third months
	tsæ mo à le ní mo p'è	gather apple-pear and poplar leaves
	k'o nì à le hə kò jọ	pull leaves off to feed the worms

| wú chæ̀ shù tì te à le ǹ tsò gɔ̀ | they lift their heads but do not eat |
| kə chæ̀ ní chæ̀ ma̱ chæ̀ à le lə lè ǹ kə gɔ̀ | lift their torsos, backs, and bellies and line up but do not swallow. |

Come back for the leaves of budding mulberry trees, the song continues, and the worms line up and swallow. They play together, they spin cocoons. But what is one to pound out the cocoons with?

7.17	t'à mo ŋə mo à le nì ka pu̱	choose two forests of pine and cedar
	kə pu̱ à le kə mà go	this makes no grain pounder's body
	bæ chr tsæ mo à le nì ka pu̱	choose two forests of Yunnan pear and apple-pear
	kə pu̱ à le kə mà go	this makes no grain pounder's body
	kò lɔ tsæ mo ní mo à le nì ka pu̱	come back and choose two forests of apple-pear and poplar
	ko̱ mo à le chù te pu̱	choose trees in a forest full of springs
	kə pu̱ à le ko̱ wo ga	this makes a grain pounder's body

Make the pounder's yoke from apple-pear, the mortar from a big stone, the pestle from cedar. A seventy-year-old man pounds, a seventy-year-old woman sweeps the pounded cocoons back into the pestle. But what do you fashion the loom with?

7.18	t'à jò à le jɔ̀ wú pe̱	make the top bars from pine
	tsæ mo à le jɔ̀ bu pe̱	make the bottom bars from apple-pear
	tsæ mo à le jɔ ŋə̀ pe̱	make the posts from apple-pear
	si̱ cæ à le jɔ̀ sæ̀ pe̱	make the comb from yellow wood
	mo cæ à le jɔ̀ chi pe̱	make the teeth from golden bamboo
	shó chi à le yè ní pe̱	take pains to thread the warp
	chæ̀ nà mæ ts'i jɔ	weave into tight, fine cloth
	n chæ̀ à le mæ sa dɔ	I have not sung of rolling into three bundles
	shó pɔ̀ à le mæ ni p'a	take pains to make red and green cloth
	ma pà lu à le mæ sa p'a	three colors even without flowers
	jé pɔ̀ hɔ wo ga	clothing for that eagle
	jé pɔ̀ p'a wo ga	bedding for that eagle

At first, this song seemed familiar to my small group of transcribers. After all, we had worked on many laments that detailed every step in the process of making hemp cloth to wrap the dead. However, no one had ever heard of silk production in Júzò. Mulberry trees, the food of silkworms, do not grow in these mountains, and looms for weaving hemp are not suitable for weaving silk. The emphasis on apple-pear wood, not the best choice for building pounders and looms, was also strange: *tsœ mo*, apple-pear, was a tree associated with harmful ghosts, the tree with trembling leaves in which the eagle built its nest. Moreover, the mutual labor of kin, central to laments about making cloth, is completely absent from this song, which mentions only the wise old man and woman, originators and guardians of ritual practices, who may be construed as aspects of the singer himself. The colored silk swaddles the uncanny couple, shaman and eagle, together in the nest. Àp'ìmà reminded us that red and green were the colors of the cloth with which the *àpip'ò* bound the eagle's claws to his staff, the topic of a song to come.

The songs of cradling and swaddling in the monkey and underworld sets might be seen as tracing the movement of the soul in time. As everyone knows, immediately after death, the soul is confused and alone. Uncertain whether it is dead or alive, the soul wanders about in fear, feeling abandoned. Eventually, it settles in a pine tree on the mountain. The soul must be rescued from this nest in the forest, where its only company is river deer and muntjac and its only gifts are cattle murdered by wild dogs. After its rescue, the soul may be placed in a coffin, raised high above the courtyard, wrapped in quilts and blankets, and given sacrifices by sons and daughters.

These songs might also be seen to trace the movement of the dead soul in historical time—a history of the dead from the point of view of the victors. At one time, Lòlopò burned their dead, the smoke rising into the sky to dissolve in mists and clouds, subject to no authority but that of the shaman. After the defeat of a Lòlopò rebellion in the mid-nineteenth century, under severe pressure from local authorities and the influence of a massive influx of Han migrants, Lòlopò began to bury their dead, making them subject to the Chinese-speaking underworld king, and wrapping them in a tissue of obligation and exchange with their living kin.

The songs of the eagle set interrupt this settling and domestication of the dead soul. In these songs, death itself comes to occupy the nest, looking down on the deaths of wild animals, dressed in silks as befits a king. The eagle is dressed by nameless hands, it looks down on sacrifices of animals killing each other, and it remains unburied, not subject to the authority of the underworld and its laws. The eagle will eventually be required to submit to a return that insists on the sovereignty of the underworld and its laws. But before that, the eagle set proliferates, generating three more songs than any of the other vertical sets. The inhabitants of the eagle's nest have until now been death and death's end, enemies and allies. The "song of generations of ancestors," *tsí zò tsí sa chœ*, transforms this alliance into the dead soul's own forebears, who look down from the nest upon wild animals dying.

7.19 ni tsí p̀ʌ̀ tsạ tẹ le mà ma ma your ancestors cradled high to see the unseen
   lò tsạ tẹ ma   see tigers cradled high
   zì mo tsạ tẹ ma   see leopards cradled high
    vè pọ te do ma   see wild boars emerge
    dò vẹ le ma je ma   see fierce wild dogs
    dò vè le wu ru ma   see wild dogs die of poison arrows
    chi p'ɔ̀ lo p'ɔ̀ ma je ma   see the river deer and muntjac
    ma je mà mo gɔ̀   shot with crossbows

The "song of talons bound with cloth," *jé wò kạ bœ chœ*, is about the cloth that binds the eagle's talons to the singer's staff. It rehearses again the eagle's dive into the courtyard to grab a chick, its swoop into the forest, and its death by the shaman's arrow. The "song of dancing beneath eagle's claws," *jé t'ɔ̀ gu t'ɔ̀ chœ*, brings the eagle's flight into the field of speech, sacrifice, and exchange. This is a labor narrative, devoted to the fashioning of the gourd-pipe used to lead the thieves dance (excerpt 3.10).

In the eagle set, death takes the form of an affinal relation negotiated in war, mediated by the shaman's crossbow bolt and words. Like every such relation, it includes three parties: in this case, the eagle of death, the shaman who conquers death, and the line of ancestors that culminates in the dead soul. In these songs, the *àpipʌ̀* does not negotiate with the dead on the behalf of the living. He explores the conditions of the world of the dead by becoming an ally of and enemy to the power of death itself. Death has the character of this active relation—the wild, contingent flight of the eagle, the arrows and words of the shaman intersecting with that flight, the line of ancestors emerging from this collision. The "song of talons bound with cloth" and "song of dancing beneath eagle's claws" refer this relation to the social field of mourners gathered for the ritual. In this context, this structured meeting of lines of flight might even be called a "war machine," opposed to the power of life and life's laws that will be consolidated in the songs of return.[1] This machine will be further developed in the songs of exemplary beings.

Songs of Return

Monkey, underworld, and eagle sets all end in songs of return, each taking the underworld as their topic, monkey and eagle appearing only in the titles. Most verses are common to all three songs in both versions of the chant. The songs begin, after the introductory section, with an invocation of the underworld

---

1. The term comes from Clastres (2010 [1980]) via Deleuze and Guattari (1987 [1980]).

king (here quoting the Sleeping in the Forest version, with the syllables *à le* inserted in the center of each line).

7.20	tè pi̱ à le je̱ cæ ru	some pigeons return early
	tè pi̱ à le je̱ p'i ru	some pigeons return late
	mó mi à bùi à le **ts'ì** ma jù	the underworld king sees your fate
	mó mi à bùi à le **zæ** ma jù	the underworld king sees your life
	mó kə à le kà lì p'ì	discarded into underworld and graveyard
	cè kə **zæ** kə à le á dù p'ì	breath and life discarded through the door
	ts'ì p'ì à le lá gò yi	fate discarded, step through
	ts'ì p'ì á le lá kò lɔ	fate discarded, step back

The pair *zæ* and *ts'ì* are obviously central here. I have glossed them as "life" and "fate" respectively, but they replace each other easily, both giving the sense of life's preordained portion or quantity. In the "song of eagle's life returned," *jé wò ts'ì kò chæ*, the couplet about the underworld king (lines two and three of excerpt 7.11) is modified, *ma*, meaning "to see," is replaced with *ǹ*, a negative particle, transforming its meaning.

7.21	mó mi à bùi ts'ì **ǹ** jù	the underworld king is not reborn
	mó mi à bùi zæ **ǹ** jù	the underworld king does not live

The songs specify the life to be returned: hundreds of golden horses, a barn of cattle, herds of bleating sheep, a corral of black goats, a sty of pigs, a courtyard full of chicks. In the Sleeping in the Forest version of the "song of monkey's life returned," *mò wò ts'ì kò chæ*, the singer adds a couplet about daughters and daughters-in-law, emphasizing that the return of life also makes possible the exchanges that bring wives:

7.23	te fú lò kò à le kæ t'è kò	return a courtyard of daughters exchanged for cattle
	chì jú lò da à le kæ t'è jɔ	a courtyard full of daughters-in-law

Life returns at a specific location: the door to the underworld in the graveyard. Life comes first to the bell and eagle's talons of the *àpi̱p'ò*. It then spreads out through the world, following series after series of beings, before settling finally on the descendants of the dead.

7.24	ts'ì sa dù mà jɔ	what is the sound of life?
	ju zò ts'ì sa dù	my bell is the sound of life
	ju zò sa ne go	we ring this bell for you
	ts'ì ma ts'ì nì dù	your two lives return here
	jé chi ts'ì ju do	come to life at my eagle's talons
	jé chi jó ne kò	return to my eagle's talons

ts'ì wò da k'ə lə̀ lə̀ go	returned life rings noisily
ts'ì wò da k'ə sa sa go	returned life rings happy
t'à ŋə̀ le mì t'è jẹ	drops on the tips of pines
t'à ŋə̀ le mì t'è je	falls from the tips of pines
wú ŋə̀ le mì t'è jẹ	drops on the tips of chestnut trees
wú ŋə̀ le mì t'è je	falls from the tips of chestnut trees
tsǽ ŋə̀ le mì t'è jẹ	drops on the tips of apple-pear trees
tsǽ ŋə̀ le mì t'è je	falls from the tips of apple-pear trees
vè ne le wú t'è jẹ	drops on the black pigs' heads
vè ne le wú t'è je	falls from the black pigs' heads
zò lí le p'à pí jẹ . . .	drops in the aprons of sons and grandsons . . .
ts'ì kò zæ tẹ lə̀ lə̀ kò	babbling life returns as long life
ts'ì kò zæ tẹ sa sa kò	noisy life returns as long life

The *nèpi* makes it clear that life (*zæ*) is a generative force shared by all beings. Unlike the lives of wild animals, human life is measured into specific quantities (*ts'i*). A quantity of life is discarded through the door of the underworld; the same quantity, measured into other portions (*t'ù*), returns through the same door. This logic of quantification makes life subject to contractual exchange. Dead souls can grant or withhold the return of life in response to the actions of the living, who provide the dead with care and nurture in the form of food and clothing. And the bureaucracy of the underworld king enforces the contract.

When the dead return life they do not relinquish it. The return of life doubles it, and the dead continue to live in the underworld, requiring sustained care from the living. The idea of the continuing life of the dead is expressed in many ways in lament and *nèpi*. For instance, the little chant used to buy water from the river to use in funeral ritual urges the dead to drink that water its whole life (*zæ*).

7.25	**zæ** bɔ bɔ dɔ ve	drink your fill all your life
	ni jɔ jɔ dɔ ve	drink every day of your existence
	k'o bɔ bɔ dɔ ve	drink your fill every year

And life (*zæ*) is doubled in a little speech made when sons, daughters, nieces, nephews, and grandchildren place hemp shrouds in the coffin:

7.26	mó mi mæ p'ə̀ dè	hemp is money in the underworld
	ni mùi **zæ zæ** ne zə̀ yi	you go spend it as long as the sky lives
	ni mi **zæ zæ** ne zə̀ yi	go spend it as long as the earth lives
	ni ma, ma p'u yi zə̀ yi[2]	go spend each eye as a silver coin

2. The eyes of the hemp cloth are the gaps between the crossed threads of a tabby weave. See Mueggler (1998) for a discussion.

Such doubling is present, too, in the logic of sacrifice. When a goat is killed at a funeral, its blood, meat, and skin are consumed by the living, but its life (*zæ* again) is given to the dead. The goat lives on in the underworld, joining a herd of goats that sustains the dead soul. This investment in nurture and care allows the life to continue to return to the living as generative power.

The *nèpi* stacks the planes of the monkey, underworld, and eagle sets, tacking between them with parallel verses, slightly shifted in each set, to build up a tightly coordinated multidimensional subject, the intensive body of the dead. This body has a vertical structure, lifted up, seeing without being seen. It has a double core, formed of an alliance on each of its three planes. This core is wrapped with cloth on all three strata: with the skins of abandoned children, with the suffering of daughters and daughters-in-law, with the effects of the shaman's silk-weaving words. We might think of the threads that cross these three planes and bind them together into a complex distributed subject as guided by the needles of three forms of power. First, there is the simple freedom of the abandoned child, subject to no authority. Second, there is the power of life (*zæ*), with its clear-cut law of return, binding dead souls to the living under the authority of the underworld king. Coincident with the power of life but neither engaging nor intersecting it is the force of death (*shr*). If life subjects the dead to a contract with the living, enforced by the bureaucratic authority of the underworld king, death allies with the charismatic power of the shaman to place the dead high in the eagle's nest with their ancestors. If life moves in an endless circuit, death moves as lines of flight intercepting other lines—the flight of the eagle as it snatches a chick, the flight of the crossbow bolt that halts the eagle's swoop. To be sure, we might speculate that these images accreted during the historical transition from cremation to burial, coinciding with the defeat of rebellion and the more secure absorption of Lip'ò and Lòlop'ò communities into the system of regular administration. Yet whatever their historical origins, the *nèpi* has drawn all these images into a tightly structured engine of the soul, finding in each an essential tool for its assemblage of a dead subject, distributed along three strata, stitched together with three differently colored threads of force.

Songs of Exemplary Beings

We have seen that the *nèpi* devotes many verses of the monkey, underworld, and eagle sets to reaffirming the implacable law of life. In coordination with the introductory and concluding passages of each song, the chant performs the practical task of clearly outlining the terms of a contract between living and dead. But the *nèpi* also repeatedly performs the intersecting lines of flight of the eagle and the shaman's arrow. Though this line has its point of origin in the parallel vertical sets of monkey, underworld, and eagle, it quickly pierces their structured boundaries. Squeezed between these block-like sets are other, intermediary songs that further develop this line of flight, working out in far more detail the actual contours of the shaman's authority and the logic of the arrow that slays death. These are the songs of exemplary beings, which trace possible routes of escape from the law of life.

The "song of green pigeons," *tè pi chæ̀*, is unique in that it is positioned in widely separated places in the two versions of the chant. In this middle part of the chant, it appears as the first song in the Tenth-Month Sacrifice version and the last song in the Sleeping in the Forest version, and I have used it to divide both chants into three parts. Because in this chapter I have described songs in sets rather than in order of performance, we have already met the eagle many times. However, in the Tenth-Month Sacrifice version, the "song of green pigeons" introduces this force of death into the world. The eagle first appears as an answer to what seems to be a question:

7.27	wú shr ma t'à shr	your head dies but not your corpse
	kə shr ní t'à shr	your torso dies but not your heart
	ni kò ni kə shr	return to die in your torso
	ni kò ni ma hè	return to sleep in your corpse
	ká pə t'à no jò	the cuckoo calls from the pines
	bɔ̀ ŋa tsí ŋa pẹ	the leeches speak from the fields
	ni sà kæ̀ me ma	your eyes are clear as the stars
	ni me ma mà pẹ	look sharply with your eyes

The song does not mention life (*zæ*). The issue is not whether life remains in some of the body's parts. The question is whether death (*shr*) has penetrated the entire body. The soul (*yeho*) has departed, but for the body to truly die, the soul must return. Living people lose their souls all the time, causing them to act dazed, lose interest in things, and perhaps fall ill. To lose a soul does not mean to die, and reuniting a soul with a body does not bring life to the dead. The song calls on the soul to return to the corpse, for only there will it gain the clarity of its senses. In the same way, bringing a soul into an effigy is necessary so it might see offerings and hear speech.

The eagle now emerges. It circles in the sky, dives into the courtyard, grabs a chick, and plunges into the chestnut forest. The eagle is unnamed in this first appearance—it is only *jé ne*, a generic category of dark-colored predatory bird. Only later will it be further specified and divided into father and son. A pair of hands—also belonging to no named subject—braid a silver cord, spin

a golden cord, string a crossbow, and shoot the offending bird. The power to
slay death immediately becomes a power of generation.

7.28	tè pi̱ sa p'i lò	one green pigeon becomes three
	chì ka̱ sa ka̱ lò	one nest becomes three nests
	chì ji sa ji lò	one branch becomes three branches
	sa ji kò tu ka̱	three branches root buckwheat sprouts
	tè pi̱ chæ̀ sa sè	a green pigeon carried away
	n shr tè lo do̱	an undying pigeon emerges
	wò p'ə tè pi̱ do̱	green pigeon born of the cock
	wò mo tè lo do̱	pigeon born of the hen

I have been using the term "soul" loosely in this chapter, as a shorthand to refer
to the paired, wrapped, folded intensive body of the dead. Yet the soul that
returns to the body so that it might die is not this structured intensive body.
This soul is the *yeho*, the singularity without form or content, without senses
or personality, which is given a home in a crushed and charred chick immediately after death. In this song and the other songs of exemplary beings, there
is no structured entity that might be called an intensive body—a dead subject.
It is even misleading to call the actors here beings, for the song mentions only
active parts: claws that grasp, hands that make and shoot. These songs are
about powers to act and arcs of movement: the power to seize and the swoop
of wings, the power to shoot and the flight of the arrow, the power to regener-
ate and to multiply. This last power is not given as a term of a contract between
living and dead. It emerges from these powers to seize and kill, as an intersection of vectors of flight. This regime of powers and movements is the creative
force of the shaman, whose words sweep the sky and fall to earth. The power
of regeneration described in this song simply sidesteps the regime of life (*zæ*)
in which regeneration is the product of exchange between living and dead.

What are the origins of this power and the conditions under which it may
be exercised? The "song of shaman and ghost," *pi p'ò nè p'ò chæ̀*, falling between
the life set and the underworld set in the Sleeping in the Forest version, is devoted to this question. This song extends the eagle's flight into the beginning
of a narrative about the shaman, which, taken up in further songs, threads
through the remainder of the chant. It begins with the great shaman Pi̱mæ̀nelì
at a loss for words:

7.29	pi̱ mæ̀ ne lì rɔ̀	that Pi̱mæ̀nelì
	m pi̱ n̂ tu̱ lu	his speech would not come
	pi̱ jù lu n̂ jɔ	nothing to speak with
	n kɔ́ n̂ tu̱ lu	his skill would not emerge
	kɔ́ jù lun̂jɔ	nothing to carry his skill

Seeking something to carry his speech and his skill, Pimæneli wanders the world, from market to market.

7.30	k'ù zò lò ji mæ̀	the fine wine market at K'ùzò
	k'ù zò lò ji do	the best wines set out at K'ùzò
	ju̠ vùu ji ǹ do	no bells sold there
	ju væ ji ǹ do	no bells bought there
	nè mi ŋɔ̀ bò mæ̀	fine gathering places in the ghost world
	cí mi ti̠ chà mæ̀	fine sitting places in the spirit world

He attends the wheat market at Kəji, the wine-pot market at Rɔp'è, the salt market at Tsɔ̀dù. He tours fifteen markets, all within a few days' walk of Júzò, and visits the gathering places of the ghost and spirit worlds. Nine of these markets are among the twelve named in the "song of sky and earth." The shaman looks for bells at each and finds none. Finally, he goes to the market at Siluyaŋ in Líjæ/Lijiang 麗江. This is a long way, the most distant place on his itinerary. Here, he finds guns set out for sale, and next to the guns, bells. He finds bells for officials and kings and bells for farmers and herders. At last, he finds bells with flared clappers, bells from three places, bells to carry a shaman's speech.

Now Pimæneli confronts the bird of prey, specified as the eagle's criminal son, who has seized a chick from the courtyard and taken refuge in a pine and cedar forest. The shaman shoots the eagle's son, carries him back, and severs his talons. But he has nothing with which to bind the talons to his staff. He walks to a market in the nearest county town, Lòcho/Yongren 永仁 , where he finds stacks of cotton cloth; he tears a strip of cloth to tie the talons to his staff. He now has two tools to carry his speech and support his skill. But he still lacks the third, the shaman's knife. He searches through strange places and familiar places, among men skilled at working in copper and iron. He travels to the ghost world and to the spirit world, where he finds abundant knives, and he brings one back. These three implements give him the power to overcome ghosts:

7.31	ni nè pə pi̠ pə t'e̠ lè lɔ	compare a ghost's due to a shaman's due
	pi̠ pə tsɨ pə nɔ	shamans receive kings' portions
	nè pə chì p'a p'o	one pile of shit for ghosts
	nè pə nì p'a p'o	two piles of shit for ghosts
	nè pə ŋo p'a p'o	five piles of shit for ghosts

Compare a ghost's voice to a shaman's voice, he continues in a passage I quoted in excerpt 5.2. A shaman's voice is a bell's voice, sharper than any ghost's voice, a shaman's talons are an eagle's talons, sharper than any ghost's claws.

The shaman's power to speak is gathered from the broad world of general-ized sociality, of negotiation and exchange across difference. As the "song of sky and earth" made clear, markets index the form of affinity, which emerges prior to the generative relations that produce human persons. They are the place where actual exogamous alliances can emerge, against which the preferred form of cross-cousin marriage is constructed. As he gains his bell, the shaman gathers the power of generalized sociality from markets; as he steals the eagle's talons, he seizes the power of ritualized words from the force of death; as he attains his knife, he gathers the creative power of sacrifice from the ghost and spirit worlds.

The song continues with the story of how the great shaman failed to resurrect his cremated son and invented the rituals of burial. Liyoŋcipʼò, whom my small team of transcribers consulted on difficult passages, offered us a prose version of this story as a way of supplementing and interpreting the song. His version replaces the narrative of the origins of the shaman's power in bell, eagle's talons, and knife with a story of how the shaman gained a medicine to undo death:

> Pị̈mæ̈nelì was a basket maker. Every day he went down to the stream to soak and weave bamboo. He discovered that every day, two boas came down to the place he worked to drink. He watched for three days. On the fourth day, he cut a small piece of bamboo into the shape of a knife and stuck it into the snakes' path. The female snake came down first, holding up her head. The bamboo knife split her belly from head to tail, and she died there. Then the male snake came down, sniffed its partner's belly once, looked over her body, and left. Pị̈mæ̈nelì followed.
>
> The snake climbed a cliff, stopped at a bush and picked two leaves with its mouth. It brought the leaves to where its partner lay, placed one on the ground, and wiped the other along her wound from head to tail. The wound closed following the leaf, and her partner led her away. Pị̈mæ̈nelì went back and dug the bush up by the roots to take home. He brought the bush to a shady place, chopped it into little pieces, and placed the pieces into three big cisterns. From that time forward, whenever someone in his family died, he placed some of this resurrection medicine (*n shr ts'i*) in the corpse's mouth, and the dead lived.

In the song version, once the shaman attains his bell, talons, and knife, the power of his speech spreads out over the earth.

7.32	mi pị ǹ tụ lu	all who could not speak
	mi ji bu zò jɔ	all the earth's people
	bu pị bu kó ga	speak and people begin
	bu pị bu tụ ga	speak and people emerge
	bu pị 'æ̀ lì tụ	speak and people spring up
	bu pị 'é lì tụ	speak and people become agile

"People" in this excerpt are *bu*. While *tsʾɔ* are people as distinguished from ghosts and spirits and thus alive, *bu* are people as distinguished from animals and thus not specified as living or dead. Speech here is *pi*, the speech that accompanies sacrifice, rather than any form of ordinary speech. The shaman uses the medicine of his speech to reanimate dead bodies.

After Pịmæ̀nelì's fame spreads, a dragon invites him to the sky to practice his medicine:

7.33 mù̀ lɔ lù kɔ́ no	the dragon in the sky hurt his crest
pị kà mi tsu chi	consulted the shaman on the earth
pị mæ̀ ne lì rɔ̀ te yi	Pịmæ̀nelì tried to go
pị kɔ́ mù̀ tso te ǹ kɔ́	he could speak, but he could not ascend
ni nà mù̀ zɔ̀ ŋɔ	"you are a child of the sky
ŋɔ nà mi zɔ̀ ŋɔ	I am a child of the earth"
pị kɔ̀ mù̀ tsɨ te ǹ kɔ́	the shaman could not climb the sky's seams
kɔ́ kɔ̀ mù̀ tsɨ te ǹ tʾe kɔ́	the skilled one could not climb the sky's creases
rɔ̀ kɔ́ pị lə lə	he [the dragon] needed that shaman
pị pʾɔ̀ ŋɔ̀ sa tụ	"I will reward your speech with 3,000 cattle
pi pʾɔ̀ rɔ sa tụ	reward your speech with 3,000 sheep
kɔ́ pʾɔ̀ ŋɔ̀ sa ho gɔ̀ bɛ	reward your skill with 300 cattle," he said
te sɔ̀ tsæ ka tsɨ sh.a te	he [the shaman] climbed up an apple-pear tree
à sà ní ǹ tsæ	whose hearts are evil?
bù̀ ro cæ ní ǹ tsæ	yellow ants' hearts are evil
tsǽ ka tsɨ rɔ̀ kʾɔ̀ pə	ants chewed down the apple-pear tree.
pị mæ̀ ne lì rɔ̀	Pịmæ̀nelì, he
yi kɔ́ kò ǹ kɔ́	could go but could not return
kò kɔ́ yi ǹ kɔ́	could return but could not go

Liyoŋcipˇɔ̈'s prose version filled in the event that occurred in Pịmæ̀nelì's absence.

Hearing of Pịmæ̀nelì's fame, the dragon in the sky sent down to ask for a cure. "I have heard that you are a great healer. I have hurt my crest, and I want you to come up to the sky to treat me."

Pịmæ̀nelì told his only son, "I am going to the sky to cure the dragon. Our house has three big pots of medicine. Do not open them when the sun shines through the doorway, for if the sun sees the medicine, he will steal it." But his son forgot this warning and let the sun steal the medicine away.

Pịmæ̀nelì climbed an apple-pear tree to get to the sky. At the top, he blinked, and he was in the sky. As he was treating the dragon, a messenger came to announce his only son's death. He said to the messenger, "I am not afraid of my son's death. If my son has truly died, cry out until the clouds part (*tsạ wú mù k'u k'æ̀*). The cry will be heard in the sky. The smoke will ascend to the sky (*k'ə̀ sí mùù lɔ tẹ*)"

The messenger returned to earth and did as he was told. He cried out and burned incense. Pịmæ̀nelì heard and left for the earth. But the apple-pear tree had fallen, so he had to go the long way around, to one of the four corners where posts support the sky. By the time he got home his son had already been cremated. He opened the three pots, but he found that the medicine was gone.

Song and prose versions use exactly the same words to select two acts from funeral ceremonies. First, the "cry to heaven" (*tsạ wú*) that the three thieves make as they begin to dance around the coffin or effigy. Second, the smoke of incense burned at the coffin's head. The song version also selects a third ritual gesture, the flight of the crossbow bolt. During the Tenth-Month Sacrifice ritual, after the "cry to heaven," a crossbow bolt is shot into the sky and then retrieved and hung on the effigy for the dead soul:

7.34	pị mæ̀ ne lì zò tí shr ǹ jo	Pịmæ̀nelì's only son did not fear death
	pị mæ̀ ne lì zò tí no ǹ jo	Pịmæ̀nelì's only son did not fear pain
	pị mæ̀ ne lì zò tí ǹ hə	Pịmæ̀nelì's only son was careless
	pị mæ̀ ne lì zò tí shr tụ yé rɔ̀	when Pịmæ̀nelì's son died, he said,
	tsạ wú mùù k'u k'æ̀	"cry out until the clouds part
	k'ə̀ sí mùù lɔ tẹ	smoke will ascend to the sky
	ché pạ mùù zò tsa gə̀ lɔ	shoot an arrow at that thief in the sky"
	dà tị ppə̀ zò t	he spoke these words
	n ŋɔ lu ǹ ŋɔ	and so it was to be
	k'ə̀ sí mùù lɔ te lɔ ga	the smoke ascended to the sky
	tsạ wú mùù k'u k'æ̀ lɔ ga	cried out and the clouds opened
	mùù wú mùù tsæ jɔ	followed the sky to its end
	pị mæ̀ ne lì rɔ̀	Pịmæ̀nelì, he
	pị p'ə̀ ŋə̀ sa ho	received 3,000 cattle for his speech
	kɔ́ p'ə̀ rɔ sa tụ wo ga	received 3,000 sheep for his skill
	mùù wú jɔ kò lɔ	returned from the top of the sky
	mi mæ jɔ kò lɔ	returned to the tail of the earth
	n shr ts'ì sa wụ	three pots of resurrection medicine
	n no mè sa ve	three loads of ointment for all pain
	chì wụ li hɔ ve	peered into one pot on tiptoes
	wú lo chì wụ hə̀	put his head in a pot
	lò ve chì pə lò ga	the load of tiger's medicine was gone

jò lɔ chì wu̜ hə̀	stood before another pot
mè chì pə lò ga	the pile of ointment was gone
chi lɔ chì wu̜ hə̀	approached another pot
sæ̀ chì pə lò ga	the pile of berries had vanished
mo jɔ lɔ lɔ wu̜ lé	washed the pot where the mother was
zò jɔ bæ lɔ chì ji tɔ gɔ̀ lɔ	poured out a bowl where the son lay

Here, the song moves directly to the final, repeated concluding passages. Liyoŋcipò's version clarified the last, cryptic couplet of this excerpt and supplied the conclusion:

> Pimæneli rinsed the three pots with water and sprinkled the water on the ashes; a corpse formed, but there was no way to put breath into it. He could think of nothing to do, so he called his daughters and his wife's brothers, put hemp socks on the corpse, and invented the rules for the funeral process, including all the different funerals, the greatest of which was Tenth-Month Sacrifice. Before this, people were cremated and that was all.

The story gives the conditions under which the shaman ceded his authority over death to the law of life. Before the introduction of burial, death was a movement between earth and sky. Death descends, the eagle stooping to snatch a chick, the snake slithering down to the river. The shaman's crossbow bolt ascends, negotiating an alliance with the eagle of death; the shaman's bamboo knife rears up from the path, negotiating an alliance with the boa of death. The line of flight of the shaman's arrow/knife/words makes the shaman the partner of death, its enemy and ally. With the "resurrection medicine" of his words, the shaman folds the relational matrix of the world into a power that regenerates directly, without detouring through the nurturing relation of parents and children. This line of flight is brought down to earth by a consanguineal relation: the shaman's authority over death may be complete, but his authority over his son is not. While ascent is easy, a matter of climbing a tree and blinking (anyone can die), descent is difficult. He has to take the long way around like the dead soul in the "song of the sky and earth road." His son's betrayal has diminished his power to the point where his medicine/words can only recompose a corpse, and with it all the "rules and procedures" of funeral ceremonies. Hereafter, the dead, beneath the earth in material bodies, are subject to the law of life.

The story sutures itself at pivotal points to the sequence of funeral ritual, the "cry to heaven," the smoke of incense, and the crossbow bolt ascending to slay death all indicating the shaman's ascendant authority during the vigil, the corpse's descent into the earth marking the ceding of that authority by the underworld. This parallel might even lead us to see funeral ritual as reenacting the history of the transition from cremation to burial and the contemporaneous consolidation of local administrative authority. Yet we can also understand these correlations as effects of the soul-building machine of the *nèpi̠*, as it folds parallel planes into a lavishly multivalent dead subject. We have seen how the force of death traverses the meticulously organized strata of monkey, underworld, and eagle. With these songs, the *nèpi̠* allows the forces of death and direct regeneration to deeply inflect the layered structure of the dead subject, even as it continues to insist on the implacable authority of the law of life. The spectacular "song of shaman and ghost" does not actually complete this narrative; it cuts off the moment before Pi̠mǽnelì must assemble the ashes of his son into a corpse. After some more songs of exemplary beings, the *nèpi̠* will take up the story again.

Cautionary Songs

While the "song of green pigeons" and the "song of shaman and ghost" intensify the force that death exerts on the intensive body of the dead, two further intermediary songs bring orthogonal forces to bear. The "song of the underworld tiger," *mó vǣ lò vǣ chǽ*, and the "song of the hunt," *ni ka̠ zò lí chǽ*, engage directly with the underworld. These songs might be seen as subjecting the law of life to questions or stresses. The power of the underworld administration, however implacable, does not remain uncontested. The "song of the underworld tiger" intervenes after the underworld set. The story is unlike anything else in the *nèpi̠*, and it seemed incomplete, yet none of my acquaintances could tell me of any similar story that might supplement it. I quote the Sleeping in the Forest version:

7.35	cǽ cæ yì zò rɔ̀	siblings of the other world
	lò kə cǽ ŋɔ bɛ	they say tigers were involved
	cǽ cǽ jɔ dù rɔ̀	siblings playing in the existing world
	shú kə cǽ ŋɔ bɛ	they say incense was involved
	cǽ cæ yì zò rɔ̀	siblings of the other world
	lò wu tʼu to te̠	trapped a tiger in chains
	cǽ cǽ jɔ dù rɔ̀	siblings playing in the existing world
	shú wu tʼu tʼo te̠	burned incense for the trapped one
	cǽ cæ yì zò rɔ̀	siblings of the other world
	lò tʼu lò m mæ	chained the tiger but did not finish him
	cǽ cǽ jɔ dù rɔ̀	siblings playing in the existing world

shú t'u shú wo ga	found incense to burn
shú wu ni k'ò lɔ	burned incense to bring him back
cǽ cæ yì zò rɔ bɛ ne	siblings of the other world spoke
tà ti̠ pɛ gɔ̀ ti̠	they spoke the truth
t'à chu shú t'à chu	"do not burn incense, do not burn!
shú chu lò mè ŋɔ́ lɔ hə	burn incense and the tiger's end will come
t'à chu shú t'à chu	do not burn incense, do not burn!"
tà ti̠ bɛ gɔ̀ ti̠	they spoke the truth
cǽ cæ à na zò rɔ̀	those mischievous children
n hə shú chu pi̠	burned incense anyway
n ŋɔ lu̠ ǹ ŋɔ	what should not be was
shú chu lò mè ŋɔ́ lɔ ga	burned incense and the tiger's end came
lò p'ə à bæ zè zè t'è	that tiger with glittering belly fur
ts'i nì kà lì lá kə yi	stepped into twelve graves
ts'i nì kà lì lá kə yi	stepped into twelve graves

The Tenth-Month Sacrifice version pairs the tiger (*lò*) with a leopard (*zì*), making it clear that the beast in question is not an ox (also *lò*), as in the sacrifice that created the world:

7.36	la jà le lú và ti̠	they crouch in lush riverside meadows
	mó mi k'o chì ti̠	sit in underworld meadows
	k'o bò le zì mo ti̠	on that side the leopard crouches
	he bò lò mo ti̠	on this side the tiger sits
	à bæ zè zè t'è	with sparkling belly fur

The *lò* of the tiger is the *lò* of Lòlo, valued human persons. In this version too, another phonetic pair, *yi/næ*, which discerns elder from younger brother, makes it clear that the siblings are parallel rather than cross:

7.37	**yi** shr **næ** mà chǽ	elder brother dies, younger brother carries the corpse
	næ shr **yi** mà chǽ	younger brother dies, elder brother carries the corpse

In other words, the story is neither about generative sacrifice nor about the generative power of cross siblings.

The song reflects the uncanny doubling that the underworld introduces into the world, the siblings of the living world (*jɔ dù*, "place of existence") paralleled by siblings in the underworld, issuing a warning for the living brothers. The warning is at the song's center. There is no other mention of incense in the *nèpi̠*, though my friends believed the smoke that announced the death of Pi̠mæ̀neli̠'s son to be incense smoke. In this light, the admonition, "do not burn incense, do not burn!" coming from the underworld where bureaucratic

authority reigns, might be read as an echo of the many injunctions by political
authorities not to burn that spurred the transition from cremation to burial
in the nineteenth century. The warning comes from the siblings' underworld
doubles, and the result of their infraction is the tiger's descent into twelve
graves, much as the outcome of Pịmæneli̇'s son's cremation was his burial.
This story, too, is correlated with the procedures of funeral ritual, where incense is burned at the head of the coffin before the corpse is finally sent to the
underworld. The dead siblings' warning not to burn refracts the plea of the
eagle, "please do not bury this king, this eagle wants to be a king." The matter
of burning or burial is made an issue at various points in the *nèpi* as a contest
over the authority of the underworld, an authority that inserts a fracture into
the "world of existence," by creating a double of that world, and by repeating
or doubling the life of that world, to shape the law of life.

The "song of the hunt" takes another perspective on the dead soul's possible fates. In nearly every case that relations of descent appear in the chant,
they are patrilineal. In contrast, this song uses many verses to describe the
dead mother, tracing lines of nurture (*ho*) through both her daughters and her
daughters-in-law.

7.38	chì p'u væ zò ho	[she] raised the sons of white daughters
	chì ne væ zò ho	nursed the sons of black daughters
	yæ nà yi bæ̣ ho	raised the little ones from far away
	væ̀ nà me jó ho	nursed the big ones under her eyes
	lí nà hɔ jó ho	raised grandchildren in her armpits

White daughters are those who have married out and whose children grow up
far away; black daughters are daughters-in-law whose children grow up under
their grandmother's eyes. "Her daughter-in-law sent her to the underworld,"
the song continues; "her daughter-in-law led her to the riverside." Then:

7.39	a ts'a rɔ̀ ci shọ	what's all the fuss about?
	chi p'ɔ̀ wò cæ t'à mo jɔ ŋɔ bɔ	a golden-breasted musk deer
	sị yi hò tsa tị	sits at the root of a thorn tree
	chi p'ɔ̀ wò cæ t'à mo jæ̀ lu jɔ jo	hunt the golden-breasted musk deer
	mi kà le mὺ te yi	go chase it from earth to sky
	mὺ kà le mi je lɔ . . .	come chase it from sky to earth . . .
	rɔ̀ lè p'u je thὺ	the right hand plucks the silver bowstring
	væ̀ lè cæ mo nà	the left hand grasps the golden bow
	chi p'ɔ̀ væ̀ k'ò lɔ	carry the musk deer back
	chi mæ̣ le he jɔ ga	hunt the musk deer down

Àp'ìmà told a fuller version of this story, about a daughter who refused to marry. Warned by a honeybee that a bumblebee would carry her away some day, her parents watched her carefully during the day and locked her in a bureau at night (thus complying with her refusal, for bees are courting youths who gather the nectar of marriageable daughters). They let her out only to attend a Tenth-Month Sacrifice ceremony. As she sat in the midst of the crowd, a musk deer sprang out of the graveyard above, and when everyone gave chase, the daughter floated away, as her parents ran beneath, eventually lodging on a cliff face from which she was not able to climb up or down.[3] Though the song selects from this story only the bit about the musk deer, its emphasis on mothers and daughters gestures towards the rest. Never one to fear stating the obvious, Lichink'æp'ò, sitting with us, declared, "The musk deer was a dead soul!" Yet if the deer leaps out of the grave to traverse earth and sky, it does not escape for long. It is hunted down and made into a corpse—drawn back into the economy of corpses and their circuit of exchange with the living.

These last two cautionary songs do not speak of a force in direct competition with the power of life and the authority of the underworld. Instead they gently contest that authority from within its parameters. Living siblings disobey the injunction of their underworld selves not to burn, and the tiger (the Lòlo community) is trapped forever beneath twelve graves. A dead soul in the shape of a musk deer escapes the grave and the endless circuit of life for life, only to be hunted down and returned. Squeezed between the parallel blocks of the monkey, underworld, and eagle sets of songs, these cautionary songs are eddies of force that subtly inflect the intricate structure of the dead subject. The circuit of life for life is not an utterly implacable power that can be opposed only by the fierce alliance of shaman and eagle. It may also be distorted from within, through playful disobedience—"those mischievous children burned incense anyway"—and fleeting escape.

Conclusion: The Imperialism of Life

Having brought into being a world of series piled upon series, these songs folded a segment of that world into multiple planes, joined by shifting points of coordination, shot through with orthogonal forces. They brought into this assemblage of dead subjects the historical experience of the living, subjected to the power of a bureaucratic administration, from which Lòlop'ò ancestors had sometimes ventured to escape, most recently in Li Zixue's rebellion of

3. This story is told more fully in Mueggler (2001, 68).

1850–1864. These songs subjected the dead to the imperialism of life, bound them to life by politico-economic means—gifts from the living paid out in unending imbursements forcing unending payments. They reminded the dead repeatedly that what distinguishes Lòlo from all other beings is that they honor contracts, most particularly between generations of consanguines. Life for life is the rule of this imperialism, enforced by the regime of burial, which keeps the dead anchored in place forever under the millstone-sized eyes of the Chinese-speaking underworld king. The despotism of the imperial rule of life is cemented into the chant's form, repeatedly emphasized in the block-like parallel segments of the songs of cradling, clothing, and return, the only songs in the *nèpi* to display such comprehensive parallelism. Yet the circuit of life is repeatedly disrupted by lines of movement emerging from other songs— the flight of the eagle ending in a flurry of feathers, the flight of a crossbow bolt ending in the eagle's death, the ascent of the "cry to heaven" and the smoke of incense, the leap of the musk deer from the grave. These lines, even those that are caught and bent back around, are signs that *àpip'ò*, directly involved through their shamanic persona in the dead's subjectivity, divined other possibilities for them—perhaps of escape, perhaps of a direct leap to regeneration, short-circuiting the rule of life.

If the intensive bodies of the dead sediment the historical experience of their living interlocutors through the transition from cremation to burial, these bodies might also be taken as sketches of possible shapes for living subjects. If so, they might prompt us to describe subjectivity in new ways—as configured along several different planes or folds, these planes bent by various transverse forces but nevertheless assembled into an awkward whole by being coordinated at scattered points of parallelism or differential repetition. If we see the *nèpi* as coming into being through a dialog between living and dead subjects, we can also imagine that the intensive bodies of the dead might have served as resources for the subjectivity of the living, demonstrating to the living that between the building blocks of even the most instrumental regimes of power are possibilities for creativity, flight, and escape—possibilities that, as chapter 5 indicated, Li Bicong may have put into practice in his own life. Yet subjects, living or dead, require material bodies. Having assembled the intensive bodies of the dead, the *nèpi* proceeds, in its third and final section, to theorize their substantive bodies, which extend into the world of the living.

8

Body Work

We have seen the great chant, or *nèpi̱*, for Tenth-Month Sacrifice and Sleeping in the Forest bring a world into being; we have seen it fold this world into the several coordinated planes of the composite souls of the dead, their intensive bodies. We have seen these souls drawn along each of their differential planes into relations with the living, as they are retrieved from the forest and lifted up to look down upon sacrifices that bind them into contracts, subject to the law of the underworld.

From this precarious perspective, always traversed by lines of flight that draw dead souls into other possible fates, the songs of the *nèpi̱* may be seen to fold the varied series of the world into textures that provide purchase for the living to grasp, so as to force the dead to labor at the work of returning life. The third and final part of the *nèpi̱* explores the parallel between the intensive bodies of the dead and their material bodies, given to them by participants in ritual. We might even say that while the world is actualized in souls it is realized in bodies (Deleuze 1993 [1988], 105). This is not to say that material bodies are made real; they have no more or less reality than souls. Bodies realize what is actual in the soul, the soul's social relations with living persons. Bodies complete this actualization as the media through which social relations with the living unfold.

At Tenth-Month Sacrifice, the dead were given two bodies: the ancestral effigy, created after Dawn-to-Dusk Sacrifice, and the great *bu* constructed for the purposes of this ritual and cremated afterwards. As we have already seen, material bodies flesh out dead souls with images of relations in which dead persons were presumed to have been suspended in life and index the intentions of the living to bind themselves into contracts with the dead. Without material forms, even when folded into the textured forms of intensive bodies, dead souls cannot truly have social relations. They can only have positions—in regard to each other as members of a couple bound together and raised high, in regard to the sacrifices below them, which they cannot yet grasp or receive. Given material bodies, the dead perceive sacrifices and take ownership of gifts and, in this way, become persons embedded in relations with living persons.

The songs of the *nèpí*'s third part may be divided into three sets. The first set of songs inquires into the nature and origin of the ancestral effigy. The second set of songs theorizes the *bu* of Tenth-Month Sacrifice. The third set of songs sends the dead couple on their final journey to the underworld and to the eagle's nest, now revealed as places of terror, and makes a final appeal to the dead to participate in generative labor, carried out on a creaking bed before midnight. The songs of the ancestral effigy and *bu* trace a journey from intensive body to extensive body. In both cases, the journey takes the form of a series: loss ⇒ search ⇒ encounter ⇒ assembly ⇒ destruction. Father and mother disappear; a search is mounted; father is recognized in a pine tree on the mountain, mother in a chestnut tree, affines in a bamboo stalk; all these are assembled into a material body; the body is eventually destroyed. This journey begins with the singular impersonal soul, detours through the manifold seriality of the material world, then encounters the entire world, social and material, reassembled. One's dead parents reveal one's world—the sum of one's relations viewed through an image of the sum of theirs. In daily life this sum is obscure, buried in virtual shadows. The journey of loss, search, encounter, assembly, and destruction—which is another way to construe the journey of grief (*shú*)—makes this sum determinate, known, actual. This is true of any death, but in the deaths of parents, the focal zones of one's virtual world and of the world reassembled in one's parents' dead bodies converge more exactly than in any other death. The songs about the ancestral effigy and the *bu* engage with the mystery at the core of this series, the mystery of the parallel between a soul and a material body. In these songs, the soul disappears. It is lost in the depths of a spring, along twelve streams, in a puff of smoke from a corpse. Only later, and after an extensive search, is it encountered again among the series of the world. How might this newly assembled material body become a body for this particular soul? The *nèpí*'s answer is strange and spectacular: matching soul and body requires a sacrifice and an alliance, the body of the shaman exchanged part for part with the body of the dead, just as the body of the ox was divided and distributed to become the world corpse.

In these songs of loss, search, encounter, assembly, and destruction, the *nèpí* engaged substantially with the ritual action of Tenth-Month Sacrifice and Sleeping in the Forest. Some songs in the other two parts also engaged directly with ritual action, notably the songs grouped into the "preparation set" in table 7.2: the "song of funerals that drive you away," *ma ru ma kà chæ̀*, the song called "making the temporary offering," *vɔ̀ chæ̀ ve chæ̀ pe*, and the "song of the courtyard," *kæ pe chæ̀*. Other preparation songs extend into this third part: the "song of setting it all up," *la pe chæ̀*, and the "song of trees," *sɨ tæ chæ̀*. In Li Bicong's performance, these were all very brief songs, which the *àp̱ip̱ò* sang as he performed discrete preparatory acts like setting up a table on the ritual site and sweeping the ground around it to make a "courtyard." In contrast, the songs about the ancestral effigy and *bu* engaged with ritual activities that were central and focal—not merely for the *àp̱ip̱ò* but for all other participants as well. For this reason, this chapter includes accounts of the ritual processes of Tenth-Month Sacrifice and Sleeping in the Forest. The former was a boisterous ceremony, involving hundreds of participants working, from their own perspectives, on the central problem that troubled this third part of the *nèpi̱*: how to find lost souls, embed them in material things, assemble those things into bodies, and engage materially with them, then how to uproot those bodies, move them through space, and reestablish them in new places. While this work required close attention to technical procedures, it also required collective effort to cultivate and shape affect: the warm lively feeling of bodies pressed together in a dance, the gaiety and sense of sexual possibility of mock antiphonal love songs.

After weeks of intense, line-by-line study of Li Bicong's songs, the single, revived Tenth-Month Sacrifice ritual that Lichink'æpò and I were able to attend in the outlying village of Wòdɔwò was a revelation to us. While the *àp̱ip̱ò* was absorbed in his quiet, layered dialog with the dead, other participants made speeches, sang funny, competitive, dialogical songs about love and loss, wept, danced, whooped the "cry to heaven," stole offerings, and mimed buggering each other with pine branches, all the while working through the steps of encountering the lost soul on the mountain, transporting it down the mountainside, assembling it into a body, wrapping the body in clothing, making offerings to it, and demanding that it return generative capacity.

So far as we could discover, Sleeping in the Forest was never revived anywhere after its final performance in Júzò in the fall of 1949. In Sleeping in the Forest, most participants were concerned not with sacrifice, exchange, or lament, but with performing the desired final result: procreative power. Though the *àp̱ip̱ò* was apparently as serious as ever, for others, Sleeping in the Forest was all about drink, play, and lovemaking. This chapter alternates descriptions of songs about the origins and nature of the material bodies of the dead, with accounts of the ritual action of Tenth-Month Sacrifice and Sleeping in the Forest. This chapter seeks to explore this terrain between the specialized language of the *nèpi̱* and the broader vocabularies used by ordinary participants, to discover more precise answers to the questions that have been at the heart of this book. What are dead people? Why do they need bodies? How do they get bodies? And what role do the persons and bodies of the dead play in the personhood of the living?

Preliminary Embodiments

Àp'ìmà was the earthly embodiment of the seventy-year-old woman who participated in creation, combining an unsurpassed devotion to the arcana of ritual with the creative, scurrying activity of the little yellow mouse of the underworld. Though Lichink'æp'ò and I solicited many descriptions of how the Tenth-Month Sacrifice ceremony had been conducted, Àp'ìmà's account was by far the most detailed. She had planned a Tenth-Month Sacrifice for her parents in 1956, and she had attended many before then. She spent days teaching us how one orchestrates this great gathering, giving us the sense that by writing down each step, we were creating a textual *nèpi* together, a song that made and combined series, creating intricate productive machines, folded into shifting layers, entangled along many points, revealing dense concatenations of relations. After Lichink'æp'ò and I returned from Wòdɔwò, we sat with Àp'ìmà again, methodically comparing the ceremony we had observed to her account of the ritual in Júzò. Always generous of imagination, Àp'ìmà expressed faith that our collaboration would be transformed from my scrawl into printed characters, bound into book, and studied by people seeking guidance as to the proper ways to treat with the dead. For my part, I see this anthropological work as analogous to the work of the ritual—materializing virtual bodies, unfolding ideal images of relations, hoping to put an end to ghostly repetition.

Tenth-Month Sacrifice was preceded by weeks of preparation and discussion. The dead couple's sons and daughters and the dead man's brothers' sons were the host parties; the dead woman's brothers were the lead guests. The hosts borrowed stacks of firewood and as much grain as was possible. They made a dozen big rice loaves, a foot in diameter, three or four hundred smaller loaves, fist-sized, and at least a hundred jin of bean curd. The host's manager caught a live squirrel or rat and some mud eels. The night before the ceremony, neighbors brought over stacks of bowls, and a hundred bowls were prepared, each containing one large round piece of bean curd topped by three smaller square pieces. "The round piece below is the *vedù*," Àp'ìmà said, "since that family is the foundation. The other three are the dead couple's daughters and granddaughters, and the dead man's brother's sons and daughters." A special bowl was prepared for the central *avɔ*, the round foundational piece of bean curd topped by a piece of boiled dried goat meat. The bowls were set out on the bed below the ancestral effigies, head to foot, as many as would fit in a single row, the rest lined up on the floor in rows and columns. It was already a body for the dead. The number one hundred—like one thousand or ten thousand—represented an innumerable quantity, an uncountable number of persons involved directly or by proxy in relations that had composed the dead couple in life, with each round image of a person made of more images of relations. "The bean curd is for the living," Àp'ìmà explained. "Bean curd always stands for living people." This body of bowls of bean curd was divided and distributed at dawn—first to those who came in support of the central *avə*, then to the central daughter's supporters though there were often not even enough for the *avə*'s group. "The manager had to make all this clear to the dead," Àp'ìmà said. "'I'm taking this food out now. I'm serving it to those who have come to help.'" In the meantime, the *avə* assembled a "bird on a pine branch"—the contraption of bamboo and cloth dangled over the head of the dead at every funeral—and hung it over the woman's bed, opposite the ancestral effigies. The room itself, with an outside (the woman's bed), paralleling the inside (man's bed), was becoming an image of the dead couple bound together, the man's side looking up at the effigies of his ancestors, the woman's side gazing up at the "bird in a pine branch," a fluttering conduit of the world's beauty. A single small rice loaf was placed on the bed below the "bird on a pine branch," with a pair of live grass seedlings sprouting from its soft white belly.

That night, a skilled old man was invited to sing lament in the inner room, standing just inside the threshold, facing the effigies above the bed. His lament, called "leading verses" (*wútsitə*), spoke of the gifts to be offered and the relations of labor and affect required to produce the gifts, much in the style of the "weeping songs" described in chapter 4. This was the sole lament performed that night. The door to this inner room was propped open all night, while outside on the porch, kin and friends warmed themselves around a fire and kept company with the dead. Bigger fires were built in the courtyard; a gourd-pipe player was recruited; and the three "thieves"—one each for *zòmæ̀*, *avə*, and *vɛdù*—led the vigorous "thieves' dance," men clasping hands in a circle, goat hooves dangling from their capes. It is "to welcome the soul (*yɛho nó*)," said a pair of men in Wòdɔwò when we asked them why they dance, a phrase often used in Júzò to speak of dance at weddings (Mueggler 2002). The verb *nó* means "to restore," "to recover," or "to welcome," and it is used in the common verb phrase *wònó*, "to rest" or "to restore strength." At weddings, dance uproots the bride's living soul from her parents' house and reestablishes it in her new home, and it detaches the souls of her brothers and other intimate kin from hers so they might return to their own homes. Dance moves souls in particular directions. Thus one might welcome a soul "away from" (*kò yi*) or "back to" (*kò lɔ*) a place, usually a house or room. Such intensely inhabited places materialize the affective qualities of social relations through time. The living souls that hang about the hearth and ancestral effigies are points of intersection between mundane activity in the present and these virtual layers of the intimately lived material world. A dead soul is little different. A dead soul, too, requires the collective warmth and liveliness of dance to uproot it from its place and prepare it to move on.

The "Three-Person'd God"

A flourish of long-stemmed trumpets announced the dawn; the fires were quenched and disassembled; and the courtyard was swept clean. The one hundred bowls of bean curd were given out to one hundred guests, and everyone else was served from a large pot of bean curd placed on a table in the courtyard. The youngest orphaned son took the dead couple's ancestral effigy down from its perch over the inner bed, placed it in a wooden pan of cooked rice, and carried it to the front porch. There, blaring double-reed trumpets heralded the effigy's arrival and the host's manager stood before it to make a speech. At Wòdɔwò, this speech was the simplest form of ritual language, addressed in a loud voice to the effigy, with the crowd in the courtyard attending:

> Ah, Yin Chang and Yin Chang's wife! Don't say you don't understand, don't say you do not see! Don't be angry if I call out your birth names. Don't block your ears, don't close your eyes! Listen closely from afar, look carefully from nearby. Examine all with care. See how none suffer more than your son Yin De, see how none suffer more than your sorrowful daughter. Don't drop these goats' lead ropes, don't drop these bowls of grain. Feel free to sell them, feel free to rent them out.

8.1	ni á tí lè lè jɔ go	as for all the places you will pass
	su pi̲ dù ni tȅ bɛ mo̲	the shaman will talk you through
	ni wo le ṅ ŋɔ ni nè ts'ɨ̀	you are no wild ghost, you are an ancestral effigy
	ju kà ni t'à yi	do not walk above the road
	ni ju kò ni t'à yi	do not walk below the road
	n do̲ lé ni ju mo yi	walk nowhere but on the main road
	n do̲ lé ni ju ká yi	walk nowhere but in the road's center
	pi̲ m ni tȅ ja dæ mo̲	the shaman will guide you
	ni ṅ sa t'à bɛ, ṅ ma t'à bɛ	don't say you don't understand, don't say you don't see!

The walk to the ritual site was a journey for the dead couple, where their gifts of goats and grain were already useful to buy off the wild ghosts that might hinder them. This journey required the collective effort of a procession, generating safety in numbers and in the warm, lively feeling that souls find attractive. The double-reed trumpet players led the procession; behind them the "bird on a pine branch" dangled over the shoulder of a man from the daughter's group; next came the orphaned son bearing the ancestral effigy in its warm pan of rice; and the rest of the participants followed. After the crowd passed, elderly widowers scattered wads of paper money to distract random kinless ghosts. At the flat site below the graves, the *àp̱ip̱ö̀* stood beside a table with his bell, his eagle-talon staff, and his broad-brimmed felt hat. The orphaned son set the ancestral effigy before him, and he chose a man, not yet widowed, to guard it all day. Drunks playing the part of rapacious ghosts would come to steal it, and if they succeeded the guard was required to pay a ransom of a j̱i̱n of alcohol. At the day's end, the guard was rewarded with the pan full of rice on which the effigy rested.

The ancestral effigy having arrived, the assembly built three great bonfires, and the three groups of participants gathered in their proper positions relative to the *àp̱ip̱ö̀*'s table: the brothers-in-law's group (*avə*) at the head, the daughters' group (*zòmæ̀*) at the sides, the sons' or host's group (*vɛdù*) at the foot. The *àp̱ip̱ö̀* swept the ground around the table and erected an effigy for his spirit familiar, building a square arbor of willow posts, about two feet high, roofing it with pine needles, and planting six small saplings inside, three of pine and three of chestnut. He then began his chant, which would continue until late afternoon.

The third part of the *nèp̱i* is largely an inquiry in to the origin and nature of effigies. The first song of this part, the "song of strange things," *hǫ p̱ǫ chæ̀*, tells of stars that plunge down, axe blows from heaven that split trees in two. Again, the prototype of human death is the death of trees, struck by lightning or meteorites. Next are two songs about sacrificial offerings. The "song of the quirt," *j̱ù j̱à chæ̀*, speaks of an old man herding goats. "Startle the goats and they clatter, startle them and they scramble, with what shall he startle them?" The old man borrows a silver knife from an official, a gold knife from a king, a chopping knife from a shaman, an iron knife from a carpenter; he then cuts a tapered bamboo quirt and returns to startle the goats. The "song of the road," *j̱ɒ p̱ǫ chæ̀*, briefly describes making a path to the sacrifice site that "goats with dangling earrings" will walk.

These three songs preface the pivotal "song of the ghost in its bamboo cradle," *mè p̱ö̀ nè p̱ǫ chæ̀*," which tells of the origins of the ancestral effigy. A man rode out on his golden horse, diligent not to lose it, refusing to lend it out or to exchange its services for human labor. He slept at a cousin's house, and he then led the horse home through eleven gullies and over twelve ridges. I quote the more complete Sleeping in the Forest version, with the characteristic extra two syllables in each line:

8.2 mùi he à le tsɨ ka nǽ	when the night grew too dark to see
yi dù à le m mæ hè	followed closely as it went
lɔ dù à le m mæ hè	followed closely as it came
si̱ vǽ à le mò p'æ du̱	tied the horse to a big tree
ká vǽ à le mò p'æ du̱	hung the saddle on a thick branch
shɨ̀ wú à le mo yi vi	seven raucous monkeys appeared
si k'ə à le si mà k'ə	in the dead of the night
mo jù à le ho t'è je̱	a monkey dropped into the saddle
ho jù à le mò t'è je̱	the saddle dropped onto the horse
mò jù à le t'ə̀ ka tə̀	the horse jumped into the spring
kò lɔ à le tsɨ lɔ p'u chá ve	turned and borrowed an official's silver staff
mà lɔ à le cæ cha ve	borrowed a king's golden staff
kə́ lɔ à le hə̀ cha ve	borrowed a carpenter's iron staff
pi̱ lɔ à le bæ̀ cha ve	borrowed a shaman's wooden staff
sa cha à le ŋo ve va	I borrowed three staffs together
mò va à le mò ma pɔ̱	probed for the horse without finding it
kò lɔ mò cæ à le cha ru va	turned and borrowed a tapered bamboo
mò va à le mò ma pɔ̱	probed for the horse without feeling it
t'à zɔ̀ à le sa tsi pɔ̱	probed with three pine trees
wu zɔ̀ à le sa cha pɔ̱	probed with three tapered chestnut trees
t'à zɔ̀ à le à bò pe̱	made the pines into father
wu zɔ̀ à le à mo pe̱	made the chestnuts into mother
nè vǽ à le nè mà pe̱	there is no greater nè than this nè
nè k'u à le nè ts'ì pe̱	bound the nè together to make a nèts'ì

In the Tenth-Month Sacrifice version of the song, the man seeks his horse along twelve streams. Pine trees and chestnut trees block the man's way, and he understands the pines are his father and the chestnuts his mother. The series official, king, carpenter, and shaman appears as the man borrows knives to cut a pine tree, a chestnut tree, and a tapering bamboo stalk. Once he ties pine and chestnut together and weaves a bamboo cradle, he sacrifices a goat to lift the cradle high and place it facing east, with its head to the west and its feet in the stars, husband and wife mingled together. He sacrifices a goat to take the effigy out the door; he sacrifices a sow to wrap in the apron with it—for at the end of the ritual, a small pig will be strangled and placed in the orphaned son's apron along with the ancestral effigy so the latter may be transported back home.

A man rides out on the horse of his parent's coffin. The man's journey bends back towards home at his cousin's house, a parallel cousin (*yì zò*)—which is to say he does not ride out beyond the territory for endogamous marriage. The man's journey home is cut short, the abandoned soul of his parent attaching to the effigy of the coffin in the slapstick sequence, monkey to saddle, saddle to horse, horse to the depths of the spring, the coffin disappearing forever, leaving the soul with no material support. Earlier in the song, a conventional passage about gifts ends with a couplet unique to this song that seems to come from the time when the dead were cremated at the mountain's foot and their ashes buried beneath small stones:

8.3   a k'ɔ̀ ŋə t'ɔ̀ t'à sḭ ŋɔ́ tsɛ   smoke ascends along paired green pines
        kà lì pḛ mo gɔ̀   gave you a wide gravesite

While the smoke of corpses no longer settles on green pines, the smoke of incense and bonfires remains a material link between the dead body and the pines and chestnuts growing on the mountainside. While the coffin has dropped out of sight, the man probes with pine and chestnut branches, feels the coffin, understands that pines are father and chestnuts mother, and binds pine and chestnut together into an effigy.

This "song of the ghost in its bamboo cradle" may be heard only through the series of equivalents that the chant has already produced. The *nèpḭ* is confronting its final task, embedding relations and intentions already outlined in the resistant flesh of material bodies, characterized by "impenetrability, inertia, impetuosity and attachment."[1] The journey of the dead is merely a series in two dimensions: traveler matched to place names. When the journey stops, the road compresses into multiple folds: monkey, saddle, horse, spring, then pine and chestnut bound together. Yet each fold expresses all the series that have brought its components into being—pine and chestnut, for instance, express the genetic series of "rules and seeds" where the proto-bodies of trees were sown in rows and columns over the crumpled body of the earth. It has been necessary to bring an entire world into being, and then to fashion an intensive body for the dead, in order to arrive at this point, where ideal and material are interleaved, where actual relations and intentions are folded into a

---

1. Deleuze (1993 [1988], 47), reading Leibnitz (1996 [1765], chap iv, §124).

virtual body in material form, where classificatory relations (mother, father, mother's brother) are reduced by means of pine, chestnut, and bamboo into a particular instance, this "three-person'd God," greatest of all *nè*.[2]

"Who Asked You to Knock on My Door?"

While the *àpipò* built his spirit familiar's effigy and prepared to sing, the orphaned son, with companions, and the brother-in-law's thief, also with an escort, walked up the mountain to the family's gravesite to retrieve the dead soul once again. This was where pine and chestnut trees were found to fashion the ancestral effigy. Now, orphan and thief searched for materials for the other body for the dead, the great *bu*. At Wòdɔwò, the orphaned son soon came trudging down the mountain bearing in hands held behind his back two live sprouts of grass in a bowl of water and mud. Then came the thief, shoeless. Behind the thief came his companions, dragging a massive pine tree, complete with root ball, which they had uprooted from the mountain. Others came bringing twelve pine saplings, each about eight feet tall, their lower trunks stripped of branches, and twelve chestnut saplings of the same height, also stripped (figure 8.1).

The thief sang as he came down, and a woman chosen from the daughter's group, standing in a cluster of women in the midst of the assembled guests, answered him. Their improvised dialog was modeled on playful antiphonal courting songs, banned by the Communist Party in Júzò's central villages in the 1950s, if not in this peripheral place. The most popular context for courtship singing had once been the collective work of rice transplanting in late spring, which created a heated, eroticized atmosphere. Groups of boys, standing on paddy margins or on the hillsides above, improvised songs together, the ablest poets feeding the singer lines. Groups of girls, stooping in the mud, improvised witty, cutting replies. The verses of each group projected voices of typical social personae of their respective genders. The dialog between the thief and the woman chosen to answer him borrowed from this tradition and modified it, moving through a series of different projected personae.

Bakhtin (1981, 1984, 1986) used the concept of voice to show how oral or written utterances project recognizable social personae. After rediscovering Bakhtin in the 1980s, linguistic anthropologists used the concept to explore the

2. From John Donne's poem, "Batter my heart, three person'd God; for you" (Grierson 1921, 88). The reference to categorical kinship being reduced and particularized draws on Viveiros de Castro (2001, 25).

FIGURE 8.1 Building the great *bu*.

heterogeneous ways different voices are produced and recognized in speech
(Lempert 2006, 2007). A variety of devices have been shown to participate in
the production of contrasting voices (Wortham and Locher 1996, Wortham
2001). Among these are shifts in lexical register, shifts in participant framework, and shifts in pronouns and other anaphora (Urban and Smith 1998).
Agha has suggested that the alternation of recognizable lexical registers (say,
between lament and courting songs) is often central, as speakers initiate a
playful dialectic between these attributes of patterned speech and local ideologies of personhood and affectivity (Agha 2005). Others have lavished close
attention on the gestural and spatial interactions that can also make different
voices recognizable (Lempert 2011, 2012; Lempert and Silverstein 2012). Here
I invoke voice, lexical register, and participant framework solely for ethnographic purposes—to make my description of the dialog between the thief and
his female opponent more clear. In this song, shifts in lexical register, participant framework, pronouns, and spatial location were all in play, as the voices
of different personae were rapidly taken up and discarded.

As he followed the orphaned son down from the mountain, the thief projected the voice of the dead couple taking pride in their fine family. This was
not the typical dead couple of lament who began life immersed in poverty
and hardship and were then brought to better times by the hard work of their
children after Liberation, decollectivization, or tax reform, depending on the

generation. Instead, the song projected the personae of a mature couple secure in the beauty, skills, and wealth of their adult children:

8.4	zò t'e p'a yi do	this stylish handsome boy
	zò t'e hɔ go ga	the better looking the more you look
	zò t'e ro wu ga	a handsomer husband you will not find
	zò t'e go ga ba	a finer boy you will never see
	ŋǽ mà ne lu ba	our fate is outstanding
	ŋǽ ló mi jè wú p'a	we herd the fattest goats
	ŋǽ tsæ dù ts'ɔ tsæ do	our house produces talented men

"We raised a fine, able son," the thief continued. "Our daughters found fine husbands. Our only son, rich from trading, has come today, his friends have come,
he stands before us, our daughter-in-law stands before us."

The thief then shifted lexical registers and, at the same time, shifted participant frameworks—the multiple roles into which speaker and hearer may
be stratified in talk—as he echoed some verses from the register of lament:

8.5	ŋǽ lò lo le ni ja	we Lòlo count on our fingers
	ce p'ò p'æ tsɨ ja	as Han count on their clothing
	ni tsæ ǽ ni ja	we counted the propitious day
	ni tsæ ǽ ni chi	the propitious day is today

With this shift, the implied authors of the speech, which had been the dead
couple, became the ancestral authors of lament. The principal—the person
committed to the song's content (Irvine 1996)—shifted from the orphaned
son, praised by his parents for his beauty and wealth, to the more generic persona of the mourning offerant. The living participants, overhearing the song,
faded into the background as ratified bystanders. The lines were mock serious in tone and content, but the crowd soon began chatting and laughing as
they became aware that the speech singled me out among the ratified bystanders by poking playful fun at the persona the singer ascribed to me, of a *Cep'ò*, a
rich urban Han.

Another less dramatic shift in participant framework followed, as the song
began to formally address the assembled crowd of the dead, listening from the
mountainside graveyard behind the thief:

8.6	ni æ mæ bò no lɔ	now come listen
	ni mó mi bɔ̀ sɔ̀ lɔ	wake up in the underworld
	p'è sí p'è mè ba mà lɔ	bring all your parents and children
	à tá à lɔ	your elder brothers

Here, the daughter's representative, who had been ladling water onto the ground and scattering bits of rice cake, managed to break in, shouting her verses over the voice of the thief. The participant framework for her song paralleled that of the thief's initial verses. The authors were the dead, the addressees were the living crowd, the (covert) principal was the orphaned daughter, praised for her beauty. Yet this singer's aspect was more serious, and her song was already in the melody of lament rather than the tune from the repertoire of love songs initially used by the thief.

8.7	ŋo mi t'e ni pe do	we've borne the most beautiful girl
	ne ho ni pe ho	we've raised the loveliest daughter
	ne ho nó lí la	to see her is to love her
	kə tsæ p'a yi lu	a body like a flower
	n tsæ n̂ jɔ pe	nothing if not beautiful
	p'a ni mæ bo pe	trailing flowers
	mà li mæ bo pe	draped in embroidery
	mò ca tsæ ga ba	her beauty blossomed early
	mò ca p'a ga ba	her skills arrived early

This singer, too, then moved into the lexical register of lament, which required all the shifts of participant framework that the thief had already managed. The author became the lament tradition, the principal became the mourning daughter, the focal addressees became the dead couple, and the ratified bystanders became the crowd.

8.8	ŋǽ ku kæ wú li pe	the courtyard makes our heads ache
	ŋǽ ni̱ mà le lɔ́ t'ɔ̀ pe	our hearts fall from our chests
	ni̱ mo le chr̀ la̱ p'a̱	our hearts rot away

Having descended to the edge of the crowd, the thief now approached to within about ten yards of his interlocutor. He interrupted her, demolishing the serious tone she had adopted and sending parts of the crowd into gales of laughter. Taking up the *p'a̱* from *la̱ p'a̱*, "to rot," in the woman's last line, replacing it with its near homonym *p'à*, "to change" as in "to change clothing," and enlarging on the theme of rich Han obsessed with their own sartorial magnificence, the thief sang as though in the voice of the women, while mocking them at the same time. This shift of voice was signaled by the first person plural pronoun *ŋǽ* in the last line:

8.9	p'à ce p'à lo ga	let's change back
	p'à ce ts'ɔ ja p'à kò lo	change back into high-class people
	ŋǽ ce mo sɨ sɨ p'à me p'à kò lo	let's change back to look just like Han girls

Guffaws from the men, outrage among the women. "The creep is making fun of
us!" exclaimed one of the women clustered around the female singer. The thief
continued, casting aspersions on his opponent's skill as a singer, her attractive-
ness as a possible bride, and even her mother's virtue. This final shift of voice
projected a more intimate but still fluid social persona. This was the persona of
a young lover taunting a conquest within earshot of her friends, but it also approached a persona that the man playing the thief, an older man confident that
he was besting his opponent in this dialogue, may have called his own.

8.10   mæ̀ ne rò kɔ́ bɛ chì po jɔ   some people say you young ladies are
                                              witty
       mé və ho la rò   they say you want a lover
       n nə ǹ bɛ ga   you can hardly speak
       a gɔ̀ no ho ga   you'll never get a husband
       n à mo ne te ni   you are your mother's
                                              daughter
           ŋo m bɛ ni lo ŋo á   I said nothing and you
           dù ti lɔ   came knocking at
                                                     my door

The female singer responded in a corresponding voice, dropping her lament
and addressing her opponent directly. In the first stanza of excerpt 8.11 below, she repeatedly used the first person plural pronoun (ŋǽ) to contrast with
her opponent's first person singular (ŋo), gaining some distance and supporting her higher moral tone by voicing her friends' and supporters' collective
condemnation of his character. The first-person pronouns disappeared in the
second stanza, as she countered her opponent's accusation that she (or the
persona of the young woman she was voicing—a deliberate lack of clarity) had
come knocking at his door. Her confession was staged in a voice that corre-
sponded to that adopted by her adversary: a girl retaliating against her former
lover's taunts, approaching the voice of a mature woman furious with a former
friend for exposing her in public:

8.11   ŋǽ à bɛ ka ka bɛ   to us your slander is wanton
       ŋǽ ts'ɔ pẹ sa go bɛ   to be a person is to speak civilly
       ŋǽ ǹ tsæ p'u t'e do   we all see your ugliness
       ŋǽ ni kà ŋǽ ba ni   we feel sorrow for you
       ŋǽ ǹ tsæ jr ǹ jɔ kæ   we don't mind being ugly

       a sa lò ho á dù ŋɔ   who asked you knock on my door?
       n tsæ ni t'à lɔ   If I am so ugly do not come in!
       n tsæ ǹ bɛ də   you speak of ugliness
       n tsæ ǹ hi hæ̀ lu   so why did you lead this ugly girl away?

In this dialog, shifts in voice, lexical register, and participant framework accompanied the thief's movement down from the graveyard to the edge of the living crowd. He spoke initially from the graveyard in the voice of the dead couple, addressing the living arrayed below. As he approached the assembly's edge, he shifted to the register of lament, as though looking back on the mountain of the dead, addressing them in the voice of a mourner poised between worlds, body with the living, soul clinging to the dead. It was only after he entered the crowd of the living and faced his opponent that he addressed first the cluster of women around the singer then the singer herself, first voicing the persona of ugly Lipò girls longing to look like Han girls, then projecting the ambiguous persona of a taunting young lover or an older amour. Though his opponent stood in one place, ladling water and scattering bits of rice loaf, her song followed every step of his journey, mirroring his shifts of voice, register, and framework with corresponding shifts of her own.

As the thief sang his dialog with the daughter's supporter, the orphaned son carried the two sprouts of grass to the space the *àpipò* had cleared beside his table, where they would become the innermost core of the new *nègu*, the *bu* for the dead. The men who had dragged the uprooted pine tree down from the mountain positioned it with its crown pointing at this space. The dead soul had made another journey, from graveyard to ritual site. Like the journey that had been folded into the convergent layering of the ancestral effigy, the simple series of this journey would be transformed into a complex, inclusive form in the *bu*. Yet it was in the interests of the living descendants to carve a particular path of intention through the world that the material bodies of the dead would enfold. The dialog between the brother-in-law (or brother-in-law's son) and daughter, through their proxies of thief and supporter, drew the entire assembly, living and dead, into a playful expression of the intention to bend the soul's journey towards the generative power of lovemaking. While this journey had been traced by the feet of the thief and orphaned son, it was also outlined in voices—the voices of the dead that began the song shifting to the voices of their younger selves taunting each other during lovemaking, this shift cycling forward to the possible unity of the children of their daughter and son. At the same time, the dialog exposed the layered entanglement of persons and relations involved in every act of lovemaking. The dead are present, for they are the force that couples youths in love and graces love with issue. The mourning children of the dead are present, for it is their suffering that seals the contract with the dead and retrieves the power of generative fertility from beyond the door of the tombstone. And of course the grandchildren, the issue of cross siblings, are the persons whom everyone desires to make love. However, love also condenses a fluctuating panoply of orientations to other and self: desire, ambition, disparagement, self-congratulation, self-denigration, betrayal, anger, scorn, and disavowal, all folded into this explosive core of uprooted tree and grass seedlings, transported down from the mountain to create the *bu*.

Assembling an Extensive Body

The orphaned son dug a small hole, lined it with hemp cloth, planted the two sprouts of grass into a small rice loaf, and placed the loaf in the lined hole. He cut a boiled egg in two and positioned the cut sides of both halves against the rice loaf. Loaf, egg, hemp, and earth surrounded the grass seedlings like a womb surrounding a fetus. At Wòdɔwò, the great uprooted tree lay with its tip pointing towards this wrapped, swollen, sprouting rice loaf: "who asked you to knock on my door?" This tree was but a crude, high-mountain innovation, my friends in Júzò protested, never used in their civilized valley, where less blatant imagery was preferred. As the dead couple at Wòdɔwò had children, the *bu* would be oriented to face east, so the great pine tree trailed off to the west (a *bu* for a couple without children would face west). Many of the songs of the *nèpi* repeated:

8.12	tsạ wú pi kə nè	cradled head to the west
	tsạ p'à pi do nè	cradled facing east
	tsạ chì shr̀ na nè	cradled feet in the stars

Now a man from the brothers-in-law's (*avə*) group took over building, driving four stakes into the ground around the hole, one in each of the four directions. He tied the bases of three pine saplings and three chestnut saplings to each stake and tied all twenty-four saplings together at their tips to create an eight-foot-high arch, with abundant foliage of pine needles and chestnut leaves. At one corner, the "bird on a pine branch" was planted; at a second corner was planted a bamboo pole sharpened at the end and stuck into the corpse of a rat or squirrel; at a third corner was planted a bamboo pole split at the end and woven into a basket into which brine shrimp and mud eels were placed.

"Brine shrimp and mud eels are our 'exotic delicacies' (shanzhen haiwei 山珍海味)," a participant at Wòdɔwò told me, using the common Chinese phrase, which had an effete ring in this context. "We are giving the dead all the highest classes of foods," he continued. "We give you everything that crawls on the earth as your playthings." In Júzò, people talked about the medicinal effects of eels. "You cut their throats, dribble the blood into sorghum wine, and use this medicine to cure injuries from falls, fractures, blows, and sprains," one healer told me. "The eels' blood enlivens the blood that has stagnated in a wound or bruise. Everyone has taken this medicine. The eels' blood makes your whole body ache suddenly as all the blood in your body begins to move more quickly. This is probably why it was used in the *bu*."

After being assembled, the *bu* was clothed. The daughters' supporters contributed two rolls of cloth, winding twelve turns of white hemp and six turns of black cotton around the clustered pine and chestnut saplings. Then layer after layer of clothing was tied over the cloth—new nylon or cotton men's clothing, richly embroidered black cotton women's blouses, aprons, and trousers. Each central family in the three groups was expected to contribute one set of nine items of men's clothing and one set of seven items of women's clothing. Over the clothing were tied layers of square black embroidered child-carrying cloths, contributed by the daughter and her supporters. The orphaned son then dumped a bowl of cooked sticky rice with two pieces of pork fat over the grass seedlings in their hole. One of the orphaned son's supporters had bought water from the river-dwelling *ci*; he set the bucket next to the assembled *bu*, and the daughter began to ladle water into the hole with the grass seedlings, now covered with cooked rice. Women of the daughters' group dug a small gutter out away from the hole for the water to flow down and scattered grain into the gutter, mirroring the empty rectangle of Dawn-to-Dusk Sacrifice, when water was spooned into the hole where the corpse's head once lay, running down a gutter through the empty body. The old man who had been hired to lament during the night wept again, in the "weeping for the dead" (*shrtsiŋɔ*) style. After emptying small traveling bamboo rice boxes of cooked rice and pork fat over the grass seedlings at the *bu*'s center, women allied with the orphaned daughter sat on benches placed around the *bu* and sang "weeping songs" (*ɔchɔŋɔ*), lamenting the dead couple and asking them to convey the singers' words, tears, and offerings to their own intimate dead. A gourd-pipe player led the three thieves, armed with pig-killing knives and bamboo staffs, in a dance around the *bu* and lamenters. They danced three rounds backwards, whooped the "cry to heaven," and danced three rounds forwards. The brother-in-law's thief picked up a crossbow, shot an arrow towards the sun, and hung the bow on the *bu*. The host's manager brought out about six <u>sheng</u> (1.5 gallons) of a mixture of oats, honey, and hemp seed—all high-mountain foods—and tossed handfuls at the *bu*'s four corners, shouting, "all you ghosts of wild mountains (*saká*), all you dead that belong to others (*nèŋa*), all who are hungry, now come and eat!" He scattered a third of what remained on the ground and left the rest out for people to take as they saw fit. "They grab it at random," said Apima, "like all the knifeless ghosts."

While women tied clothing onto the *bu*, men built fires, killed and butchered goats, and boiled the goat meat. A winnowing basket was placed on the table before the *bu*, and there the host's manager presided over *jì'ítị*, the exchange of meat, rice loaves, and grain at the center of every death ritual. As at Emerging from the Courtyard and Dawn-to-Dusk Sacrifice, *jì'ítì* exchange foregrounded images of each of the relations presumed to have composed the couple in life. The bodies of goats and rice loaves were partitioned along the lines of those relations, bringing each relation to the fore in the act of dissevering it. My friends in Júzò found a few variations specific to Tenth-Month Sacrifice worth mentioning. Three or four hundred small rice loaves, prepared by the host family, were piled on a winnowing basket at the tail of the *bu* and then distributed. Sixty small rice loaves were given to each of the brothers-in-law (*avə*) to distribute to their supporters, and if sixty were not enough, the *avə* would ask for more. Sixty were given to each daughter to give to her supporters, thirty to each of the granddaughters, twenty or thirty to the wife's sisters, and twenty or thirty to the husband's bothers' sons and daughters. In practice, this giant pile of fist-sized rice loaves was often depleted by thieves when the orphaned son and host's manager were attending to other matters. These rice loaves comprised a significant outlay of grain for the host family. Having taken in far more grain during Emerging from the Courtyard and Dawn-to-Dusk Sacrifice than they distributed, they expended much of that excess here.

After the four to eight hours of *jì'ítì* exchange, and the "*avə* handover," a tableau of corpses was created as an offering to the ancestral effigy. The host family killed a ram and a nanny goat and laid out their bodies facing each other, the nanny goat with hemp fiber in its mouth streaming towards its tail, representing everything unclean, with which the goat was said to be running away. The orphaned son placed a piglet in a hemp bag and asked the host's thief to strangle it. This was the only animal in all of death ritual aside from the "soul's chick" to be killed without slitting its throat and gathering the blood. "Its body is clean, free of blood, so the dead soul is happy to go back home with it," was Àp'ìmà's comment. Like the "soul's chick," the piglet was yet a virtual body, undivided, undistributed, not made the image of any particular relation, potentially containing every relation—a fit receptacle for a soul still not entirely subject to the instrumental intentions of its descendants. The piglet was placed between the dead ram and nanny goat with its mouth to the nanny's teat, an image of generative unity created from bodies classified not by their form but by what they were capable of—the ram of insemination, the nanny of giving birth, the piglet of being born—powers controlled by the dead, which could still be withheld according to their whim.

The pelts of the ram and nanny goat were given to the *àpipò* as part of his fee; later he crafted them into bags in the shape of a small sheep and goat, which he brought back to the host to fill with two <u>sheng</u> of unhusked rice, half a big rice loaf, and three small rice loaves. The meat of these sacrifices was divided among the three thieves and the host's manager. The *avɔ* helped the orphaned son carefully wrap the strangled pig together with the ancestral effigy in his hemp apron, and the two walked back to the orphaned son's house, followed by his most intimate kin. There, the orphaned son's wife or daughter placed the effigy, now renewed with a new woven bamboo platform and new threads binding the male and female figurines together, on the wall beside the effigies of its ascendants. The strangled piglet was laid out on the bed below it, and a last meal was served to the guests. At the ritual site, other guests dismantled the *bu*. The orphaned daughter directed one of her supporters to take the "bird on a pine branch" up the mountain and place it on the grave. The soul had been returned to house and grave where it had resided before the ritual began. Those who had placed clothing on the *bu* reclaimed it. The hemp that had been wound around the saplings was distributed to the three thieves and the gourd pipe player. The core of the *bu* was bundled up, carried to a gully, and cremated.

Virtual Wholes, Actual Parts

The *bu* may be understood in the same way as the body for the dead assembled for the Emerging from the Courtyard ritual. A singular, impersonal soul, evanescent and without content, is folded into layers that attach it to elements of the immanent world with all their affective associations and entailments— the egg split around the rice loaf and grass seedlings; the bed of hemp and earth; the sticky rice and fat heaped on them; the river water ladled over them; the twelve pine saplings and twelve chestnut saplings, male and female elements of the twelve-month cycle of the world, arced over them; the squirrels, mud eels, and brine shrimp standing in for all the world's crawling and swimming creatures, dangling from bamboo poles beside them; the "bird on a pine branch" concentrating all the world's visual beauty, fluttering above them. These corporeal parts all display "impenetrability, inertia, impetuosity and attachment." It takes the world-building effort of the *nèpi* chanted beside the *bu* to force each part to include infinite series: all the world's birds, beasts, and bugs, all the rules and seeds that clothe the earth in trees, and so on. At the same time, the qualities of these materials are employed to create a defined intentional path through the varied series of the world. With its imagery of grass, rice loaf, hemp, egg, chestnut, and pine, the *bu* is a forceful attempt to draw a particular power out of the dead soul, the power of generative union. The core of the *bu,* like the core of any dead body, is wrapped in images of the relations of love and care that surrounded the body while alive, branching out into relations of relations, each male donor multiplying into nine, each female into seven. It is then further wrapped in images of other varied relations. The myriad exchanges of goats and rice loaves image and dissever hundreds of living relations; the mourners ask the dead soul to pass gifts on to other dead.

All this is predictable, drawn from the analysis in chapters 2 and 3. However, the *nèpi* also theorizes the *bu*, and in quite a different way. As the *bu* was being built, as the daughter's allies lamented, and as *jì'íti* exchange proceeded, the *àpìpò* did not cease to chant, working through the songs already mentioned. After the songs of the ancestral effigy, the *àpìpò* performed a set of songs about the *bu*: four brief preparatory songs followed by a long song about origins. The "song of grasses," *cí pe chœ*, is about selecting the small, hairy species of crabgrass at the *bu*'s center. Grasses may be selected during the fourth month, when the rain falls three times a day. All living creatures on earth select grasses, lambs select grass leaves, rabbits select grass roots:

> 8.13   bùi hò á lí zò   dogs of flying ants
>   lú zò cí ŋa bɛ   criminals speak of grasses
>   da zò cí ŋa bɛ   killers speak of grasses

Spear grass is the grass of kings and officials, the song continues. The grass used to call lambs is the grass of farmers and herders, but along the bluffs grows a kind of crabgrass, and that is the chosen grass, the grass of ghosts cradled with their heads to the west, facing east, feet in the stars. The "song of the silver of old age," *ts'ì p'u zœ p'u chœ*, continues the theme of the materials used in the *bu*, working through the series of pine, chestnut, and bamboo. The song tells of an old man herding goats. He follows his goats along a gully where he sees tapered green bamboo. He sets the bamboo up as thick clothing for his dead father and colorful clothing for his dead mother. He follows his goats to the high, forested mountains where he sees three pairs of pines; he follows his goats along the road where he sees three tapered chestnuts. He sets the pine up as father, he sets the chestnut up as mother.

The "song of the cry," *kǒ yi kǒ le chœ*, folds the "cry to heaven" voiced by the dancing thieves into the *bu*. The thieves' voices echo the cry of the messenger who brought news of Pìmæneli's son's death to his father in the sky:

> 8.14   mi kǒ mùi tɛ yi   a cry from earth ascends to the sky
>   mùi kǒ mi je lɔ   a cry from the sky descends to the earth

Having ascended to heaven, the cry descends as Pìmæneli descended—the shaman's cry, the *àpìpò*'s ringing voice. In the "song of the cry," the cry descends on pine and on chestnut, on black goats and black sacrificial pigs, on the aprons of sons and grandsons—moving out from the core of the *bu* into the concentric rings of relations that surround it. Finally, the "song of animal sacrifices," *jè kə̀ mà kə̀ chæ̀*, speaks of all the live offerings for the *buɯ*:

8.15   à sà jè dǫ sǫ   who brought this animal?
        ni zò kǽ væ̀ jè dǫ sǫ . . .   your eldest son brought it . . .

The song works in this fashion through the series of kin: elder sons, younger sons, younger daughters, wife's elder brothers, wife's younger brothers, wife's elder sisters, wife's younger sisters, elder sons (again), younger sons (again), elder children of sons, younger children of sons, elder great-grandchildren, younger great-grandchildren, husband's elder sisters, husband's younger sisters, elder children of daughters, younger children of daughters. While this series does not precisely match the order of sacrifice and exchange (table 3.3), it includes all of the categories in that list. In these songs, the *nèpi* again moves out from the fleshy core of the *nègu* into the folds of relations in which it is wrapped.

This set of songs culminates in a long song that repeats and continues the story of how Pịmæ̀nelì attempted to resurrect his dead son's ashes. This song has two titles: "song of setting up an effigy bound with cloth," *buɯ tsì buɯ tǫ p̀a ní sì lè chæ̀*, in Tenth-Month Sacrifice and "song of seventy body parts," *shr̀ ts'i buɯ mo chæ̀*, in Sleeping in the Forest. In this version of the story, it is Pịmæ̀nelì's son, now named as Àgò'àtə̀, who makes the "resurrection medicine" from a snake, traveling to a hundred places to cure the dead of their deaths before he himself dies of cold and hunger. When Pịmæ̀nelì is asked to treat the dragon he demands medicine for himself, in addition to his fee of three thousand sheep and three hundred cattle. Here he is, describing the enervating effects on his body of having to speak. Incipient human body series have appeared in other songs: heart, eyes; head, torso, feet. But only in this song is the living human body extended into a full series, as elaborate as the ox-body series out of which the world is made:

8.16   pị pị ŋo wú no   I speak and my head hurts
            ts'ì wú ŋo gò̀ lɔ   give me medicine for my head
        pị pị ŋo lu no   I speak and my tongue hurts
            ts'ì lu ŋo gò̀ lɔ   give me medicine for my tongue
        pị pị ŋo ji no   I speak and my skin hurts
            ji k̀o tsú gò̀ lɔ   stick my skin back together
        pị pị ŋo chi no   I speak and my feet hurt
            chi t'ì bò̀ gò̀ lɔ   keep me from stumbling
        pị pị ŋo ní no   I speak and my heart hurts
            ní ts'ì hò̀ gò̀ lɔ   give me heart medicine

pi̱ pi̱ ŋo sɨ no	I speak and my liver hurts
sɨ ts'ɨ́ ká gɔ̀ lɔ	dig up liver medicine for me
pi̱ pi̱ ŋo pɯ no	I speak and my lungs hurt
pɯ ts'ɨ́ ká gɔ̀ lɔ	dig up lung medicine for me
pi̱ pi̱ ŋo je̱ no	I speak and I get cold
je̱ ts'ɨ́ ts'a gɔ̀ lɔ	gather cold medicine for me
pi̱ pi̱ ŋo mæ no	I speak and my penis hurts
mæ mo ŋo gɔ̀ lɔ	take care of my penis
ts'ɨ̀ mæ ŋo gɔ̀ lɔ	give me penis medicine

The idea that ritual speech depletes the speaker of strength and warmth, eas-ily making him ill, was commonly held among ritualists. It was one reason that some believed that Li Bicong's sale to me of these verses helped bring on his death two years later. In this version of the story of Pi̱mæneli̱'s attempt to resurrect his dead son, it helps explain Àgò'àta̱'s death of cold and hunger after he used his snake medicine to reanimate hundreds of dead.

Here the shaman is clearly speaking of his own body. However, immediately after his demand for penis medicine, the focus of his speech shifts to the corpse of his son lying before him, reconstituted from ashes with the dregs of the res-urrection medicine. In all previous songs, the word used for corpse is *ma* (as in, "your head dies but not your corpse," *wú shr ma tà shr*, in excerpt 7.27). Here, however, the specialized word *bɯ* is used. I have been referring to the *nègu* for the dead used at Tenth-Month Sacrifice as the *bɯ*, but the word can also mean corpse or, more commonly, statue. The prototypical *bɯ* is the god of salt re-puted to stand over the salt works at Baiyanjing near the former regional capital of Tsòdù/Yanfeng, as noted in the introduction. The old man who discovered salt there was made into a god as his reward, by an official who slaughtered an ox, wrapped the man in its hide, and stood him up in the sun to dry into the shape of a statue. The most fearsome *bɯ* are statues in Buddhist temples, immobile corpses that infect all who encounter them with disaster or death, requiring a *nèpi̱* called "sacrifice to the *bɯ*" to counter. The song continues:

8.17	bɛ pi̱ æ̀ lè tṵ	I speak and he rises up
	bɯ pi̱ í lè tṵ	I speak to the *bɯ* and his hands move
	í lè tṵ lɔ ga	his hands begin to move
	mṳ̀ do mṳ̀ hə	to the top of heaven
	mi gə mi tè lɔ	through earth's corners
	bɯ pi̱ bɯ tṵ ga	I speak and the *bɯ* emerges
	bɯ pi̱ bɯ kó ga	I speak and the *bɯ* begins
	bɯ pi̱ bɯ lí ga	I speak and the *bɯ* flourishes
	bɯ wo ni ní shr	a *bɯ* for your heart's content

The final four lines of this excerpt are variations on the lines that describe Pịmæ̀nelì's reanimation of all his dead kin in the "song of shaman and ghost," replacing *bu*, "people" with *buɯ* (as in "speak and people begin," *bu pị bu kó ga*, and "speak and people emerge," *bu pị bu tụ ga*, in excerpt 7.32). As Pịmæ̀nelì's speech depletes his body from head to penis, it reanimates the corpse of his son part by part—thus the title, "song of seventy body (*buɯ*) parts," in the Sleeping in the Forest version. The chanting *àpịpǒ*, Pịmæ̀nelì's descendant and avatar, is speaking to the *buɯ* standing before him, striking the top of the effigy as he sings, "I speak and my head hurts, give me medicine for my head," and proceeding down the corpse of the *buɯ* as he moves through the series, thus the title, "song of setting up an effigy bound with cloth," in the Tenth-Month Sacrifice version.

Much the same procedure, involving different bodies, was used after the ancestral effigy arrived at the house. The strangled piglet was laid on the bed below the ancestral effigies, head upstream, facing east. The *àpịpǒ* lay a handful of pine needles on the piglet's head, then struck the corpse with the needles in seven places as he chanted: head, neck, shoulder, loin, rump, hocks, tail:

8.18	ma ǹ dæ̀ ǹ do	if I do not point you will not receive
	ma dæ̀ wú ká jẹ	I point out this head
	wú ka jẹ yi ka	receive this head
	mà li ká jẹ	receive this neck
	li ká jẹ p'æ gɔ	this neck tied with a rope
	ma ǹ dæ̀ ǹ do	if I do not point, you will not receive
	ma dæ̀ p'æ ká jẹ	I point out this shoulder
	p'æ wú nè hɔ̀ va	a shoulder where ghosts stand
	p'æ jò ne yi hạ	a shoulder is a sea of bubbling wine

After walking his speech down to the tail, the *àpịpǒ* picked a bright coal out of the fire with tongs and touched the pig with the coal in each of the seven places while repeating the chant. Then he swept the pig from head to foot with a chestnut bough.

These are alliances, made using the mediating substance of the *àpịpǒ*'s "cry" that ascends to the sky, then works through the body series while descending to earth. They are alliances among bodies given as wholes and bodies made as assemblages: the shaman's body and the *buɯ*, the pig's body and the ancestral effigy. Every body is a virtual body until sacrifice divides it into parts; only then is the body actualized as an assemblage of parts that enter into relations with other parts. In the world of the *nèpị*, the shaman has gained a body for the first time—a body now divided part from part, each part allied with a part of the *buɯ*. These exchanges differ from sacrifices only in that, where the intention is the impossible task of reanimating the bodies of the dead, the whole is more explicitly foregrounded before being divided—an ordered progression from head to tail (*mǽ*) or head to penis (also *mǽ*)—for in the world of the *nèpi̱* there is no whole that is not actualized into a series. The whole is foregrounded because only as a whole does the body have that impersonal but singular spark of life that the shaman transfers to the *bu* and the *àpipȍ* transfers to the ancestral effigy (literally a spark, a burning ember). In sacrifice, the spark of life transfers over the threshold to the underworld, where the dead will raise the goat's soul. Here, in the world of matter and affect, the spark of life moves from one extensive body to another.

These procedures are little different from the procedure used by the deaf-mute in differentiating and actualizing the virtual whole of the world, where the shaman's unspeaking double produces a full body series as he sacrifices the ox. The earth is but a *bu*, a corpse animated by sacrifice. This great *bu* is populated with markets, the virtual form of the relation of alliance, which gives rise to all generative relations. The earth is clothed with trees, intensive forms out of which extensive bodies are fashioned to contain specific contractual relations and intentions. *Bu* and ancestral effigy are made by choosing, cutting, and assembling parts from the vast effigy of the earth. In the "song of rules and seeds," abstract unspecified "rules and procedures" generate these impersonal indeterminate bodily forms, which the acts and words of shamans manufacture into actual bodies. Every virtual whole is partitioned; every actual part enters into relations with other parts. However, to be a body, the *bu* must become a whole, rather than merely an assemblage of determinate parts, and it can only borrow this wholeness from a living body. In lament, this sense of wholeness is borrowed from the memory of the living parent. Here, it is borrowed from the living body of the shaman, as he makes an alliance between his body and the reconstituted corpse of his son, the body of the effigy.

Sleeping in the Forest

The power to procreate was hard-won, made through suffering together to produce gifts for the dead, to bind the dead into contracts, and to force the dead to work for the living. Yet all funeral rituals imaged and dissevered relations with the dead, and the power to procreate became freely available only as these relations finally faded, leaving the dead free to dissolve into sky and earth. If the major funerals are taken in chronological order from Emerging from the Courtyard to Sleeping in the Forest, the theme of procreation becomes increasingly dominant, emerging gradually from layers of other concerns. Because Sleeping in the Forest was abandoned six years before Tenth-

Month Sacrifice, and because even in the 1940s it was performed only for an estimated one-third of the dead, most in Júzò who remembered anything about it had only attended as children. Most people who could talk about the ceremony at all dwelled on the opportunities for playful courting it provided. As always, Àp'ìmà was the exception. She said she had participated in seven Sleeping in the Forest rituals as a daughter's supporter and attended many others for more distant kin.

Sleeping in the Forest was performed two or three generations after a death. "My mother will never give my grandmother a Sleeping in the Forest ritual," said Àp'ìmà. "But I may give her one after I am old. If I do not, it will be up to my children. Usually, it was the great-grandchildren's responsibility." All Sleeping in the Forest rituals in Júzò were performed in the same place: a grove of old-growth trees just below the flat, treeless site where people from Chezò and parts of Chemo performed Tenth-Month Sacrifice. Most of the "rules and procedures" for the ritual repeated those of Tenth-Month Sacrifice. The most prominent difference was that the concern of Tenth-Month Sacrifice with producing a *bu*, a material dead body, was replaced in Sleeping in the Forest by a ubiquitous emphasis on procreation.

Sleeping in the Forest began the same way as Tenth-Month Sacrifice—a hundred bowls of bean curd were prepared the night before and distributed in the morning, and an elderly man was asked to sing lament in the inner room. In the morning, *ji'íti̯* exchange was performed in the courtyard, but it involved no animal sacrifice, only rice loaves and grain. At about noon, the ancestral effigy was removed from the wall and carried in procession to the ritual site, along with an enormous pile of firewood, two big steamers of maize, a steamer of buckwheat, a piglet in a hemp bag, and at least two big goats, all donated by the host family. The daughter's supporters brought pots of homemade sweet rice beer. Inside the grove, the ground was littered with small erect stones, exactly like the stones that had once been set up over the buried ashes of cremated dead. Each stone was identified with a patrilineage. The *àpip'ö* built the *nègu* for his spirit familiar on the hillside above the appropriate stone, establishing the stone's "head," and the assembly took up their positions around the stone as *avǝ*, *zòmæ̀*, and *vɛdu*. The central roles in these groups had to be reestablished on the basis of inheritance, the central daughter's role (*zòmæ̀ kachì*) being inherited matrilineally. The two goats contributed by the hosts were killed, portions of their meat given as fees to the *àpip'ö* and the master of ceremonies, the rest chopped and divided into hundreds of piles on a bed of pine needles. The networked modeling of relations effected by *ji'íti* exchange was absent from this ritual site. Instead, equal portions of goat meat were distributed directly to the participants. The only relations imaged were those of each individual participant to the host family, identical with the procedure followed at exorcism rituals. The host's thief strangled the piglet in its bag and placed it before the àpipò, who began his songs by midafternoon, chanting rapidly until after dark, when three huge bonfires were built, one for each of the three groups. Women of the daughters' group spent the night serving out rice beer to every participant, first splashing a bit from each pot into a bowl placed at the stone's head. At dawn, the avə wrapped the strangled piglet in the orphaned son's apron along with the ancestral effigy, and the most intimate guests followed the host home to help reinstall the effigy on the wall.

Everyone remembered the ritual's lighthearted tone. "There was no grief, only play," said Àp'ìmà. No one sang lament, but older people sang other genres of mèkòbɛ, songs of growth and renewal. "The best thing was to just show up in the grove without going to the house first," an elderly male ritualist told us. "You did not have to bring a thing, and no one cared. You could just sit there and get drunk all night, so the grove was full of people for the entire tenth month." "There was no shame," Lichink'æpò whispered while Àp'ìmà sipped her tea, pretending not to hear. "Those with relations of shame could not sit together. You had to be careful of that, because if you sat near your mother, she would see you listening when people told dirty jokes." Lichink'æpò had been only ten years old at Liberation, so his memories were those of a child. Children leapt over the fires; youths played flutes and mouth harps, courting instruments normally not played when generations were together. Boys made bamboo water guns to squirt girls and each other. "One reason the fires were so big was so the pretty girls could dry themselves out after getting soaked by crowds of boys." Meanwhile, couples disappeared into the darkness beyond the firelight: the weather was still warm enough during the tenth month that a couple could lie together on a pair of goatskins, perhaps warmed by a small private fire.

Songs of the Terrible End and Raucous Beginning

The nèpi's final songs escort the soul to its destination and celebrate the return of life. Three of these songs further develop the topic of the soul ascending to the eagle's nest and descending to the underworld, though these songs do not share the formal parallel features of the previous sets of songs about these topics. The affective engagement with the dead soul in these songs is more intense than in earlier songs, and the songs reveal that, from the dead soul's perspective, the eagle's nest and underworld are ghoulish, terrifying places. Inserted between these songs is the enigmatic "song of the pounder and silkworm," which, in Àp'ìmà's interpretation, further develops the topic of the dead person's material body. The last song of the chant, kept secret from all but older married men, is explicit about the intended final result of the ritual.

The "song of sleeping in the ghost's nest," *nè pʼə yì pʼə chæ̀*, begins by encouraging the soul to go "sleep in terrifying places" with the kin of its lineage:

8.19	tsə yì yi sə sə	your lineage sleeps soundly
	ni nè yì yi sə sə	you ghost, go sleep soundly
	tsə yì cì mò mò	your lineage sleeps with many kin
	ni yì cì mò mò	you sleep with many kin

The song rehearses the flight of the eagle for a final time. This time, the eagle seizes not a chick but a "boa with a painted tail," carrying it to its nest, where the eagle dies, pierced by the shaman's arrow. This is where the soul must now settle down to sleep:

8.20	æ̀ jé wú chì ŋə	in a corner of the eagle's nest
	cæ ne sì chì pə̣	a pile of snake's blood
	æ̀ jé tu̧ chì pʼə	where the eagle flapped his wings
	tsæ mo ká chì jì	on a branch of an apple-pear tree
	cæ̀ me sì chì pə̣	a pile of snake's blood
	shi mo hə̣ chì pə̣	a pile of green bottle fly maggots
	yì yi sɛ sɛ	go sleep in terror
	mó yì yi sɛ sɛ	go sleep in the terrifying underworld
	tsæ yì ŋə mò mò	the apple-pear tree's leaves flutter
	nè yì ŋə mò mò	flutter in the bed of ghosts

"Those lines about fluttering leaves give you the most terrible feeling," Lichin-kʼæpʼò said, and he ventured his own interpretation. "The song is about a time when an eagle was eating all the chickens in a village. No one could kill the eagle, but an old Lòlo man shot it in its nest. When he climbed up to the nest to get it, he saw, amongst piles of blood, all the jewelry of all the people the eagle had killed." Though eagles cannot kill people, the equivalence the *nèpi* had established between chicks and humans as the eagle's victims was strong enough for this story to ring true.

After the "song of the pounder and silkworm," which I will discuss out of sequence below, two final songs urge the dead on into the underworld. The "song of the ghost freely departing," *nè pʼu yì pʼu chæ̀*, appearing only in the Sleeping in the Forest version, varies in its title by only one repeated phoneme from the "song of sleeping in the ghost's nest," *nè pʼə yì pʼə chæ̀* (excerpts 8.19 and 8.20), as the *nèpi* continues to track eagle's nest and underworld through scattered coordinates of parallel verses and phrases. In a few verses set between the introductory and concluding segments, the "song of the ghost freely departing" encourages the soul to leave peacefully in its old age, "take the road to the underworld, others walk the same road, go to the sky's heights without lingering, go to the earth's tail without stopping." Finally, the much longer "song of the underworld road," *mi ŋè jo mó chœ*, begins with the corpse on the bed, "wrapped in black and white quilts, wrapped in red and gold quilts." It then points out the path to the underworld, step by step:

8.21	mo cæ ŋə̀ ga pǫ	lie on your bamboo mat
	kó tə mo tʼè ŋə̀	approach the side of the bed
	kó tə mo tʼè pǫ	lie beside the bed
	á dù tị̀ tʼè ŋə̀	approach the threshold
	á dù tị̀ tʼè pǫ	lie against the threshold
	tsʼi nì kæ ka ŋə̀	approach twelve courtyards
	tsʼi nì kæ ka pǫ	lie in twelve courtyards
	tsʼi nì kà lì ŋə̀	approach twelve gravesites
	tsʼi nì kà lì pǫ	lie in twelve gravesites

"Enter the ghost world, approach the spirit world . . . here is a wallet full of money, I count it as paper money, you count it as copper money . . . tigers beg beside the road, leopards beg in the road, toss the money with your right hand, scatter it with your left." Arriving at the threshold to the underworld, the soul is confronted with the terrifying sight of the underworld king:

8.22	mó mi yà lò wù	Yan Luo Wang of the underworld
	nó pɔ là ka le	ears like millstones
	me sæ̀ kǽ mo le	eyeballs like stars
	lè và hə və̀ le	forearms like iron pillars
	lè pǫ tsʼə pǫ le	biceps like mortars
	lè ni hə̀ kạ le	fingers like iron bars
	m bə̀ ǹ shr lu	never falls ill, never dies
	n ə̣ ǹ æ lu	never stops, never starts
	kʼo nì tʼà mo jɔ	there is such a one
	kʼo nì tʼà jo sὲ	don't you fear him
	kʼo nì tʼà ŋò sὲ	don't you turn in terror
	ni si gò wù má chɔ	plow a straight, true furrow

"Go use these livestock for a thousand years," the song continues, "use this silver for a thousand years." And in a final exhortation, in case the *nèpi* has not been sufficient despite its length, "do as I have sung, do even what I have not sung."

At Wòdɔwò, it was almost dusk. The *àpip'ò* had at long last finished chanting. The coupled souls had been sent off for a final time to their terrible fates. The ancestral effigy had been wrapped with the strangled piglet in the orphaned son's apron and carried down the hill to its home. The *bu* had been disassembled, thrown in the gully, and burned. Most the guests had scattered, leaving only a cluster of older men at the ritual site—the *àpip'ò*, the *avə*, the *avə*'s thief, and a few others. "Those who stay behind are mostly drunkards," I was told, "or men with very thick skins." When the ancestral effigy departed, a few kind souls urged me to go with it, hoping to spare me embarrassment, but Lichink'æp'ò, sensing some residual excitement, insisted that we both stay. After some confused discussion, the remaining men gathered about the *àpip'ò* and the central *avə*. The *avə* donned a wool-felt vest, unusual garb in this area, where everyone wore goatskins. The *àpip'ò* cut a terminal leader, about three feet long, from a pine tree. He held this in one hand while he handed the *avə* a slice of boiled goats blood with the other. The *avə* swallowed the blood, and then the *àpip'ò* sprang at him and chased him around the ritual field, jabbing at his buttocks with the pine terminal leader, chanting at the top of his voice, while the onlookers laughed uproariously.

Li Bicong did not include this final chant in his performance, but several other *àpip'ò* told us about it, giving it the Chinese name <u>jiaoweijing</u> 交尾經, which might be rendered "song of mating." Dolecip'ò, a frail, elderly *àpip'ò* whom we sometimes consulted on arcane *nèpi* that others had difficulty explaining, said that he remembered the song, but he could not be induced to perform it. Instead, he summed it up quickly, mumbling under his breath over a cup of tea, "He asks mothers to fuck sons, father to marry daughters, sisters to fuck brothers, grandmothers to marry grandsons."

Eventually, Qi Wenping heard that we had been asking about the song and sent word that he would perform it for us himself. In contrast to most of the *àpip'ò* we consulted, who lived in Júzò's large central villages of Chemo and Chezò, Qi Wenping was from the valley's sparsely populated "shady" (or west-facing) slope in the village of Me'abò (literally "opposite slope"). His *nèpi* were unorthodox, with verses and passages we never heard on the valley's sunny side. Qi Wenping had a huge frame by local standards and an expansive personality. He was perhaps the last person in the valley who could shoot a crossbow accurately and one of the last men who could sing lament. His poverty and love of drink meant that he could be relied upon to play the role of thief at virtually any funeral ritual. We met him at his house where, having no tea to serve us, he apologized good-humoredly for his poverty, "One daughter and one pig are all I have in this world, and the pig is kinder to me."

He led us outside to perform the "song of mating," including a severely truncated version of the introductory section common to all Li Bicong's songs:

8.23 á sa le te do yi   I have come out
      te lò vǽ sa yi   chaff in my dangling bag
      cá wo je̠ sə yi   cattle on my lead rope
        də̀ wò t'à lo yi   the rabbit hops below the branch
        də̀ p'æ hə lo yi   the weasel creeps above
          zò sa æ mæ chè he   Let all below heaven now
          sa tu̠ lɔ   understand.

      chì bù chì bù ba ǹ də̀   billy goats, goats in rut
        chì bù te lè k'a ba ǹ də̀   goats do it on a tilt
      chì bù chì bù ba ǹ də̀   billy goats, goats in rut
        chì bù á dù mò ba ǹ də̀   goats do it like doors slamming
      rɔ bù rɔ bù ba ǹ də̀   rams, rams in rut
        rɔ bù kə ts'ə go ba ǹ də̀   sheep do it until their forelocks wither
      vè bù vè bù ba ǹ də̀   boars, boars in rut
        vè bu mí rɔ chɤ a ba ǹ də̀   pigs do it with twisted ropes
      mò bù mò bù ba ǹ də̀   stallions, stallions in rut
        mò bù lá t'ú dæ ba ǹ də̀   horses do it with beating hammers
      ye bù ye bù ba ǹ də̀   cocks, cocks in rut
        ye bù chì pɯ je ba ǹ də̀   chickens do it and vomit
      ŋə̀ bù ŋə̀ bù ba ǹ də̀   bulls, bulls in rut
        ŋə̀ bù le tə kə ba ǹ də̀   bulls do it with slim needles

      mùɯ t'ə̀ mùɯ ǹ t'ə̀   the sky is not yet light
        sæ k'ə sæ ǹ k'ə   midnight has not arrived
          wò bə wò m bə   the rooster has not crowed
            a ts'a mi ce cho̠   what is that sound?

      gə wú gə mæ tsí tsá ma tsá   the bed creaking and rattling, head to tail
        chì pe̠ zæ pe̠ ba   the work of making new generations
        chì pè zæ pè ba   the task of making generations

No mention of incest, but the general idea could not be more clear. This is
what is brought to the living by the contract with the dead: domestic animal
procreation along with human, human procreation merely the culmination
of the series.

Thuds and Cries: An Anti-nèpi̠

Inserted among the last songs of the *nèpi̠* was the "song of the pounder and
silkworm," *pǒ wò bùɯ lɔ chæ̀*. It seemed out of place to me, even though it took

the same position in both versions of the chant, directly following the eerie "song of sleeping in the ghost's nest." It was neither about the *bu*, like the songs that preceded it, nor about the soul's path to its final resting place like the songs that followed it. The grain pounder first appeared in the "song of the eagle's portion," where it was mentioned as a tool in the long process of manufacturing silken clothing (excerpts 7.16–7.18). The "song of the pounder and silkworm," however, makes the pounder its focus, referring to it frequently with the noun *bùù*, which usually indicates an insect or worm. My consultants on this song— Àp'ìmà, Lichink'æp'ò, and the latter's brother Li Guoshan—decided that, while *bùù* indeed indicated the grain pounder in many lines, *bùù* referred to the silkworm (*bùù t'ù*) in others. They did not share my puzzlement about the placement of the song. To them it seemed quite natural to mention the grain pounder at the end of the chant. Attempting to explain why, they engaged in a lively discussion of grain pounder lore, and Àp'ìmà told a story about the origin of one of the pounder's parts—a story that both interprets the song and reflects on the *nèpi* as a whole.

A foot tilt-hammer grain pounder (*ts'ə*) has a long body made of a pine log with a pestle or "mouth" (*ts'ə mè*) fashioned of cedar attached to one end, the head. The body is set on a yoke (*ts'ə pə*) that acts as a fulcrum, placed so that the pestle falls with some force into a stone mortar (*ts'ə k'ù*) set into the ground. To operate it, one person steps onto the body's flattened tail, lifting her foot to let the pestle fall repeatedly into the mortar, while another continuously sweeps the overflowing grain back into the mortar.[3] Pounders are used to husk rice, to make cooked sticky rice congeal into a loaf, to separate fibers of hemp in preparation for spinning, and in this song to loosen silk from cocoons so it might be unraveled and spun. Predictably, the song decomposes the pounder into the series of its parts. "Don't use pine and cedar for the

---

3. The foot tilt-hammer grain pounder is a very old technology, used continuously for at least 2,200 years and probably much longer. The well-known glazed earthenware mortuary figurines of the Han dynasty include models of foot-tilt hammer grain pounders constructed almost exactly like those still in use in the mountains of north-central Yunnan. At least two extant figurines show a farmer's courtyard. In both, a man is operating the grain pounder with a dog looking on, and to the side is a hand-operated rotating mill, as in courtyards in Juzò. One figurine shows chickens poised to peck grain out of the mortar; another figurine includes a rotating winnowing machine of a more complicated design than the winnowing baskets and sieves used in Júzò. The two figurines are in the collection of the Nelson-Atkins Museum of Art in Kansas City, Missouri, items 34-210/1 and 34-210/2. A photograph of one courtyard figurine is included in Needham and Wang (1965, plate CLVI, figure 415). A photograph of another appears in Smith and Wen (1973, 67).

pounder's yoke," it instructs, "use apple-pear and bottle-gourd trees. Make the mortar from a stone, make the foot pedal from cedar,"

8.24	bù tí tə̀ tə̀ t'e	pound with a knocking
	bù tí tsa tsa t'e	pound with a thudding
	bù tí bù wo ga	once the pounder is made
	mè p'ò hà wo p'a wo	bedding and clothing to your
	ni ní shr	heart's content

Grain pounders are associated in many ways with death and birth. At weddings, a pounder becomes a kind of *nègu* and is offered rice and alcohol, perhaps because the squeal of the moving yoke and thud of the pestle entering the mortar in rhythmic alternation echo human procreative activity. But this sound and motion can easily tilt the other way, towards intimate violence: it is as close to beating with fists or a club as it is to sex. Perhaps for this reason, pounders are powerful conduits for the spread of pollution from those who have died of violence. Pounders must not be used for seven or nine days after a violent death or for three days after any death, except to make rice loaf offerings, a prohibition still widely observed in Júzò, even as many other such rules have been abandoned.

Àp'ìmà's story gathered up all these associations, delving more deeply into the problematic of the transfer of life among material bodies that death entails, and helping explain the pounder's presence here at the very end of the *nepi*, where the most terrible fates of the dead are placed in the closest proximity to the work of making new life.

Long ago, the pounder's yoke was invented by a deaf-mute who could hear and speak. When the deaf-mute's wife got pregnant, he visited her mother. She gave him a gift of eggs. "Take these home, break them into boiling water, and give them to your wife to eat. Pregnant women are very hungry, hungry enough to eat a man."

On his way home, he came to a spring and broke the eggs into the bubbling spring water. At home, his wife asked him what her mother had given him. "She gave me six eggs. I put them in the spring's boiling water. Go eat them." She carefully explained the difference between a boiling pot and a bubbling spring.

The deaf-mute grew very angry. "Blame your mother!" he shouted. "She said you would be hungry enough to eat a man, so I didn't dare break the eggs in front of you!" He laid her over the yoke of the grain pounder and beat her so hard that he thought he beat her to death. He covered her body with a straw rain cape and went into the house to find some hemp to wrap her with so he might go out and bury her.

While he was inside, she found a log, wrapped it in the rain cape, placed it over the pounder's yoke where she had been lying, and ran away. He wrapped the log in hemp, carried it off, and buried it. His wife sneaked back into the house and covered the yoke with the rain cape again. When he saw the cape lying over the pounder's yoke, he said to himself, "It seems that the pounder's yoke has died along with my wife." When he used the pounder it made a noise: "yii! yii!" And he said,

ŋo mæ̀ zò "yii" n̂ ŋɔ!	it is not my wife who cries "*yii!*"
tsə pɔ̰ à mo le "yii" ba!	The yoke's mother [the pounder's main body] cries "*yii!*"

So many devious substitutions, not least Àp'ìmà's insertion of a matrilineal theme here at the end of our patrilineal-minded *nèpi*. Beginning with the invention that is not an invention, and the deaf-mute (always the shaman's shadowy double) who is neither deaf nor mute, nothing is as it appears, except to the clever injured wife who manipulates her husband's series of misrecognitions. This series produces a series of alliances that look both like and unlike the incarnation of a dead soul in a material body. The mother hopes to convey eggs, the undifferentiated prototypes of living souls, to her daughter, but they go into the depths of the spring like the dead soul's horse, not to be recovered for the sake of procreation as in the *nèpi* but lost forever. The wife's beaten body becomes a *bu* in the log, which is wrapped in hemp as every corpse or *bu* must be wrapped, before it is buried. Then again, her body becomes the *bu* of the pounder's yoke, allied with the body of her mother and put to work. The husband's fist takes the place of the shaman's cry as the agent of this transubstantiation—though the shaman also thrashes the *bu* with his knife as he exchanges his body, part for part, with its body. And there is a "cry to heaven," the "*yii!*" of the woman being beaten, the "*yii!*" of her mother, which can be recognized in every squeak of every grain pounder as it produces rice loaves and hemp cloth for the dead.

It is the act of wrapping that produces the deaf-mute's/shaman's/husband's misrecognitions; all the bodies are clothed, first in the rain cape, then in hemp, then in the cape again. While the husband wraps his wife's dead body himself, mother and daughter provide the cloaks that enable misrecognition (they plait the cape; they weave the hemp). We know wrapping as the work of making the body social by clothing it in all the alliances that nurtured it in life. Here, wrapping conceals the true nature of the dead: the body, the *bu*, wrapped into relations with its living survivor and put to work for him, is not the dead person at all. It is a log that is buried and a yoke that is put to work, complaining, in the courtyard: the wife herself, while staying close enough to pull the cloak over her husband's eyes, is footloose.

Àp'ìmà's story was an anti-*nèpi*, reprising the central themes of this final part of the chant and casting them as a series of misrecognitions. But if Àp'ìmà was a trickster, upsetting all the pots and pans of the verses we had spent so much time filling up and laying out, she nevertheless remained our Virgil as well. The "song of the underworld" had just pointed out a path through the rings of this hell, layered like the "layered bamboo of the seventh month," passing from the "fine places of the ghost world," into the "gathering places of the spirit world," from whence a last portal opened up onto the creaking bed of the "song of mating." With her story, Àp'ìmà invited us into this secret, upstream chamber to catch a glimpse of the hidden side of procreation, deliberately ignored by the boisterous men buggering each other with pine branches. This was procreation's "hidden abode," where the cries and thuds of sexual pleasure turned so easily to the thuds and "cries to heaven" of intimate violence. If these parallel sounds accompanied the work of the dead, the "task of making new generations," they were often also the sounds of the suffering of labor that nurtured and clothed dead and living bodies. Here, "in a complex way, involving many different kinds of 'corpses,'" the realm of the dead "has become the hidden abode of production . . . the principal arena where still-unresolved struggles over labor and loyalty continue to be carried on" (Feeley-Harnik 1984, 13).[4] Àp'ìmà's anti-*nèpi* was a subversive reminder that all the work for the dead, all the incessant production of gifts of animals, rice, cloth, words, and tears, all the imaging and dissevering of relations, were the result of intimate struggles over work and loyalty, and that every lament echoed a double set of cries and thuds.

Conclusion: Skin

Three structuring series have emerged from this investigation of these world-building *nèpi*. The first is the series of genesis, positioning human bodies as the effect of difference, affinity, and personhood, and positioning the earth's geography as an effect of the movement of human bodies. This series can be summed as difference ⇒ affinity ⇒ persons ⇒ bodies ⇒ geographies. The second series shapes the intensive bodies of the dead. This second series may be summed up as abandonment ⇒ ascent ⇒ descent ⇒ return ⇒ escape. The soul is abandoned in the forest; it is lifted up to the eagle's nest to live forever in piles of snakes' blood; it is buried beneath the tomb to live forever under the millstone-sized eyes of the underworld king; it is forced to return its portion of life; it is given routes of possible escape. The third series is the

---

4. This quotation comes from an early article of Gillian Feeley-Harnik's on Sakalava work for the dead in Madagascar; her book on Sakalava royal funerals (1991) has been a source of inspiration for this book.

series of the extensive or material bodies of the dead, summarized as loss ⇒ search ⇒ encounter ⇒ assembly ⇒ destruction.

These structuring series are obviously parallel. They begin with indeterminate difference, expressed as loss or abandonment; they assemble bodies with determinate qualities; they specify relations among bodies; they end with dissolution, escape, or destruction. The great achievement of the chant is to create a precarious alignment or communication between these three bodies: the body of the earth, the intensive body of the dead, and the extensive body of the dead. This alignment is achieved with difficulty: through experiments with piling song upon song, with building systems of relays that echo from series to series, with creating grids of correspondence between a phoneme inserted into a verse and its near homonyms. The success of these efforts is never assured. Tenth-Month Sacrifice and Sleeping in the Forest were no more likely to be successful than any other effort to settle a wandering soul. To appreciate the difficulty of such coordination, we might, echoing the style of the *nèpi*, put the problem in the form of questions. First, how is a person—body and soul— to be aligned with the earth; how is a person to fit on the earth, to find a home there? Second, how is a soul to be aligned with a particular body; how is that soul to fit into that body, to find a home there?

The first question identifies a longstanding and deeply consequential historical issue for Lòlop'ò. The ancestors of Júzò's Li descent groups fled their homes in the Tiesuo Valley after a failed rebellion in the late sixteenth century. The ancestors of other descent groups drifted in later, many beginning as Han, all seeking a place where "the land was not marked and owned." The *nèpi* expresses the sense of this difficult unsettled process of aligning person to earth as it guides the dead on several circuits of the known world—through the lands of kings and officials, through near villages and far cities—then finally asking them to find their home in Júzò. In the present, this question continues to define Lòlopò as a people, as nearly one third of Lòlopò have sought new homes in lowland diaspora villages, and the majority of Lòlopò youths have moved to cities to seek a future that does not include farming. Like all the questions the *nèpi* asks, the question of how a person may be aligned with the earth finds an answer only in the form of an apophatic series—in historical experience as well as in verse: not there, not there, not there, but here.

The second question grapples with another historical issue, which Lòlopò were beginning to encounter in a new way during the time of the *nèpi*'s final public performances. How might a soul be aligned with a particular body? The profound difficulty of this question is expressed in the "song of the ghost in its bamboo cradle" (excerpts 8.2 and 8.3). The monkey drops onto the saddle, the saddle onto the horse, the horse into the spring, sinking into its depths.

Immediately after the dispersed, fragmented soul is assembled into a layered composite, it drops out of sight, perhaps forever. The search is mounted as a combination of will and chance—encounters in the forest with pine, chestnut, bamboo; a crossbow bolt shot into the roots of a pine tree. Yet success is difficult, and sure knowledge that the soul has been made to lie in this particular bamboo cradle is impossible. The shaman intervenes, with the "song of setting up an effigy bound with cloth"/"song of seventy body parts" (excerpts 8.16 and 8.17). Body series is aligned with body series, part exchanged for part. The vehicles for this exchange of head for head, tongue for tongue, skin for skin are the shaman's speech, the resurrection medicine, the spark of the charcoal ember. The ephemeral relation of soul to body is confirmed only by the sacrifice and dismemberment of another body. This is another way to understand grief: as the dismemberment of a living person who invests in locating, actualizing, and incarnating the soul of a dead intimate.

After 1958, when Tenth-Month Sacrifice was finally abandoned, the difficulty and uncertainty involved in matching soul to body came to dominate local political life. The state campaigns of the socialist period all insisted that identities be fixed and that people be held responsible for their attitudes, affects, and words. In innumerable ways, people in Júzò were disciplined to own the identities assigned to them during the land reform period (landlord, rich peasant, middle peasant, poor peasant, local bully, purveyor of superstition), as well as to feel approved emotions with authentic sincerity and to mouth approved phrases with heartfelt sentiment. Their response was to find the problem of aligning soul with body increasingly difficult. The illness and disability among the àpipò who had learned the great nèpi is this book's central example of this common and diverse phenomenon. The "ghosts of speech" who had once possessed the ritualists with the power to speak now possessed them with madness, chronic illness, and early death. Li Bicong survived due to a chronic differential alignment of soul and body, a negotiated compromise with his pinè, whom he deliberately allowed to possess him with the long speech of the nèpi once a year so as to hold at bay his chronic illness. Across Júzò, varied forms of madness, disease, and difficult death resulting from possession by the ghosts of those who died badly were chronic during the socialist period (Mueggler 2001).

This difficulty of aligning souls to bodies brings us back full circle to the topic of chapter 1. Lòlopò in Júzò began to inscribe the skin of tombstones with biographies, names of descendants, and revolutionary verse in the late 1950s, just as the stable coordination of living bodies with their souls was simultaneously receiving increased political emphasis and growing more difficult. In chapter 1, our example of these early inscriptions was the stone that Li Fuzhong inscribed in 1958 for his father, mother, and stepmother. On that stone, in the position where later tombstones would showcase revolutionary verse, we found a compressed echo of the songs of genesis of the Tenth-Month *nèpi*: "First there was Heaven and Earth, and then there were the ten thousand beings . . ." Opposite this, the biographical inscription begins,

人生如梦而别世矣欲身后不没之名以碑为记吾父母没之数有几下之
载 . . . 声音容貌 常在不孝之耳目过吾父刀明乃之次 . . . [5]

The lives of men are like a dream of another world. Desiring that after their deaths their names might not disappear, on this stone I record a few traces of my father and mother . . . their voices and faces often pass before the ears and eyes of this unfilial one. My father was the second-born of Li Mingnai . . .

The sense that the voices and visages of the dead linger in the spaces that living descendants inhabit was frequently expressed in lament, as in these verses that we encountered in chapter 4: "mother clutching your cane's head, I think of you stepping behind the house, I think of you standing there in the ditch." The stone aspires to materialize such traces in writing, along with the decedents' names and those of thirty-six descendants, as a partial diagram of the personhood of the dead: two sons and their two wives, three daughters and their two husbands, three sons of sons and their six wives, seven daughters of sons and their six husbands, two sons of daughters and their two wives, and one daughter of a daughter.

Writing engaged with the problem of aligning the subjectivity of the dead to a material body with a specificity and durability that pine, chestnut, and bamboo could never achieve. Stones like this one attempted to fix and materialize the flow of ritualized exchanges that composed a dead person as an ensemble of relations. At the same time, such stones were an early expression of the "modern" sense that persons are a chain of specific biographical events, which women would develop fully in the lament of the late twentieth and early twenty-first centuries. Stones worked the names and biographical details of an absent person's intensive body into the material form of an extensive body. They aspired to a full and permanent alignment of soul and body during this period when the pressing necessity for such a fixed coordination was being felt and subverted by the living. As our exploration of the *nèpi* has revealed, tombstones were doors to the underworld, the gateway through which life was deposited and through which it must return. Stones were crucial valves in a machine built to subjugate the dead to the practical requirements of the living, operating under the regulatory gaze of the

5. The internal ellipse indicates two unreadable characters.

underworld king and his bureaucratic subordinates, the "mountain spirits," or shanshen 山神, who kept guard over each individual family graveyard. After 1960, the skins of these stone bodies were inscribed with formulae and sentiments, in the form of revolutionary verse, that the underworld king's new avatar, the socialist state, had begun to insist that people feel in their hearts, and demonstrate in words. The assiduous and detailed work of aligning soul and body through inscription acknowledged this unified assemblage as the fundamental key to socialist power. Finally, by fixing all of this—a biographical life, relational personhood, and a subject's thoughts and affects—on the skin of a permanent body, stones engaged with a possible future in which the dead were answerable not only to the community of intimates involved in their personhood but also a wider world of officials and strangers. In short, tombstones engaged with all the complex dimensions of personhood and subjectivity with which people in Júzò found themselves struggling during the late twentieth and early twenty-first centuries.

As my friends in Júzò were lamenting the loss of the great chants of Tenth-Month Sacrifice and Sleeping in the Forest, they continued to create ever more elaborately inscribed tombstones for a minority of their ascendants. After examining a version of these chants (however occluded, however spectral), it now seems clear that inscribed tombstones continue their project. The nèpi layered together images from two possible worlds for the dead, drawn from the older conditions of cremation, on the one hand, and the newer conditions of burial, on the other, as it encountered the problems of grief, subjugation, compassion, and power. Tombstones layer those worlds with yet a newer world, in which the alignment of body and earth is no more certain, yet a new field of struggle has opened up around the coordination of body and soul. In stones, as in the nèpi, Lòlopò continue to work with the dead to model, grapple with, and experiment with forms of personhood, subjectivity, and materiality in which the living also participate.

Epilogue

The only body I have left for him is a photograph. The face is my own face, except fuller and more rugged, the smile more open. One large hand is visible, resting on the handle of an oar. His heavily muscled arms are bare. His chest is clothed in a life vest, a cap covers his head. He is on a river, crossing a river, the rock wall of a canyon a blurred background. His eyes cannot be seen, as befits a dead body; they are hidden behind sunglasses. His eyes have receded from each of the few photographs I have of him; after all these years I cannot see them anymore. The strong, fleshy hand and arms speak to me more than the face. They remain so unbearably alive. The pliable flesh of the little boy, the joyful carved flesh of the young man. The flesh of the corpse that I never saw yet see repeatedly—so crushed, mangled, and frozen, when it was finally excavated with the corpses of his two friends from beneath the avalanche that crushed their tent, that it was deemed unsuitable for viewing and kept enclosed in the coffin.

Dead brothers form a submerged series in this book about dead parents, parallel to the equally indistinct series of unsettled ghosts. The series begins, in chapter 1, with the brothers Gu Yuanzhang and Gu Yuanwei, who migrated to Júzò together in the 1820s. Though Gu Yuanwei died a decade before Gu Yuanzhang, the elder brother did not erect a tombstone for the younger; the task was left to their six sons—brothers and parallel cousins working together. Qi Ping waited decades to erect a tombstone for his elder brother, until he could simultaneously erect stones for his parents and brother-in-law. Thirty-seven years after the death of his parallel cousin, whom he also called "younger brother," Su Pingying finally inscribed a tombstone for his soul, sent wandering after his ignominious death from a wound suffered in the Guomindang

army. Luo Guiyuan inscribed the name of his long-dead adopted brother Luo
Guiyan onto the tombstone he erected for his disgraced adopted father Luo
Guotian. Twenty-two years later, he helped sponsor the extravagant funeral
mentioned in chapter 2 for his adopted brother's widow, as a final offering
to his dead brother. In chapter 3, Zhang Wenxing's family was plunged into
deep poverty when his eldest brother encountered an unspecified tragedy that
caused his wife's death and the loss of all their father's land. That brother and
Zhang Wenxing's second oldest brother both married out, giving up the status
of parallel siblings, leaving Zhang Wenxing and his younger brother to "lean
upon each other like beam and girder" until all four of his brothers died, and
Zhang Wenxing adopted his younger brother's son as heir. Finally, in chapter 7, elder and younger brothers double as dead siblings and living siblings,
warning each other not to burn but burning anyway, opening up the twelve
doors to the underworld.

    The deaths of brothers are always subordinated to the deaths of parents,
for brothers do not form the generative couplings out of which creative power
flows. Instead, they wander unsettled, and no tomb or funeral sponsored or
hosted by a brother seems to settle them. The death of a brother is parallel
to one's own death. Such deaths are one's own death torn out of time; dead
brothers throw time out of joint. This is because the difference between brothers is hardly a difference at all. Brothers are differentiated merely as elder and
younger, *yi* and *næ*, equal inheritors of the names, property, and bodies of
their parents, one quite easily substituted for the other. Their difference is not
the fertile difference of cross siblings, out of which all human kinship emerges,
nor the difference between the allied descent groups of married-out sisters. It
is a sterile difference that produces nothing, the difference between one repetition and the next. That brothers are the same yet not the same is why they
so often lock themselves into endless cycles of love and hate. "People say that
brothers' quarrels start in a previous life," one of my friends in Júzò, who had
an elder brother, said. "In the underworld, one says to the other, 'You obnox-
ious creature, I'm not finished with you. I'll follow you to the family you are
born into, and we'll continue this argument there'" (Mueggler 2001, 61).

    I could not tell my friends in Júzò about the circumstances of my little
brother's death, because it would have seemed, in their eyes, such a bad death.
Keeping this secret, I stubbornly resisted all their ideas about bad deaths as
generating monstrous ghosts that plague their kin and descendants by possess-
ing them, driving them mad, making them ill, killing them. Keeping it from
them, I insisted on the difference between their world and my world and strove
to keep these worlds separate. I insisted to myself that my brother died well,

doing what he loved, adventuring with his friends, in the sweetest and most vigorous fullness of youth. All along, and despite my convictions, I have been willing such separations. Between the world that I live and the world of this book. Between the world of ritualized action for the dead and the world of the great chant, or *nèpi*, for Tenth-Month Sacrifice and Sleeping in the Forest. Between the world of my intimate dead and the world occupied by the intensive and extensive bodies fashioned in that *nèpi*.

Yet every page of this text that attends to the language out of which such worlds are crafted attests to the obvious truth that nothing can keep different worlds apart. Between worlds is no more space than it takes to draw a single breath, no more space than between the two halves of a semantic couplet. "The rabbit hops below the branch, the weasel creeps above." "Siblings of the other world, siblings playing in the existing world." "Elder brother dies, younger brother carries the corpse, younger brother dies, elder brother carries the corpse." Between worlds is only difference: parallels, oppositions, correlations. There is no world whose being may be uttered in a different voice from the being of any other, no words that can inoculate one world against another.

I can no longer deny that the reason that my brother's death exerts such force in the present moment is that it was wrongly timed. It is not just that he was so young—only thirty-one. It is also that all deaths of brothers are untimely, for they are prototypes for one's own death without being, to all appearances, one's own death. The deaths of brothers strung through this book all generated wandering, unsettled souls. As Su Pingying put it on the stone he had inscribed for his parallel cousin whom he called younger brother, in the distancing phraseology of a language not his own, "folk tradition has it that his lonely soul (<u>guhun</u> 孤魂) is suffering in the underworld." The action of such unsettled souls is to possess with madness (*tæ*) the persons of those who love them or are descended from them. Yet the madness of possession is not to be avoided at all costs. I have shown in a previous ethnography how such madness can be received strategically by those trapped in deplorable circumstances, by those with something to say that cannot be said, or by those who have found a point upon which to press to exert leverage on the strata of politics and power. Madness has its own power, the power of frictionless slippage through the chaotic multiplicity of differences that make the world, the power to shatter all fixity, upend all settlements, negate all contracts. To choose the madness of possession would be to select, with a degree of freedom, a specific form of relation with my dead brother as other. It would be to begin to speak with his voice, to take on his bodily form, to explode the varied strata of relations that define my shape.

Àp'ìmà, the living embodiment of the clever woman of seventy who clothed the world with seeds and rules, had no illusions about separate worlds. Her kindness in patiently and repeatedly explaining each step that one must take from the moment breath ceases to the final celebration generations later was born of the sense that I needed this knowledge. It was born of the sense, which she divined through my enormously ignorant attempts to answer her questions about death ritual in my own country, that my people could use a manual of the kind she thought I should be preparing, which would explain with detailed clarity all the proper rules and procedures for parting with a loved one. She knew very well all the temptations of madness, all the power that unrestrained grief could deploy, all the permissions to alter worlds that possession could give. Yet she also knew better than anyone all the insupportable costs. Her explanations were designed to show that, with a degree of attention, a modest clarity of mind, an adequate memory, a sense of the elements of poetic language, and a patience extending through decades, another way could be crafted. The lack of an adequate supply of live black goats and of the capacity to convince my four formidable sisters to do all the work, inter alia, would have made it difficult to treat my brother as Àp'ìmà would have advised. We laughed about this, but we also discussed the possibility seriously, if in a hypothetical tone. It quickly became clear that even Àp'ìmà, with her passion for exactitude, was aware that, in a move from Júzò to elsewhere, all of her beloved procedures would be subjected to a series of relays at a distance: oppositions, correlations, resonances, echoes, distortions. Yet she insisted that their elements would nevertheless remain available.

The most fundamental of those elements are expressed in the extensive and intensive bodies of the dead. The series of relations that is my dead brother may be summed up, like any such series, in the trio of partial subjects sought and found in the "song of the ghost in its bamboo cradle." Pine, chestnut, bamboo; father, mother, affine. It matters little that he did not marry or have children; all the relations that make him can nevertheless be asserted in this trio, after being subjected to the work of substitution and displacement outlined in chapter 3. One generation above him, one position upstream of him on the wall above my bed, is the trio of our parents. Pine, chestnut, bamboo; father, mother, affine. My brother's effigy stands in the position of orphaned son to that trio of partial subjects, and upon my death, of which my brother's was the prototype, my own effigy will be positioned directly below his. Pine, chestnut, bamboo; father, mother, affine. Two parallel series, positioned in parallel relation to the series above, separated by only a few bricks on the wall of time, an upstream-downstream differential. Circulating between these two series, keeping them in relation and keeping them apart, are energies and affects of

the kind that may be called partial or virtual objects: shreds, remainders, fragments, always displaced, always lacking their own identities.[1]

In Àpìmà's terms, such partial objects might include the figure of my brother
appearing in my dream, the shape of his smile that pierces me when I look at
his photograph, the timbre of his voice that, half unaware, I sometimes hear
vibrating in my own harsher voice. Insubstantial traces that, nevertheless,
threaten to give rise to an outpouring of grief, which must then be channeled
into poetic language and expressed in a suitably ritualized setting. Other such
partial objects may be half signs—the voice of the wind or the sour odor of a
burning building—that may, with little warning, cohere with other half signs
into the most powerful and deplorable of virtual beings, a *chènè*, or wild ghost.
In the "song of the ghost in its bamboo cradle," such a partial or virtual object
appears in the distributed form of the seven raucous monkeys that come in
the dead of the night, the masked shapes of unidentifiable dead children. The
energy of such partial objects circulates, keeping the terms of the relational
series distinct—a monkey drops into the saddle, the saddle drops onto the
horse, the horse drops into the spring, the spring is probed with bamboo, pine,
and chestnut; affine, father, and mother.

The procedures of death ritual gradually wear away these partial virtual
objects, disguised sources of grief's power, involuntary remnants of memory,
unassimilable shreds of affect. As their energy dissipates, little remains to
keep the differentially positioned series from collapsing into each other. The
relational series of my dead brother's body, cut out of me and made other during grief-strewn vigils immediately after his death, returns to my own series;
pine, chestnut, bamboo. The wall of time becomes empty time, the image of
time. Between the prototype of my death and my own death remains only this
empty image of time, ensuring their coexistence; my death is the subjective
experience of empty time. My brother is in me (as he always has been); he is
not other than me (for I have chosen against that freedom and cage); he is me
(and I him). This is not a subject identical with itself. It is the differential folds
of the intensive dead body, plane coordinated with plane through a system
of relays, coordinates, parallels, and substitutions, the folded strata bent by
forces from other directions. Taken as a whole, this intensive body is fractured by the experience of empty time, the experience of death that cannot
be other than one's own. This is the meaning of the sympathy with the dead

---

1. I borrow this vocabulary of partial virtual objects from Deleuze (yet again) for whom an
outstanding example is Lacan's *objet petit a*, demonstrated in exemplary fashion in Lacan's classic essay on Edgar Allan Poe's short story, "The Purloined Letter" (Deleuze 1994 [1968], 100–102;
Lacan 1972 [1955]).

expressed in the Tenth-Month Sacrifice *nèpi̠*, the final effort to release the
dead from their practical obligations to serve life. It is easy enough to accept
that the dead are us; they can be none other than us. What is more difficult
is to know that we are the dead. There is no language that can keep worlds
apart, no voice other than the one voice of difference. We are the dead; death
belongs to no other.

Appendix

In this book Chinese and Lòloŋo are distinguished by underlining words in Chinese inserted into the text (and transcribed into Roman characters with the <u>hanyu pinyin</u> system) and italicizing words in Lòloŋo inserted into the text (and transcribed with a modified form of the International Phonetic Alphabet, described below). Local place names or ethnonyms are not underlined, but when they are in Chinese, they are often clarified with written characters in the text or a footnote.

Lòlopò in Júzò call their language Lòloŋo, the "Lòlo tongue." Lòloŋo may be considered a dialect of Lipo 里颇, which is a member of the very large Southeastern subfamily of Tibeto-Burman languages (Bradley 2002), also known as Burmic (Shafer 1974), Burmese-Lolo (Benedict 1972), and Lolo-Burmese (Matisoff 2003). Lòloŋo belongs to the largest and most diverse subgroup of Southeastern Tibeto-Burman, which has been known as Loloish (Bradley 1979) and, among Chinese linguists, the Yiyuzhi 彝语支, "Yi-language branch" (Chen 2010). Recently, Lama (2012) has introduced the term Nisoic, and Bradley has proposed Ngwi, based on autonyms (Bradley 2005, Pelkey 2011, Gao 2015). Ngwi comprises ninety-eight known languages, most spoken in Southwestern China, with a few spoken in Burma, Laos, Vietnam, and Thailand (Lewis et al. 2014). These languages are spoken by all the diverse groups designated by the Chinese state as belonging to the Yi 彝 nationality, with nearly eight million members, as well as by smaller nationalities such as Lisu, Hani, and Akha. The most recent taxonomies of Ngwi list four branches: Northern, Southern, Southeastern, and Central (Pelkey 2011, Lama 2012, Bradley 2017). Lipo and twenty-three other known languages are classed in the Central branch. Two dialects are currently recognized: a Western dialect, spoken mainly in the three contiguous counties of Dayao, Yao'an, and Yongren, and an Eastern

TABLE A.1 Consonants.

	Labial	Dentilabial	Dental	Retroflex	Palatal	Velar
Voiceless stop	p		t			k
Aspirated stop	p'		t'			k'
Voiced stop	b		d			g
Voiceless affricate			ts	j	j	
Aspirated affricate			ts'	ch	ch	
Voiceless fricative		f	s	sh	c	h
Voiced fricative			z			
Nasal	m		n			ŋ
Lateral			l			
Voiced flap			r			
Continuants	w				y	

dialect, centered in Wuding and proximate counties (Lewis et al. 2014; Lama 2012, 80–81).

Distinct orthographies were used to write ritual texts in three branches of Ngwi languages. While based on principles similar to those of Chinese writing, these logographic systems share no characters with Chinese (Pu 2004, Bradley 2011). Three new "standardized" orthographies were introduced in the last half of the twentieth century, founded on the traditional orthographies but intended for writing ordinary language (Bradley 2009). No traditional orthographies developed in the Central group of Ngwi languages, and no writing system for their language has been adopted by Lipo speakers.

Chinese linguists have adapted a version of the International Phonetic Alphabet to represent Tibeto-Burman languages. I have modified this system to minimize the use of exotic symbols. The system of transcription that has resulted (based on Mueggler 2001), while far from phonetically perfect, is sufficient to make necessary phonemic distinctions. Consonants are transcribed as single letters or sequences of two letters already familiar in conventions of English-language writing (table A.1). An initial glottal stop is represented only by the absence of an initial graph before a vowel. The voiceless affricate *j* and aspirated affricate *ch* are palatal before the front vowels *i*, *ɨ*, *e*, *ɛ*, *æ*, and their "tense" or laryngealized variations (which I mark with an underline [*u̲*]), and retroflex before other vowels (table A.2). The velar voiced stop *g* varies a great deal, frequently becoming fricative.

Both dialects of Lipo display an extreme phonological poverty at the end

TABLE A.2 Vowels.

i, ɨ	ɯ	u	r
e	ə	o	
ɛ	a	ɔ	
æ			

TABLE A.3 Tones.

high, level	á
mid, level	a
low, falling	à

of the syllable. Consonants are used only as initials except in loan words from Chinese. Even in the form its speakers call Lòloŋo, spoken only in Júzò (the administrative villages of Zhizuo 直苴 and Bozhedi 波者地), there is a great deal of microregional variation. My friends often pointed out distinct variations that could be heard simply by walking across the small gully that separated Júzò's two large villages, Chemo and Chezò. Most of the examples of poetic speech represented in this book, whatever their origin, passed through the ears and mouths of speakers from these two villages during the process of transcription, which tended to standardize them, even as to the variations across the two villages, which I learned, of necessity, to adapt to a Chemo standard, which my friends, even those from Chezò, considered proper.

This system is ethnographically oriented, intended to make necessary phonemic distinctions to show poetic patterning in transcriptions. It is too conservative to provide a fully accurate phonetic representation of every line of text. The only other published list of values for a Western Lipo subdialect is Lama's, based on elicitation from two speakers from Dayao County. Lama lists thirty-seven initials, thirty-five vowels, and three tones (table A.3). The vowels are twenty-six monophthongs, including laryngealized variations, eight diphthongs, including laryngealized variations, and one triphthong (Lama 2012: 81, 89–107). Lama's approach, though perhaps useful for divining genetic relationships among languages, is overly meticulous for most purposes. Some of the phonemes he discerns have little phonemic value, and they vary from speaker to speaker and, even more, from village to village. Huang's list of values for the closely related Lolopo of Nanhua County is far more modest, including thirty-three initials and twenty-three vowels (including laryngealized variations) (Huang B. 1992, 685–686); Merrifield lists thirty initials and twenty-one vowels (including laryngealized variations) for Lolopo in Yao'an County (Merrifield 2012, 10, 14).

Bibliography

Adams, Kathleen M. 2006. *Art as Politics: Re-crafting Identities, Tourism, and Power in Tana Toraja, Indonesia, Southeast Asia—Politics, Meaning, and Memory.* Honolulu: University of Hawai'i Press.

Agha, Asif. 2005. "Voice, Footing, Enregisterment." *Journal of Linguistic Anthropology* 15 (1): 38–59.

Ahearn, Laura. 2001. *Invitations to Love: Literacy, Love Letters, and Social Change in Nepal.* Ann Arbor: University of Michigan Press.

Ahern, Emily. 1973. *The Cult of the Dead in a Chinese Village.* Stanford, Calif.: Stanford University Press.

Allen, Nicholas. 1976. "Sherpa Kinship Terminology in a Diachronic Perspective." *Man* 11: 569–587.

Anagnost, Ann. 1997. *National Past-times: Narrative, Representation, and Power in Modern China.* Durham, N.C.: Duke University Press.

Anagnost, Ann. 2004. "The Corporeal Politics of Quality (*Suzhi*)." *Public Culture* 16 (2): 189–208.

Anagnost, Ann. 2008. "From 'Class' to 'Social Strata': Grasping the Social Totality in Reform-era China." *Third World Quarterly* 29 (3): 497–519.

Apter, David E., and Tony Saich. 1994. *Revolutionary Discourse in Mao's Republic.* Cambridge, Mass.: Harvard University Press.

Ariès, Philippe. 1982 [1975]. *The Hour of Our Death.* Translated by Helen Weaver. New York: Vintage Books.

Asad, Talal. 2003. *Formations of the Secular: Christianity, Islam, Modernity.* Stanford, Calif.: Stanford University Press.

Asad, Talal. 2009. *Geneaologies of Religion: Discipine and Reasons of Power in Christianity and Islam.* Baltimore: Johns Hopkins University Press.

Atkinson, Jane Monnig. 1989. *The Art and Politics of Wana Shamanism.* Berkeley: University of California Press.

Austin, John L. 1962. *How to Do Things with Words.* Oxford: Clarendon Press.

Bakhtin, Mikhail. 1981. *The Dialogic Imagination: Four Essays.* Translated by Caryl Emerson and Michael Holquist. Austin: University of Texas Press.

Bakhtin, Mikhail. 1984. *Problems of Dostoevsky's Poetics*. Translated by Caryl Emerson. Minneapolis: University of Minnesota Press.

Bakhtin, Mikhail. 1986. *Speech Genres and Other Late Essays*. Translated by Vern W. McGee. Austin: University of Texas Press.

Ballantyne, Tony. 2011. "Paper, Pen, and Print: the Transformation of the Kai Tahu Knowledge Order." *Comparative Studies in Society and History* 53 (2): 232–260.

Barabantseva, Elena V. 2009. "Development as Localization: Ethnic Minorities in China's Official Discourse on the Western Development Project." *Critical Asian Studies* 41: 225–254.

Bauman, Richard, and Charles Briggs. 1990. "Poetics and Performance as Critical Perspectives on Language and Social Life." *Annual Review of Anthropology* 19: 59–88.

Bell, Catherine. 1997. *Ritual: Perspectives and Dimensions*. Oxford: Oxford University Press.

Benedict, Paul K. 1972. *Sino-Tibetan: A Conspectus*. Cambridge: Cambridge University Press.

Bergeton, Uffe. 2013. "From Pattern to 'Culture'?: Emergence and Transformation of Metacultural Wén." Ph.D. dissertation, University of Michigan.

Bernstein, Anya. 2013. *Religious Bodies Politic: Rituals of Sovereignty in Buryat Buddhism*. Chicago: University of Chicago Press.

Besnier, Niko. 1995. *Literacy, Emotion, and Authority: Reading and Writing on a Polynesian Atoll*. Cambridge: Cambridge University Press.

Blake, C. Fred. 1978. "Death and Abuse in Marriage Laments: the Curse of Chinese Brides." *Asian Folklore Studies* 37 (1): 13–33.

Blake, C. Fred. 1979. "The Feelings of Chinese Daughters Towards their Mothers as Revealed in Marriage Laments." *Folklore* 90: 91–97.

Blomaert, Jan. 2008. *Grassroots Literacy: Writing, Identity and Voice in Central Africa*. New York: Routledge.

Bol, Peter. 1992. *This Culture of Ours: Intellectual Transitions in T'ang and Sung China*. Stanford, Calif.: Stanford University Press.

Bourdieu, Pierre. 1977. *Outline of a Theory of Practice*. Translated by Richard Nice. Cambridge: Cambridge University Press.

Bourke, Angela. 1993. "More in Anger than in Sorrow: Irish Women's Lament Poetry." In *Feminist Messages: Coding in Women's Folk Culture*, edited by Joan Newlon Radner, 160–182. Urbana: University of Illinois Press.

Bradley, David. 1979. *Proto-Loloish*. London: Curzon Press.

Bradley, David. 2002. "The Subgrouping of Tibeto-Burman." In *Medieval Tibeto-Burman Languages*, edited by Christopher Beckwith, 73–112. Leiden: Brill.

Bradley, David. 2005. "Sanie and Language Loss in China." *International Journal of the Sociology of Language* 173: 161–178.

Bradley, David. 2007. "Birth-order Terms in Lisu: Inheritance and Contact." *Anthropological Linguistics* 49 (1): 54–69.

Bradley, David. 2009. "Language Policy for China's Minorities: Orthography Development for the Yi." *Written Languages and Literacy* 12 (2): 170–187.

Bradley, David. 2011. "Problems of Orthography Development for the Yi in China." In *Handbook of Language and Ethnic Identity*, edited by Joshua A. Fishman and Ofelia García, 180–191. Oxford: Oxford University Press.

Bradley, David. 2017. "Tibeto-Burman Languages of China." In *Encyclopedia of Chinese Language and Linguistics*, edited by Rint Sybesma. Accessed February 27, 2017. doi:http://dx.doi.org/10.1163/2210-7363_ecll_COM_00000419.

Briggs, Charles. 1993. "Personal Sentiments and Polyphonic Voices in Warao Women's Ritual Wailing: Music and Poetics in a Critical and Collective Discourse." *American Anthropologist* 95 (4): 929–957.

Brightman, Marc, Vanessa Elisa Grotti, and Olga Ulturgasheva. 2012. *Animism in Rainforest and Tundra: Personhood, Animals, Plants, and Things in Contemporary Amazonia and Siberia.* New York: Berghahn Books.

Brose, Michael. 2005. "Uyghur Technologists of Writing and Literacy in Mongol China." *T'ong Pao* 9 (4–5): 396–435.

Burns, Kathryn. 2010. *Into the Archive: Writing and Power in Colonial Peru.* Durham, N.C.: Duke University Press.

Candea, Matei, and Lys Alcayna-Stevens. 2012. "Internal Others: Ethnographies of Naturalism." *Cambridge Anthropology* 30 (2): 36–47.

Chau, Adam Yuet. 2005. *Miraculous Response: Doing Popular Religion in Contemporary China.* Stanford, Calif.: Stanford University Press.

Chen Jiujin 陈久金, Lu Yang 卢央, and Liu Yanhan 刘尧汉, eds. 1984. *Yizu tianwenxue shi* 彝族天文学史 [History of Yi Astronomy]. Kunming: Yunnan renmin chubanshe.

Chen Kang 陈康. 2010. *Yiyu fangyan yanjiu* 彝语方言研究 [A Study of Yi Dialects]. Beijing: China Minzu University Press.

Chen Wen 陳文, ed. 1995 [1455]. *[Jingtai] Yunnan tujing zhishu* [景泰]雲南圖經志書 [(Jingtai-period) Illustrated Record of Yunnan]. Shanghai: Shanghai guji chubanshe.

Cheng, Francois. 1982. *Chinese Poetic Writing, with an Anthology of T'ang Poetry.* Translated by Donald A. Riggs and Jerome P. Seaton. Bloomington: Indiana University Press.

Chien Mei-ling 簡美玲. 1999. *Guizhou dongbu gaodi Miaozu de qinggan yu hunyin* 貴州東部高地苗族的情感與婚姻 [Sentiment and Marriage among the Miao of the Eastern Guizhou Plateau]. Guiyang: Guizhou University Press.

Childs, Geoff H. 2008. *Tibetan Transition: Historical and Contemporary Perspectives on Fertility, Family Planning, and Demographic Change.* Leiden: E. J. Brill.

Clastres, Pierre. 2010 [1980]. *Archaeology of Violence.* Translated by Jeanine Herman. Los Angeles: Semiotext(e).

Clewell, Tammy. 2004. "Mourning Beyond Melancholia: Freud's Psycholanalysis of Loss." *Journal of the American Psychoanalytic Association* 52 (1): 43–67.

Cohen, Myron. 1992. "Family Management and Family Division in Contemporary Rural China." *China Quarterly* 130: 357–377.

Cooper, Eugene. 1993. "Cousin Marriage in Rural China: More and Less than Generalized Exchange." *American Ethnologist* 20 (4): 758–780.

Cooper, Eugene, and Meng Zhang. 1993. "Patterns of Cousin Marriage in Rural Zhejiang and in *Dream of the Red Chamber.*" *Journal of Asian Studies* 52 (1): 90–106.

da Col, Giovanni, and Caroline Humphrey, eds. 2012. "Future and Fortune: Contingency, Morality, and the Anticipation of Everyday Life [special issue]." *Social Analysis* 56 (2).

Day, Alexander. 2013. *The Peasant in Post-Socialist China: History, Politics, and Capitalism.* Cambridge: Cambridge University Press.

Dayao Xian Renmin Zhengfu 大姚县人民政府 [People's Government of Dayao County]. 1993. *Yunnan Sheng Dayao Xian di ming zhi* 云南省大姚县地名志. [Place-name Gazetteer of Dayao County, Yunnan Province]. Dayao Xian: Dayao Xian Renmin Zhengfu.

de Heusch, Luc. 1985. *Sacrifice in Africa: A Structuralist Approach.* Bloomington: Indiana University Press.

Delanda, Manuel. 2002. *Intensive Science and Virtual Philosophy*. London: Bloomsbury.

Deleuze, Gilles. 1989 [1969]. *The Logic of Sense*. Translated by Mark Lester with Charles Stivale. New York: Columbia University Press.

Deleuze, Gilles. 1993 [1988]. *The Fold: Liebniz and the Baroque*. Translated by Tom Conley. Minneapolis: University of Minnesota Press.

Deleuze, Gilles. 1994 [1968]. *Difference and Repetition*. Translated by Paul Patton. New York: Columbia University Press.

Deleuze, Gilles. 2001. *Pure Immanence: Essays on a Life*. Translated by Anne Boyman. New York: Zone Books.

Deleuze, Gilles. 2004 [1967]. "How Do We Recognize Structuralism?" In *Desert Islands and Other Texts, 1953–1974*, edited by David Lapaujade, 170–192. Los Angeles and New York: Semiotext(e), distributed by Cambridge: MIT Press.

Deleuze, Gilles. 2014 [1978]. "On Spinoza." In "Lectures by Gilles Deleuze." Accessed 06/09/2015. http://deleuzelectures.blogspot.com.

Deleuze, Gilles, and Felix Guattari. 1986 [1975]. *Kafka: Toward a Minor Literature*. Translated by Dana Polan. Minneapolis: University of Minnesota Press.

Deleuze, Gilles, and Felix Guattari. 1987 [1980]. *A Thousand Plateaus: Capitalism and Schizophrenia*. Translated by Brian Massumi. Minneapolis: University of Minnesota Press.

Derrida, Jacques. 1976 [1967]. *Of Grammatology*. Translated by Gayatri Spivak. Baltimore: Johns Hopkins University Press.

Descola, Philippe. 2013. *Beyond Nature and Culture*. Translated by Janet Lloyd. Chicago: University of Chicago Press.

Desjarlais, Robert R. 1993. *Body and Emotion: The Aesthetics of Illness and Healing in the Nepal Himalayas*. Philadelphia: University of Pennsylvania Press.

Diamant, Neil J. 2000. *Revolutionizing the Family: Politics, Love, and Divorce in Urban and Rural China, 1949–1968*. Berkeley: University of California Press.

Dickens, Charles. 1883. *Our Mutual Friend*. 2 vols. New York: J. W. Lovell Company.

Douglas, Mary. 2007. *Thinking in Circles: an Essay on Ring Composition*. New Haven: Yale University Press.

Duffy, Carol Ann. 2007. *The Hat*. London: Faber and Faber.

Dumont, Louis. 1980 [1966]. *Homo Hierarchicus: The Caste System and Its Implications*. Translated by Mark Sainsbury, Louis Dumont, and Basia Gulati. Chicago: University of Chicago Press.

Ebrey, Patricia Buckley. 1991. *Confucianism and Family Rituals in Imperial China*. Princeton, N.J.: Princeton University Press.

Ebrey, Patricia Buckley. 2003. "Cremation in Song China." In *Women and the Family in Chinese History*, 144–164. New York: Routledge.

Eco, Umberto. 2009. *The Infinity of Lists: From Homer to Joyce*. London: MacLehose.

Empson, Rebecca M. 2011. *Harnessing Fortune: Personhood, Memory, and Place in Mongolia*. Oxford: Oxford University Press.

Evans-Pritchard, E. E. 1956. *Nuer Religion*. Oxford: Clarendon Press.

Fan, Chuo 樊綽. 1962 [864]. *Man shu jiaoju* 蠻書校注 [Annotated Book of Barbarians], edited and annotated by Xiang Da 向達. Beijing: Zhonghua shuju.

Feeley-Harnik, Gillian. 1984. "The Political Economy of Death: Communication and Change in Malagasy Colonial History." *American Ethnologist* 11 (1): 1–19.

Feeley-Harnik, Gillian. 1991. *A Green Estate: Restoring Independence in Madagascar*. Washington, D.C.: Smithsonian Institution Press.

Feld, Stephen. 1995. "Wept Thoughts: The Voicing of Kaluli Memories." In *South Pacific Oral Traditions*, edited by Ruth Finnegan and Margaret Orbell, 85–108. Bloomington: Indiana University Press.

Fernandez, James W. 1986. *Persuasions and Performances: The Play of Tropes in Culture*. Bloomington: Indiana University Press.

Fjeld, Heidi. 2008. "When Brothers Separate: Conflict and Mediation within Polyandrous Houses in Central Tibet." In *Conflict and Social Order in Tibet and Inner Asia*, edited by Toni Huber and Fernanda Prie, 241–262. Leiden: Brill.

Fox, James J., ed. 2006. *To Speak in Pairs: Essays on the Ritual Languages of Eastern Indonesia*. Cambridge: Cambridge University Press.

Freud, Sigmund. 1917. "Mourning and Melancholia." In *The Standard Edition of the Complete Psychological Works of Sigmond Freud*, edited by James Strachey, 243–258. London: The Hogarth Press.

Gamliel, Tova. 2014. *The Aesthetics of Sorrow: The Wailing Culture of Yemenite-Jewish Women*. Detroit: Wayne State University Press.

Gao, Katie B. 2015. "Assessing the Linguistic Vitality of Miqie: An Endangered Ngwi (Loloish) Language of Yunnan, China." *Language Documentation & Conservation* 9: 164–191.

Geary, Patrick J. 1991. *Furta Sacra: Thefts of Relics in the Central Middle Ages*. Rev. ed. Princeton, N.J.: Princeton University Press..

Geertz, Clifford. 1973. *The Interpretation of Cultures: Selected Essays*. New York: Basic Books.

Geertz, Hildred, and Clifford Geertz. 1964. "Teknonymy in Bali: Parenthood, Age-grading and Genealogical Amnesia." *Journal of the Royal Anthropological Institute of Great Britain and Ireland* 94 (2): 94–108.

Gell, Alfred. 1996. "Vogel's Net: Traps as Artworks and Artworks as Traps." *Journal of Material Culture* 1 (1): 15–38.

Gell, Alfred. 1998. *Art and Agency: An Anthropological Theory*. Oxford: Clarendon Press.

Gell, Alfred. 1999. "Strathernograms, or, the Semiotics of Mixed Metaphors." In *The Art of Anthropology: Essays and Diagrams*, 29–75. London: Athlone Press.

Germano, David, and Kevin Trainor. 2004. *Embodying the Dharma: Buddhist Relic Veneration in Asia*. Albany: State University of New York Press.

Gernet, Jacques. 1963. "La Chine, Aspects et Fonctions de L'écriture." In *L'écriture et la Psychologie des Peuples, 22e Semaine de Synthèse*, edited by Marcel Cohen, 29–49. Paris: Armand Colin.

Goffman, Erving. 1979. "Footing." *Semiotica* 25: 1–30.

Goldstein, Melvyn. 1975. "Preliminary Notes on Marriage and Kinship." *Contributions to Nepalese Studies* 2: 57–69.

Gong Yin 龚荫. 2000. *Zhongguo tusi zhidu* 中国土司制度 [China's Native Hereditary Chieftan System]. Kunming: Yunnan minzu chubanshe.

Goode, Leslie. 2009. "'Creating Descent' after Nancy Jay: A Reappraisal of Sacrifice in Relation to Social Reproduction." *Method and Theory in the Study of Religion* 21 (4): 383–401.

Goodman, Jane. 2003. "The Proverbial Bourdieu: Habitus and the Politics of Representation in the Ethnography of Kabylia." *American Anthropologist* 105 (4): 782–793.

Goody, Jack, and Ian Watt. 1963. "The Consequences of Literacy." *Comparative Studies in Society and History* 5 (3): 304–345.

Graham, A.C. 1986. *Yin-yang and the Nature of Correlative Thinking*. Singapore: Institute of East Asian Philosophies.

Greenberg, Joseph H. 1988. "The Present State of Markedness Theory: a Reply to Scheffler." *Journal of Anthropological Research* 43 (4): 367–374.

Greenberg, Joseph H. 1990 [1980]. "Universals of Kinship Terminology: Their Nature and the Problem of Their Explanation." In *On Language: Selected Writings of Joseph H. Greenberg*, 310–327. Stanford, Calif.: Stanford University Press.

Greenberg, Joseph H. 2005 [1966]. *Language Universals: With Special Reference to Feature Hierarchies*. The Hague: Mouton & Co.

Grierson, Herbert J. C., ed. 1921. *Metaphysical Lyrics & Poems of the Seventeenth Century, Donne to Butler; Selected and Edited with an Essay by Sir Herbert John Clifford Grierson*. Oxford: Clarendon Press.

Gu Yuejuan 谷跃娟, ed. 2007. *Nanzhao shi gaiyao* 南詔史概要 [Outline of Nanzhao History]. Kunming: Yunnan daxue chubanshe.

Guo Xiexi 郭燮熙. 1968 [1922]. *Yanfeng Xian zhi* 鹽豐縣志 [Gazetteer of Yanfeng County]. Taipei: Taiwan xuesheng shuju.

Harrell, Stevan. 1989. "Ethnicity and Kin Terms Among Two Kinds of Yi." In *Ethnicity and Ethnic Groups in China,* edited by Chiao Chien and Nicholas Tapp, 179–197. Hong Kong: Chinese University Press.

Harrell, Stevan. 1993. "Geography, Demography, and Family Composition in Three Southwestern Villages." In *Chinese Families in the Post-Mao Era,* edited by Deborah Davis and Stevan Harrell, 77–102. Berkeley: University of California Press.

Harvey, Graham, ed. 2014. *The Handbook of Contemporary Animism*. New York: Routledge.

Henare, Amiria, Martin Holbraad, and Sari Wastell, eds. 2007. *Thinking Through Things: Theorising Artifacts Ethnographically*. London: Routledge.

Herman, John E. 1997. "Empire in the Southwest: Early Qing Reforms to the Native Chieftain System." *Journal of Asian Studies* 56 (1): 47–74.

Herman, John E. 2007. *Amid the Clouds and Mist: China's Colonization of Guizhou, 1200–1700*. Cambridge, Mass: Harvard University Press.

Hershatter, Gail. 2011. *The Gender of Memory: Rural Women and China's Collective Past*. Berkeley: University of California Press.

Hertz, Robert. 1960 [1907]. *Death and the Right Hand*. Glencoe, Ill.: Free Press.

Hertzfeld, Michael. 1993. "In Defiance of Destiny: The Management of Time and Gender at a Cretan Funeral." *American Ethnologist* 20 (2): 241–255.

Hinton, William. 1967. *Fanshen: A Documentary of Revolution in a Chinese Village*. New York: Monthly Review Press.

Holbraad, Martin. 2012. *Truth in Motion: The Recursive Anthropology of Cuban Divination*. Chicago: University of Chicago Press.

Holst-Warhaft, Gail. 2000. *The Cue for Passion: Grief and Its Political Uses*. Cambridge, Mass.: Harvard University Press.

Howard, Angela. 1997. "The Dharani Pillar of Kunming, Yunnan: A Legacy of Esoteric Buddhism and Burial Rites of the Bai People in the Kingdom of Dali (937–1253)." *Artibus Asiae* 57 (1): 33–72.

Hsu, Francis L. K. 1945. "Observation on Cross-Cousin Marriage in China." *American Anthropologist* 47 (1): 83–103.

Hua Lin 华林. 1997. "Yunnan shaoshu minzu wenzi lishi shike dang'an shuping 云南少数民族文字历史石刻档案述评 [Inscribed stone archives of the history of Yunnan's minority languages]." *Xinnan minzu xueyuan xuebao (zhexue shehui kexueban)* 西南民族学院学报 (哲学社会科学版) [Journal of the Southwest Institute of Nationalities (Philosophy and Social Sciences Edition)] 18 (3): 36–41.

Huang Bufan 黄布凡, editor-in-chief. 1992. *Zangmian yuzu yuyan cihui* 藏缅藏语族语言词汇 [A Tibeto-Burman Lexicon]. Beijing: Zhongyang minzuxueyuan chubanshe.

Huang, Shu-min. 1992. "Re-examining the Extended Family in Chinese Peasant Society: Findings from a Fujian Village." *Australian Journal of Chinese Affairs* 2 (7): 25–38.

Huang Zhaizhong 黄宅中. 1849. *Daoguan Dading Fu zhi* 道光大定府志 [Daoguan-period gazetteer of Dading Fu]

Hubert, Henri, and Marcel Mauss. 1964 [1899]. *Sacrifice: Its Nature and Function*. Chicago: University of Chicago Press.

Hull, Matthew. 2012. *Government of Paper: The Materiality of Bureaucracy in Urban Pakistan*. Berkeley: University of California Press.

Hume, David. 1888 [1738]. *A Treatise of Human Nature*. Oxford: Clarendon Press.

Humphrey, Caroline, and James Laidlaw. 1994. *The Archetypal Actions of Ritual: A Theory of Ritual Illustrated by the Jain Rite of Worship*. Oxford: Clarendon Press.

Hymes, Dell. 1981. "Breakthrough into Performance." In *In Vain I Tried to Tell You: Essays in Native American Ethnopoetics*, 79–141. Philadelphia: University of Pennsylvania Press.

Irvine, Judith. 1996. "Shadow Conversations: The Indeterminacy of Participant Roles." In *Natural Histories of Discourse*, edited by Michael Silverstein and Greg Urban, 131–159. Chicago: University of Chicago Press.

Jakobson, Roman. 1987 [1960]. "Linguistics and Poetics." In *Language in Literature*, edited by Krystyna Pomorska and Stephen Rudy, 62–94. Cambridge, Mass.: Harvard University Press.

Jay, Nancy B. 1992. *Throughout Your Generations Forever: Sacrifice, Religion, and Paternity*. Chicago: University of Chicago Press.

Johnson, Elizabeth L. 1988. "Grieving for the Dead, Grieving for the Living: Funeral Laments of Hakka Women." In *Death Ritual in Late Imperial and Modern China*, edited by James L. Watson and Evelyn Sakakida Rawski, 135–163. Berkeley: University of California Press.

Johnson, Elizabeth L. 2003. "Singing of Separation, Lamenting Loss: Hakka Women's Expressions of Separation and Reunion." In *Living with Separation in China: Anthropological Accounts*, edited by Charles Stafford, 27–52. London: Routledge Curzon.

Kantorowicz, Ernst Hartwig. 1957. *The King's Two Bodies: A Study in Mediaeval Political Theology*. Princeton, N.J.: Princeton University Press.

Keane, Webb. 1995. "The Spoken House: Text, Act, and Object in Eastern Indonesia." *American Ethnologist* 22 (1): 102–124.

Keane, Webb. 2003. "Semiotics and the Social Analysis of Material Things." *Language and Communication]* 23: 409–425.

Keane, Webb. 2007. *Christian Moderns: Freedom and Fetish in the Missionary Encounter*. Berkeley: University of California Press.

Keane, Webb. 2012. "The Evidence of the Senses and the Materiality of Religion." In *The Objects of Evidence: Anthropological Approaches to the Production of Knowledge*, edited by Matthew Engeleke, 105–121. Chichester, England: Wiley-Blackwell.

Keane, Webb. 2013. "On Spirit Writing: Materialities of Language and the Religious Work of Transduction." *Journal of the Royal Anthropological Institute* 19 (1): 1–17.

Kipnis, Andrew. 2006. "Suzhi: A Keyword Approach." *China Quarterly* 186: 295–313.

Kipnis, Andrew. 2011. "Subjectification and Education for Quality in China." *Economy and Society* 40: 289–306.

Kligman, Gail A. 1988. *The Wedding of the Dead: Ritual, Poetics and Popular Culture in Transylvania.* Berkeley: University of California Press.

Knapp, Ronald. 1990. *The Chinese House.* Hong Kong: Oxford University Press.

Kohn, Eduardo. 2013. *How Forests Think: Toward an Anthropology Beyond the Human.* Berkeley: University of California Press.

Küchler, Susanne. 1987. "Malangan: Art and Memory in Melanesian Society." *Man* 22 (2): 238–255.

Küchler, Susanne. 1988. "Malanggan: Objects, Sacrifice, and the Production of Memory." *American Ethnologist* 15: 625–637.

Küchler, Susanne. 1992. "Making Skins: Malanggan and the Idiom of Kinship in New Ireland." In *Anthropology, Art, and Aesthetics,* edited by Jeremy Coote and Anthony Shelton, 94–112. Oxford: Clarendon Press.

Lacan, Jacques. 1972 [1955]. "Seminar on 'The Purloined Letter,'" translated by Jeffrey Mehlmann. *Yale French Studies* 48: 39–72.

Lama, Ziwo Qiu-Fuyuan. 2012. "Subgrouping of Nisoic (Yi) Languages: A Study from the Perspectives of Shared Innovation and Phylogenetic Estimation." Ph.D. dissertation, University of Texas, Arlington.

Lambek, Michael. 2007. "Sacrifice and the Problem of Beginning: Meditations from Sakalava Mythopraxis." *Journal of the Royal Anthropological Institute* 13 (1): 19–38.

Laplanche, Jean. 1989. *New Foundations for Psychoanalysis.* Translated by David Macey. New York: Basil Blackwell.

Laqueur, Thomas W. 2015. *The Work of the Dead: A Cultural History of Mortal Remains.* Princeton, N.J.: Princeton University Press.

Leach, Edmund. 1951. "The Structural Implications of Matrilateral Cross-cousin Marriage." *Journal of the Royal Anthropological Institute of Great Britain and Ireland* 81 (1/2): 23–55.

Lebner, Ashley. 2016. "La redescription de l'anthropologie, selon Marilyn Strathern." *L'Homme* 218: 117–150.

Lee, James. 1985. "Food Supply and Population Growth in Southwest China, 1250–1850." *Journal of Asian Studies* 41 (4): 711–746.

Lee, Nancy C. 2002. *The Singers of Lamentations: Cities Under Siege, from Ur to Jerusalem to Sarajevo.* Leiden: E. J. Brill.

Leibniz, Gottfried Wilhelm Freiherr von. 1996 [1765]. *New Essays on Human Understanding.* Cambridge: Cambridge University Press.

Lemon, Alaina. 2001. "Russia: Politics of Performance." In *Between Past and Future: The Roma of Central and Eastern Europe,* edited by Will Guy, 227–141. Hatfield: University of Hertfordshire Press.

Lempert, Michael. 2006. "Disciplinary Theatrics: Public Reprimand and the Textual Performance of Affect at Sera Monastery, India." *Language and Communication* 26 (1): 15–33.

Lempert, Michael. 2007. "Conspicuously Past: Distressed Discourse and Diagrammatic Embedding in a Tibetan Represented Speech Style." *Language and Communication* 27 (3): 258–271.

Lempert, Michael. 2011. "Barack Obama, Being Sharp: Indexical Order in the Pragmatics of Precision-Grip Gesture." *Gesture* 11 (3): 241–270.

Lempert, Michael. 2012. *Discipline and Debate: The Language of Violence in a Tibetan Buddhist Monastery.* Berkeley: University of California Press.

Lempert, Michael, and Michael Silverstein. 2012. *Creatures of Politics: Media, Message, and the American Presidency.* Bloomington: Indiana University Press.

Levin, Samuel K. 1962. *Linguistic Structures in Poetry.* The Hague: Mouton.

Levine, Nancy. 1988. *The Dynamics of Polyandry: Kinship, Domesticity, and Population on the Tibetan Border.* Chicago: University of Chicago Press.

Levinson, Stephen C. 1988. "Putting Linguistics on a Proper Footing: Explorations in Goffman's Participation Framework." In *Goffman: Exploring the Interaction Order,* edited by Paul Drew and Anthony Wooton, 161–227. Oxford: Polity Press.

Lévi-Strauss, Claude. 1969. *The Elementary Structures of Kinship.* Translated by James H. Bell and John R. von Sturmer. Boston: Beacon Press.

Lewis, M. Paul, Gary F. Simons, and Charles D. Fennig, eds. 2014. *Ethnologue: Languages of the World,* 17th ed. Dallas: SIL International. Online version: http://www.ethnologue.com.

Lewis, Mark Edward. 2006. *The Flood Myths of Early China.* Albany: State University of New York Press.

Li Yunfeng 李云峰, Li Zixian 李子贤, and Yang Fuwang 杨甫旺, eds. 2007. *Meige de wenhua xue jiedu* 梅葛的文化学解读 [Deciphering the Culture of Meige]. Kunming: Yunnan daxue chubanshe.

Liebenthal, Walter. 1947. "Sanskrit Inscriptions from Yunnan I: And the Date of Foundation of the Main Pagodas in That Province." *Monumenta Serica* 12: 1–40.

Lietard, Alfred. 1913. *Au Yun-nan: Les Lo-lo p'o.* Munster: Aschendorffsche Verlagsbuch-handlung.

Lin, Wei-Ping. 2015. *Materializing Magic Power: Chinese Popular Religion in Villages and Cities.* Cambridge, Mass.: Harvard University Press.

Lin, Xiaodong. 2013. *Gender, Modernity, and Male Migrant Workers in China: Becoming a "Modern" Man.* New York: Routledge.

Lin, Yi. 2007. "Ethnicization through Schooling: The Mainstream Discursive Repertoires of Ethnic Minorities." *China Quarterly* 192: 933–948.

Lin, Yi. 2011. "Turning Rurality into Modernity: Suzhi Education in a Suburban Public School of Migrant Children in Xiamen." *China Quarterly* 206: 313–330.

Lindskog, Benedikte V. 2000. "We Are All Insects on the Back of Our Motherland: Space, Place, and Movement Among Halh Nomads of Mongolia." Ph.D. dissertation, University of Oslo.

Litzinger, Ralph A. 2000. *Other Chinas: The Yao and the Politics of National Belonging.* Durham, N.C.: Duke University Press.

Liu, James J.Y. 1962. *The Art of Chinese Poetry.* Chicago: University of Chicago Press.

Liu Rongfu 劉榮黼. 1845. *Dayao Xian zhi* 大姚縣志 [Dayao County Gazetteer].

Liu Yaohan 刘尧汉. 1980. *Yizu shehui lishi diaocha yanjiu wenji* 彝族社会历史调查研究文集 [A Collection of Papers on the Historical Investigation of Yi Society]. Beijing: Minzu chubanshe.

Liu Yaohan 刘尧汉, ed. 1985. *Zhongguo wenming yuantou xin tan: Daojia yu Yizu hu yuzhouguan* 中国文明源头新探：道家与彝族虎宇宙观 [New Investigations into the Origins of Chinese Civilization: Daoism and Yi Tiger Cosmology]. Kunming: Yunnan renmin chubanshe.

Liu Yaohan 刘尧汉, ed. 2002. *Yi xiang Shacun she qu yan jiu* 彝乡沙村社区研究 [Research on the Yi Village of Shacun]. Kunming: Yunnan renmin chubanshe.

Liu Yaohan 刘尧汉, ed. 2007. *Yizu wenhua fangyan* 彝族文化放言 [Discussions on Yi Culture]. Wuhan: Hubei jiaoyu chubanshe.

Liu Yaohan 刘尧汉 and Lu Yang 卢央, eds. 1986. *Wenming Zhongguo de Yizu shiyue li* 文明中国的彝族十月历 [The Ten-Month Yi Calendar of Civilized China]. Kunming: Yunnan renmin chubanshe.

Lloyd, John C. 2003. "Toponyms of the Nanzhao Periphery." Masters thesis, University of Massachusetts Amherst.

Lu, Hui. 1989. "Preferential Bilateral Cross-Cousin Marriage Among the Nuosu in Liangshan." In *Perspectives on the Yi of Southwest China*, edited by Stevan Harrell, 68–80. Berkeley: University of California Press.

Luo, Changpei. 1945. "The Genealogical Patronymic Linkage System of the Tibeto-Burman Speaking Tribes." *Harvard Journal of Asiatic Studies* 8 (3–4): 349–363.

Ma, Jianxiong. 2013. *The Lahu Minority in Southwest China: A Response to Ethnic Marginalization on the Frontier*. New York: Routledge.

Ma, Jianxiong. 2014. "The Zhaozhou *Bazi* Society in Yunnan: Historical Process in the *Bazi* Basin Environmental System During the Ming Period (1368–1643)." In *Environmental History in East Asia: Interdisciplinary Perspectives*, edited by Ts'ui-jung Liu, 131–155. New York: Routledge.

MacKinnon, John Ramsay. 2000. *A Field Guide to the Birds of China*. Oxford: Oxford University Press.

Makley, Charlene. 2002. "Sexuality and Identity in Post-Mao Amdo." In *Amdo Tibetans in Transition. Society and Culture in the Post-Mao Era. PIATS 2000. Proceedings from the Ninth Seminar of the International Association of Tibetan Studies, Leiden 2000*, edited by Toni Huber, 53–98. Leiden: Brill.

Malinowski, Bronislaw. 1965. *Coral Gardens and Their Magic*. Bloomington: Indiana University Press.

Mannheim, Bruce. 1998. "'Time, Not the Syllables, Must Be Counted': Quechua Parallelism, Word Meaning, and Cultural Analysis." *Michigan Discussions in Anthropology* 13: 238–281.

Marcus, Joyce 1976. "The Origins of Mesoamerican Writing." *Annual Review of Anthropology* 5: 35–67.

Maschino, Thomas. 1992. "To Remember the Faces of the Dead: Mourning and the Full Sadness of Memory in Southwestern New Britain." *Ethos* 20 (4): 387–420.

Matisoff, James A. 2003. *Handbook of Proto-Tibeto-Burman*. Berkeley: University of California Press.

Mazard, Mireille. 2016. "The Algebra of Souls: Ontological Multiplicity and the Transformation of Animism in Southwest China." *Social Analysis* 60 (1): 18–36.

McCraw, David. 2006. "Criss-Cross: Introducing Chiasmus in Old Chinese Literature." *Chinese Literature: Essays, Articles, Reviews (CLEAR)* 28: 67–124.

McLaren, Anne E. 2008a. "Making Heaven Weep: Funeral Laments in Chinese Culture." *Journal of the Oriental Society of Australia* 39–40: 369–384.

McLaren, Anne E. 2008b. *Performing Grief: Bridal Laments in Rural China*. Honolulu: University of Hawai'i Press.

Merrifield, W. Scott. 2012. "Yáo'àn Central Yi Phonology." *SIL Electronic Working Papers* 2012-002.

Moore, Henrietta L. 2011. *Still Life: Hopes, Desires, and Satisfactions*. Cambridge: Polity.

Morgan, Lewis Henry. 1870. *Systems of Consanguinity and Affinity of the Human Family*. Washington, D.C.: Smithsonian Institution.

Mosko, Mark S., and Frederick H. Damon. 2005. *On the Order of Chaos: Social Anthropology and the Science of Chaos*. New York: Berghahn Books.

Mueggler, Erik. 1998a. "A Carceral Regime: Violence and Social Memory in Southwest China." *Cultural Anthropology* 13 (2): 167–192.

Mueggler, Erik. 1998b. "The Poetics of Grief and the Price of Hemp in Southwest China." *Journal of Asian Studies* 57 (4): 979–1008.

Mueggler, Erik. 1999. "Spectral Subversions: Rival Tactics of Time and Agency in China." *Comparative Studies in Society and History* 41 (3): 458–481.

Mueggler, Erik. 2001. *The Age of Wild Ghosts: Memory, Violence, and Place in Southwest China*. Berkeley: University of California Press.

Mueggler, Erik. 2002. "Dancing Fools: Politics of Culture and Place in a 'Traditional Nationality Festival.'" *Modern China* 28 (1): 3–38.

Mueggler, Erik. 2011a. "Bodies Real and Virtual: Joseph Rock and Enrico Caruso in the Sino-Tibetan Borderlands." *Comparative Studies in Society and History* 53 (1): 6–37.

Mueggler, Erik. 2011b. *The Paper Road: Archive and Experience in the Botanical Exploration of West China and Tibet*. Berkeley: University of California Press.

Mundy, Barbara. 1996. *The Mapping of New Spain: Indigenous Cartography and the Maps of the Relaciones Geográficas*. Chicago: University of Chicago Press.

Needham, Joseph, and Ling Wang. 1965. *Science and Civilization in China*, vol. 4, part 2, *Mechanical Engineering*. Cambridge: Cambridge University Press.

Oppitz, Michael, and Elizabeth Hsu. 1998. *Naxi and Moso Ethnography: Kin, Rites, Pictographs*. Zurich: Völkerkundemuseum.

Owen, Stephen. 1977. *Early Tang Poetry*. New Haven, Conn.: Yale University Press.

Owen, Stephen. 1985. *Traditional Chinese Poetry and Poetics: Omen of the World*. Madison: University of Wisconsin Press.

Paleček, Martin, and Mark Risjord. 2013. "Relativism and the Ontological Turn Within Anthropology." *Philosophy of the Social Sciences* 43 (1): 3–23.

Pedersen, Morten A. 2011. *Not Quite Shamans: Spirit Worlds and Political Lives in Northern Mongolia*. Ithaca, N.Y.: Cornell University Press.

Pelkey, Jamin. 2011. *Dialect as Dialectic: Interpreting Phula Variation*. Berlin: Mouton de Gruyter.

Plaks, Andrew H. 1990. "Where the Lines Meet: Parallelism in Chinese and Western Literatures." *Chinese Literature: Essays, Articles, Reviews (CLEAR)* 10 (1/2): 43–60.

Pu, Zhongliang. 2004. "Policies on the Planning and Use of the Yi Language and Writing Systems." In *Language Policy in the People's Republic of China: Theory and Practice Since 1949*, edited by Minglang Zhou and Hongkai Sun, 257–275. Boston: Kluwer.

Pullinger, Debbie. 2014. "Infinity and Beyond: The Poetic List in Children's Poetry." *Children's Literature in Education*. doi:10.1007/s10583-014-9230-2.

Qin, Zhaoxiong. 2001. "Rethinking Cousin Marriage in Rural China." *Ethnology* 40 (4): 347–360.

Rappaport, Joanne, and Tom Cummings. 2011. *Beyond the Lettered City: Indigenous Literacies in the Andes*. Durham, N.C.: Duke University Press.

Rappaport, Roy. 1999. *Ritual and Religion in the Making of Humanity*. Chicago: University of Chicago Press.

Rilke, Rainer Maria. 2005 [1905]. *Rilke's Book of Hours: Love Poems to God*. Translated by Anita Barrows and Joanna Macy. New York: Penguin Group.

Robbins, Joel. 2005. "Introduction. Humiliation and Transformation: Marshall Sahlins and the Study of Cultural Change in Melanesia." In *The Making of Global and Local Modernities in Melanesia*, edited by Joel Robbins and Holly Wardlow, 3–22. Aldershot: Ashgate.

Rock, Joseph Francis Charles. 1947. *The Ancient Na-Khi Kingdom of Southwest China.* Cambridge, Mass.: Harvard University Press.

Rock, Joseph Francis Charles, and Klaus Ludwig Janert. 1965. *Na-Khi Manuscripts.* Wiesbaden: F. Steiner.

Rofel, Lisa. 2007. *Desiring China: Experiments in Neoliberalism, Sexuality, and Public Culture.* Berkeley: University of California Press.

Rose, Gillian. 1996. *Mourning Becomes the Law: Philosophy and Representation.* Cambridge: Cambridge University Press.

Rui Zengrui 芮增瑞. 2000. "Yizu wenhua liang ti 彝族文化两题 [Two Questions on Yi Culture]." *Chuxiong shizhuan xuebao* 楚雄师专学报 [Journal of the Chuxiong Teachers' College] (2): 1–4.

Sahlins, Marshall. 1992. "The Economics of Develop-man in the Pacific." *Res* 21: 13–25.

Sahlins, Marshall. 2013. "Colloquium: On the Ontological Scheme of *Beyond Nature and Culture.*" *Hau: Journal of Ethnographic Theory* 4 (1): 281–290.

Santner, Eric. 2011. *The Royal Remains: The People's Two Bodies and the Endgames of Sovereignty.* Chicago: University of Chicago Press.

Schieffelin, Bambi. 2002. "Marking Time: The Dichotomizing Discourse of Multiple Temporalities." *Current Anthropology* 43 (supplement): S5–S17.

Schuler, Sidney Ruth. 1987. *The Other Side of Polyandry: Property, Stratification, and Non-marriage in the Nepal Himalayas.* Boulder: Westview.

Selden, Mark. 1993. "Family Strategies and Structures in Rural North China." In *Chinese Families in the Post-Mao Era*, edited by Deborah Davis and Stevan Harrell, 139–164. Berkeley: University of California Press.

Sen, Tansen. 2004. *Buddhism, Diplomacy, and Trade: The Realignment of Sino-Indian Relations, 600–1400.* New Delhi: Manohar Publishers.

Severi, Carlo. 2014. "Transmutating Beings: A Proposal for an Anthropology of Thought." *Hau: Journal of Ethnographic Theory* 4 (2): 41–71.

Shafer, Robert. 1974. *An Introduction to Sino-Tibetan.* 4 vols. Wiesbaden: Harrassowitz.

Smith, Bradley, and Wan-Go Wen. 1973. *China: A History in Art.* New York: Harper & Row.

Smith, W. Robertson. 1889. *Lectures on the Religion of the Semites.* Edinburgh: A. and C. Black.

Solomon, Frank, and Mercedes Nino-Murcia. 2011. *The Lettered Mountain: A Peruvian Village's Way with Writing.* Durham, N.C.: Duke University Press.

Stasch, Rupert. 2009. *Society of Others: Kinship and Mourning in a West Papuan Place.* Berkeley: University of California Press.

Strathern, Marilyn. 1988. *The Gender of the Gift: Problems with Women and Problems with Society in Melanesia.* Berkeley: University of California Press.

Strathern, Marilyn. 1990. "Out of Context: The Pursuasive Fictions of Anthropology." In *Modernist Anthropology: From Fieldwork to Text*, edited by Marc Manganaro, 80–132. Princeton, N.J.: Princeton University Press.

Strathern, Marilyn. 1991. *Partial Connections.* New York: Rowman & Littlefield.

Strathern, Marilyn. 1992a. *After Nature: English Kinship in the Late Twentieth Century.* Cambridge: Cambridge University Press.

Strathern, Marilyn. 1992b. "Parts and Wholes: Refiguring Relationships." In *Reproducing the Future: Essays on Anthropology, Kinship, and the New Reproductive Technologies*, 90–117. Manchester: Manchester University Press.

Strathern, Marilyn. 1999. *Property, Substance, and Effect: Anthropological Essays on Persons and Things*. London: Athlone Press.

Strathern, Marilyn. 2005. *Kinship, Law, and the Unexpected: Relatives Are Always a Surprise*. Cambridge: Cambridge University Press.

Strathern, Marilyn. 2012. "A Comment on 'the Ontological Turn' in Japanese Anthropology." *Hau: Journal of Ethnographic Theory* 2 (2): 402–405.

Sun, Wanning. 2009. "Suzhi on the Move: Body, Place, and Power." *Positions* 17 (3): 617–642.

Swancutt, Katherine. 2012. *Fortune and the Cursed: The Sliding Scale of Time in Mongolian Divination*. Oxford: Berghahn Books.

Swancutt, Katherine. 2016. "The Art of Capture: Hidden Jokes and the Reinvention of Animistic Ontologies in Southwest China." *Social Analysis* 60 (1): 74–91.

Teiser, Stephen F. 1988. *The Ghost Festival in Medieval China*. Princeton, N.J.: Princeton University Press.

Tolbert, Elizabeth. 1994. "The Voice of Lament: Female Vocality and Perforative Efficacy in the Finnish-Karelian Itkuvirsi." In *Embodied Voices: Representing Female Vocality in Western Culture*, edited by Leslie C. Dunn and Nancy A. Jones, 179–194. Cambridge: Cambridge University Press.

Tomlinson, Matt. 2004. "Ritual, Risk, and Danger: Chain Prayers in Fiji." *American Anthropologist* 106 (1): 6–16.

Toren, Christina, and Joao Pina-Cabral, eds. 2011. *The Challenge of Epistemology: Anthropological Perspectives*. Oxford: Berghahn.

Trautmann, Thomas R. 1981. *Dravidian Kinship*. Cambridge: Cambridge University Press.

Tumarkin, Nina. 1983. *Lenin Lives!: The Lenin Cult in Soviet Russia*. Cambridge, Mass.: Harvard University Press.

Turner, Victor. 1967. *The Forest of Symbols: Aspects of Ndembu Ritual*. Ithaca, N.Y.: Cornell University Press.

Turner, Victor. 1969. *The Ritual Process: Structure and Anti-Structure*. Chicago: Aldine.

Turner, Victor. 1974. *Dramas, Fields, and Metaphors: Symbolic Action in Human Society*. Ithaca, N.Y.: Cornell University Press.

Turner, Victor. 1982. *From Ritual to Theatre: the Human Seriousness of Play*. New York: Performing Arts Journal Publications.

Urban, Greg, and Kristin M. Smith. 1998. "The Sunny Tropics of Dialogue?" *Semiotica* 121 (3/4): 263–281.

Van Gennep, Arnold. 1960 [1908]. *The Rites of Passage*. Chicago: University of Chicago Press.

Verdery, Katherine. 1999. *The Political Lives of Dead Bodies: Reburial and Postsocialist Change*. New York: Columbia University Press.

Vinding, Michael. 1998. *The Thakali: A Himalayan Ethnography*. London: Serindia Publications.

Viveiros de Castro, Eduardo. 2001. "GUT Feelings About Amazonia: Potential Affinity and the Construction of Sociality." In *Beyond the Visible and the Material: The Amerindianization of Society in the Work of Peter Rivière*, edited by Laura Rival and Neil Whitehead, 19–43. Oxford: Oxford University Press.

Viveiros de Castro, Eduardo. 2004. "Perspectival Anthropology and the Method of Controlled Equivocation." *Tipití: Journal of the Society for the Anthropology of Lowland South America* 2 (1): 3–20.

Viveiros de Castro, Eduardo. 2009. "The Gift and the Given: Three Nano-essays on Kinship and

Magic." In *Kinship and Beyond: The Genealogical Model Reconsidered*, edited by James Leach and Sandra Bamford, 237–268. Oxford: Berghahn Books.

Viveiros de Castro, Eduardo. 2014. *Cannibal Metaphysics: For a Post-Structural Anthropology*. Translated by Peter Skafish. Minneapolis: University of Minnesota Press.

Volkman, Toby Alice. 1990. "Visions and Revisions: Toraja Culture and the Tourist Gaze." *American Ethnologist* 17 (1): 91–110.

Wagner, Roy. 1986. *Asiwinarong: Ethos, Image, and Social Power Among the Usen Barok of New Ireland*. Princeton, N.J.: Princeton University Press.

Wagner, Roy. 1991. "The Fractal Person." In *Big Men and Great Men: The Personifications of Power*, edited by Maurice Godelier and Marilyn Strathern, 159–173. Cambridge: Cambridge University Press.

Wakeman, Frederik. 1988. "Mao's Remains." In *Death Ritual in Late Imperial and Modern China*, edited by James L. Watson and Evelyn Sakakida Rawski, 254–288. Berkeley: University of California Press.

Watkins, Joanne. 1996. *Spirited Women: Gender, Religion, and Cultural Identity in the Nepal Himalaya*. New York: Columbia University Press.

Watson, Burton. 1971. *Chinese Lyricism*. New York: Columbia University Press.

Watson, James L., and Evelyn Sakakida Rawski, eds. 1988. *Death Ritual in Late Imperial and Modern China*. Berkeley: University of California Press.

Watson, Rubie S. 1996. "Chinese Bridal Laments: The Claims of a Dutiful Daughter." In *Harmony and Counterpoint: Ritual Music in the Chinese Context*, edited by Bell Yung and Evelyn Sakakida Rawski, 107–129. Stanford, Calif.: Stanford University Press.

Wellens, Koen. 2010. *Religious Revival in the Tibetan Borderland: The Premi of Southwest China*. Seattle: University of Washington Press.

Wickett, Elizabeth. 2010. *For the Living and the Dead: The Funerary Laments of Upper Egypt, Ancient and Modern*. London: I. B. Tauris.

Wilce, James M. 1998. *Eloquence in Trouble: The Poetics and Politics of Complaint in Rural Bangladesh*. Oxford: Oxford University Press.

Wilce, James M. 2005. "Traditional Laments and Postmodern Regrets: The Circulation of Discourse in Metacultural Context." *Journal of Linguistic Anthropology* 15 (1): 60–71.

Wilce, James M. 2009. *Crying Shame: Metaculture, Modernity, and the Exaggerated Death of Lament*. Maiden, Mass.: Wiley-Blackwell.

Willerslev, Rane. 2007. *Soul Hunters: Hunting, Animism, and Personhood Among the Siberian Yukaghirs*. Berkeley: University of California Press.

Willerslev, Rane. 2013. "Taking Animism Seriously, but Perhaps Not too Seriously?" *Religion and Society: Advances in Research* 4: 41–45.

Wortham, Stanton. 2001. *Narratives in Action*. New York: Teachers College Press.

Wortham, Stanton, and Michael Locher. 1996. "Voicing on the News: An Analytic Technique for Studying Media Bias." *Text* 16: 557–585.

Xie Zhaozhe 謝肇淛. 1972 [1567–1624]. *Dian lüe* 滇略 [Brief History of Yunnan]. Taipei: Taiwan shang wu yin shu guan.

Yan Hairong. 2008. *New Masters, New Servants: Migration, Development, and Women Workers in China*. Durham, N.C.: Duke University Press.

Yan, Yunxiang. 1997. "The Triumph of Conjugality Structural Transformation of Family Relations in a Chinese Village." *Ethnology* 36(3): 191–212.

Yang Fuwang 杨甫旺. 2008. *Minzuxue shiye zhong de Menglian Yi cun: bianqian yu fazhan* 民族学视野中的勐连彝村:变迁与发展 [Ethnology of Menglian Yi villages: Change and Development]. Kunming: Yunnan Daxue chubanshe.

Yang Fuwang 杨甫旺 and Yang Qiongying 杨琼英. 2000. "Yizu huozang wenhua chugai 彝族火葬文化初探 [A Preliminary Study of the Crematory culture of the Yi nationality]." Yunnan Shifan Daxue xuebao 云南师范大学学报 [Journal of Yunnan Normal University 32 (6): 65–70.

Yongren Xian Renmin Zhengfu 永仁县人民政府 [Yongren County People's Government]. 1992. *Yunnan Sheng Yongren Xian di ming zhi* 云南省永仁县地名志 [Place-name Gazetteer of Yongren County, Yunnan Province]. Yongren Xian: Yongren Xian Renmin Zhengfu.

Yunnan Sheng minzu minjian wenxue Chuxiong diaochadui 云南省民族民间文学楚雄调查队 [Yunnan Province nationalities folk literature Chuxiong research team]. 1978. Meige: Yizu minjian shishi 梅葛: 彝族民间史詩 [Meige: A Yi Folk Epic]. Kunming: Yunnan renmin chubanshe.

Index

achārya (asheli), 40

affective register, of funeral procedures, 73

affinity: consanguinity and, 179, 202; vs. descent, 71, 71n2, 124–25, 133; emergence of persons and, 227, 252, 294; jì'íti exchange and, 124–25; Viveiros de Castro on, 71n2, 201

Agàmisimo, 49, 225

Agha, Asif, 271

Àgò'àtə, 281, 282

Ailao Mountains, 35, 37

alienation, 97, 99

Althusser, Louis, 25

ancestral effigies: aging and destruction of, 47–48; bed's-head spirit and, 50, 229; as bodies of immaterial beings, 92; description of, 46–47; drawing of, 47; as extensive bodies of the dead, 187, 191; genders represented by, 119–20; hanging of, 20; intensive bodies of the dead as analogues of, 229; materializing the cremated corpse, 68; placement above man's bed, 81; recovery of soul from mountain and, 83, 145, 146, 191; sacrifice to, in case of illness, 80; Sleeping in the Forest and, 285, 286; songs about, 30, 46, 262, 263, 267–70; soul residing with, 49, 83, 146; Tenth-Month Sacrifice and, 261, 265, 266, 267, 278, 279, 283–84, 289; trees used for fashioning of, 270

animism, 75

animist ontology, 11

anthropology of death, 73–74

Àp'ìmà, 12–13, 14, 79–83; on àpip'ö, 168, 172; on àpip'ö's staff with eagle's claws, 244; asking about book on death ritual, 183–84; death of, 184; on friend's encounter with underworld, 90–91; on grain pounder, 291, 292–94; on great chants, 168; helping with translations

of chants, 182, 198–99, 238, 240–41; knowledge of Tenth-Month Sacrifice, 264–65, 278; on love, 79–80, 92; memories of Sleeping in the Forest, 285–86; on ritual uses of laying hen, 87–88; summarizing jì'íti exchange, 122; telling story about daughter who refuses to marry, 259; telling story about monkeys, 238–39, 242; wisdom of, 302

àpip'ö, 169–71; as authors of great chants, 168; compact discs of verses sent to, 184; extreme hardship for, beginning in 1958, 22, 172–73, 296; helping with translation of taped nèpi, 180, 182; Li Bicong's story about, 177; pain caused by suppression of, 169; performing in Wòdɔwò, 183, 184, 185, 270, 289; Qi Wenping as, 289–90; at Sleeping in the Forest, 285–86; at Tenth-Month Sacrifice in Júzò, 267, 278, 283; tools of, 169–70, 172, 246, 251–52, 267. See also great chants; Li Bicong; ritualists

apophatic series, 211, 212, 216, 295

Ariès, Philippe, 163

Asad, Talal, 13, 14

assembly and partition of dead bodies, 97–98, 99, 133

Atkinson, Jane Monnig, 13, 14

avə (brothers-in-law) group, 56–57; alcohol not offered by, 121; bilateral cross-cousin marriage and, 108–9; building the great bu, 276; carrying out of coffin and, 130; as classificatory relationship, 98; cooked grain offerings of, 88, 91; at Dawn-to-Dusk Sacrifice, 145–46; location and orientation of grave and, 130–31; possibilities for insult to, 81; Qi Ping's erection of tombstones and, 58–61, 67; retrieval of soul from mountain and, 144–45; role in funeral events, 57, 100, 101–2, 103; in sacrifice and exchange,